Law Collections from Mesopotamia and Asia Minor

D0023956

Writings from the Ancient World
Society of Biblical Literature

Simon B. Parker, General Editor

Associate Editors

Jo Ann Hackett
Harry A. Hoffner, Jr.
Peter Machinist
Patrick D. Miller, Jr.
William J. Murnane
David I. Owen
Robert R. Ritner
Martha T. Roth

Volume 6
Law Collections from Mesopotamia and Asia Minor
by Martha T. Roth
Edited by Piotr Michalowski

Law Collections from Mesopotamia and Asia Minor

SECOND EDITION

by
Martha T. Roth

With a contribution by
Harry A. Hoffner, Jr.

Volume editor
Piotr Michalowski

Society of Biblical Literature
Writings from the Ancient World Series

Scholars Press
Atlanta, Georgia

LAW COLLECTIONS FROM MESOPOTAMIA AND ASIA MINOR
Copyright © 1995, second edition © 1997
Society of Biblical Literature

The Society of Biblical Literature gratefully acknowledges a grant from the National Endowment for the Humanities to underwrite certain editorial and research expenses of the Writings from the Ancient World series. Published results and interpretations do not necessarily represent the view of the Endowment.

Library of Congress Cataloging-in-Publication Data

Roth, Martha Tobi.
Law collections from Mesopotamia and Asia Minor / by Martha T. Roth with a contribution by Harry A. Hoffner, Jr. ; volume editor, Piotr Michalowski. — 2nd ed.
p. cm. — (Writings from the ancient world ; vol. 6)
Includes bibliographical references and index.
ISBN 0-7885-0378-2 (pbk. : alk. paper)
1. Law, Sumerian—Sources. 2. Law, Assyro-Babylonian—Sources. 3. Law, Hittite—Sources. 4. Law, Ancient—Sources. I. Hoffner, Harry A. II. Michalowski, Piotr. III. Title. IV. Series: Writings from the ancient world ; no. 6.
KL210.R68 1997
340.5'3—dc21 97-24359
CIP

Printed in the United States of America
on acid-free paper

Contents

Series Editor's Foreword

Writings from the Ancient World is designed to provide up-to-date, readable, English translations of writings recovered from the ancient Near East.

The series is intended to serve the interests of general readers, students, and educators who wish to explore the ancient Near Eastern roots of Western civilization, or compare these earliest written expressions of human thought and activity with writings from other parts of the world. It should also be useful to scholars in the humanities or social sciences who need clear, reliable translations of ancient Near Eastern materials for comparative purposes. Specialists in particular areas of the ancient Near East who need access to texts in the scripts and languages of other areas will also find these translations helpful. Given the wide range of materials translated in the series, different volumes will appeal to different interests. But these translations make available to all readers of English the world's earliest traditions as well as valuable sources of information on daily life, history, religion, etc. in the preclassical world.

The translators of the various volumes in this series are specialists in the particular languages and have based their work on the original sources and the most recent research. In their translations they attempt to convey as much as possible of the original texts in a fluent, current English. In the introductions, notes, glossaries, maps, and chronological tables, they aim to provide the essential information for an appreciation of these ancient documents.

Covering the period from the invention of writing (by 3000 B.C.E.) down to the conquests of Alexander the Great (ca. 330 B.C.E.), the ancient Near East comprised northeast Africa and southwest Asia. The cultures represented within these limits include especially Egyptian, Sumerian, Babylonian, Assyrian, Hittite, Ugaritic, Aramean, Phoenician, and Israelite. It is hoped that Writings from the Ancient World will eventually produce translations of most of the many different genres attested in these cultures: letters—official and private, myths, diplomatic documents, hymns, law collections, monumental inscriptions, tales, and administrative records, to mention but a few.

The preparation of this volume was supported in part by a generous grant from the Division of Research Programs of the National Endowment for the Humanities. Significant funding has also been made available by the Society of Biblical Literature. In addition, those involved in preparing this volume have received financial and clerical assistance from their respective institutions. Were it not for these expressions of confidence in our work, the arduous tasks of preparation, translation, editing, and publication could not have been accomplished or even undertaken. It is the hope of all who have worked on these texts or supported this work that Writings from the Ancient World will open up new horizons and deepen the humanity of all who read these volumes.

Simon B. Parker
Boston University School of Theology

Chronological Table

Third Dynasty of Ur	2112–2004 B.C.E.
Ur-Namma (2112–2095 B.C.E.)	
Shulgi (2094–2047 B.C.E.)	
Larsa Dynasty	2025–1763 B.C.E.
First Dynasty of Isin	2017–1794 B.C.E.
Lipit-Ishtar (1934–1924 B.C.E.)	
First Dynasty of Babylon	1894–1595 B.C.E.
Hammurabi (1792–1750 B.C.E.)	
Middle Assyrian State	ca. 1400–950 B.C.E.
Ashur-uballiṭ (1363–1328 B.C.E.)	
Tukultī-Ninurta I (1243–1207 B.C.E.)	
Tiglath-pileser I (1114–1076 B.C.E.)	
Neo-Assyrian Empire	ca. 950–627 B.C.E.
Neo-Babylonian (or Chaldean) Dynasty	625–539 B.C.E.
Nabopolassar (625–605 B.C.E.)	
Nebuchadnezzar II (604–562 B.C.E.)	
Nabonidus (555–539 B.C.E.)	
Persian Empire	538–331 B.C.E.
Cyrus II (The Great) (538–530 B.C.E.)	

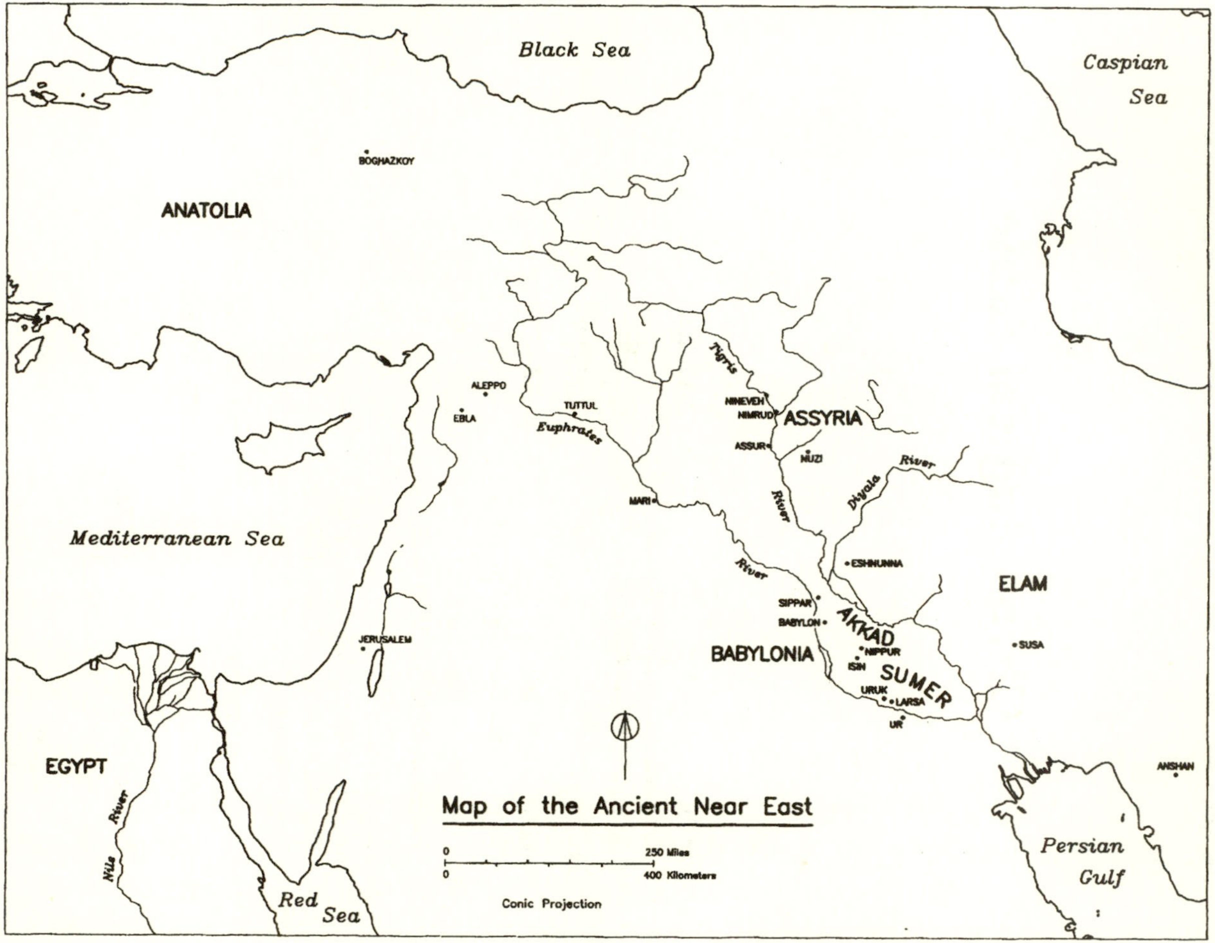
Black Sea
Caspian Sea
ANATOLIA
BOGHAZKOY
ALEPPO
EBLA
TUTTUL
Euphrates
Tigris
NINEVEH
NIMRUD
ASSYRIA
ASSUR
NUZI
Diyala River
River
MARI
River
ESHNUNNA
ELAM
SIPPAR
BABYLON
AKKAD
NIPPUR
ISIN
SUMER
URUK
LARSA
UR
SUSA
BABYLONIA
ANSHAN
Persian Gulf
Mediterranean Sea
JERUSALEM
EGYPT
Nile River
Red Sea
Map of the Ancient Near East
0 250 Miles
0 400 Kilometers
Conic Projection

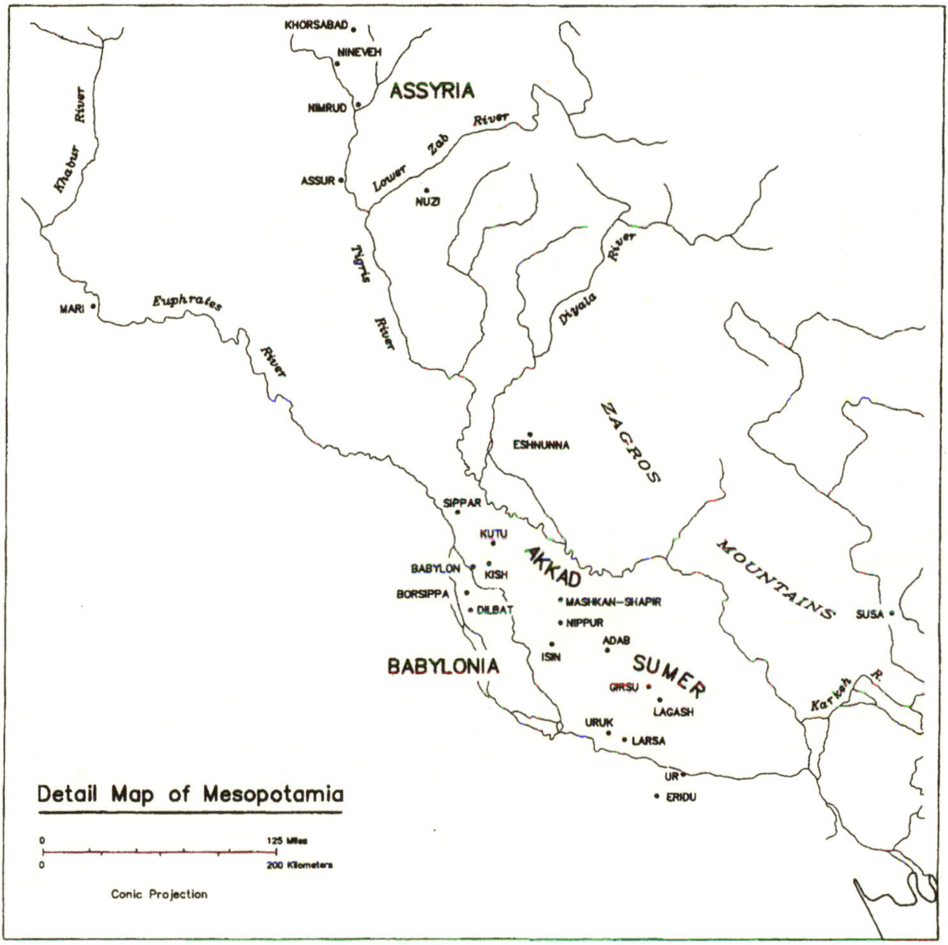
KHORSABAD
NINEVEH
ASSYRIA
NIMRUD
River
Zab
Lower
ASSUR
NUZI
Khabur River
Tigris
River
MARI
Euphrates
River
River
Diyala
River
ZAGROS
ESHNUNNA
SIPPAR
KUTU
AKKAD
BABYLON
KISH
BORSIPPA
DILBAT
MASHKAN-SHAPIR
NIPPUR
ADAB
ISIN
MOUNTAINS
SUSA
BABYLONIA
SUMER
GIRSU
LAGASH
Karkeh R.
URUK
LARSA
UR
ERIDU
Detail Map of Mesopotamia
0
125 Miles
0
200 Kilometers
Conic Projection

Explanation of Conventions, Signs, and Abbreviations

The typographical conventions and sigla used here follow generally accepted Assyriological practice. These include the differing typography marking the different languages: lower case roman (with morphemes separated by hyphens) for Sumerian; lower case italics (with hyphens when not normalized) for Akkadian; upper case roman (with periods) for logograms or Sumerograms of uncertain reading.

In the English translations, some proper nouns are given in their commonly accepted English spellings rather than in the more accurate transcription (Babylon rather than Bābili, Shalmaneser rather than Shulmānu-asharidu, Hammurabi rather than Ḫammu-rapī, etc.). In the English translations, I transcribe the phoneme /š/ as /sh/ (Shamash rather than Šamaš), but sometimes retain the velar fricative /ḫ/ (pronounced as in German "auch"), and the emphatics /ṣ/ and /ṭ/. Other notations and symbols include the following:

[ ] Full square brackets mark restorations to broken text in the original.
⸢ ⸣ Half square brackets mark damaged but likely readings.
< > Pointed brackets mark modern insertions of text omitted by the ancient scribe.
« » Double pointed brackets mark deletions of text erroneously included by the ancient scribe.
( ) Parentheses enclose material added to the English translation.
... Ellipses mark untranslatable text or a gap.

The only bibliographic abbreviations used are:

AHw See von Soden 1959–81.
CAD See Oppenheim, Reiner, et al. 1956–.

The law collections in this volume are identified by the following abbreviations:

HL	Hittite Laws
LE	Laws of Eshnunna
LH	Laws of Hammurabi
LL	Laws of Lipit-Ishtar
LNB	Neo-Babylonian Laws
LOx	Laws about Rented Oxen (Ox Laws)
LU	Laws of Ur-Namma
LX	Laws of X
MAL	Middle Assyrian Laws
MAPD	Middle Assyrian Palace Decrees
SLEx	Sumerian Laws Exercise Tablet
SLHF	Sumerian Laws Handbook of Forms

Additional abbreviations used:

col.	column
obv.	obverse of tablet
r.	reign
rev.	reverse of tablet

Chronologies follow Brinkman 1977.

Weights and Measures

Weights and measures have been converted in the translations into basic units, to facilitate comparisons between and within the laws. Thus, silver and other commodities usually weighed are reduced to shekels, area measures to ikus, and capacities to silas. Although the correspondences varied during the three-thousand-year history of their attested uses, the measurement systems used in the Sumerian and Akkadian law collections are consistent.

The cuneiform writing systems almost always indicated numbers, measurements, and commodities using logograms, usually without phonetic complements, and the grammatically correct Akkadian readings often are impossible to determine. In transcribing weights and measures I render the numeral either in Akkadian or logographically in Arabic numerals and fractions, the measurement notation in the absolute state, and the commodity in the appropriate grammatical case: e.g., 1 *mana kaspam išaqqal,* "he shall weigh and deliver 1 mina of silver" (passim), or 6 *mana šipātum ana* 1 *šiqil kaspim,* "360 shekels of wool for 1 shekel of silver" (LE ¶ 1); so, too, when the commodity is understood but not written, as in 12 *uṭṭet idūšu,* "12 barleycorns is his hire" (LE ¶ 7), with *kaspum,* "silver," understood. The distributive is rendered here with the locative-adverbial ending *-um,* with the associated commodity in the appropriate grammatical case: thus, e.g., *ana* 1 *burum* 60 *kur še*ʾ*am imaddad,* "he shall measure and deliver 18,000 silas of grain per 18 ikus of land" (LH ¶ 255); see Goetze 1956: 36; and Borger 1979: 114 ad ¶ 44.

Table of Weights and Measures

Weight measures (used for silver, gold, tin, wool, etc.)

1 *biltu* (gún) "talent" (ca. 30 kilograms) = 60 "minas"
1 *manû* (ma-na) "mina" (ca. 500 grams) = 60 "shekels" [Hittite "mina" = 40 "shekels"]
1 *šiqlu* (gín) "shekel" (ca. 8.33 grams) = 180 "barleycorns"
1 *uṭṭetu* (še) "barleycorn" (ca. 0.046 grams)

Capacity measures (used for grain, etc.)

1 *kurru* (gur) "kur" (ca. 300 liters) = 5 "bariga"
1 *pānu* (bariga) "bariga" (ca. 60 liters) = 6 "seahs"
1 *sūtu* (bán) "seah" (ca. 10 liters) = 10 "silas" [Neo-Babylonian "seah" = 6 "silas"]
1 *qû* (sìla) "sila" (ca. 1 liter) = 60 "shekels"

Surface measures (used for fields, houses, etc.)

1 *buru* (bùr) "bur" (ca. 64,800 sq. meters or ca. 6.5 hectares) = 18 "ikus"
1 *ikû* (iku) "iku" (ca. 3600 sq. meters or ca. 0.36 hectares) = 100 "sars"
1 *mušaru* (sar) "sar" (ca. 36 sq. meters or ca. 0.0036 hectares)

Length measures (used for walls, textiles, etc.)

1 *nindānu* (ninda) "ninda" (ca. 6 meters) = 12 "cubits" [Neo-Babylonian "ninda" = 14 "cubits")
1 *qanû* (gi) "reed" (ca. 3 meters) = 6 "cubits" [Neo-Babylonian "reed" = 7 "cubits"]
1 *ammatu* (kùš) "cubit" (ca. 50 centimeters) = 30 "fingers" [Neo-Babylonian "cubit" = 24 "fingers"]
1 *ubānu* (šu-si) "finger" (ca. 1.66 centimeters) = 6 "barleycorns"
1 *uṭṭetu* (še) "barleycorn" (ca. 0.28 centimeters)

Table 2. The standard Old Babylonian weights and measures as used in the Sumerian and Akkadian law collections. Akkadian terms are indicated in normalized italics, Sumerian terms in (hyphenated) syllabic roman, and English translations within quotation marks. The different equivalencies in the Hittite and Neo-Babylonian systems are indicated within square brackets. See Powell 1987 and van den Hout 1987.

Acknowledgments

It is a pleasure to offer my acknowledgments to many people. Sections of this volume have been in preparation for many years, since the mid-1970s, and the final product owes much to numerous conversations with teachers, colleagues, and students. Especially valuable have been the insights from colleagues in legal history at the University of Chicago, whose questions and promptings helped shape my translations, and I thank in particular Charles Gray and James Lindgren. I first studied the Mesopotamian law collections at the University of Pennsylvania under the direction of Barry Eichler and Åke W. Sjöberg, to both of whom I am grateful for lessons in philology and methodology. Portions of the manuscript, in various drafts, were read and commented on by several colleagues at the Oriental Institute: Miguel Civil, who also allowed me access to his hypertext files, and Walter Farber, Erica Reiner, and Matthew W. Stolper; John A. Brinkman made available to me his draft translations of the Laws of Hammurabi and of the Middle Assyrian Laws. The manuscript was read with great care by the volume editor, Piotr Michalowski. I thank all these colleagues for their cooperation, suggestions, and insights.

Editorial assistance for this volume was provided by Stephanie Endy, Linda McLarnan, and Helen Rosner (for the Sumerian and Akkadian collections), and by Scott Branting (for Harry Hoffner's translation of the Hittite Laws). The maps were prepared by Peggy Sanders, Archaeological Graphic Services; the indexes were prepared with the assistance of Rachel Dahl. I am grateful for the patience and editorial guidance of the two series editors, Burke O. Long and Simon B. Parker. Numerous questions relating to computer problems were always cheerfully answered by John Sanders. The Oriental Institute and its Director, William Sumner, provided essential material support. Manuscript preparation was aided by a 1993 National Endowment for the Humanities Summer Stipend.

I have been able to collate many of the original cuneiform documents for the Sumerian and Akkadian law collections, including all those in the University Museum, Philadelphia, by courtesy of Åke W. Sjöberg; in Yale University, New Haven, by courtesy of W. W. Hallo; in the Free Library of Philadelphia, by courtesy of the Curator of the Rare Books Department; in the Oriental Institute, Chicago, by courtesy of J. A. Brinkman; in the British Museum, London, by courtesy of the Trustees of the British Museum;[1] in the Musée du Louvre, Paris, by courtesy of the Trustees of the Musée du Louvre.

I dedicate this book to my family: to Bryon, Helen, Joseph, and Lillian.

Note

1. For the LU, Finkelstein (1969a: 66) noted that he was able to make "collations of the Ur fragments in the British Museum"; the tablets are now in Baghdad, at the Iraq Museum, and have not been recollated.

Introduction

The law collections presented in this volume are compilations, varying in legal and literary sophistication, recorded by scribes in the schools and the royal centers of ancient Mesopotamia and Asia Minor from the end of the third millennium through the middle of the first millennium B.C.E. Some of the collections, like the famous Laws of Hammurabi, achieved a wide audience throughout Mesopotamia for centuries; others, like the Laws about Rented Oxen, were scribal exercises limited to a local school center. All, however, reflected and influenced contemporary legal practice in the scribes' recordings of contracts, administrative documents, and court cases, and also provide the modern historian with evidence of abstractions of legal rules from cases.

Cuneiform Script

The cuneiform script—a system of wedges impressed into damp clay tablets or, in imitation, impressed into wax, incised into stone or metal, or painted on other surfaces—was used throughout the ancient Near East from the late fourth millennium B.C.E. until the first centuries C.E. In the local languages and dialects, cuneiform was used to record a range of private and public documentation: accountings of incomes and disbursements and ration lists, private letters and diplomatic correspondence, contracts and lawsuits, literary compositions and historical annals, medical and astronomical treatises, mathematical problems, ritual and religious compilations, lexical lists, and so on. In Mesopotamia, these texts in Sumerian and in the Semitic Akkadian dialects of Babylonian and Assyrian entered (or sometimes were composed for) the curricula of the schools where scribes were trained in the ancient and accepted formal traditions of their craft, both practical and esoteric: from how to draft a letter or produce an inventory, to how to record an astronomical observation. (For an introduction to cuneiform writing, with further bibliography, see Walker 1987.)

The Scribal Curriculum

One of the skills necessary for the scribe was mastery of the legal terminology and clauses that he would use in recording a formal court case or in drawing up a contract or agreement between private parties. To this end, the scribal curriculum included such works as *ana ittišu* (Landsberger 1937)—a multitablet series of thousands of Sumerian and Akkadian legal terms and formulas which would be copied and memorized by the aspiring student—or the Laws about Rented Oxen (LOx, in this volume)—an exercise collecting a small series of laws or contract formulas relating to a single theme. Most students would later use the lessons learned from these to draft the daily contracts of local life. But the rare and fortunate scribes might be called upon to help collect, organize, and publicize a larger formal collection of laws and cases, possibly one with a royal sponsor and patron. One such collection is that promulgated under the name of King Hammurabi of Babylon about 1750 B.C.E., which was copied and recopied in the scribal centers for over a thousand years.

The Formats and Structures of the Law Collections

Some of the earlier Sumerian and Babylonian collections frame the body of legal provisions with a historical-literary prologue and epilogue (the Sumerian Laws of Ur-Namma, Laws of Lipit-Ishtar, Laws of X, and the Akkadian Laws of Hammurabi). These frames establish a political context for the compositions, relating the series of laws to the role of king as the divinely authorized guardian and administrator of justice. The high literary style and language of the prologue and epilogue contrast with the dry legal and contractual style of the laws, but the essential link between the laws and their literary frame must not be severed. The prologue and epilogue outline the historical circumstances that allow the ruler to present himself as a worthy recipient of the gods' favor and support, the highest mark of which is his ability to administer and dispense justice throughout his realm. In return for his able exercise of these powers, he demands absolute loyalty from his subjects. Surely it is no coincidence that the very first legal provisions in the Laws of Hammurabi, after a lengthy prologue establishing Hammurabi's credentials, deal with the consequences of false accusations (i.e., in the political realm, treason) and establish the state's right to impose a death penalty, and that the last provision, after more than 275 laws, deals with the consequences of a slave's challenge to his master (i.e., insurrection). The political context of the laws is emphasized by these associations with the prologue and epilogue frame.

The law cases or legal provisions included in the collections are formulated in a variety of styles (Yaron 1988: 96-110). The most frequently used is the casuistic formulation that first describes a situation and then sets out the resolution or sanction that restores balance: "If a man (or an ox, or a slave, etc.) does such and such, then he shall weigh and deliver so many shekels (etc.)." This characteristic formulation predominates throughout most of the collections in this volume: in the Sumerian Laws of Ur-Namma, Laws of Lipit-Ishtar, Laws of X, Ox Laws, and Sumerian Laws Tablet (tukum-bi lú, etc.), in the Akkadian Laws of Eshnunna, Laws of Hammurabi, Middle Assyrian Laws, Middle Assyrian Palace Decrees (*šumma awīlum*, etc.), and also in the Hittite Laws (*takku* LÚ-*an*). A variation of this casuistic formulation is the relative construction "A man who . . ." (*amēlu ša*), which is almost the only style used in the latest collection in this volume, the Neo-Babylonian Laws, and in the Middle Assyrian Palace Decrees. The relative construction is also found, along with other styles, in the Laws of Eshnunna, Middle Assyrian Laws, and Middle Assyrian Palace Decrees. Also less common is a negative apodictic statement, much like the "Thou shalt not" injunctions of the biblical commandments; a few of these formulations are found in the Laws of Eshnunna, Laws of Hammurabi, Middle Assyrian Laws, and Middle Assyrian Palace Decrees. Finally, in addition to legal rules, the Laws of X, Laws of Eshnunna, and Laws of Hammurabi also include wage and price regulations, helping to assess the relative values of labor and commodities; these should be compared to the standardizations established in the prologue of the Laws of Ur-Namma, again clearly linking the literary frame to the legalistic body.

Each "rule" or unit—casuistic clause, relative construction, negative apodictic statement, or wage and price regulation—usually (but not always) begins with a new line on the cuneiform tablet or stela; there is often no other marking, ruling, or indentation that would distinguish one unit from the next. The designation by seriatim numbers or letters of these units and the division of the text into "laws," "provisions," or "paragraphs" is purely the work of modern scholarship and not of the native compilers. The prologue and epilogue sections consist of continuous cuneiform text, and the paragraphing in these narrative sections also is a modern editorial innovation.

The sequences and groupings of legal situations within each law collection vary. In any one collection, there is a complex interplay of literary and compositional principles, of legal requirements, and of unusual cases and common circumstances. Associative principles draw law provisions together into larger blocks, and certain cases in the provisions serve as bridges linking together such blocks (see Petschow 1965, Petschow 1968, Sauren 1989). These blocks (or "chapters") were sometimes consciously marked by the ancient scribes, as seen in the few subject headings found in some late Old Babylonian copies of the Laws of Hammurabi. Within these larger groups of laws, two compositional principles—presentation of polar cases with maximal variation and juxtaposition of individual legal cases—dictate sequencing of the provisions (Eichler 1987). The entire tablet of Middle Assyrian Laws A, with more than fifty-five provisions, deals almost exclusively with offenses involving women as victims or perpetrators and with sexual offenses (including charges of sodomy); these are best studied along with the Middle Assyrian Palace Decrees, which record the decrees formulated by Assyrian rulers to regulate the behavior and etiquette of the palace women and of those royal officers whose functions demand proximity to them. The more fragmentary collections (such as the Laws of X) and the less polished and shorter exercises, excerpts, or drafts (such as Sumerian Laws Exercise Tablet or the Neo-Babylonian Laws) are more difficult to dissect and explain.

The Nature and Function of the Law Collections

The legal function of the law collections has been the subject of much debate throughout the twentieth century, ever since the stela of the Laws of Hammurabi was first published in 1902; and the debate has, predictably, centered on that most famous and largest of the collections. None of the collections is comprehensive or exhaustive, and it is clear that none attempts to set out a complete "law of the land"; but it is not clear what conclusions follow. Certainly, a lack of comprehensiveness does not, in itself, detract from the legal import or applicability of a set of laws. There are scholars who view the collections as codifications of existing practice, providing precedents for the courts and the administration of justice (see Haase 1965: 22ff.). In recent decades, the weight of scholarly opinion has come down strongly in recognition of the collections as products of the scribal schools, and as manifestations of the intellectual processes that developed other scientific treatises, including such topically diverse treatises as the god lists, tree lists, professions lists, mathematical lists, star lists, omen lists, pharmacopoeia, etc. (Kraus 1960; Bottéro 1992; Westbrook 1985). Others maintain that the connection of the law collections with their royal sponsors is paramount, and that the laws must be read with other products of the royal administration of justice (such as the edicts and debt remissions) as royal apologia with political and historical implications (Finkelstein 1961).

Throughout Mesopotamian history, the concern of the king with justice and the legal process is emphasized in royal inscriptions, royal epithets, iconographic representations, and literary allusions. Whether or not the king was always himself an active participant in the administration of the legal system, he was always its guardian, for the application of justice was the highest trust given by the gods to a legitimate king. This point was made in a letter from eighteenth-century B.C.E. Mari on the upper Euphrates, which reports the message conveyed by a prophet of the god Addu of Aleppo to the Mari ruler Zimri-Lim: "I (Addu) gave the entire country to (your father) Yaḫdun-Lim . . . He abandoned me and so I gave the country which I had given to him instead to Samsi-Addu (of Assyria) . . . (Later) I restored you to the throne of your father's house . . . Now heed this one matter: When anyone makes an appeal to you for a judgment, saying, 'I have been wronged!' you be present and render a judgment for him! Respond to him with righteousness! This alone I ask of you!" (Durand 1993: 43-45). This important message was delivered on several occasions and reappears in yet another communication from the god to the same king: "Am I not Addu, lord of Aleppo, who raised you in my bosom and who restored you to the throne of your father's house? I ask nothing else of you but that when a man or woman who has been wronged appeals to you, you be present and render a judgment for them! This alone I ask of you" (Lafont 1984: 9-11). Any ruler would certainly take such admonitions seriously, and the law collections in this volume provide numerous examples (both in the literary prologues and epilogues and in the body of the legal provisions) of the king as the ultimate authority in the day-to-day affairs of the courts and the judicial process, and as the moral leader maintaining the divinely inspired and ordained ideals of justice.

These law collections are not the sole evidence of the law from the ancient Near East. Tens of thousands of surviving cuneiform tablets record lawsuits, court cases, and legal agreements and transactions (real estate sales and leases, loans, pledges, marriages, adoptions, inheritance dispositions, slave transfers, etc.), and any comprehensive treatment of a legal subject in a given time and place within the three millennia of the cuneiform record must rely on these functional and practical legal documents and not exclusively on the law collections. One must ask, then: What are the relationship and the degree of legal concord between the provisions of the law collections and the contemporary transactional documents?

In numerous studies of a range of legal situations, little correspondence has been found between the provisions in the law collections and contemporary practice. Furthermore, no court document or contract makes a direct reference to any of the formal law collections. From such an absence of linking evidence some scholars have concluded that the law collections had little or no impact on the daily operation of legal affairs. There is, however, one Old Babylonian letter which does make reference to a "stela" (Akkadian *narû*) upon which wages were inscribed, reminding us of the provisions in LH ¶¶ 273-74, which establish daily wages for several categories of workmen. The letter was sent by an administrator to one of his team leaders in response to a complaint he received about unreasonable demands made by some weavers. The text reads, in full:[1]

> (1-3) Speak to Nabi-Shamash, thus says Alammush-naṣir: May the gods Shamash and Marduk keep you in good health!
>
> (4-6) Concerning the woven-textile workers whom you brought in (to work) and who spoke to you as follows: (6-10) "15 barleycorns of silver is the daily wages per man. If you will not weigh and deliver 15 barleycorns of silver, then we (as a group) will take (payment in rations of) 20 silas of grain, 5 silas of beer, and 4 silas of bread per day." (10-11) Thus they spoke to you and thus you wrote to me. (12-13) The wages for a hired worker are recorded on the stela. (14-16) In accordance with what they spoke to you, either in grain or in silver, do not withhold their wages! (rev. 17-20) And when I come there, I will investigate the matter personally and I will deduct their wages from their work assignment.
>
> (21-24) Furthermore, the mat which is to be produced should not require 3600 shekels (of fiber materials)! Rather 1800 shekels for the woof, 600 shekels for the warp, in all 2400 shekels is enough for one mat. (25-27) Let them make that mat 12 cubits long and 7 cubits wide.
>
> (28-29) Furthermore, appoint a trustworthy person and let him supervise them!

The wages demanded by the workers in this letter are triple the daily wages set out in LH ¶ 274. But from that fact one cannot conclude that the economic parameters set forth in the law collection were out of touch with the reality of the market (Sweet 1958: 111). Furthermore, of course, there is no reason to assume that the wages set out in the Laws of Hammurabi were not *minimum* wages rather than *maximum* wages; the regulations in the Laws of Hammurabi, for example, could protect workers from exploitation. This would be in keeping with the intent and claims of the prologue as well. Nonetheless, whether or not the letter's reference in lines 12-13 to the stela is indeed an allusion to the stela of Hammurabi upon which his laws were inscribed, the tone of the entire letter is one of outrage—both at the workers' audacity in demanding high wages and at their attempt to cheat the administrator by using 50 percent more wool than necessary to accomplish their task. His response indicates neither acquiescence in the face of labor's demands nor acceptance of the inconsequence of the "stela"; rather, he orders his on-site representative to make the work progress at whatever cost, and promises that he himself will rectify the abuses when he arrives to assess the situation in person. Thus it is entirely possible that the writer referred to the Laws of Hammurabi (or to another collection of laws written and displayed on a stela, see below) and would keep in mind its provisions in his final settlement with his workmen. His comment, "The wages for a hired worker are recorded on the stela," confirms the publicity and publication value of the law collection in its contemporary context.

Another piece of evidence from the same period, but from outside of Mesopotamia, also refers to a stela that publicized prices and wages. This is an early nineteenth century B.C.E. stamped mudbrick from Susa, the Elamite capital, the entire text of which reads (Scheil 1939: 5 No. 3):

> Addaḫushu, the shepherd[2] of the god Shushinak, the sister's-son[3] of Shilḫaḫa, set up the stela (listing) correct (prices) in the market place, (and thus) the god Shamash will instruct him who does not know the correct price.

The stela celebrated in this brick inscription has not been recovered, and it is possible that it recorded, in addition to prices and wages, the kinds of laws and cases we find in the Sumerian and Babylonian collections presented in this volume.

Ultimately, such questions as Is there any concord between the formal law collections and the transactional contracts? or Is the daily operation of the law constrained by the rules of the formal law collections? are not really answerable and, moreover, miss the intimate connections between law and society. The many and varied manifestations of the law—including the law collections, the scholastic exercises, the court cases, the royal edicts and remissions, and the daily transactional contracts and agreements—are all evidence of the law as a function of social life. The collections translated in this volume—which range from the sophisticated, self-conscious articulations of legal rules, of administrative measures, and of judicial reforms, to the purely scholastic handbook or the crude student exercise—are all products of the cultural assumptions and values of their drafters and copyists and are clear reflections of the ancient Near Eastern concern for justice.

About the Translations

The English translations of the Sumerian and Akkadian law collections in this volume reflect a deliberate awareness of all the others and aim for consistency in translational conventions and devices. Where possible, I use the simplest, most neutral English word, in order to avoid imposing my interpretations on the texts. Thus, for example, verbal forms of *dâku* (Akkadian) and gaz (Sumerian) are always translated with forms of "to kill" (thus, "they shall kill her," or "he shall be killed," etc.)—and not, depending on varying context, with "to execute," "to put to death," or "to die."

The translations remain faithful to the moods and tenses of the original languages as well, and thus a passive "he shall be killed" should not be confused with an active "they shall kill him," which implies actors for which there might be no evidence. In the apodosis, the third person imperfect-future tense usually is translated here with the auxiliary "shall" which in formal legal contexts conveys both the senses of ordering and permitting; however, when there can be no question but that the verbal form implies an optional action, the auxiliary "may" is used in the translation instead. Injunctions expressed with Akkadian *la* are translated "he shall not . . . ," and the simple negation with Akkadian *ul* is translated "he will not . . ." (thus *imât ul iballuṭ* is translated "he shall die, he will not live").

The protasis constructed with *šumma* includes preterite verbal forms expressing the simple conditional (translated, e.g., "If he rents"), perfect verbal forms expressing the hypothetical conditional ("If he should rent"), present verbal forms expressing intention ("If he intends to rent"), and stative verbal forms expressing states. Subsequent or sequential action is expressed by following a preterite form with a perfect form (translated usually, e.g., "If he rents . . . and then breaks . . . ," but if the sequence is obvious in the English, "then" or another similar word is not always supplied).

In order to preserve the appropriate nuances and to convey the differing commodities (used in the penalty clauses or wage scales, for example), instead of translating "to pay" indiscriminately throughout, I translate "to weigh and deliver" for Akkadian *šaqālu* and Sumerian lá (always used with silver, gold, tin, etc.); "to measure and deliver" for Akkadian *madādu* and Sumerian ág (always used of grain, etc.); "to give" for Akkadian *nadānu* and Sumerian sum (or "to give for silver" or "to sell" for *ana kaspim nadānu*).

The most difficult question of translation involves the terms used to identify the subjects of the provisions and touches upon the larger and elusive question of the purpose and function of these law collections. The most frequent subject throughout is Sumerian lú, Akkadian *awīlum* (*a'īlu, amēlu*), usually a term referring to "man," "person," "someone," "anyone," etc. It is in this sense, as the unmarked, the indefinite subject, that I understand the term throughout. However, within some sets of law provisions, lú or *awīlum* is used as a marked subject and is deliberately juxtaposed with terms referring to specific social or legal classes and age or gender groups. Thus, when one provision identifies the subject as an *awīlum*, and the following one varies the provision in identifying the subject as a *muškēnum* or a *wardum*, it is clear that the *awīlum* is a member of the elite or upper class (mostly males), consciously opposed by the drafter of the composition to a member of the "commoner" class or of the "slave" class. In the latter such provisions, therefore, I have translated *awīlum* as "member of the *awīlu*-class"; in all other cases, I assume *awīlum*, etc., to be the unmarked subject, without respect to age and social or legal class. The translation used in all these other cases, then, is "man." Furthermore, I have tried throughout to avoid anachronistic translations or translations using terms with well-established modern or Western connotations. Thus such translations as "citizen" or "seignior" for *awīlum*, or "nun" for *nadītum*, can only confuse the reader who understands the "citizen" as a voting member of a *polis* or modern state, or the "nun" as a female religious living under vows of poverty and chastity. Instead I have sought and used the least encumbered or least loaded terms possible, and when such were not forthcoming, I have allowed the native terminology to remain untranslated. The minor annoyance of these Akkadian or Sumerian terms in the English translations should be alleviated by recourse to the glossary, and compensated for by the avoidance of misplaced cultural assumptions.

I have tried to remain conservative in both my restorations and my translations. When restorations are conjectural, I mark the corresponding translations with square brackets. I have been unable completely to avoid the occasional translation that may be more literal than literary, especially when the original Akkadian or Sumerian syntax is particularly complex and I have not wanted to obscure the provision's legal reasoning. Throughout I have been guided by a concern to prevent an unwary user from drawing unwarranted conclusions from nonexistent text; thus, I have sought a balance between uncritical translation and interpretive paraphrase. This has been particularly difficult to achieve with the minimal footnotes permitted by the format of this series, but I hope that the resulting translations find some acceptance from both Assyriologists and comparative legal historians, as well as serve the needs of the general reader.

About the Transliterations and Transcriptions

A few comments about the transliteration and transcription of the Sumerian and Akkadian texts is in order. Assyriologists usually publish their critical editions using syllabic transliteration, in full score, with critical apparatus and citation of all textual variants. Such editions allow each manuscript to be reconstructed separately, and give full voice to each variant tradition or dialect. The value of such a publication remains undeniable for the cuneiformist. However, for both the general reader and the specialist, there is also a place for an edition that carries the critical edition to another level, to the publication of the *results* of the editor's autopsy of the cuneiform sources. In such an enterprise, as presented in this volume, all variants and discrepancies are of course examined and weighed by the editor-translator, but only those essential to the *interpretation* of the text are noted (and not those the value of which is strictly philological or lexicographical). The benefit of having the original language text along with the translation should be obvious: readers with only an introductory knowledge of the languages should have little difficulty following the transcriptions, and even readers with no experience at all of any of the cuneiform languages should be able to find the essential key words in using these sources for their own research.

For the transcriptions or normalizations of the Akkadian texts I refer the reader to the standard grammars, especially to the comprehensive *GAG* (von Soden 1969). The transcriptional conventions follow those of the

Chicago Assyrian Dictionary (*CAD*), which diverge from those used in the German-language grammars and dictionaries; many of these conventions are noted in Brinkman 1966.

Notes

1. The letter, A 3529, in the collections of the Oriental Institute, belongs to a small archive and can be dated to about the tenth year of Samsuiluna, the immediate successor of King Hammurabi (thus to ca. 1740 B.C.E.); the archive probably comes from Kish, less than ten miles east of the dynastic capital in Babylon. The only publications are in two University of Chicago Ph.D. dissertations (Sweet 1958: 104–11 and Stuneck 1927: 25f. and 57f.).

2. "Shepherd" is an epithet referring to the king, evoking the image of his responsible care for the population placed in his charge by the deity.

3. The designation "sister's-son" (Sum. dumu-nin, Akk. *mār aḫāti*, Elamite *ruḫu-šak*) is part of the royal titulature, asserting the legitimacy of the ruler (in this case, possibly a usurper). The preferred line of succession in early second millennium Elam apparently was through the sister of a previous ruler, and the identification as "sister's-son" is not necessarily an indication of descent from an incestuous union; see van Soldt 1990.

Translations

A. Sumerian

1

Laws of Ur-Namma (LU) (ca. 2100 B.C.E., Ur)

The beginning of the prologue, where the royal sponsor would have been identified, is not well preserved. Current opinion attributes this law collection either to King Ur-Namma of Ur (r. 2112–2095 B.C.E.) or to his son and successor on the throne, Shulgi (r. 2094–2047). Not all of the historical events recounted in the prologue can be placed within the reign of Ur-Namma, and Shulgi is known for his acts of administrative and judicial reform. See the summary of the arguments in Michalowski and Walker 1989: 384–86.

Ur-Namma achieved the independence of the city of Ur from the overlord Utu-ḫegal of Uruk. During his eighteen-year reign, Ur-Namma founded the Third Dynasty of Ur, uniting for only the second time in history the city-states of southern ("Sumer and Akkad") and northern Mesopotamia after the collapse of the Dynasty of Akkad (ca. 2334–2193 B.C.E., founded by Sargon the Great). Ur-Namma's centralized bureaucracies and administration of resources allowed him to undertake the building of the magnificent ziggurats (stepped temple-towers) and other labor-intensive projects, including local temple restorations and maintenance and expansions of the canal systems. The stability of the kingdom was maintained during the forty-eight-year reign of his son Shulgi, who introduced administrative and organizational reforms into the bureaucracy that are documented in tens of thousands of surviving cuneiform tablets. This period saw, too, a great flowering of Sumerian literature—hymns, prayers, and epic cycles revolving around the palace and temple.

About the Laws

Only the prologue and fewer than forty laws are preserved; the total number of provisions and the size of the epilogue in the original, complete composition are unknown. It is possible that, after a gap, the last twenty laws and the epilogue are represented by the composition separately edited in this volume as LX. The prologue recounts the political and economic accomplishments of the king, including providing a peaceful climate for sea and land trade to flourish and regularizing and standardizing weights and measures. The first law provision of the collection provides for the death penalty for homicide and is followed by provisions dealing with various illegal or unlawful acts, the ownership of children of unions between slaves and free persons, sexual offenses, marriage, bodily injuries, insubordination, false witnesses, and agricultural offenses. Each provision is introduced by the Sumerian tukum-bi, "if."

The principal class of persons considered in the Laws of Ur-Namma is the free person (lú, "man"), which includes the wife (dam), the first-ranking wife (nitadam), the native-born woman (dumu-gi$_7$) and the widow (nu-ma-su), and probably also the young man (guruš) involved in royal- or temple-sponsored ventures; the laws also refer to the male and female slave (arad and géme).

About the Sources

The three sources used in the reconstruction of the Laws of Ur-Namma come from three—or perhaps two—different sites: the Nippur tablet preserves the beginning of the prologue and laws ¶¶ 4-20; the Ur tablets preserve ¶¶ 7-37; and the "Sippar" tablet, which might also come from Nippur,[1] completes the prologue and provides the first ten laws.

The line numbering and provision numbering present some problems. First, the Nippur and Sippar tablets (A and C) were first published with line numbers running consecutively (rather than beginning anew with each tablet column), and most previous editions have used the consecutive line numbers. Although this practice can make for difficulty in locating provisions, it has been retained—with the addition of the column numbers—for the sake of consistency. Second, Yıldız's publication of the "Sippar" source (C) in 1981, which fully preserves the first provisions, revealed that earlier estimates of the number of missing or fragmentary provisions were incorrect; the provision numbers have been adjusted accordingly and conform to the numbering initiated by Yıldız.

Prologue

(A i 1-30) ... [...] ba [...] bi [...] an [^{d}Ur]-^{d}Nam[ma nita ka]lag-g[a lugal] Úri[^{ki}-ma lugal K]i-en-[gi Ki-uri] dingir [...] bi [... (about 8 lines broken) ... ka]lam$^{?}$-ma-š[è ...] itu-da 90 še-gur 30 udu 30 sìla ì-nun sá-dug$_4$-šè mu-na-ni-gar

... Ur-Namma, the mighty warrior, king of the city of Ur, king of the lands of Sumer and Akkad ... he established 21,600 silas of barley, 30 sheep, 30 silas of butter, per month, as regular offerings ... in the land.

(A i 31-42) ud An-né ^{d}En-líl-le ^{d}Nanna-ar nam-lugal Úri^{ki}-ma ⌜mu-na-sum⌝-mu-uš-a-ba ⌜ud-ba ^{d}Ur⌝-^{d}Namma-ke$_4$ dumu tu-da ^{d}Nin-súna-ka ⌜émedu⌝ ki-ág-gá-ni-ir níg-si-sá-ni-šè ⌜níg-gi⌝-[na]-ni-šè (A i 43-ii 74) [...] x [...] x [...] mu [...] x [...] x [...] a [...] a [...] x [... (about 20 lines broken) ...] dingir [...] x x 7-bi ḫu-mu-un-da-an-⌜sum$^{?}$⌝ (A ii 75–86) Nam-ḫa-ni énsi Lagaš^{ki}-ke$_4$ ⌜ḫé-mi-íl⌝ ki-sar-ra má Mágan^{ki}-na ^{d}Nanna á ^{d}Nanna lugal-⌞gá⌝-ta ḫé-mi-gi$_4$ Úri^{ki}-ma ḫa-ba-zálag

When the gods An and Enlil turned over the kingship of the city of Ur to the god Nanna, at that time, for Ur-Namma, son born of the goddess Ninsun, for her beloved house-born slave, according to his (the god Nanna's) justice and truth ... gave to him ... I promoted Namhani to be the governor of the city of Lagash. By the might of the god Nanna, my lord, I returned Nanna's Magan-boat to the quay(?), and made it shine in the city of Ur.

(A ii 87-92) ud-ba a-šà *ni-is-kum* ì-gál-la-àm nam-ga-eš$_8$ má-laḫ$_4$ ga[l] ì-gál-la-àm (A iii 93–103) [...] x-e [... gud] dab$_5$ [... udu] dab$_5$ [...]-àm [...] x [(about 7 lines damaged)]

At that time, the *nisku*-people had control of the fields, the sea-captains had control of the foreign maritime trade. ... those who appropriate(?) [the oxen] ... those who appropriate(?) [the sheep ...]

(A iii 104-113) [ud-ba ^{d}Ur-^{d}N]amma [nita kalag]-ga [lugal Úri^{ki}]-ma [lugal Ki-en-gi] Ki-uri [á ^{d}]Nanna [lugal-g]á-ta [inim g]i$^{?}$-na [^{d}Utu(?)]-ta [níg-s]i$^{?}$-sá$^{?}$ [kalam-ma(?) ḫ]u-mu-ni-gar

[At that time, (I)], Ur-Namma, [mighty warrior, lord of the city of Ur, king of the lands of Sumer and] Akkad, [by the might] of the god Nanna, my lord, [by the true command of the god Utu(?)], I established [justice in the land(?)].

(A iii 114-124) [...] x ḫé-mi-gi$_4$ nam-ga-eš$_8$ má-laḫ$_4$ gal ùtul-e gud dab$_5$ udu dab$_5$ anše dab$_5$ uri lú gi[r$_5$-ra] Ki-en-g[i Ki-uri-a] šu ba-a[n-bar]

[...] I returned. I established freedom for the Akkadians and foreigners(?) in the lands of Sumer and Akkad, for those conducting foreign maritime trade (free from) the sea-captains, for the herdsmen (free from) those who appropriate(?) oxen, sheep, and donkeys.

(A iii 125–134, C i 1-10[2]) ud-ba Akšak^{ki} Mára-da^{ki} Gír-kal^{ki} Ka-zal-lu^{ki} ù maš-gán-bi Ú-ṣa-ru-um^{ki} níg An-ša$_4$-an^{ki}-a nam-arad ḫé-éb-ak-e á ^{d}Nanna lugal-gá-ta ama-ar-gi$_4$-bi ḫu-mu-gar

At that time, by the might of Nanna, my lord, I liberated Akshak, Marad, Girkal, Kazallu, and their settlements, and Uṣarum, whatever (territories) were under the subjugation of Anshan.

(A iii 135–iv 149, C i 11-21) urudu ba-rí-ga ḫu-mu-dím 60 sìla-àm ḫé-ge-en urudu ba-an ḫu-mu-dím 10 sìla-àm ḫé-ni-ge-en urudu ba-an si-sá lugal-la ḫu-mu-dím 5 sìla-àm ḫé-ni-ge-en na$_4$ 1 gín kù zag 1 ma-na-⌈šè?⌉ ḫé-ni-ge-en zabar 1 sìla ḫu-mu-dím 1 ma-na-àm ḫé-ni-ge-en

I made the copper bariga-measure and standardized it at 60 silas. I made the copper seah-measure, and standardized it at 10 silas. I made the normal king's copper seah-measure, and standardized it at 5 silas. I standardized (all) the stone weights (from?) the pure(?) 1-shekel (weight) to the 1-mina (weight). I made the bronze 1-sila measure and standardized it at 1 mina.[3]

(A iv 150–161, C i 22-ii 29) ud-ba gú ^{id}Idigna gú ^{id}Burun gú íd dù-a-bi add[ir si ḫé-em-mi-sá-sá] kas$_4^{?}$ šà [...] é ḫé-em-mi-in-[dù] ^{giš}kiri$_6$ [ḫé-b]í-í[b-gub] šandana lugal-e ḫé-éb-tuk

At that time, [I regulated] the river-boat traffic on the banks of the Tigris River, on the banks of the Euphrates River, on the banks of all rivers. [I secured safe roads for] the couriers(?); I [built] the (roadside) house.[4] [I planted] the orchard, the king placed a gardener in charge of them.

(A iv 162–168, C ii 30–39) nu-síg lú níg-tuku-ra ba-ra-na-an-gar nu-mu-un-su lú á tuku-ra ba-ra-na-an-gar lú 1 gín-e lú 1 ma-na-ra ba-ra-na-an-gar lú 1 udu-e lú 1 gud-ra[5] ba-ra-na-an-gar

I did not deliver the orphan to the rich. I did not deliver the widow to the mighty. I did not deliver the man with but one shekel to the man with one mina (i.e., 60 shekels). I did not deliver the man with but one sheep to the man with one ox.

(A iv 169–170, C ii 40-51) GÌR.NITÁ + GÌR.NITÁ-mu-ne ama-mu-[n]e šeš-šeš-mu-ne su-a-[su-a-ne]-ne ki ḫa-b[a-

I settled (in independent settlements?) my generals, my mothers, my brothers, and their families; I

ni-gar]-re-eš á-[ág-gá-ne]-ne-a ba-ra-ba-[gu]b-bé-en kin ba-ra-[b]a-ni-gar níg-érim níg-á-zi i-^{d}Utu ug-gu ḫé-ni-dé níg-si-sá kalam-ma ḫu-mu-ni-gar

did not accept their instructions(?), I did not impose orders. I eliminated enmity, violence, and cries for justice. I established justice in the land.

(C iii 52) ud-ba

At that time:

Laws

(C iii 52–54) tukum-bi lú-ù sag-giš bí-in-ra lú-bi ì-gaz-e-dam

¶ **1** If a man commits a homicide, they shall kill that man.

(C iii 55–56) tukum-bi lú-ù sa-gaz-šè in-ak in-gaz-e

¶ **2** If a man acts lawlessly(?), they shall kill him.

(A iv 195, C iii 57–60) tukum-bi lú-ù ḫeš$_5$-šè in-ak lú-bi en-nu-gá ì-ti-le 15 gín kù-babbar ì-lá-e

¶ **3** If a man detains(?) (another), that man shall be imprisoned and he shall weigh and deliver 15 shekels of silver.

(A v 196–198, C iii 61–64) tukum-bi arad-dè géme á-áš-a-ni in-tuk «x x» arad-bi ama-ar-gi$_4$-ni ì-gá-gá é-ta nu-ub-ta-è

¶ **4** If a male slave marries a female slave, his beloved, and that male slave (later) is given his freedom, she/he will not leave (or: be evicted from?) the house.

(A v 205–215, C iii 65–75) tukum-bi arad-dè dumu-gi$_7$ in-tuk dumu-nita 1-àm lugal-a-ni-ir in-na-an-gub-bu dumu lugal-a-ni-ir in-na-ab-gub-bu-da níg-ga é ad-da-[na] BAR-bi é-gar$_8$ é [...] dumu dumu-gi$_7$ lugal-da n[u-me-a] nam-arad-d[a$^{?}$-šè] la-ba-an-[ku$_4$-re]

¶ **5** If a male slave marries a native woman, she/he shall place one male child in the service of his master; the child who is placed in the service of his master, his paternal estate, ... the wall, the house, [...];[6] a child of the native woman will not be owned by the master, he will be pressed into slavery.

(C iv 76–80) tukum-bi dam guruš-a a nu-gi$_4$-a níg-á-gar-šè lú in-ak-ma a bí-in-gi$_4$ nita-bi ì-gaz-e

¶ **6** If a man violates the rights of another and deflowers the virgin wife of a young man, they shall kill that male.

(A v 225–231, B i 1-10, C iv 86-92[7]) tukum-bi dam guruš-a ní-te-a-ni-ta

¶ **7** If the wife of a young man, on her own initiative, approaches a

lú ba-an-ús-ma úr-ra-né ba-an-ná munus-bi ì-gaz-e nita-bi ama-ar-gi$_4$-ni ì-gá-gá

man and initiates sexual relations with him, they shall kill that woman;[8] that male shall be released.

(A v 232–235, B i 11–19, C iv 81–85) tukum-bi géme lú-ù a nu-gi$_4$-a níg-á-gar-šè lú in-ak-ma a bí-in-gi$_4$[9] 5 gín kù-babbar ì-lá-e

¶ **8** If a man acts in violation of the rights of another and deflowers the virgin slave woman of a man, he shall weigh and deliver 5 shekels of silver.

(B i 20–24, C iv 93–97) tukum-bi lú-ù dam nitadam-a-ni in-tag$_4$-tag$_4$ 1 ma-na kù-babbar ì-lá-e

¶ **9** If a man divorces his first-ranking wife, he shall weigh and deliver 60 shekels of silver.

(A vi 246–249, B i 25–29, C iv 98[10]) tukum-bi nu-ma-su ì-tag$_4$-tag$_4$ ½ ma-na kù ì-lá-e

¶ **10** If he divorces a widow, he shall weigh and deliver 30 shekels of silver.

(A vi 250–254, B i 30–36) tukum-bi nu-ma-su dub ka-kéšda nu-me-a lú úr-ra-na ba-an-ná kù nu-lá-e

¶ **11** If a man has sexual relations with the widow without a formal written contract, he will not weigh and deliver any silver (as a divorce settlement).

(A vi 267–269, B i 37) tukum-bi [(gap of about 10 lines) ...] x x [x] x bi lú x x x x

¶ **12** If [...]

(A vi 270–vii 280, B ii 1–2) tukum-bi nam-x-x lú lú-ra in-da-ab-lá dÍd-lú-ru-gú-šè in-túm dÍd-lú-ru-gú um-dadag lú in-túm-mu (...) 3 gín kù[11] ì-lá-e

¶ **13** If a man accuses another man of ... and he has him brought to the divine River Ordeal but the divine River Ordeal clears him, the one who had him brought (i.e., the accuser) (...[12]) shall weigh and deliver 3 shekels of silver.

(B ii 3-12) tukum-bi dam guruš-a-da úr-ra ná-a lú ì-da-lá Íd-dè ù-um-dadag lú ì-da-lá-[a] ⅓ ŠA [kù] ì-[lá-e]

¶ **14** If a man accuses the wife of a young man of promiscuity but the River Ordeal clears her, the man who accused her shall weigh and deliver 20 shekels of silver.

(B ii 13-23) tuk[um-bi] mí-ús-[sa tur] é ú-[ùr-ra-na-ka] ì-[in-ku$_4$] ú-ù[r dam-a-ni] ègir-[ni-ta] lú [ku-li-ni-ir]

¶ **15** If a son-in-law [enters] the household of his father-in-law but subsequently the father-in-law

ba-a[n-na-sum] níg-[dé-a in-túm-a-ni] a-rá [2-kam-ma] ì-[na-lá-e]

[gives his wife to his (the son-in-law's) comrade], he (the father-in-law) shall [weigh and deliver to him (the jilted son-in-law)] twofold (the value of) the prestations [which he (the son-in-law) brought (when he entered the house)].

(B ii 24–34) tuk[um-bi] x [...] x [...] ba-[...] ki-[...] ì-[...] x [...] lú [...] x x [...] 2 gín [kù] ì-n[a-lá-e]

¶ **16** If [...], he shall weigh and deliver to him 2 shekels of silver.

(A vii 314–323) [tukum-bi ...] géme [...]-a ki-sur-ra uru-na-ka íb-te-bal lú im-mi-gur lugal sag-gá-ke_4 lú im-mi-in-gur-ra [x] gín kù-babbar ì-lá-e

¶ **17** If [a slave or(?)] a slave woman [...] ventures beyond the borders of (his or) her city and a man returns (him or) her, the slave's master shall weigh and deliver [x] shekels of silver to the man who returned (the slave).

(A vii 324–viii 330, B ii 35-41[13]) tukum-bi [lú lú-ra ...]-a-ni [gì]ri-ni in-ku_5 10 gín kù-babbar ì-lá-e

¶ **18** If [a man] cuts off the foot of [another man with ...], he shall weigh and deliver 10 shekels of silver.

(A viii 331–338) tukum-bi lú lú-ra ^{giš}tukul-ta gìr-pad-du al-mu-ra-ni in-zi-ir 1 ma-na kù-babbar ì-lá-e

¶ **19** If a man shatters the ...-bone of another man with a club, he shall weigh and deliver 60 shekels of silver.

(A viii 339–344, B ii 42–47) tukum-bi lú lú-ra x-x-ta $kiri_4$-ni in-ku_5 $2/3$ ma-na kù-babbar ì-lá-e

¶ **20** If a man cuts off the nose of another man with ..., he shall weigh and deliver 40 shekels of silver.

(A viii 345–349, B ii 48–54) tukum-bi [lú lú-r]a [...-t]a [in-ta]-ku_5 [...]-àm [x gín kù-à]m [ì-lá]-e

¶ **21** If [a man] cuts off [the ... of another man] with [..., he shall] weigh and deliver [x shekels of silver].

(B ii 55–iii 4) [tukum]-bi [lú lú-ra ...-t]a z[ú-ni] i[n-...] 2 g[ín kù-àm] ì-[lá-e]

¶ **22** If [a man knocks out another man's] tooth with [...], he shall weigh and deliver 2 shekels of silver.

(B iii 5) tu[kum-bi ...]

¶ **23** If [...]

(gap)

(B iii 34–44) [tukum-bi ...]-a ḫa-ba-túm-mu tukum-bi géme nu-tuku 10 gín kù-babbar-àm ḫé-na-lá-e tukum-bi kù nu-tuku níg-na-me «nu» na-ab-sum-mu

¶ **24** [If...], he shall bring [a slave woman]; if he has no slave woman, he shall instead weigh and deliver 10 shekels of silver; if he has no silver, he shall give him whatever of value he has.[14]

(B iii 45–51) tukum-bi géme lú nin-a-ni-gin$_7$ dím-ma-ar áš ì-ni-dug$_4$ 1 sìla mun-àm ka-ka-ni ì-sub$_6$-bé

¶ **25** If a slave woman curses someone acting with the authority of her mistress, they shall scour her mouth with one sila of salt.[15]

(B iii 52–55) tukum-bi géme lú nin-a-ni-gin$_7$ dím-ma-ar in-ni-ra [...]

¶ **26** If a slave woman strikes someone acting with the authority of her mistress, [...].

(gap)

(B iv x–33) [tukum-bi ... x] x x x

¶ **27** [If ...]

(B iv 34–40) tukum-bi lú lú-ki-inim-ma-šè íb-ta-è lú ní-zuḫ ba-an-ku$_4$ 15 gín kù-babbar-àm ì-lá-e

¶ **28** If a man presents himself as a witness but is demonstrated to be a perjurer, he shall weigh and deliver 15 shekels of silver.

(B iv 41–46) tukum-bi lú lú ki-inim-ma-šè íb-ta-è nam-erím-ta e-gur níg-di-ba en-na-gál-la íb-su-su

¶ **29** If a man presents himself as a witness but refuses to take the oath, he shall make compensation of whatever was the object of the case.

(B iv 47–v 1) tukum-bi $^{\text{a-šà}}$aša$_5$ lú níg-á-gar-šè lú ì-ak ba-an-uru$_4$ di bí-dug$_4$ gú in-ni-šub lú-bi á-ni íb-ta-an-e$_{11}$-dè

¶ **30** If a man violates the rights of another and cultivates the field of another man, and he sues (to secure the right to harvest the crop, claiming that) he (the owner) neglected (the field)—that man shall forfeit his expenses.

(B v 2-7) tukum-bi $^{\text{a-šà}}$aša$_5$ lú lú a-da bí-GUB a-šà 1 iku 3 še-gur ì-ág-gá

¶ **31** If a man floods(?) another man's field, he shall measure and deliver 900 silas of grain per 100 sars of field.

(B v 8–17) tukum-bi lú lú $^{a\text{-}\check{s}\grave{a}}$aša$_5$ apin-lá-šè ì-na-sum nu-un-uru$_4$ šà-su-ga ì-gar 1 iku 3 še-gur ì-ág-gá

¶ **32** If a man gives a field to another man to cultivate but he does not cultivate it and allows it to become wasteland, he shall measure out 900 silas of grain per 100 sars.

(B v 18–20) tukum-bi lú lú [...]-a [(break of about 25 lines)]

¶ **33** If a man ... another man ...

(gap)

(B vi 1) [...] ì-na-lá-e[16]

¶ **37** [...] he shall weigh and deliver to him.

(remainder broken)

Notes

1. The first publication of source C, Si. 277 (in Yıldız 1981), reported that the tablet came from the Sippar collection, although a Nippur provenience later was reported by V. Donbaz apud Lieberman 1989: 243.

2. For the passage, see Steinkeller 1987: 19 n. 1, with collation of P. Michalowski for C i 3 (= A iii 125, where the geographical name is lost in the break); the change to first person does not demand that the passage be assigned to King Shulgi.

3. The order of the final two of this group of five metrological standardizations is reversed in A and differs in some details.

4. Restored following suggestions offered by M. Civil.

5. C ii 34 incorrectly marks the subject and object markers—lú 1 udu-ra(for -e) lú 1 gud-e(for -ra); the clause is omitted in A.

6. The precise sense of the second clause in ¶ 5 is uncertain but probably deals with the inheritance rights to the master's estate of the child placed in service.

7. C reverses the order of ¶¶ 7 and 8; text follows C, although the order of the provisions follows A and B.

8. B: "the man shall kill that woman."

9. So C; B: é bí-gi$_4$ lú-bi "... deflowers ..., that man (shall weigh and deliver ...)."

10. C iv 98 ends the tablet with a catchline: tukum-bi nu-mu-su lú in-tuk "If a man marries a widow," either an error or evidence of a variant tradition.

11. So B; A: ⸢2⸣[+1? gín kù]-babbar.

12. Frymer-Kensky (1977: 138–44) understands the provision to deal with an accusation of sorcery (although the surrounding provisions all deal with accusations of sexual offenses). Interpretation of the provision is hampered by two uncertainties: first, the signs indicating the nature of the offense (accusation of which must be resolved by the River Ordeal) remain unclear; second, the coherence of the provision as suggested by the transcription is misleading: the bulk of the provision comes from Source A only (col. vi 270-278, end of column), and the final two lines

come only from Source B (col. ii 1-2) with a possible—but not certain—overlap at the line recording the monetary penalty (the traces at the beginning of A vii do not conflict with the readings in B, but could easily be reconciled with a number of other readings, see the previous note).

13. Kramer's numbering of the lines in B ii needs to be adjusted in accordance with Finkelstein's suggestion that U.7740 ii "36" follows immediately after U.7739 ii 37. The resulting provision in B is a single variant provision conflating the two in A (¶¶ 18 and 19), and reads tuk[um-bi] gìr-pa[d-du] x [...] [...] x [in-t]a-ku_5 [x gín k]ù-àm [ì-l]á-e "If ... he severs a bone ..., he shall weigh and deliver [x shekels] of silver."

14. Text (error) "he will not give him anything."

15. Different interpretations of this difficult provision are given by Finkelstein 1969a: 70, Römer 1982: 22, and Sauren 1990: 41–42.

16. Source B, which has four columns on the obverse, has inscribed signs on the reverse on only one column (B v) and on the first line of another (B vi 1), leaving blank almost three full columns.

2

Laws of Lipit-Ishtar (LL) (ca. 1930 B.C.E., Isin)

The royal authority behind this collection of laws is Lipit-Ishtar (r. 1934-1924), fifth ruler of the First Dynasty of Isin (founded after the collapse of the Third Dynasty of Ur). Members of the dynasty ruled the city of Isin and consolidated military and political power in the cities of Lower Mesopotamia. Although political and military dominance in the region shifted to Larsa to the south soon after Lipit-Ishtar's reign, the city of Isin, which was a major cultic center for worship of the goddess of healing, continued to be an important cultic and strategic center throughout Mesopotamian history.

In Babylonia, from the end of the third millennium through the middle of the second, there was in use a sequential dating system involving "year names," formulaic statements commemorating an event of military or cultic importance during the preceding year and used to identify the year in all dated documents. One such year name in the reign of Lipit-Ishtar could include a reference to the erecting of the stela on which this composition was inscribed: "The year in which Lipit-Ishtar established justice in the lands of Sumer and Akkad." The commemoration in a year name of the king's act of justice is an indication of the importance of this royal responsibility.

About the Laws

A prologue, an epilogue, and almost fifty provisions are extant. The prologue includes a self-praise of Lipit-Ishtar's benevolence for all of Sumer and Akkad, lists the southern Mesopotamian cities under the care of his divinely sanctioned rule, and stresses his role as restorer of justice and the social order. The first laws securely identifiable with this collection deal with boats and are followed by laws dealing with agriculture, fugitive slaves, false testimony, foster care and apprenticeship, marriage and associated property rights, and rented oxen. Each law provision is introduced by Sumerian tukum-bi, "if." The epilogue, after reiterating the fair application of justice under the rulership of Lipit-Ishtar, invokes blessings on any future king who honors and respects the monumental stela recording this composition and curses anyone who would desecrate or mutilate it.

The laws in this composition are concerned primarily with the free person (lú, "man"), which includes the child (dumu) in the context of adoption or apprenticeship and inheritance and the free-born or native son (dumu-gi$_7$), three categories of priestess or devotee (*nadītu*, *qadištu*, and *ugbabtu*), the wife (dam), and the first-ranking wife (nitadam). Insofar as the rights of the free person are affected, the laws also refer to the male and female slave (arad and géme) and to the palace dependent or client (*miqtu*).

About the Sources

Almost all the sources for the LL come from Nippur, which had active scribal schools during the Old Babylonian period and from which archaeological excavations in this century have yielded rich cuneiform finds. Source R apparently comes from Kish, and source N from Sippar, both sites that have also yielded other law collections of the early second millennium B.C.E.

The LL is known from more than a dozen manuscripts,[1] but difficulties in reconstruction and placement of fragments remain. Thus, for example, the first provisions given here, identified as ¶¶a–g, might not belong to the composition at all. The large tablet which originally held the entire composition (sources B, C+H, and G, all from the same tablet although they cannot be physically joined) was thought by Steele to include ten columns on each side; in fact, there are the remains of wedges in a column to the right of the first well-preserved column on the reverse (Steele's "column XI"), and there were therefore at least eleven columns per surface.

Prologue

(i 1–19 [A i 1-19, B i 1'-2']) [ud An]-gal [a-a dingir-re]-ne-ke$_4$ [^{d}En]-líl [lugal kur-kur]-ra-ke$_4$ [en nam-tar]-re-dè [^{d}Nin]-ì-si-na [dumu A]n-na-ra [nin s]un$_5$-na [nam-nir-gá]l-la-ni-šè [íb-š]i-ḫúl-la [i]gi-bar zalag-ga-ni-šè mu-un-ši-in-⸢gá-gá⸣ Ì-si-in^{ki} in-dub-ba An-né gar-ra-na bala ša$_6$-ga nam-lugal Ki-en-gi [Ki]-uri im-ma-an-sum-mu-uš-a

[When] great [god An, father of the gods], and the god Enlil, [king of the lands, the lord who determines] destinies, gave a favorable reign and the kingship of the lands of Sumer and Akkad to the goddess Ninisina, child of An, pious lady, for whose reign [...] rejoicing, for whose brilliant glance ..., in the city of Isin, her treasure house(?), established by the god An,

(i 20–37 [A i 20–ii 13, B i 3'-5']) ud-[ba] ^{d}*Li-pí-it-Ištar* sipa giš-tuku mu pà-da ^{d}Nu-nam-nir-ra níg-si-[sá] kalam-ma gá-gá-dè i-^{d}Utu ka-ta ḫa-lam-e-dè níg-érim níg-á-zi giš-tukul gi$_4$-gi$_4$-dè Ki-en-gi Ki-uri su-ba du$_{10}$-ge-dè An-né ^{d}En-líl-le ^{d}*Li-pí-it-Ištar* nam-nun kalam-ma-šè mu-un-pà-dè-eš-a-ba

At that time, the gods An and Enlil called Lipit-Ishtar to the princeship of the land—Lipit-Ishtar, the wise shepherd, whose name has been pronounced by the god Nunamnir —in order to establish justice in the land, to eliminate cries for justice, to eradicate enmity and armed violence, to bring well-being to the lands of Sumer and Akkad.

(i 38–55 [A ii 14–iii 8]) ud-ba ^{d}*Li-pí-it-Ištar* sipa sun$_5$-na Nibru^{ki} engar zi Úri^{ki}-ma muš-nu-túm-mu Eridu^{ki}-ga en me-te Unu^{ki}-ga [lugal] Ì-[si-in^{ki}-na lu]gal Ki-e[n-gi Ki-uri š]à-ge-tú[m-a] ^{d}Inanna-ka me-en inim ^{d}En-líl-lá-ta níg-si-sá [Ki-e]n-gi Ki-uri [ì-ni-i]n-gar-ra-aš

At that time, I, Lipit-Ishtar, the pious shepherd of the city of Nippur, the faithful husbandman of the city of Ur, he who does not forsake the city of Eridu, the befitting lord of the city of Uruk, the king of the city of Isin, king of the lands of Sumer and Akkad, the heart's desire of the goddess Inanna, by the command of the god Enlil, I established justice in the lands of Sumer and Akkad.

(ii 1–15 [A iii 9–23]) [ud-b]i-a [dumu-ní]ta dumu-munus [Nib]ru^{ki} [dumu-ní]ta dumu-munus [Ú]ri^{ki}-[ma] [du]mu-níta dumu-munus Ì-si-in^{ki}-na [dumu]-níta dumu-munus [Ki-en]-gi Ki-uri [lú gú-b]i-a [šudul(?)] nam-arad [ḫu-m]u-ni-íb-ak [am]a-ar-gi$_4$-bi [ḫu]-mu-gar ki-bi-šè ḫé-bí-dab$_5$

At that time, I liberated the sons and daughters of the city of Nippur, the sons and daughters of the city of Ur, the sons and daughters of the city of Isin, the sons and daughters of the lands of Sumer and Akkad, who were subjugated [by the yoke(?)], and I restored order.

(ii 16–24 [A iii 24–26, iv 1–6]) dub$^{?}$-sag-ta ad-da dumu-ne-ne-er ḫu-mu-ne-en-íl dumu ad-da-b[i-ir] ḫu-mu-ne-e[n-íl] ad-da dumu-ne-[ne-da] ḫu-mu-ne-gub-b[a-àm] dumu ad-da-bi-[da] ḫé-eb-da-gub-ba-àm

With a ... decree(?) I made the father support his children, I made the child support his father. I made the father stand by his children, I made the child stand by his father.

(ii 25–40 [A iv 7–22, B ii 1'-5']) é ad-da é [šeš-šeš-a-ka] dù-a-[bi] ḫé-su$_8$-

I imposed service (equally) on the household of a living father and on

ga-[àm] ^{d}*Li-pí-it-Ištar* dumu ^{d}En-líl-lá me-en é ad-da é šeš-šeš-a-ka 70 ḫé-gub é guruš sag aša-ta itu-da ud 10-àm ḫé-gub [...] ... [...] ... [...] dam-lú [...] dumu-lú [...] a [...]

the undivided household [of brothers]. I, Lipit-Ishtar, son of the god Enlil, obligated those in a household of a living father and in an undivided household of brothers to service for seventy (days per year), I obligated those in a household of dependent workers to service for ten days per month. ... the wife of a man ... the son of a man ... [(more than two columns lost)]

(B v 1–3) ugnim-ke$_4$ [x (x)]-gál-la [x x]-àm ... (B vi 1–3) níg-gur$_{11}$ é ad-da x-x-ga-bi [...] ba ... (B vii 1-3) dumu GÌR.NITÁ dumu šà é-gal x-nu-[...]-ni

[...] the troops, ... (col. vi) ... the property of the paternal estate ... (col. vii) ... the son of the governor, the son of the palace official, ...

[ud-ba]

[At that time:]

Laws

(gap)

(P rev. ii' 2'–7') tukum-[bi] gud áb-ùr-ra lú [in-ḫun] mu 2-àm addi[r-šè] 8 še-gur in-na-ág-ág gud áb-sag murub$_4$ addir-[šè] 6 še-gur in-na-ág-ág

¶ **a** If a man rents an ox for the rear of the team, he shall measure and deliver 2400 silas of grain for two years as its hire; if it is an ox for the front or middle, he shall measure and deliver 1800 silas of grain (for two years) as its hire.

(P rev. ii' 8'–11') tukum-bi lú ba-ug$_7$ dumu-nita nu-un-tuku dumu-munus dam nu-un-du$_{12}$-a ibila-a-ni m[e-eš]

¶ **b** If a man dies without male offspring, an unmarried daughter shall be his heir.

(P rev. ii' 12'–15') tukum-[bi lú ba-ug$_7$] dumu-munus-a-ni [...] níg-gur$_{11}$ é ad-da-na [...] nin$_9$ bàn-da murgu$_x$ (LUM) é x [...]

¶ **c** If [a man dies] and his daughter [is married(?)], the property of the paternal estate [...], a younger sister, after [...] the house [...]

(P rev. iii' 2'–6') tuku[m-bi ...] x dumu-munus lú-[ka i-ni-in]-ra níg-

¶ **d** If [a ...] strikes the daughter of a man and causes her to lose her

šà-[ga-n]a šu mu-u[n-da-an-lá] ½ ma-na [kù-babbar ì-lá]-e

fetus, he shall weigh and deliver 30 shekels of silver.

(P rev. iii' 7'–8') tukum-b[i b]a-ug$_7$ nita-bi ì-[gaz]-e

¶ e If she dies, that male[2] shall be killed.

(P rev. iii' 9'–13') tukum-bi x-x géme lú-ka i-ni-in-ra níg-šà-ga-na šu mu-un-da-an-lá 5 gín kù-[babbar ì-lá]-e

¶ f If a ... strikes the slave woman of a man and causes her to lose her fetus, he shall weigh and deliver 5 shekels of silver.

(P rev. iii' 14'–15') tukum-[bi ...] x x [...]

¶ g If [...]

(gap)

(C xiii 9–11) x [...] má [...] má íb-[su-su]

¶ **4** [If ... the] boat [is lost], he shall [replace] the boat.

(C xiii 12–23) tuku[m-bi] lú-ù má in-ḫun kaskal inim-dug$_4^{du}$-a in-na-an-gar [e-n]e kaskal-bi in-kúr ki-ba[3] má-u$_5$ sa-gaz-šè ba-ak lú má i[n-ḫun-e] má í[b-su-su] ù [á-bi ì-ág-e]

¶ **5** If a man rents a boat and an agreed route is established for him, but he violates its route and the boat ... in that place—he has acted lawlessly; the man who rented the boat shall replace the boat and [he shall measure and deliver in grain its hire].

(C xiv 6–8) ì-n[a-x ...] níg-ba-[ni-šè] íb-ba-a[n-sum-e]

¶ **6** [...] he shall give as his gift.

(C xiv 9–22, R 1'–6') tukum-bi[4] kiri$_6$-ni nu-kiri$_6$-ra ḫun-kiri$_6$ e$_{11}$-dè-dè in-na-an-sum nu-kiri$_6$-ke$_4$ lugal kiri$_6$-ra [...] in-da-gub-ba ^{giš}nimbar-ba igi-10-gál-bi-im zú-lum-bi in-da-gu$_7$-e

¶ **7** If he leases his orchard to a gardener in an orchard-lease, the gardener shall plant [...] for the owner of the orchard, he (the gardener) shall have the use of the dates from one-tenth of the palm trees.

(C xiv 23–25, R 7') tukum-bi lú-ù [...]

¶ **7a** If a man [...]

(C xv 3-7, D i 1-11, E i 1-11) tukum-bi lú lú-ù kiri$_6$ giš gub-bu-dè kislaḫ in-na-an-sum kislaḫ-bi kiri$_6$ giš gub-

¶ **8** If a man gives another man fallow land for the purpose of planting an orchard but he does not

bu-dè nu-ni-in-til lú kiri$_6$ in-gub-ba šà ḫa-la-ba-na-ka kislaḫ ba-ra-ab-tag$_4$-a in-na-ab-sum-mu

complete the planting of the orchard, they shall give the fallow land which he neglected to one who is willing to plant the orchard as his share.

(C xv 8–14, D i 12–15, E i 12–15) tukum-bi lú-ù kiri$_6$ lú-ka ì-in-e$_{11}$ nam-nú-zuḫ-šè ba-dab$_5$ 10 gín kù-babbar ì-lá-e

¶ **9** If a man enters the orchard of another man and is seized there for thievery, he shall weigh and deliver 10 shekels of silver.

(C xv 15–19, D i 16–20, E i 16–18) tukum-bi lú-ù kiri$_6$ lú-ka giš in-sìg $^1/_3$ ma-na kù-babbar ì-lá-e

¶ **10** If a man cuts down a tree in another man's orchard, he shall weigh and deliver 20 shekels of silver.

(D i 21–ii 13, E ii 1–15) tukum-bi lú é-e ús-sa-ni kislaḫ lú al-tag$_4$ lugal é-a-ke$_4$ lú kislaḫ-ra kislaḫ-zu al-tag$_4$ é-mu lú ì-bùr-dè é-zu kala-ga-ab in-na-an-dug$_4$ inim ka-kéš-du-bi un-da-an-ge-en lugal kislaḫ-a-ke$_4$ lugal é-a-ra níg-ù-gu-dé-a-ni in-na-ab-su-su

¶ **11** If a man—adjacent to whose house another man has neglected his fallow land—(if this) householder declares to the owner of the fallow land: "Your fallow land has been neglected; someone could break into my house. Fortify your property!" and it is confirmed that this formal warning was given, the owner of the fallow land shall restore to the owner of the house any of his property that is lost.

(D ii 14–22, E ii 16–18) tukum-bi géme arad lú-ù šà-uru-ka ba-záḫ é lú-ka 1 itu-àm ì-tuš-a ba-an-ge-en sag sag-gin$_7$ ba-ab-sum-mu

¶ **12** If a man's female slave or male slave flees within the city, and it is confirmed that the slave dwelt in a man's house for one month, he (the one who harbored the fugitive slave) shall give slave for slave.

(D ii 23–iii 2, E iii 4–7) tukum-bi sag nu-tuku 15 gín kù-babbar ì-lá-e

¶ **13** If he has no slave, he shall weigh and deliver 15 shekels of silver.

(C xvi 1–4, D iii 3–13, E iii 8–17) tukum-bi arad-lú-ke$_4$ lugal-a-ni-ir nam-arad-da-ni ba-an-da-gur lugal-

¶ **14** If a man's slave contests his slave status against his master, and it is proven that his master has

a-ni-ir nam-arad-da-ni a-rá 2-àm un-ge-en arad-bi al-búr-e

been compensated for his slavery two-fold, that slave shall be freed.

(C xvi 5–8, D iii 14–17, E iii 18-21) tukum-bi *mi-iq-tum* níg-ba lugal-kám nu-ub-da-an-kar-re

¶ **15** If a *miqtu*-person is a gift of the king, he will not be appropriated.

(C xvi 9–15, D iii 18–25, E iv 1–8) tukum-bi *mi-iq-tum* ní-te-a-ni-ta lú-ù un-ši-gen lú-bi nu-un-tag-tag ki šà-ga-na-šè ḫa-ba-gen

¶ **16** If a *miqtu*-person goes (into service) to a man of his own free will, that man will not restrict(?) him, but he (the *miqtu*) shall go wherever he wishes.

(D iv 1–9, E iv 9–18) tukum-bi lú lú-ù á nu-gar-ra-ta inim nu-zu-ni in-da-lá lú-bi nu-un-ge-en inim in-da-lá-a nam-i-ni-tag-ba íb-íl-e

¶ **17** If a man, without grounds(?), accuses another man of a matter of which he has no knowledge, and that man does not prove it, he shall bear the penalty of the matter for which he made the accusation.

(D iv 10–22, E iv 19–20) tukum-bi lugal é-a ù nin é-a-ke_4 gú-un é-a in-šub-bu-uš lú kúr-e in-íl mu 3-kám-ma-ka nu-ub-ta-è-e lú gú-un é-a in-íl-la é-bi ba-an-tùm lugal é-a-ke_4 inim nu-um-gá-gá-a

¶ **18** If the master or mistress of an estate defaults on the taxes due from the estate and an outsider assumes the taxes, he (the master) will not be evicted for three years; (but after three years of defaulting on the taxes) the man who has assumed the tax burden shall take possession of the estate and the (original) master of the estate will not make any claims.

(B xvi 1'–9', D iv 23–24) tukum-bi lugal é-a-ka [...] ... in-da-a[n-x]

¶ **19** If the master of the estate [...]

(B xvi 10'–14') tukum-bi lú-ù dumu túl-ta šu ba-ra-an-kar giri-[na šu bí-in-ti ...]

¶ **20** If a man rescues a child from a well, he shall [take his] feet [and seal a tablet with the size of his feet (for identification).[5]]

(gap)

(N ii 1') ud x x lú á-è-a

¶ **20a** ... when ... fosterage.

(N ii 2'–5') tukum-bi lú-ù dumu á-è-[a] á-kala-ni-gin$_7$ nu-bùlug-[e-dè] igi di-kud-dè-šè un-ge-en ama tu-du-na ba-an-ši-gur-ru

¶ **20b** If a man does not raise the son whom he contracted to raise in an apprenticeship, and it is confirmed before the judges, he (the child) shall be returned to his birth mother.

(N ii 6'–8') [tukum-bi lú]-ù dumu-munus á-è-[a ...]-x-na-a-e-na [...]

¶ **20c** If a man [does not raise] the daughter whom he contracted to raise [...]

(gap)

(B xvii 1'–11') [tukum-bi ...] in-du$_{12}$ níg-ba é ad-da-na-ka ba-an-na-ba-a ibila-ni-im ba-an-tùmu [...] (O rev. i' 1'–6') [tukum-bi ...] dam-e ba-an-sum níg-ba é ad-da-na-ka ba-an-na-ba-a šeš-a-ne-ne nu-um-da-ba-e-ne ù [...]

¶ **21**[6] (B) [If ...] marries, the (marriage) gift which is given by(?) her/his paternal estate shall be taken for her/his heir. [...] (O) [If ...] is given to a wife, her/his brothers will not include for division (among their inheritance shares) the (marriage) gift which had been given by(?) her/his paternal estate, but [...]

(B xvii 12'–18') tukum-bi ad-da ti-la dumu-munus-a-ni-ir nin-dingir lukur ù nu-gig ḫé-a ibila-gin$_7$-nam é ì-ba-e-ne

¶ **22** If, during a father's lifetime, his daughter becomes an *ugbabtu*, a *nadītu*, or a *qadištu*, they (her brothers) shall divide the estate considering her as an equal heir.

(B xvii 19'–20', M ii 5–9) tukum-bi dumu-munus é ad-da-ka ti-la dam-ra la-ba-[an-sum] šeš-a-ne-ne dam-ra in-na-an-sum-mu

¶ **23** If a daughter is not given in marriage while her father is alive, her brothers shall give her in marriage.

(M ii 10–18) [tu]kum-bi [nam]-arad in-tuku [x]-a-x ba-ug$_7$ [...] lú kúr-e [...] ... [...-a]n-tuku-tuku-a [...]

¶ **23a** If he takes a slave [...] he dies [...] an outsider [...] marries(?) [...]

(M ii 19–20) [tuku]m-bi [lú]-ù [...]

¶ **23b** If a man [...]

(B xviii 1'–5', F i 1–13, J ii' 1'–7') [tuku]m-bi [dam eg]ir-ra [ba-a]n-

¶ **24** If the second wife whom he marries bears him a child, the

du_{12}-a [du]mu in-ši-in-tu-ud sag-rig_7 é ad-da-na-ta mu-un-túm-ma dumu-na-ka dumu dam-nitadam ù dumu dam-egir-ra níg-gur_{11} ad-da-ne-ne téš-a sì-ga-bi ì-ba-e-ne

dowry which she brought from her paternal home shall belong only to her children; the children of the first-ranking wife and the children of the second wife shall divide the property of their father equally.

(B xviii 6'–19', F i 14–25, J ii' 8'–19', O ii' 1'–7') tukum-bi lú-ù dam in-du_{12} dumu in-ši-in-tu-ud dumu-bi ì-ti ù géme lugal-a-ni-ir dumu in-ši-in-tu-ud ad-da-a géme ù dumu-ne-ne ama-ar-gi_4-bi in-gar dumu géme-ke_4 dumu lugal-a-na-ra é nu-un-da-ba-e

¶ **25** If a man marries a wife and she bears him a child and the child lives and a slave woman also bears a child to her master, the father shall free the slave woman and her children; the children of the slave woman will not divide the estate with the children of the master.

(B xviii 20', F i 26–ii 6, G xix 11–12, J ii' 20', M iii 1', O ii' 8'–9') [tuk]um-bi [dam]-nitadam-a-ni [ba]-ug_7 [eg]ir dam-a-na-ta [géme]-ni nam-dam-šè [ba-a]n-du_{12}-du_{12} [dumu] dam-nit[adam-a-na] ibi[la-a-ni ì-me-en] dumu géme lugal-a-ni-[ir] in-ši-in-tu-ud dumu dumu-gi_7-gin_7-nam é-a-ni íb-dùg-g[e]

¶ **26** If his first-ranking wife dies and after his wife's death he marries the slave woman (who had borne him children), the child of his first-ranking wife shall be his (primary) heir; the child whom the slave woman bore to her master is considered equal to a native free-born son and they shall make good his (share of the) estate.

(F ii 7–25, G xix 13–17, M iii 2'–8') tukum-bi lú-ù dam-a-ni dumu nu-un-ši-in-tu-ud kar-kid-da tílla-a dumu in-ši-in-tu-ud kar-kid-ba še-ba ì-ba síg-ba-ni in-na-ab-sum-mu dumu kar-kid-dè in-ši-in-tu-ud-da ibila-ni ì-me-en ud dam-a-ni a-na-ti-la-aš kar-kid dam-nitadam-ra é-a nu-mu-un-da-an-tuš

¶ **27** If a man's wife does not bear him a child but a prostitute from the street does bear him a child, he shall provide grain, oil, and clothing rations for the prostitute, and the child whom the prostitute bore him shall be his heir; as long as his wife is alive, the prostitute will not reside in the house with his first-ranking wife.

(B xix 1'–8', F ii 26–iii 6, J iii 1'–6', L i 1'–5') tukum-bi lú-ù dam-nitadam-a-ni igi-ni ba-ab-gi_4 ù šu ba-an-lá-lá é-ta nu-ub-ta-è dam-a-ni dam

¶ **28** If a man's first-ranking wife loses her attractiveness or becomes a paralytic, she will not be evicted from the house; however, her hus-

galam-na ba-an-du$_{12}$-du$_{12}$ dam-egir-ra dam-nitadam in-íl-íl

band may marry a healthy wife,[7] and the second wife shall support the first-ranking wife.[8]

(B xix 9'–19', F iii 7-20, J iii 7'–20', L ii 1'–2') tukum-bi mí-ús-sá-tur é ur$_7$-ra ì-in-ku$_4$ níg-mí-ús-sá in-ak egir-bi-ta im-ta-an-è-eš dam-a-ni ku-li-ni-ir ba-na-an-sum-mu-uš níg-mí-ús-sá in-túm-a-ni in-na-ab-tab-e-ne dam-bi ku-li-ni nu-un-du$_{12}$-du$_{12}$

¶ **29** If a son-in-law enters the household of his father-in-law and performs the bridewealth presentation, but later they evict him and give his wife to his comrade, they shall restore to him twofold the bridewealth which he brought, and his comrade will not marry his wife.

(B xix 20'–29', F iii 21–iv 5, J iii 21'–iv 8, L ii 3'–4', K iii 1'–5') tukum-bi guruš dam-du$_{12}$ kar-kid-dè tílla-a in-du$_{12}$-àm kar-kid-bi-ir nu-un-ši-gur-ru-da di-kud-e-ne in-na-an-eš egir-bi-ta dam-nitadam dam-a-ni ba-an-tag$_4$ kù dam-tag$_4$-a-ni ù-na-an-sum kar-kid-bi nu-un-du$_{12}$-du$_{12}$

¶ **30** If a young married man has sexual relations with a prostitute from the street, and the judges order him not to go back to the prostitute, (and if) afterwards he divorces his first-ranking wife and gives the silver of her divorce settlement to her, (still) he will not marry the prostitute.

(F iv 6-14, G xx 1'–7', J iv 9-19, K iii' 6'–12') tukum-bi ad-da ti-la dumu igi-na ša$_6$-ga níg-ba in-na-an-ba kišib in-na-an-sar egir ad-da ba-ug$_7$-a-ta ibila-e-ne é ad-da ì-ba-e-ne ḫa-la ba-a nu-un-gá-gá-ne inim ad-da-ne-ne a-a nu-un-ne-ne

¶ **31** If a father, during his lifetime, gives his favored son a gift for which he writes a sealed document, after the father has died the heirs shall divide the (remaining) paternal estate; they will not contest the share which was allotted, they will not repudiate their father's word.

(G xx 8'–16', J iv 20-22, L iii 1'–6') tukum-bi ad-da ti-la dumu šeš gal-a-ni-ir níg-mí-ús-sá in-na-a[n-sum] igi ad-da ti-l[a-šè] dam ba-an-du$_{12}$ egir ad-da [ba-ug$_7$-a-ta] ibila-[e-ne] é-a x [...] é ad-[da-ta] níg-mí-ús-[sa] in-x-[...] níg-mí-ús-[sa ...]

¶ **32** If a father, during his lifetime, designates the bridewealth for his eldest son and he (the son) marries while the father is still alive, after the father has died the heirs [shall ...] the estate [...] from the paternal estate [...] the bridewealth they shall [...] the bridewealth [...]

(B xx 1') [...]-x-ne

¶ **32a** [...]

(B xx 2'–8') [tuk]um-bi dumu-munus lú é nu-gi$_4$-a giš ì-zu lú ba-ab-dug$_4$ giš nu-un-zu-a un-ge-en 10 gín kù-babbar ì-lá-e

¶ **33** If a man claims that another man's virgin daughter has had sexual relations but it is proven that she has not had sexual relations, he shall weigh and deliver 10 shekels of silver.

(B xx 9'–13') tukum-bi lú-ù gud in-ḫun sa-sal-KU-a bí-in-sil igi-3-gál šám-ma-kám ì-lá-e

¶ **34** If a man rents an ox and cuts the hoof tendon, he shall weigh and deliver one-third of its value (in silver).

(B xx 14'–17', L iv 1'–2') tukum-bi lú-ù gud in-ḫun igi-bi in-ḫul šu-ri-a šám-ma-kám ì-lá-e

¶ **35** If a man rents an ox and destroys its eye, he shall weigh and deliver one-half of its value (in silver).

(B xx 18'–21', L iv 3'–6', S 1'–4') tukum-bi lú-ù gud in-ḫun si-bi ìb-ta-an-kud igi-4-gál šám-ma-kám ì-lá-e

¶ **36** If a man rents an ox and breaks its horn, he shall weigh and deliver one-quarter of its value (in silver).

(B xx 22'–26') tukum-bi lú-ù gud in-ḫun kun-bi íb-ta-an-kud-ru igi-4-gál šám-ma-kám ì-lá-e

¶ **37** If a man rents an ox and breaks its tail, he shall weigh and deliver one-quarter of its value (in silver).

(G xxi 1–4, J v 1'–3', K iv' 1'–4') [tukum-bi ...] in-ak [...]-e [... ì-l]á-e

¶ **38** [If a man ...], he shall weigh and deliver (in silver).

Epilogue

(xxi 5–17 [G xxi 5–17, J v 4'–17', K iv' 5'–11']) [inim g]i-na ^{d}Utu-ta [Ki]-en-gi Ki-uri di gi-na ḫé-bí-dab$_5$ ka-ta-è ^{d}En-líl-la-ta ^{d}*Li-pí-it-Ištar* dumu ^{d}En-líl-lá me-en níg-érim níg-á-zi dug$_4$-ge ḫé-mi-gi ér a-nir i-^{d}Utu di-bi níg-gig-ga ḫé-ni-ku$_4$ níg-zi níg-gi-na pa-è ḫé-mi-ak su Ki-en-gi Ki-uri ḫu-mu-du$_{10}$ [...]

In accordance with the true word of the god Utu, I made the lands of Sumer and Akkad hold fair judicial procedure. In accordance with the utterance of the god Enlil, I, Lipit-Ishtar, son of Enlil, eradicated enmity and violence. I made weeping, lamentation, shouts for justice, and suits taboo. I made right and truth shine forth, and I brought well-being to the lands of Sumer and Akkad. [...]

(xxi 36–48 [B xxi 1'–14', L vi 1'–7', M v 1'–13']) [...]-kal-la [...] ... sag gi$_{6}$ ud tag-ga-ba ud níg-si-sá Ki-en-gi Ki-uri i-ni-in-gar-ra-a na$_{4}$-bi ki ḫé-im-ma-ni-tag lú á níg-ḫul dím-ma nu-ub-ši-ág-gá-a níg-dím-ma-mu nu-ub-zi-ri-a mu-sar-ra-ba šu bí-íb-ùr-a mu-ni li-bí-íb-sar-ri-a nam-ti zi ud-sù-gál sag-e-eš ḫé-rig$_{7}$-ga É-kur-ra gú an-šè ḫé-ni-in-zi sag-ki zalag-ga ^{d}En-líl-lá-ka an-ta ḫé-ib-gi$_{4}$

[...] all humankind. When I established justice in the lands of Sumer and Akkad, I erected this stela. He who will not do anything evil to it, who will not damage my work, who will <not> efface my inscription and write his own name on it – may he be granted life and breath of long days; may he raise his neck to heaven in the Ekur temple; may the god Enlil's brilliant countenance be turned upon him from above.

(xxi 49–60 [B xxi 15'–26']) lú á níg-ḫul dím-ma íb-ši-ág-gá-a níg-dím ma-mu íb-zi-ri-a é-níg-gur$_{11}$-ra ì-ni-ku$_{4}$-ku$_{4}$ ki-gub-ba-bi íb-kúr-ru-a mu-sar-ra-ba šu bí-ìb-ùr-ru-a mu-ni bí-íb-sar-re-a [áš-bala-ba]-ke$_{4}$-eš lú kúr [šu ba-a]n-zi-zi-a lú-bi lugal ḫ]é-a [en ḫé]-a [ù lú énsi ḫé-à ...]

(But) he who does anything evil to it, who damages my work, who enters the treasure room, who alters its pedestal, who effaces this inscription and writes his own name (in place of mine), or, because of this curse, induces an outsider to remove it—that man, whether he is a king, an *ēnu*-lord, or an ensi-ruler [... may he be completely obliterated ...]

(gap)

(xxii 6–16 [G xxii 1'–9', S rev. 1-7]) [...] dumu-sag ^{d}En-líl-lá-ke$_{4}$ [nu]-un-da-an-te numun$^{!}$ na-an-ni-ku$_{4}$ [...] ...-ne kalag-ga numun [...] tukul-a ba-an-da-an-kar [é-a]-na ú-mu-na-ni-in-ku$_{4}$ [ibila]-a-ni nam-me [...] ^{d}Ašnan ^{d}Sumukan [en ḫé-g]ál-la-ke$_{4}$-ne [an k]i-a ba-an-da-an-[kar$^{?}$-r]e-eš

May [... the god ...], primary son of the god Enlil, not approach; may the seed not enter; ... the mighty one, the seed, ... May he who escapes from the weapon, after he enters (the safety of) his house, may he not have [any heirs]. May [the gods ...], Ashnan, and Sumukan, lords of abundance, [withhold(?) the bounty of heaven and] earth. [...]

(gap)

(xxii 34–52 [B xxii 1'–19']) [...] ^{d}En-líl-[lá] níg-ba-a É-kur-[ra] ìl-la-na

May [...] the god Enlil [...] revoke the gift of the lofty Ekur temple.

inim ḫé-im-mi-ib-gi$_4$-gi$_4$ ^{d}Utu di-kud-an-ki-ke$_4$ [x] inim maḫ-da [ḫa-b]a-an-da-an-kar [x] x-ma-na [x]-na-ni úr-bi [é]-a-ni-a mu-tùm [x] x in-sar$^{?}$ [ur]u^{ki}-bi du$_6$-du$_6$-ra ḫé-en-šed ma-da-na úr-bi na-an-gi-ni lugal-bi nam-me ^{d}Nin-urta [ur]-sag kala-ga [dumu-^{d}En-l]íl-la [ḫé]-šub-bé [...]

May the god Utu, judge of heaven and earth, remove the august word. [...] its foundation bring into his house(?) ... May he make his cities into heaps of ruins. May the foundations of his land not be stable, may it have no king. May the god Ninurta, mighty warrior, son of the god Enlil, [...]

(remainder broken)

Notes

1. There are two fragments of a stone stela that could be Lipit-Ishtar's original monument on which the laws were inscribed: Biggs 1969: 40 No. 49 and Legrain 1926: pl. 17 No. 47 (here source T) are nonjoining fragments that preserve narrative belonging to the prologue of this collection.

2. The term is used elsewhere in the law collections (nita in LU, *zikaru* in LH) to refer to the "other man," the "not-husband" who violates the husband's exclusive procreative rights by engaging in illicit sexual intercourse; by using the same term here (in ¶e and probably to be restored at the beginning of ¶d) to identify the man responsible for a miscarriage, the violation of the husband's rights is extended beyond the sexual act.

3. Text UD.

4. Var. adds lú-[ù], "(If) a man ..."

5. The restoration is based on *ana ittišu* III iii 39ff., in Landsberger 1937: 44–45, and see *CAD* Š/2 298 s.v. *šēpu* mng. 1a-5' and Leichty 1989: 349–56.

6. It is not clear whether manuscripts B and O preserve nonoverlapping (or variant) portions of one provision, or if these lines in O preserve a new provision.

7. Var. dam-2-kam-ma "a second wife."

8. Var. "he shall support the second wife and the first-ranking wife."

3

Laws of X (LX) (ca. 2050–1800 B.C.E.)

The text does not preserve the name of the ruler who might have commissioned the composition (Michalowski and Walker 1989: 386, 395).[1] It is possible that this is not a separate, new Sumerian law composition but the end of the Laws of Ur-Namma.

About the Laws

Fewer than twenty law provisions are preserved, each beginning with Sumerian tukum-bi, "if." The often fragmentary laws deal with deposits; marriage; fees for physicians, weavers, and other craftsmen or laborers; loans and interest; and real estate sale and rental values. An epilogue records curses against any future ruler who damages or dishonors the monumental inscription recording the laws.

The surviving laws deal only with the free person (lú, "man"), including both the husband and wife (dam) and several professionals.

About the Sources

The text is extremely fragmentary, preserving only the lower portions of the three columns of the reverse face of the tablet, and has been put together from a number of quite small pieces. Michalowski and Walker did not assign numbers to the provisions, in the expectation that additional joins will further the restoration of the law collection or make its relationship to other surviving collections more certain. In recognition of the provisional state of this, the most recently recovered cuneiform law collection, I have assigned consecutive alphabetic sigla to the provisions, without regard for column gaps; this assignment should make it easier to accommodate the improvements and reconstructions of future editions.

Laws

(rev. i' 1'–4') tukum-bi lú-ù é lù [...] é-a-ni x [...] lugal še-ke$_4$ nam-érim [...-kud] lugal é-e-ke$_4$ še níg-gu NE x [...]

¶ **a** If a man [...-s] the house of another man, his house [...] the owner of the grain shall swear the assertory oath, and the owner of the house [shall ...] the grain.

(rev. i' 5'–8') tukum-bi lú-ù é lú x [...] x x-ke$_4$ [...] ki-inim-ma x x [... lugal é]-e-ke$_4$ še šà-bi x [...]

¶ **b** If a man [...-s] the house of another man, [...] testimony [... the owner of the house ...] out of the grain [...]

(rev. i' 9'–10') [tu]kum-bi lú-ù é lú-k[a ...] ... addir-bi [...]

¶ **c** If a man [...-s] the house of another man, [...] its rental [...]

(rev. i' 11'–12') [tuku]m-bi munus-e dam-a-ni [...] x in-na-an-x da[m ...] ḫa-[...]

¶ **d** If a woman [...-s] her husband, the wife [...]

(rev. i' 13'–14') [tukum-b]i lú-ù dam-a-[ni ...] ...

¶ **e** If a man [...-s] his wife [...]

(gap)

(rev. ii' 1'–2') tu[kum-bi lú-ù ...] a-zu ì-[silim ...]

¶ **f** If [a man ...-s and] a physician [heals him, ...]

(rev. ii' 3'-4') tukum-bi l[ú-ù ...] a-zu ì-silim 5 gí[n kù-babbar ì-lá-e]

¶ **g** If a man [...-s and] a physician heals him, [he shall weigh and deliver] 5 shekels [of silver].

(rev. ii' 5'–6') tukum-bi x x x [...] a-zu ì-silim 4 [gín kù-babbar ì-lá-e]

¶ **h** If [a man ...-s and] a physician heals him, [he shall weigh and deliver] 4 shekels [of silver].

(rev. ii' 7'–8') tukum-bi x [...] a-zu ì-silim 1 g[ín kù-babbar ì-lá-e]

¶ **i** If [a man ...-s and] a physician heals him, [he shall weigh and deliver] 1 shekel [of silver].

(rev. ii' 9'–10') ^{géme}uš-bar tan_4-tan_4-na á ud 1-a-ka-ni [...] ^{géme}uš-bar x-x-x-da á ud 1-a-ka-ni [...]	¶ **j** A female weaver who launders(?), her hire for one day [is ...]; a female weaver who ...-s, her hire for one day [is ...]
(rev. ii' 11'–13') [...] x á-bi 2 (bán) š[e-àm] x á-bi 6 sìla š[e-àm] x x [...] x á-bi 1 (bariga) 1 (bán) še-àm	¶ **k** [...] his/her hire is 20 silas of grain; [...] his/her hire is 6 silas of grain; [...] his/her hire is 70 silas of grain.
(rev. ii' 14'–16') tukum-bi $^{munus-lú}$kurun-na-àm 1 ^{dug}Ú.SA.KA.NI lú-ra in-na-an-sum [ud] ebur-ke_4 5 (bán) še [šu ba-ab-te-g]á	¶ **l** If a woman innkeeper gives one of her vats (of beer on credit) to a man, [she shall receive] 50 silas of grain at the harvest.
(rev. ii' 17'–19') tukum-bi lú [lú-ra] 1 še gur ur_5-ra-šè [in-na-an-sum] mu 1-àm máš-bi [1 (bariga) 4 (bán) še-àm]	¶ **m** If a man [gives another man] 300 silas of grain as an interest-bearing loan, its interest rate per annum is [100 silas in grain (= 33%)].
(rev. ii' 20'–22') tukum-bi lú l[ú-ra] 10 gín kù-babbar ur_5-ra-š[è in-na-an-sum] mu 1-àm máš-bi [2 gín kù-babbar-àm]	¶ **n** If a man [gives] another man 10 shekels of silver as an interest-bearing loan, its interest rate per annum is [2 shekels in silver (= 20%)].
(rev. ii' 23'–24') tukum-bi lú x [...] ... [...]	¶ **o** If a man [...]

(gap)

(rev. iii' 1'–2') [...] x-gin_7-nam-[...]	¶ **p** [...]
(rev. iii' 3'–4') [tuku]m-bi 1 sar é-[(...) lú in-sa_{10} kù]-bi [x gín kù-babbar-àm]	¶ **q** If [a man purchases] one-sar of a (...)-house, its [price is x shekels of silver.]
(rev. iii' 5'–6') [tuk]um-bi 1 sar KI-[x x lú] in-sa_{10} kù-bi 1 gín kù-bab[bar-àm]	¶ **r** If [a man] purchases one sar of [...]-land, its price is 1 shekel of silver.
(rev. iii' 7'–8') [tuku]m-bi 1 sar é-dù-[a ...] x-e lú in-ḫun 1 gín kù-babbar ì-l[á-e]	¶ **s** If a man rents one sar of a roofed-over area [...], he shall weigh and deliver 1 shekel of silver.

Epilogue

(rev. iii' 9'–14') [lú mu]-sar-ra-ba šu bí-íb-ùr-ru-a mu-ni bí-íb-sar-re-a [áš-bal]-ba-ke_4-eš lú kúr šu ba-an-zi-zi-a <<[lú mu-s]ar-ra-ba šu bí-íb-ùr-ru-a mu-nu x-x in-na-ab-[x]-x>> [lú]-bi lugal ḫé-a en ḫé-a énsi ḫé-àm [...] x x x x x ḫé-eb-ta-dag-dag

He who effaces this inscription and writes his own name (in place of mine), or, because of this curse, induces an outsider to remove it, <<...>>[2]–that man, whether he is a king, an *ēnu*-lord, or an ensi-ruler, [...] may he be completely obliterated.

(rev. iii' 15'–20') [uru]-ni uru ^{d}En-líl nu-še-ga ḫé-a [abu]la uru-na-ke_4 gál [(x)] tag-tag [x (x)] guruš uru-na igi-nu-du_8 ḫé-me-eš [x (x)] ki-sikil uru-na ù nu-tu-du-[e]-eš [x (x)] uru-na-ke_4 ^{d}En-ki ^{d}Iškur ^{d}Aš[nan] [inim] maḫ ^{d}En-líl-lá-ka [x] x x [x] [(10 lines fragmentary)]

May his city be a city despised by the god Enlil; may the main gate of his city be left open (and undefended). May the young men of his city be blind; may the young maidens of his city be barren. May the [...] of his city <be ... by> the gods Enki, Ishkur, and Ashnan. [May] the mighty word of the god Enlil [curse him ...]

Notes

1. The suggestions and alternate readings proposed by Lieberman (1992: 130 with n. 18), upon which he based his conclusion that the tablet records not a royal law collection but rather a scholastic compilation of clauses and paradigms (comparable to SLHF) are not supported by collation.

2. A repetition with variation of the first clause ("he who erases this inscription and writes his own name"), probably a scribal error. A different and appealing interpretation is offered by Lieberman (1992: 130 n. 18), but not supported beyond doubt by collation.

4

Laws about Rented Oxen (LOx) (ca. 1800 B.C.E., Nippur)

About the Laws

A number of student exercise tablets include extracts from a series of laws dealing with issues of liability involving injury to or loss of rented oxen. The laws in this scholastic exercise reflect considerations similar to those found in groups of provisions within larger collections: LL ¶¶ 34–37, LH ¶¶ 244–49, HL ¶¶ 72–78, the SLHF col. vi, SLEx ¶¶ 9'–10' (and obverse i 36–ii 2), and in "Ai. IV Appendix" (Landsberger 1937: 68–69). It appears that there was a self-contained series consisting of such legal provisions that circulated independently of the larger and more formal collections, and, with its repetitive language and limited subject matter, lent itself to student copying and memorization. Each provision begins with the Sumerian tukum-bi, "if."

About the Sources

The student exercise tablets that preserve the Ox Laws permit a secure sequencing of the provisions for ¶¶ 1–4, ¶¶ 5–7, and ¶¶ 8–9; however, there is room for additional provisions between ¶ 4 and ¶ 5, and it is not certain that ¶¶ 8–9 belong to the composition.

(A 1', B 1'–4') tuk[um-bi] gud igi-bi í[b-ta-an-ḫul] šu-ri šá[m-ba-ka] ì-l[á-e]

¶ 1 If he (the renter) destroys the eye of the ox, he shall weigh and deliver one-half of its value (in silver).

(A 2'–5', B r. 1–5, E 1'–2') tuk[um-bi] gud si-bi íb-t[a-an]-kud igi-3-gál šám-b[a-ka] ì-lá-e

¶ 2 If he (the renter) cuts off the horn of the ox, he shall weigh and deliver one-third of its value (in silver).

(A 6', E 3'–5') tukum-bi gud sa-sal-bi íb-ta-an-síl[!] igi-4-gál šám-ba-ka ì-lá-e

¶ **3** If he (the renter) severs(?) the hoof tendon of the ox, he shall weigh and deliver one-quarter of its value (in silver).

(E 6'–7') tukum-bi gud kun-bi íb-ta-an-kud [igi-x-gál šám-ba-ka ì-lá-e]

¶ **4** If he (the renter) cuts off the tail of the ox, [he shall weigh and deliver one-... of its value (in silver)].

(gap)

(C r. 1'–4', D 1'–3') tu[kum-bi gud] x-[bi íb-ta]-an-[x] igi-4-g[ál] šám-ba-[ka] ì-lá-e

¶ **5** If he (the renter) [...]-s the ... of the ox, he shall weigh and deliver one-quarter of its value (in silver).

(A r. 1'–5', C r. 5'–8', D 4'–8') tukum-bi gud íd-da bal-da-bi gud ba-ug_7 šám til-la-bi-šè ì-lá-e

¶ **6** If an ox dies while crossing a river, he (the renter) shall weigh and deliver (silver) according to its full value.

(A r. 6'–9', C r. 9'–12', D 9'–11') tukum-bi gud [giš]šudun gíd-da-bi ur-maḫ-e ba-an-gaz nu-ub-[su-su]

¶ **7** If a lion kills a yoked ox engaged in pulling (a plow or wagon), he (the renter) will not replace (the ox).

(gap)

(F 1–3) tukum-bi gud an[še(?) ...] ki-ba ur-maḫ-e [ba-an-gaz] [nu]-ub-[su-su]

¶ **8** If a lion kills an ox or an ass(?) [...] in that place, he (the renter) will not replace (the ox).

(F 4-7) [tu]kum-bi [...] x x bal[?] [...] igi-[x-gál šám-ba-ka] ì-[lá-e]

¶ **9** If [...] crossing(?) [...] he shall [weigh and deliver] one-[... of its value (in silver)].

5

A Sumerian Laws Exercise Tablet (SLEx) (ca. 1800 B.C.E.)

About the Laws

The composition is the product of a scribal school's training and was written—either copied or taken from dictation—by an intermediate student named Bēlshunu. The provenience of the tablet is not known. The composition is commonly cited by Assyriologists by reference to the publication of the autograph copy of the cuneiform tablet in the Yale Oriental Series, as *YOS* 1 28.

The ten provisions on the legible reverse involve cases of bodily injury resulting in miscarriage, violation of contracted use, repudiation of adoption, rape, and injury to rented oxen. Each provision is introduced by Sumerian tukum-bi, "if" (for which also see further below). Other legal situations are referred to on the unpublished fragmentary obverse, which originally had three columns, now effaced and mostly illegible. The signs or phrases that can be understood refer to a range of cases: gàr-ra ì-dá-a nam-kù-ga in-na-an-sum, "he marked him with a slave-hairdo, he sold him for silver" (i 5–6); nam-lugal-la-ni-šè ì-ág-e, "he shall measure and deliver grain to its owner" (i 18–19). A few casuistic clauses, either contractual clauses or complete law provisions, also can be read: tukum-bi kišib ú-gu ba-an-dé nagar-e-ne gaz-e-dè ..., "if he has lost a seal, the herald [shall announce] that it is invalid ..." (i 20–23; see Roth 1979: 54); [tukum-bi] gud ú-gu ba-an-dé gud gud-gin$_7$ bí-ib-su-su, "if he has lost an ox, he shall replace ox for ox" (i 37–ii 2; cf. Ox Laws in this volume); tukum-bi má má-laḫ$_4$ ..., "if a boat man [...-s] a boat ..." (ii 7–8); tukum-bi é a-šà ..., "if a house (or) a field ..." (iii 2–3); 10 gín kù-babbar ì-lá-e, "he shall weigh and deliver 10 shekels of silver" (iii 17). Although the entire text is replete with ambiguities and mistakes, not all of which can be eliminated by a modern editor, the assortment of provisions decipherable on the reverse reflects situations known from the formal law collections as well as from contracts; for example, ¶¶ 5 and 6 offer alternate repudiation clauses for an adoption contract.

The extant provisions on the reverse deal only with the free person (lú), including the free woman (dumu-munus lú, "daughter of a man"); the slave (arad) is mentioned only in the context of private property, and also on the poorly preserved obverse (see above).

The tablet closes with an invocation for the patron deities of the scribal arts, Nisaba and her consort Ḫaja. Such blessings are not usually found on tablets written in Nippur or Ur, the major tablet-yielding sites of the early second millennium.

About the Source

The less-than-professional character of the tablet is revealed by the repetitive copying and recopying of selected basic phrases. For example, in the middle of the first column, the scribe tried to write tukum-bi, the Sumerian word translated here "if," which begins each casuistically formulated provision in all the Sumerian law collections. tukum-bi is a compound logogram composed of the five signs ŠU.GAR.TUR.LÁ.BI; three times the scribe wrote the compound defectively as ŠU.GAR.LÁ.BI (i 11–13). To reinforce his mastery of the correct sequence of signs, he later wrote ŠU.GAR.TUR.LÁ.BI again three times (ii 17-19). The well-preserved reverse of the tablet, although easier to read, is still obviously the work of a scribe-in-training and not the polished product of the accomplished professional.

For consistency, the paragraph numbering here follows that established by Finkelstein (1969c), but the reader must be aware that the largely indecipherable obverse also included legal provisions, and that ¶ 1' is the first preserved provision on the reverse and not the first of the composition.

Laws

(iv 1–5) tukum-bi dumu-munus lú zag an-ús níg-šà-ga-ni a im-šub-šub[1] 10 gín kù-babbar ì-lá-e

¶ 1' If he jostles the daughter of a man and causes her to miscarry her fetus, he shall weigh and deliver 10 shekels of silver.

(iv 6–10) tukum-bi dumu-<munus> lú ba-an-sìg níg-šà-ga-ni a im-šub-šub $^1/_3$ ma-na kù-babbar ì-lá-e

¶ 2' If he strikes the daughter of a man and causes her to miscarry her fetus, he shall weigh and deliver 20 shekels of silver.

(iv 11–18) tukum-bi kaskal dug_4-ga-ni in-ri-bal má ú-gu ba-an-dé en-na

¶ 3' If he alters his agreed route and thus causes the loss of the boat,

má e-gibil$_4$ á-bi ba-ma-ta nam-lugal-la-a-ni-šè ì-ág-e

until he restores the boat he shall measure and deliver one-half of its hire in grain to its owner.

(iv 19–29) tukum-bi ad-da-ni ù ama-ni nu ad-da-mu nu ama-mu ba-an-dug$_4$ é a-šà kiri$_6$ arad-arad níg-gur$_{11}$-ra íb-ta-è-a ù kù-bi šám til-la-a-ni-šè in-na-ab-sum-mu

¶ **4'** If he (the adopted son) declares to his father and mother, "You are not my father," or "You are not my mother," he shall forfeit house, field, orchard, slaves, and possessions, and they shall sell him for silver (into slavery) for his full value.

(iv 30–33) ad-da-ni ù ama-ni nu dumu-[mu]-meš ba-an-na-ab-dug$_4$ ub$^?$ é-ta bar-ra-è-a

¶ **5'** (If) his (adoptive) father and mother declare to him, "You are not our son," they shall forfeit ... the estate.

(iv 34–v 2) tukum-bi ad-da-ni ù ama-ni nu dumu-mu-meš [x-x]-x-dug$_4^?$ [é íb-t]a-è-a

¶ **6'** If his (adoptive) father and mother declare [to him], "You are not our son," they shall forfeit [the estate].

(v 3–15) tukum-bi dumu-munus lú e-sír-ra é im-gi ad-da-ni ù ama-ni nu-ba-an-zu-uš ka-ar-ab-du$_6$[2] «nam ad-ni ù ama-e»[3] ì-dug$_4$-e ad-da-ni ù ama-ni nam-dam-ni-šè in-na-ab-sum-mu

¶ **7'**[4] If he deflowers in the street the daughter of a man, her father and her mother do not identify(?) him, (but) he declares, "I will marry you"—her father and her mother shall give her to him in marriage.

(v 16–25) tukum-bi dumu-munus lú e-sír-ra(text: da) é im-gi ad-da-ni ù ama-ni ba-an-zu-uš lú é-im-gi in-zu in-kúr ká dingir-ra x-[x] in-⌈pàd⌉

¶ **8'** If he deflowers in the street the daughter of a man, her father and her mother identify(?) him, (but) the deflowerer disputes the identification(?)—he shall swear an oath ... at the temple gate.

(v 26–31) tukum-bi gud nígin-nígin-na ur-maḫ e-gu$_7$-e gaba-ri nam-lugal-la-ni-šè íb-ri-ri

¶ **9'** If a lion devours a wandering ox, the misfortune falls to its owner.

(v 32–vi 1) tukum-bi gud nígin-nígin-na gud ú-gu ba-an-dé gud gud-gin$_7$ [bí-ib-su-su]

¶ **10'** If a wandering ox is lost, he (the renter) shall replace ox for ox.

Colophon

(vi 1') [(...) 60+]130 mu-bi-im	[(...)] 190 is the number of its lines.[5]
(vi 2'–3') ti-la ^{d}Nisaba ù ^{d}Ḫa-ià	(This copy of the composition is dedicated for the scribe's) well-being (to) the goddess Nisaba and (her consort) Ḫaja.[6]
(vi 4'–5') ⌜šu⌝ *Be-el-šu-nu* [...] x x	Personally written by (the scribe) Bēlshunu [son of ...].[7]

Notes

1. The Sumerian expression seems to refer to premature rupture of the amniotic membrane.

2. The last sign of v 9 (collated) is almost certainly du_6, and I take this for *ga-ra-ab-du_{12}.

3. The entire line (v 10) is deleted here, as a scribal error confusing the following lines.

4. The translations of ¶¶ 7' and 8' given here differ considerably from previous attempts at understanding these difficult provisions; see also Finkelstein 1966: 365.

5. Each column ends with a line subtotal; for the columns of the obverse the subtotals are written on the lower edge: column i is broken but should have counted about 37 lines; column ii indicates 41 lines, although the column actually has only 36; column iii indicates 37 lines. On the published reverse the subtotals indicate 37 and 35 lines respectively for columns iv and v; column vi, which only included a few lines (now eroded) of the body of the text, would have had no more than five to eight lines. Thus the restored total of 190 is probable.

6. See Hallo 1976: 195 n. 98.

7. See Hunger 1968: 29 No. 38.

6

Sumerian Laws Handbook of Forms (SLHF) (ca. 1700 B.C.E.)

About the Laws

This late Old Babylonian prism is a Sumerian compendium of contracts and contractual clauses, legal provisions comparable to those found in the law collections, and isolated phrases such as might be found in Old Babylonian contracts. The compendium was recorded by an accomplished scribe, and displays professional organization and care.

The situations considered in the contractual clauses and provisions include: manumission, oaths, theft, house sales and leases, rape, marriage, adoption, heirship and apprenticeship, agricultural offenses and leases, violation of contracted use, damage to rented boats and oxen, slaves, and debt pledges. The law provisions and some contractual clauses are introduced by Sumerian tukum-bi, "if," as in the other Sumerian law collections; other contractual clauses that relate narrative events, and isolated formularies or verbal clauses, have no such marked beginning.

The provisions include reference to the free person (lú), including both the husband and wife (dam), to the foster or adopted child (dumu), and to the female slave (géme); although no term for male slave is preserved, the manumission procedure in column ii certainly refers to male as well as female slaves.

About the Source

The four-sided prism (approximately 19.5 centimeters in height, with three columns on each face), which is in the collection of Philadelphia Free Library, was purchased from dealers in the early part of the twentieth century, and no information relating to excavation or provenience is available.

One face of the prism is eroded beyond reconstruction; there is no preserved indication of an initial or final column, and the numbering of the columns here begins for convenience with the first preserved column.[1] Although this edition translates continuous and coherent sections into "paragraphs," such divisions are not rendered on the prism itself. In some cases, the units are clear from the context of the clauses or law provisions, but often the units are determined solely by the limits of preservation and decipherment.[2] Because of the varied and fragmentary nature of the preserved text, the translations are marked by the column and line numbers rather than by the alphabetical or numerical notations used elsewhere in this volume.

(i 1–3) [...] x-ni [x-(x)]-du$_8$ [ba]-an-du$_8$

(i 1–3) ... he released

(i 4–5) [x]-x-x-zalag [in-n]i-in-BU$^?$

(i 4–5) ...

(i 6–8) [in]-pàd [in-p]àd-dè-eš [i]n-pàd-dè-eš

(i 6–8) He swore. They swore. They swore.

(i 9–11) [in]-tag$_4$ [in]-na-an-tag$_4$ [in]-dadag

(i 9–11) He left. He left him. He cleared.

(i 12–22) [x-(x)]-KA [x]-x-x [x]-x-al-U$^?$ [x-x]-bi-x-x [x-x-(x)] lugal$^?$ [x-x]-àm [x]-x-a-NE [x-x]-x-x [x-x]-ku$_5$-da [x-x]-in-x-[x] [x-x]-x-[x-x] [...]

(i 12–22) ...

(gap)

(ii 1–3) til[la$_5$] uru^{ki}-na-ka si gù ba-ni-in-ra

(ii 1–3) In the streets of his city, he (the herald) sounded the horn.

(ii 4–6) kišib-a-ni sag-ki-ir táb-e-dè in-na-an-⌈ne⌉-eš

(ii 4–6) They ordered him to kiln-fire(?) (i.e., validate?) his document (of manumission) regarding (his) forehead.

(ii 7–9) sag-ki-ni in-dadag giš-gìri-ni in-du$_8$ dug-a-ni in-gaz

(ii 7–9) He cleared his forehead, he released his foot fetters, he smashed his pot.

(ii 10–13) ama-ar-gi$_4$-ni in-gar ù

(ii 10–13) He established his free-

kišib in-dadag-ga-ni in-na-an-tag$_4$

dom, and he executed for him the document of his having cleared him.

(ii 14) x-a-ni in-BIR

(ii 14) He ...-ed his ...

(ii 15–18) é a-šà nìg-gur$_{11}$ ù ^{giš}šu-kára a-na-me-a-bi ba-⌈ra⌉-è-dè

(ii 15–18) He shall forfeit house, field, possessions, and utensils, as much as there may be.

(ii 19–20) ⌈ù⌉ [kù-š]è [ba-an-sum-mu-uš]

(ii 19–20) And they sold him for silver.

(ii 21–25) [tuk]um-⌈bi⌉ [inim-gá]l-la [ba]-an-tuku inim-gál-⌈la⌉-bi ba-ni-ib-gi$_4$-gi$_4$

(ii 21–25) If there is a claim, he shall satisfy the claim.

(ii 26–31) ù ^{min}min$_6$-e ugu [u]gu-na [u]gu-na in-tuku [u]gu-na [l]i-bí-in-tuku

(ii 26–31) And double. Against. Against him. He has a claim against him. No one shall have a claim against him.

(ii 32–33) [in]im-inim-ni ⌈ba-an⌉-sum

(ii 32–33) He promised him.

(ii 34–36) kišib-⌈ba?⌉-a-ni $^{[na_4]}$kišib dili $^{[n]a_4}$kišib didli-ta

(ii 34–36) His document (or: seal). A single document (or: seal). Every individual document (or: seal).

(ii 37–38) [lu]gal?-e gaz-dè [ba]-an-sum

(ii 37–38) The king(?) delivered him up to be killed(?).

(ii 39–42) [bí]-ib-diri [nam]-ba-lá [ḫé-i]b-diri [ḫa-b]a-lá

(ii 39–42) It may be more but not less. It may be more or it may be less.

(ii 43–45) [mu luga]l-bi [x-x]-x [in]-pàd

(ii 43–45) He swore ... by the name of the king that.

(iii 1–2) [...] x [...]

(iii 1–2) ...

(iii 3–5) dili-[e-eš] mu-luga[l-bi] in-pàd-[dè-eš]

(iii 3–5) They swore jointly by the name of the king that.

(iii 6–7) téš-bi [mu-lugal-bi] in-⌈pàd⌉-[dè-eš]

(iii 6–7) They swore together by the name of the king that.

(iii 8–9) téš-a [sè-ga] ì-ba-e-[ne]

(iii 8–9) They shall divide equally.

(iii 10–12) tukum-bi ^{giš}má in-zuḫ su$^{!}$-šè^{3} min ḫ[é-tab-b]é

(iii 10–12) If he steals a boat, he shall double (its value) as compensation.

(iii 13–15) tukum-bi šaḫ ì-zuḫ su$^{!}$-šè min ḫé-tab-e

(iii 13–15) If he steals a pig, he shall double (its value) as compensation.

(iii 16–17) ud-na-me-ka é-mu nu-ub-bé-a

(iii 16–17) He shall never, at any time in the future, declare "It is my house."

(iii 18–19) iz-zi dal-ba-na šu-ne-ne aš-àm

(iii 18–19) They share responsibility for the common wall.

(iii 20–23) iz-zi dal-⌈ba-na⌉ 2½ ninda uš-bi [x] kùš dagal-bi 1½ ninda s[ag-bi]

(iii 20–23) The common wall measures 30 cubits as its length, [x] cubits as its width, 18 cubits as its height.

(iii 24–25) ní-t[e-ni-ta] in-dag ⌈ù⌉ [in-dù]

(iii 24–25) He tore down and rebuilt (the wall) by himself.

(iii 26–31) mu ní-te-ni-[ta] in-dag ù in-dù-a nam-á-kúš-a iz-zi dal-ba-na 1½ gín kù-babbar in-⌈na⌉-an-⌈sum⌉

(iii 26–31) Because he tore down and rebuilt (the wall) by himself, he (the second party) gave him 1½ shekels of silver for the maintenance expenses for the common wall.

(iii 32–38) ud-kúr-⌈šè⌉ é-⌈gin$_7$-nam⌉ nu-dím-me-«en» ^{giš}gag nu-ub-dù-e ^{giš}ùr-ra nu-ub-gi-na nu-mu-un-⌈na-ab⌉-bé-a

(iii 32–38) (In consideration of the sum received, the first party swore) that in the future he will not declare to him (the second party) that he may not build any structure such as a house, that he may not drive in a nail, that he may not place a beam in position (on the common wall).

(iii 39–47) tukum-bi ni-x-x ni-x-ḫu bí-ib-x-àm al-dù-e an-x-àm <x> sar [é]-dù-a ^{giš}[x-x]-da ^{giš}ig x-x-x	(iii 39–47) If ... <x> sar of a built-up house plot, a wooden ..., a door, ...
(iv 1–9) [...] x [...] é ⸢inim nu⸣-gá-gá inim nu-gá-gá-dè é-mu nu-ub-bé-a	(iv 1–9) ... house. He will not raise a claim. He will not raise a claim. He will not declare that "It is my house."
(iv 10–11) a bí-in-gi$_4$ egir a bí-in-gi$_4$	(iv 10–11) He deflowered her. After he deflowered her.
(iv 12–14) ḫul ba-an-gig kù dam-tag$_4$ ì-lá-e	(iv 12–14) He despised her. He shall weigh and deliver a divorce settlement in silver.
(iv 15–16) ^{túg}siki-ni in-kud	(iv 15–16) He cut her hem.
(iv 17–18) ⸢dam⸣ ḫé-en-du$_{12}$-du$_{12}$ dam-mu nu-ub-bé-a	(iv 17–18) (Another man) shall marry her; he (the first husband) will not declare that "She is my spouse."
(iv 19–20) dam šà-ga-ni-šè ⸢i⸣-ni-íb-sum-mu	(iv 19–20) He gave her in marriage to a spouse of her choice.
(iv 21–22) ⸢nam-dam⸣-šè ⸢in⸣-du$_{12}$	(iv 21–22) He married.
(iv 23–24) mu-lugal-la-ka-ni in-pàd	(iv 23–24) He swore by his "name-of-the-king" oath.
(iv 25–26) nam-dumu-ni-šè ba-da-ri	(iv 25–26) He has adopted him as his son.
(iv 27–28) nam-ibila-ni-šè in-gar	(iv 27–28) He has established him as his heir.
(iv 29–30) nam-á-è-ni-šè nam-bùlug-gá-ni-šè	(iv 29–30) Into the status of foster child. Into the status of apprentice-foster child.
(iv 31–34) ibila 5-àm ḫé-gál-le-eš ibila 1-gin$_7$-nam ì-ba-e-ne	(iv 31–34) Should there be even five heirs, they shall divide as one heir (i.e., as equal heirs).

(iv 35–41) tukum-bi lú-ù a-⌈šà⌉ lú ùr-ra a i-ni-in-kud-ré a-šà a ba-an-dé še ús-sa-du-ni-šè bí-íb-sì-ge

(iv 35–41) If a man diverts water into a field that a man has harrowed and floods the field, he shall replace the grain according to (the yields of the fields of) his neighbors.

(iv 42–v 11) tukum-bi lú-ù $^{[g]iš}$m[á ì-ḫun] ⌈kaskal⌉ dug$_4$-g[a-ni] in-na-a[n-gar] e-ne kaskal-b[i] in-kúr ki-ba ^{giš}má ba-su ù sa-ga[z-šè] ba-an-⌈ak⌉ ^{giš}má bí-íb-⌈su⌉-su ù á-bi ì-ág-e

(iv 42–v 11) If a man rents a boat and his agreed route is established for him, but he violates its route and the boat sinks in that place—thus he has acted lawlessly; he shall replace the boat and he shall measure and deliver in grain its hire.

(v 12–20) tukum-bi lú-ù ^{giš}má [ì]-ḫun ^{giš}x-[x-(x)-t]a ^{giš}KA-[x-(x)-d]a ba-an-[zi-i]r šu-ri-[(x)]-a šám-ba-[(x)]-kam ì-⌈lá-e⌉

(v 12–20) If a man rents a boat, and he destroys the wooden ... and the wooden ..., he shall weigh and deliver one-half of its value in silver.

(v 21–26) tukum-b[i] ^{giš}má ba-su ^{giš}má bí-ib-su-s[u] ù á-bi kar-bi-šè bí-ib-gur-re

(v 21–26) If the boat sinks, he shall replace the boat and return its hire to the quay.

(v 27–31) tukum-bi ^{giš}má ru-ru-gú ^{giš}má diri-ga ba-su ^{giš}má bí-ib-su-su

(v 27–31) If an upstream-boat sinks a downstream-boat, he (the captain/owner of the upstream-boat) shall replace the (lost) boat.

(v 32–36) tukum-bi ^{giš}má diri-ga ^{giš}má ru-ru-gú ba-su ^{giš}má nu-ub-su-su

(v 32–36) If a downstream-boat sinks an upstream-boat, he (the captain/owner of the downstream-boat) will not replace the (lost) boat.

(v 37–44) tukum-bi lú-ù má «má»-laḫ$_5$-ra mu 1-kam ^{giš}má-ni ba-an-⌈kéš⌉ ki-ulutin-bi-⌈šè⌉ á-⌈bi⌉ ì-⌈ág⌉-e

(v 37–44) If a man commits his boat to a boatman for one year, he (the boatman) shall measure and deliver in grain its hire at the completion of its term.

(v 45) 1 gud á ùr-⌈ra⌉

(v 45) One ox for the rear of the team.

(vi 1–10) [...]	(vi 1–10) ...
(vi 11–15) t[ukum-bi] gud [x-bi] í[b?-x-x-x] igi-4–[gál] ì-lá-[e]	(vi 11–15) If he (the renter) [... (damages)] the ... of an ox, he shall weigh and deliver one-quarter of its value in silver.
(vi 16–22) tuku[m-bi] gud-da-r[i-a] dag-⸢gi$_4$?-ta?⸣ gišgi-šè ⸢in-ku$_4$?⸣ ur-maḫ-[e] in-g[az] gud nu-ub-s[u-su]	(vi 16–22) If a reserve(?) ox enters(?) the canebrake from the protected area(?) and a lion kills it, he (the renter) will not replace the ox.
(vi 23–31) [tu]ku[m-bi] [g]ud ⸢íd⸣-d[a] ⸢bal⸣-e-d[è] ba-[u]g$_7$ gud bí-ib-[s]u-su gud silim-[ma] ⸢ù á-bi⸣ ur$_5$-bi-šè bí-ib-⸢gur-re⸣	(vi 23–31) If an ox dies while crossing a river, he (the renter) shall replace the ox; he shall return a healthy ox together with its compensatory hire.
(vi 32–36) tukum-⸢bi⸣ gud giš⸢šudun⸣-ta ur-maḫ-e in-gaz gud nu-ub-⸢su-su⸣	(vi 32–36) If a lion kills a yoked ox, he (the renter) will not replace the ox.
(vi 37–39) nam-érim ku$_5$-ru-⸢dam⸣ ba-an-sum-mu-uš	(vi 37–39) They handed him over to swear an assertory oath.
(vi 40–42) ki nam-érim-ma im-me-gur-ru ba-an-na-dug$_4$	(vi 40–42) He declared to him that he returned from the place of the assertory oath.
(vi 43–48) kù nu-mu-un-⸢sa$_6$?-ge⸣ mu kù nu-mu-un-da-an-x-(x) ⸢sum?⸣-mu-⸢dam⸣ ⸢kù⸣-pad-⸢du⸣ ⸢x-x⸣ nu-mu-un-tag?-tag?-g[e?] [*š*]*i-bi-ir-tum*-[*m*]*a*[4]	(vi 43–48) He did not satisfy him for the silver. Since he did not ... the silver. It is given. Unprocessed lump(s) of silver. ... he did not ... Unprocessed lump(s) of silver.
(vii 1–12) [...] [...]-nu [...]-x-ga [...] ⸢é?⸣-mu [...]-x-en	(vii 1–12) ... "My house" ...
(vii 13–27) [ba-an]-⸢na⸣-dug$_4$ [...]-x-ni-ta [...]-ra? [...]-x [...] [...] ug[u? ...] [í]b-r[a-x-x]-x [b]a-a[n-x-x]-x x-x-[x]-x b]a-da-[an?]-du$_8$ [x]-⸢nam-x-x⸣-ni-šè [x]-ga-[x-x-r]a [...]-x [...-r]a	(vii 13–27) He shall say to him ...

(vii 28–30) [...] géme ^{I}*A-lí-ba-aš-ti* mu-ni

(vii 28–30) ... slave woman, Ali-baštī is her name.

(vii 31–33) íd-da a-rá 1-kam pú-ta a-rá 2-kam ⌈a⌉ bí-ib-tag$_{4}$-tag$_{4}$

(vii 31–33) In(?) the river once, in(?) the river twice, he shall ... her with water.

(vii 34–36) $\frac{1}{3}$ ma-na siki éš-gàr nam-munus-a al$^{?}$-x ḫé-e

(vii 34–36) 20 shekels of wool, the assigned work quota of "womanhood" ...

(vii 37–45) máš$^{?}$-ta-àm àm-ur$_{5}$-re àm-NI ḫé-e x-x-x-x-x x-[...] [...]-x [...]-x [...]-an

(vii 37–45) Interest(?) ... Accrues as interest ...

(viii 1–2) [x-(x)]-bi [x]-x-e

(viii 1–2) ...

(viii 3–10) [t]ukum-⌈bi⌉ [ba]-⌈ug$_{7}$⌉ [ba-an]-záḫ-a ⌈ú⌉-gu ba-an-dé ù tu-ra ba-an-TU á-giš-gar-ra-ni-šè bí-ib-si-si$^{?}$-ge

(viii 3–10) If she (the pledge) dies, flees, disappears, or falls ill, he (the debtor) shall compensate in full for her assigned work quota.

(viii 11–15) géme ù kù-babbar igi-ne-ne-du$_{8}$ ud kù mu-un-tùmu-da géme-ni ⌈ba-an⌉-tùm-mu

(viii 11–15) The slave woman (as pledge) and the silver (owed as debt) are considered equal; when he brings the silver, he shall retrieve his slave woman.

(viii 16–19) [na]m-uru$_{4}$-lá-šè ⌈á mu ú-a-šè⌉ [i]gi-⌈4-gál⌉-šè íb-ta-an-è

(viii 16–19) He leased for cultivation at the rate of one-quarter of the annual crop.

(viii 20–21) kù máš a-šà-ga-ke$_{4}$ šà-ga-ni al-dùg

(viii 20–21) He (the lessor) has been satisfied with the silver for the portion of the rent of the field paid in advance.

(viii 22–25) išin$^{?}$(PA$^{?}$.ŠE$^{?}$) a-šà-ga gál-la-bi lugal a-šà-ga-ke$_{4}$ mu-⌈un⌉-dab$_{5}$

(viii 22–25) The owner of the field has taken the crops of the field while on the stalk, as much as there may be.

(viii 26–30) ud e[bur]-ka še [a-š]à-ga

(viii 26–30) At the time of the har-

gál-la-⌜bi⌝ šà igi-4-gál-ka ì-bu-re-m[a]

vest, he shall take(?) one-quarter of the grain of the field, as much as there may be.

(viii 31–34) lugal a-šà-ga-ke$_4$ níg-gál-⌜la⌝ é-g[al] é saḫar ⌜a-šà⌝-g[a] ba-ni-⌜ib⌝-[gi$_4$-gi$_4$]

(viii 31–34) The owner of the field is responsible for maintaining the property belonging to the palace and the earthworks of the field.

(viii 35–43) tuku[m-bi] a-šà a x [...] ù x [...] 10 gín [kù-babbar] x-x-[...] a x [...] KA [...]

(viii 35–43) If the field, water ... and 10 shekels [of silver] ... water ...

(ix 1–11) é-[dù-a] ½ ninda 1 [kùš] al-[bal-e] egir-b[i x-(x)] kislaḫ-[bi x] sila dag[al-la x] da é [PN] ki *Ì-[lí-x-x-*ta] lugal é-[ke$_4$] ᴵGìri-ni-[ì-sa$_6$] in-ši-in-s[a$_{10}$]

(ix 1–11) A built-up house plot—7 cubits; a second story; its rear ...; its threshing floor ...; the main thoroughfare ...; adjacent to the house of [so-and-so]—Girini-isa purchased from Ili-..., the owner of the house.

(ix 12–14) 1½ ⌜ma⌝-na kù-bab[bar] šám ⌜til⌝-la-bi-šè in-na-an-lá

(ix 12–14) He weighed and delivered to him 90 shekels of silver, its full price.

(ix 15–25) ud-kúr-šè ud-na-me-a-k[a] ᴵ*Ì-lí-x-[x]* ibi[la]-ni ù [...] ù [x]-x-[x]-x-x é x-[x]-x-[x] kù? ⌜ù⌝-[x-x] nu-na-a[b]-bé-⌜a⌝ ⌜mu lugal-bi⌝ ⌜in-pàd⌝

(ix 15–25) He (the seller) has sworn by the name of the king that, at any time in the future, Ili-..., his heirs, and ... and ... will not declare that the house [was not sold] nor (that) the silver [was not paid].

(remainder of column ix and columns x–xii broken)

Notes

1. Column i includes verbal paradigms recalling the verbal paradigms with which *ana ittišu* begins (see Landsberger 1937) and providing support on contextual grounds for this column as the "beginning" of the prism.

2. There is a single incised line following vii 12, and a double incised line appears to follow ix 25.

3. Text: BA-šè.

4. The Akkadian translates Sumerian kù-pad-du.

Translations

B. Babylonian

7

Laws of Eshnunna (LE) (ca. 1770 B.C.E., Eshnunna)

The date of the collection is determined by the fragmentary date formula at the beginning of Source A, which probably refers to events in one year of the reign of Dadusha, a ruler of the kingdom of Eshnunna. During the Old Babylonian period, Eshnunna's influence extended beyond the city on the Dijala River (modern Tell Asmar) and into Assyria to the north and Babylonia to the south, becoming one of the greatest powers in the region. Dadusha was an earlier contemporary of King Hammurabi of Babylon, and his kingdom eventually fell to Hammurabi and the expanding Babylonian empire.

About the Laws

The composition as known from the extant sources has no prologue or epilogue. In beginning with a date formula in Sumerian, the composition recalls the introductions to the Old Babylonian royal edicts and remissions (*mīšaru*-edicts), recurrent enactments, at irregular intervals, which canceled private debt obligations in order to implement economic reforms (see Kraus 1984). The association with economic measures is further enhanced by the silver and grain values for basic commodities in the first two sections, the wage and price standards for services and equipment, and the silver and grain interest rates. A similar economic motivation is found in the prologue of the Laws of Ur-Namma.

In addition to these economic measures, the composition includes provisions that deal with numerous situations, including renters' liability, agricultural matters, theft, pledges, deposits and loans, debt servitude, marital rights and property and sexual offenses, fosterage and care for children of dependent classes, bodily injuries, fugitive slaves, goring oxen and vicious dogs, and collapsing walls.

The provisions are introduced in a number of ways, including (most often) *šumma*, "if" ("If a man ..."), the relative formulation *awīlum ša* ("A man who ..."), the apodictic statement ("A merchant ... will not accept ..."), and the variously formulated statements of prices and hires.

The only source that preserves the end of the composition shows that the last column concluded with a blank section (about the space of six to eight lines) in which a scribe could have placed a colophon or self-identification (as in the final column of SLEx).

The principal class with which the laws are concerned, the free person (*awīlu*), includes both men and women (*mār awīlim* and *mārat awīlim*); reference is also made to the wife (*aššatu*) and to the child (*māru*). The laws also refer to a secondary class of person, the commoner (*muškēnu*), and to the male and female slave (*wardu* and *amtu*) of free persons and of the palace (*ekallu*). Three categories of persons are mentioned whose status is uncertain but who occupy a place outside of the usual social order: the *ubaru*, the *napṭaru*, and the *mudû*. Special attention is given to the merchant or creditor (*tamkāru*) and to the woman innkeeper (*sābītu*).

About the Sources

Two large cuneiform tablets, excavated at Tell Harmal (ancient Shaduppum) in the 1945 and 1947 seasons, preserve nearly complete copies of the collection of legal rules. A third witness to the collection (Source C), a student exercise tablet recording extracts from the laws, was excavated in the early 1980's during salvage operations conducted in the Hamrin Basin at Tell Haddad.

There is a double line incised between the introductory lines 1–7 and the first provision beginning in line 8; otherwise, however, the tablets do not mark divisions between the provisions, and in fact a new provision might begin even midline; furthermore, the three sources do not configure the lines and provisions identically. The provision numbers given here follow those used in the accepted standard publications; when provisions previously kept separate are understood as a single unit, the union is represented by a single slash (e.g., ¶ 17/18); when provisions previously viewed as one are separated, the separation of the subsequent portion is represented with the addition of "A" (e.g., ¶ 18A, ¶ 47A).

Superscription

(A i 1–7) [...] ud-21-kam [...] ^{d}En-líl-lá ^{d}Nin-a-zu [...] nam-lugal Èš-nun-na^{ki} x-a é-ad-da-a-ni-šè [...]-x- ra-àm *Ṣu-pu-ur-*^{d}Utu^{ki} [...]-x bal-ri-a ^{id}Idiglat [...] mu-1-kam ^{giš}tukul-kalag-ga ba-an-díb

[...] day 21 [...] of the gods Enlil and Ninazu, [when Dadusha ascended to] the kingship of the city of Eshnunna [and entered] into the house of his father, [when] he conquered with mighty weapons within one year the cities Ṣupur-Shamash [and ... on] the far bank of the Tigris River [...].

Laws

(A i 8–17) 1 *kur še'um ana* 1 *šiqil kaspim* 3 *qa šaman rūštim ana* 1 *šiqil kaspim* 1 (*sūt*) 2 *qa šamnum ana* 1 *šiqil kaspim* 1 (*sūt*) 5 *qa nāḫum ana* 1 *šiqil kaspim* 4 (*sūt*) *ittûm*[1] *ana* 1 *šiqil kaspim* 6 *mana šipātum ana* 1 *šiqil kaspim* 2 *kur ṭabtum ana* 1 *šiqil kaspim* 1 *kur uḫūlum ana* 1 *šiqil kaspim* 3 *mana erûm ana* 1 *šiqil kaspim* 2 *mana erûm epšum ana* 1 *šiqil kaspim*

¶ **1** 300 silas of barley (can be purchased) for 1 shekel of silver. 3 silas of fine oil—for 1 shekel of silver. 12 silas of oil—for 1 shekel of silver. 15 silas of lard—for 1 shekel of silver. 40 silas of bitumen—for 1 shekel of silver. 360 shekels of wool—for 1 shekel of silver. 600 silas of salt—for 1 shekel of silver. 300 silas of potash—for 1 shekel of silver. 180 shekels of copper—for 1 shekel of silver. 120 shekels of wrought copper—for 1 shekel of silver.

(A i 18–20) 1 *qa šamnum ša nisḫātim* 3 (*sūt*) *še'ušu* 1 *qa naḫum ša nisḫātim* 2 (*sūt*) 5 *qa še'ušu* 1 *qa ittûm ša nisḫātim* 8 *qa še'ušu*

¶ **2** 1 sila of oil, extract(?)—30 silas is its grain equivalent. 1 sila of lard, extract(?)—25 silas is its grain equivalent. 1 sila of bitumen, extract(?)—8 silas is its grain equivalent.

(A i 21–23) *ereqqum qadum alpīša u rēdîša* 1 (*pān*) 4 (*sūt*) *še'um idūša šumma kaspum* 1/3 *šiqil idūša kala ūmim ireddīši*

¶ **3** A wagon together with its oxen and its driver—100 silas of grain is its hire; if (paid in) silver, 1/3 shekel (i.e., 60 barleycorns) is its hire; he shall drive it for the entire day.

(A i 23–24) *idī elippim 1 kurrum 2 qa u* [*x*] *qa idī malaḫḫim kala ūmim ireddīši*

¶ **4** The hire of a boat is, per 300-sila capacity, 2 silas; furthermore, [x] silas is the hire of the boatman; he shall drive it for the entire day.

(A i 25–26) *šumma malaḫḫum īgīma elippam uṭṭebbe mala uṭebbû umalla*

¶ **5** If the boatman is negligent and causes the boat to sink, he shall restore as much as he caused to sink.

(A i 27–28) *šumma awīlum ina nulāni elippam la šattam iṣṣabat* 10 *šiqil kaspam išaqqal*

¶ **6** If a man, under fraudulent circumstances, should seize a boat which does not belong to him, he shall weigh and deliver 10 shekels of silver.

(A i 28–29) 2 (*sūt*) *še'um idī ēṣidim*[2] *šumma kaspum* 12 *uṭṭet idūšu*

¶ **7** 20 silas of grain is the hire of a harvester; if (paid in) silver, 12 barleycorns is his hire.

(A i 29) 1 (*sūt*) *še'um idī zārî*

¶ **8** 10 silas of grain is the hire of a winnower.

(A i 30–33) *awīlum* 1 *šiqil kaspam ana eṣēdim ana agrim [lid]dinma šumma rēssu la ukīlma [e]ṣēdam eṣēdam*[3] *la ēṣissu* 10 *šiqil kaspam [išaq]qal*

¶ **9** Should a man give 1 shekel of silver to a hireling for harvesting—if he (the hireling) does not keep himself available to work and does not harvest for him, he shall weigh and deliver 10 shekels of silver.

(A i 33–34) 1 (*sūt*) 5 *qa idī niggallim u kuzīrum [ana bēl]išuma itâr*

¶ **9A** 15 silas is the hire of a sickle, and the broken blade(?) shall revert to its owner.

(A i 34–35) 1 (*sūt*) *še'um idī imērim u* 1 (*sūt*) *še'um idī rēdîšu kala ūmim ireddīšu*

¶ **10** 10 silas of grain is the hire of a donkey, and 10 silas of grain is the hire of its driver; he shall drive it for the entire day.

(A i 36–37) *idī agrim* 1 *šiqil kaspum* 1 (*pān*) *še'um ukullêšu warḫam ištēn illak*

¶ **11** The hire of a hireling is 1 shekel of silver, 60 silas of grain is his provender; he shall serve for one month.

(A i 37–40) *awīlum ša ina eqel muškēnim ina kurullim ina muṣlalim iṣṣabbatu* 10 *šiqil kaspam išaqqal [ša ina mū]šim ina kurullim iṣṣabbatu imât ul iballuṭ*

¶ **12** A man who is seized in the field of a commoner among the sheaves at midday shall weigh and deliver 10 shekels of silver; he who is seized at night among the sheaves shall die, he will not live.

(A i 41–42, B i 4–7) *awīlum ša ina bītim ša muškēnim ina bītim ina muṣlalim iṣṣabbatu* 10 *šiqil kaspam išaqqal ša ina mūšim ina bītim iṣṣabbatu imât ul iballuṭ*

¶ **13** A man who is seized in the house of a commoner, within the house, at midday, shall weigh and deliver 10 shekels of silver; he who is seized at night within the house shall die, he will not live.

(B i 8–9) *idī ašlākim* 1 *lubuštum* 5 *šiqil kaspam lībilma* 1 *šiqil idūšu* 10 *šiqil kaspam lībilma* 2 *šiqil idūšu*

¶ **14** The hire of a fuller, per one garment valued at 5 shekels of silver—1 shekel is his hire; (per one garment) valued at 10 shekels of silver—2 shekels is his hire.

(B i 10–11) *ina qāti wardim u amtim tamkārum u sābītum kaspam še'am šipātim šamnam adi mādim ul imaḫḫar*

¶ **15** A merchant or a woman innkeeper will not accept silver, grain, wool, oil, or anything else[4] from a male or female slave.

(A ii 1, B i 12) *mār awīlim la zīzu u wardum ul iqqīap*

¶ **16** The son of a man who has not yet received his inheritance share or a slave will not be advanced credit.

(A ii 2–3,[5] B i 13–15) *mār awīlim ana bīt emim terḫatam lībilma šumma ina kilallīn ištēn ana šīmtim ittalak kaspum ana bēlišuma itâr*

¶ **17** Should a member of the *awīlu*-class bring the bridewealth to the house of his father-in-law—if either (the groom or bride then) should go to his or her fate, the silver shall revert to its original owner (i.e., the widower or his heir).

(A ii 4–5, B i 16–18) *šumma īḫussima ana bītišu īrub lu āḫizānu lu kallatum ana šīmtim ittalak mala ublu ul ušeṣṣi wataršuma ileqqe*

¶ **18** If he marries her and she enters his house and then either the groom or the bride goes to his or her fate, he will not take out all that he had brought, but only its excess shall he take.[6]

(A ii 6–7, B i 19–20) 1 *šiqlum* IGI.6.GÁL *u* 6 *uṭṭet ṣibtam uṣṣab* 1 *kur=rum* 1 (*pān*) 4 (*sūt*)[7] *ṣibtam uṣṣab*

¶ **18A** Per 1 shekel (of silver) interest accrues at the rate of 36 barleycorns (= 20%); per 300 silas (of grain) interest accrues at the rate of 100 silas (= 33%).

(A ii 8–9, B i 21–22) *awīlum ša ana*

¶ **19** A man who lends against its

meḫrišu inaddinu ina maškanim ušaddan

corresponding commodity(?) shall collect at the threshing floor.

(A ii 10–13) *šumma awīlum še'am x x x x x x iddinma še'am ana kaspim uštepīl ina ebūri še'am u ṣibassu* 1 *kurrum* 1 (*pān*) 4 (*sūt*) *ileqqe*

¶ **20** If a man loans ... grain ... and then converts the grain into silver, at the harvest he shall take the grain and the interest on it at (the established rate of 33%, i.e.,) 100 silas per 300 silas.

(A ii 13–15) *šumma awīlum kaspam ana pānišu iddin kaspam u ṣibassu* 1 *šiqlum* IGI.6.GÁL *u* [6 *uṭṭet*] *ileqqe*

¶ **21** If a man gives silver for/to his/its ..., he shall take the silver and the interest on it at (the established rate of 20%, i.e.,) 36 barleycorns per 1 shekel.

(A ii 15–18) *šumma awīlum eli awīlim mimma la išūma amat awīlim ittepe bēl amtim nīš ilim i[zakkar] mimma elija la tīšû kaspam mala* ⌜*šīm*(?)⌝ *amtim išaqqal*

¶ **22** If a man has no claim against another man but he nonetheless takes the man's slave woman as a distress, the owner of the slave woman shall swear an oath by the god: "You have no claim against me"; he (the distrainer) shall weigh and deliver silver as much as is the value(?) of the slave woman.

(A ii 19–21) *šumma awīlum eli awīlim mimma la išūma amat awīlim ittepe nipûtam ina bītišu iklāma uštamīt* 2 *amātim ana bēl amtim iriab*

¶ **23** If a man has no claim against another man but he nonetheless takes the man's slave woman as a distress, detains the distress in his house, and causes her death, he shall replace her with two slave women for the owner of the slave woman.

(A ii 23–25) *šumma mimma elišu la išūma aššat muškēnim mār muškēnim ittepe nipûtam ina bītišu iklāma uštamīt dīn napištim nēpû ša ippû imât*

¶ **24** If he has no claim against him[8] but he nonetheless takes the wife of a commoner or the child of a commoner as a distress, detains the distress in his house, and causes her or his death, it is a capital offense–the distrainer who distrained shall die.

(A ii 26–28) *šumma awīlum ana bīt emi issīma emušu ikšīšuma*[9] *mārassu*

¶ **25** If a man comes to claim (his bride) at the house of his father-in-

ana [šanîm it]tadin abi mārtim terḫat imḫuru tašna utâr

law, but his father-in-law wrongs(?) him and then gives his daughter to [another], the father of the daughter shall return two-fold the bridewealth which he received.

(A ii 29–31) *šumma awīlum ana mārat awīlim terḫatam ubilma šanû balum šâl abiša u ummiša imšu'šima ittaqabši dīn napištimma imât*

¶ **26** If a man brings the bridewealth for the daughter of a man, but another, without the consent of her father and mother, abducts her and then deflowers her, it is indeed a capital offense—he shall die.

(A ii 31–34) *šumma awīlum mārat awīlim balum šâl abiša u ummiša īḫussima u kirram u rik<sā>tim ana abiša u ummiša la i[škun] ūmī šattim ištiat ina bītišu līšimma ul aššat*

¶ **27** If a man marries the daughter of another man without the consent of her father and mother, and moreover does not conclude the nuptial feast and the contract for(?) her father and mother, should she reside in his house for even one full year, she is not a wife.

(A ii 34–37, B ii 1–2) *šumma* <...>[10] *riksātim u kirram ana abiša u ummiša iškunma īḫussi aššat ūm ina sūn awīlim iṣṣabbatu imât ul iballuṭ*

¶ **28** If he concludes the contract and the nuptial feast for(?) her father and mother and he marries her, she is indeed a wife; the day she is seized in the lap of another man, she shall die, she will not live.[11]

(A ii 38–45, B ii 3–7) *šumma awīlum ina ḫarrān šeḫtim u sakpim it[tašlal] ulu naḫbutum ittaḫbat ūmī [arkūtim] ina mātim šanītimma itta[šab] aššassu šanûmma ītaḫaz u māram ittalad inūma ittūram aššassu ita[bbal]*

¶ **29** If a man should be captured or abducted during a raiding expedition or while on patrol(?), even should he reside in a foreign land for a long time, should someone else marry his wife and even should she bear a child, whenever he returns he shall take back his wife.

(A ii 45–?, B ii 8–10) *šumma awīlum ālšu u bēlšu izērma ittaḫbit aššassu šanûmma ītaḫaz inūma ittūram ana aššatišu ul iraggam*

¶ **30** If a man repudiates his city and his master and then flees, and someone else then marries his wife, whenever he returns he will have no claim to his wife.

(B ii 11–12) *šumma awīlum amat awīlim ittaqab* 1/3 *mana kaspam išaqqal u amtum ša bēlišama*

¶ **31** If a man should deflower the slave woman of another man, he shall weigh and deliver 20 shekels of silver, but the slave woman remains the property of her master.

(A iii 3–5, B ii 13–15) *šumma awīlum mārašu ana šūnuqim ana tarbītim iddinma epram piššatam lubuštam šalaš šanātim la iddin 10 šiqil kaspam*[12] *tarbīt mārišu išaqqalma mārašu itarru*

¶ **32** If a man gives his child for suckling and for rearing but does not give the food, oil, and clothing rations (to the caregiver) for 3 years, he shall weigh and deliver 10 shekels of silver for the cost of the rearing of his child, and he shall take away his child.

(A iii 6–9, B ii 16–18) *šumma amtum usarrirma mārаša ana mārat awīlim ittadin inūma irtabû bēlšu immaršu iṣabbassuma itarrūšu*

¶ **33** If a slave woman acts to defraud and gives her child to a woman of the *awīlu*-class, when he grows up should his master locate him, he shall seize him and take him away.

(A iii 9–12, B ii 19–21) *šumma amat ekallim mārаša lu mārassa ana muškēnim ana tarbītim ittadin māram lu mārtam ša iddinu ekallum itabbal*

¶ **34** If a slave woman of the palace should give her son or her daughter to a commoner for rearing, the palace shall remove the son or daughter whom she gave.

(A iii 12–13, B ii 22–23) *u lēqû ša mār amat ekallim ilqû meḫeršu ana ekallim iriab*

¶ **35** However,[13] an adoptor who takes in adoption the child of a slave woman of the palace shall restore (another slave of) equal value for the palace.

(A iii 14–17, B ii 24–28) *šumma awīlum bušēšu ana napṭarim ana maṣṣartim iddinma bītum la pališ sippu la ḫališ aptum la nasḫat bušē maṣṣartim ša iddinušum uḫtalliq bušēšu iriabšum*[14]

¶ **36** If a man gives his goods to a *napṭaru* for safekeeping, and he (the *napṭaru*) then allows the goods which he gave to him for safekeeping to become lost—without evidence that the house has been broken into, the doorjamb scraped, the window forced—he shall replace his goods for him.

(A iii 18–23, B iii 1–6) *šumma bīt awīlim luqqut itti bušê awīl maṣṣartim*[15] *ša iddinušum ḫuluq bēl bītim ḫaliq bēl bītim ina bāb Tišpak*[16] *nīš ilim izakkaršumma itti bušēka bušūja lu ḫalqū iwītam u sartam la ēpušu izakkaršumma mimma elišu ul išu*

¶ **37** If the man's house[17] has been burglarized, and the owner of the house incurs a loss along with the goods which the depositor gave to him, the owner of the house shall swear an oath to satisfy him at the gate of (the temple of) the god Tishpak: "My goods have been lost along with your goods; I have not committed a fraud or misdeed"; thus shall he swear an oath to satisfy him and he will have no claim against him.

(A iii 23–25, B 7–9) *šumma ina atḫî ištēn zittašu ana kaspim*[18] *inaddin u aḫušu šâmam ḫašeḫ qablīt šanîm umalla*

¶ **38** If, in a partnership, one intends to sell his share and his partner wishes to buy, he shall match any outside offer.[19]

(A iii 25–27, B iii 10–11) *šumma awīlum īnišma bīssu ana kaspim ittadin ūm šājimānum inaddinu bēl bītim ipaṭṭar*

¶ **39** If a man becomes impoverished and then sells his house, whenever the buyer offers it for sale, the owner of the house shall have the right to redeem it.

(A iii 28–29, B iii 12–13) *šumma awīlum wardam amtam alpam u šīmam mala ibaššû išāmma nādinānam la ukīn šûma šarrāq*

¶ **40** If a man buys a slave, a slave woman, an ox, or any other purchase, but cannot establish the identity of the seller, it is he who is a thief.

(A iii 30–31, B iii 14–16) *šumma ubarum napṭarum u mudû šikaršu inaddin sābītum maḫīrat illaku šikaram inaddinšum*

¶ **41** If a foreigner, a *napṭaru*, or a *mudû*[20] wishes to sell his beer, the woman innkeeper. shall sell the beer for him at the current rate.

(A iii 32–34, B iii 17–20) *šumma awīlum appi awīlim iššukma ittakis* 1 *mana kaspam išaqqal īnu* 1 *mana šinnu* ½ *mana uznu* ½ *mana meḫeṣ lētim* 10 *šiqil kaspam išaqqal*

¶ **42** If a man bites the nose of another man and thus cuts it off, he shall weigh and deliver 60 shekels of silver; an eye—60 shekels; a tooth—30 shekels; an ear—30 shekels; a slap to the cheek[21]—he shall weigh and deliver 10 shekels of silver.

(A iii 35–36, B iii 21–22) *šumma awīlum ubān awīlim ittakis* 1/3[22] *mana kaspam išaqqal*

¶ **43** If a man should cut off the finger of another man, he shall weigh and deliver 20 shekels of silver.

(A iii 36–37, B iii 23–24, C 1–2) *šumma awīlum awīlam ina sūqim*[23] *iskimma qāssu ištebir* ½ *mana kaspam išaqqal*

¶ **44** If a man knocks down another man in the street(?) and thereby breaks his hand, he shall weigh and deliver 30 shekels of silver.

(A iii 38, B iii 24, C 3–4) *šumma šēpšu ištebir* ½ *mana kaspam išaqqal*

¶ **45** If he should break his foot, he shall weigh and deliver 30 shekels of silver.

(A iii 39–40, C 5–6) *šumma awīlum awīlam imḫaṣma kirrašu ištebir* 1/3 *mana kaspam išaqqal*

¶ **46**[24] If a man strikes another man and thus breaks his collarbone, he shall weigh and deliver 20 shekels of silver.

(A iii 40–41, C 7–8) *šumma awīlum ina šigištim awīlam* IG-*te-el* 10 *šiqil kaspam išaqqal*

¶ **47** If a man should inflict(?) any other injuries(?) on another man in the course of a fray, he shall weigh and deliver 10 shekels of silver.

(C 9–11) *šumma awīlum ina risbatim mār awīlim uštamīt* 2/3 *mana kaspam išaqqal*

¶ **47A** If a man, in the course of a brawl, should cause the death of another member of the *awīlu*-class, he shall weigh and deliver 40 shekels of silver.

(A iii 42–44, B iv 1–3) *u ana dīnim ša kaspim ištu* 1/3 *mana adi* 1 *mana dajānū dīnam ušaḫḫazušuma awat napištim ana šarrimma*

¶ **48**[25] And for a case involving a penalty of silver in amounts ranging from 20 shekels to 60 shekels, the judges shall determine the case against him; however, a capital case is only for the king.

(B iv 4–5) *šumma awīlum ina wardim šarqim amtim šariqtim ittaṣbat wardum wardam amtum amtam iredde*

¶ **49** If a man should be seized with a stolen slave or a stolen slave woman, a slave shall lead a slave, a slave woman shall lead a slave woman.[26]

(A iv 1?–7, B iv 6–10) *šumma šakkanakkum šāpir nārim bēl têrtim*

¶ **50** If a military governor, a governor of the canal system, or any per-

mala ibaššû wardam ḫalqam amtam ḫaliqtam alpam ḫalqam imēram ḫalqam ša ekallim u muškēnim[27] *iṣbatma ana Ešnunna*^{ki} *la irdiamma ina bītišu iktala ūmī eli warḫim ištēn ušētiqma*[28] *ekallum šurqam ittišu ītawwu*

son in a position of authority seizes a fugitive slave, fugitive slave woman, stray ox, or stray donkey belonging either to the palace or to a commoner, and does not lead it to Eshnunna but detains it in his house and allows more than one month to elapse, the palace shall bring a charge of theft against him.

(A iv 7–9, B iv 11–13) *wardum u amtum ša Ešnunna*^{ki} *ša kannam maškanam u abbuttam šaknu abul Ešnunna*^{ki} *balum bēlišu ul uṣṣi*

¶ **51** A slave or slave woman belonging to (a resident of) Eshnunna who bears fetters, shackles, or a slave hairlock will not exit through the main city-gate of Eshnunna without his owner.

(A iv 10–13, B iv 14–16) *wardum u amtum ša itti mār šiprim naṣruma abul Ešnunna*^{ki} *īterbam kannam maškanam u abbuttam iššakkanma ana bēlišu naṣir*

¶ **52** A slave or slave woman who has entered the main city-gate of Eshnunna in the safekeeping of only a foreign envoy shall be made to bear fetters, shackles, or a slave hairlock and thereby is kept safe for his owner.[29]

(A iv 13–15, B iv 17–19) *šumma alpum alpam ikkimma uštamīt šīm alpim balṭim u šīr alpim mītim bēl alpim kilallān izuzzu*

¶ **53** If an ox gores another ox and thus causes its death, the two ox-owners shall divide the value of the living ox and the carcass of the dead ox.

(A iv 15–18, B iv 20) *šumma alpum nakkāpîma bābtum ana bēlišu ušēdīma alapšu la u<šē>širma awīlam ikkimma uštamīt bēl alpim* $^2/_3$ *mana kaspam išaqqal*

¶ **54** If an ox is a gorer and the ward authorities so notify its owner, but he fails to keep his ox in check and it gores a man and thus causes his death, the owner of the ox shall weigh and deliver 40 shekels of silver.

(A iv 18–19) *šumma wardam ikkimma uštamīt* 15 *šiqil kaspam išaqqal*

¶ **55** If it gores a slave and thus causes his death, he shall weigh and deliver 15 shekels of silver.

(A iv 20–23) *šumma kalbum šegīma bābtum ana bēlišu ušēdīma kalabšu la*

¶ **56** If a dog is vicious and the ward authorities so notify its owner, but

iṣṣurma awīlam iššukma uštamīt bēl kalbim ⅔ *mana kaspam išaqqal*

he fails to control his dog and it bites a man and thus causes his death, the owner of the dog shall weigh and deliver 40 shekels of silver.

(A iv 23–24) *šumma wardam iššukma*[30] *uštamīt* 15 *šiqil kaspam išaqqal*

¶ **57** If it bites a slave and thus causes his death, he shall weigh and deliver 15 shekels of silver.

(A iv 25–28) *šumma igārum iqâmma bābtum ana bēl igāri ušēdīma igāršu la u<dan>ninma igārum imqutma mār awīlim uštamīt napištum ṣimdat šar=rim*

¶ **58** If a wall is buckling and the ward authorities so notify the owner of the wall, but he does not reinforce his wall and the wall collapses and thus causes the death of a member of the *awīlu*-class—it is a capital case, it is decided by a royal edict.

(A iv 29–33) *šumma awīlum mārī wulludma aššassu īzimma šanītam ītaḫaz ina bītim u mal*[*a ib*]*aššû*[31] *innassaḫma warki ša i*-⌜*x*⌝-[*x-x*]-*ma ittallak* [*x-x*]-⌜*x*⌝ É *x-x-x*

¶ **59** If a man sired children but divorces his wife and then marries another, he shall be expelled from the house and any possessions there may be and he shall depart after the one who ..., [...] the house ...[32]

(A iv 33–37) [*šumma*] *maṣṣārum* [*bītam ina n*]*aṣārim īgûma pallišu* [*bītam ipluš*] *maṣṣār bīti ša ippalšu* [... *idu*]*kku balum* [*qa*]*brišu* [*ina pani p*]*ilšim iqqabbir*

¶ **60**[33] [If] a guard is negligent in guarding [a house], and a burglar [breaks into the house], they shall kill the guard of the house that was broken into [...], and he shall be buried [at] the breach without a grave.

Notes

1. See Stol 1988: 178, for Ì.ÍD interpreted as *ittû*, "bitumen."

2. Reading Á GURUŠ ŠE.KUD.KIN; see Moran 1957: 219, and Stol 1989: 165 n. 29.

3. Possibly to be deleted as dittography.

4. The meaning of the phrase *adi mādim* is still disputed, but is clear both from context here and from additional references; see (in addition to Yaron's summary of the treatments, 1988: 52f.) the references cited *CAD* M/1 24, and *AbB* 9 184: 10 cited by Stol 1993a: 247 with n. 12.

5. Source A conflates ¶¶ 17 and 18.

6. Subjects in the final clause are uncertain, and the resolutions outlined are not clear. Only one prestation, the bridewealth (*terḫatu*) is referred to in ¶ 17, in which following the death of one spouse the bridewealth is returned to the groom or his heir. In ¶ 18, before the death of one spouse the marriage had progressed to the stage of cohabitation which involved additional exchanges of marriage gifts, and the bridewealth is retained by its recipient (the bride's father) while only a specific but otherwise unknown payment ("excess"–of a bridewealth over a dowry?) is taken by the surviving spouse or his heir. For discussion of other possibilities and summary of solutions proposed, see Yaron 1988: 179ff.

7. Var. adds *še'am* "(100 silas) of grain."

8. See Yaron 1988: 141–42, for summary of the arguments involving the equations of the "man" (*awīlum*) of ¶ 23, the unidentified pronoun in "against him" (*elišu*), and the "commoner" (*muškēnum*) of ¶ 24. Does *elišu* refer back to and resume the *awīlum* (thus, "If a man has no claim against another man ...") or does it anticipate *muškēnum* (thus, "If a man has no claim against a commoner ...")? On balance, I find the latter resolution more satisfactory.

9. Reading *ik-ši-šu-ma* uncertain; see the suggestions reported Yaron 1988: 58 note, and see *CAD* K 294 s.v. *kašû* A discussion.

10. The text has *ḫe-pí*, "broken," a scribal notation indicating that the original from which the scribe was copying had a break at this point; if anything is lost after *šumma*, "If," it can only be *awīlum* (thus, "If a man concludes ...").

11. Yaron (1988: 284–85) maintains his earlier position that it is the lover and not the woman who is the subject of *imât ul iballuṭ* "s/he shall die, s/he shall not live," and that her punishment is left to her husband. However, on contextual, legal, and philological grounds it is certain that the provision deals with the status of the woman and the consequent punishment for her actions; see Roth 1988.

12. Reading here 10 GÍN KÙ.BABBAR, with Eichler 1987: 78 and n. 25.

13. The ambiguity of the conjunction (*u*, "and," "or," or "but") makes uncertain the relationship of ¶ 35 to ¶ 34: that which follows *u* could be (a) a continuation of the resolution outlined in ¶ 34 (thus the palace retrieves the child and also demands another); (b) an alternative resolution option (thus the palace accepts *either* the child or his replacement); or (c) a new variation, in which the one who took the child is not the same individual identified in ¶ 34 as a *muškēnum* who reared the child but one who stood in a more formal relationship to the child as adoptor or foster parent, and therefore the child is kept by his new household and a substitute is given to the palace. The weight of scholarly opinion is in favor of the first option over the second (see Yaron 1988: 167ff., Eichler 1987: 79), but the third ("But an adoptor ...") has been largely overlooked since Goetze's editions (but see the translation of Borger 1982: 36, which implies an interpretation similar to that offered here).

14. Var. *iriab*, "he shall replace (his goods)."

15. Var. omits *bušê* LÚ.

16. Var. *ina bīt Tišpak*, "(an oath to satisfy him) in the temple of Tishpak."

17. I.e., the house of the depositary, the "resident alien" (*napṭarum*) of ¶ 36.

18. Var. omits *ana kaspim*, "for silver," thus reading "intends to give."

19. So with *CAD* Q 6 s.v. *qablītu* mng. 7, understanding that the willing partner

has the option of first right of refusal; for other interpretations, see Yaron 1988: 228ff.

20. The three terms are references to categories of persons outside of the common social and jural protective networks; see Westbrook 1994.

21. "Slap to the cheek" is a reference to a physical or social assault to a person's honor.

22. The copy and photograph clearly show 1/3 (and not 2/3, an error introduced in Goetze's first publication in 1948).

23. *ina sūqim* with *CAD* S 70 s.v. *sakāpu* A mng. 1a, although the traces legible on the photograph cannot confirm the reading.

24. On ¶¶ 46, 47, 47A, see Roth 1990.

25. The readings and restorations of ¶ 48 are uncertain at several points, but the general import is clear.

26. The probable meaning of *iredde*, "he shall lead, bring along," in this context is that the party in whose possession the slave is found shall return the slave and in addition provide another of equal value.

27. Var. omits *ša ekallim u muškēnim*, "belonging to the palace or to a commoner."

28. Var. omits *ūmī eli warḫim ištēn ušētiqma*, "allows more than a single month to elapse."

29. The translation is based on understanding the *mār šiprim*, "envoy," and the *bēlu*, "owner," as two different individuals.

30. Text (error) *ikkimma*, "it gores."

31. Westbrook (1988: 72 n. 21) reads *ù ma-a[k-ku-r]i šu-ú*.

32. The interpretation of the provision is disputed, revolving around the identity (or identities) of the subjects in the subclauses of the apodosis; see the summaries of the discussion in Yaron 1988: 214ff. and in Westbrook 1988: 72ff. The final subclause (beginning with *warki*) is very uncertain; I take *ittallak* as a Gt separative, in a hendiadys with *innassaḫma*, conveying the sense of the husband departing, leaving, or going away from the estate from which he is expelled. The traces visible on the photograph do not support any of the various proposals offered for reading the damaged lines 32 and 33, and the sense remains unclear.

33. The provision is damaged, and the restorations and interpretation are uncertain; here, I follow the treatment put forward by Landsberger 1968: 102.

8

Laws of Hammurabi (LH) (ca. 1750 B.C.E., Babylon)

The collection of rules was compiled toward the end of the forty-three year reign of Hammurabi (r. 1792–1750 B.C.E.), sixth ruler of the First Dynasty of Babylon, the king who directed the great political expansion of the empire and organized a complex and sophisticated government and military bureaucracy to administer it. He defeated powerful rival kingdoms and extended his political and diplomatic influence throughout the ancient Near East in an expansion rivaled only by that achieved by his early contemporary to the north, Shamshi-Adad of Assyria. The year name formula for Hammurabi's second year, "Year in which Hammurabi established justice in the land," is a testimony to Hammurabi's concern for justice and a possible reference to his enactment of a *mīšaru*-edict (see the introductory remarks to the Laws of Eshnunna).

About the Laws

The Laws of Hammurabi is the longest and best organized of the law collections from Mesopotamia. It draws on the traditions of earlier law collections and doubtless influenced those that came later. The composition consists of a lengthy prologue, between 275 and 300 law provisions, and an epilogue. The prologue stresses the gods' appointment of Hammurabi as ruler of his people, his role as guardian and protector of the weak and powerless, and his care and attention to the cultic needs of the patron deities of the many cities incorporated into his realm. The laws of this composition, inscribed on imposing black stone stelas, stand as evidence of Hammurabi's worthiness to rule.

The law provisions refer to many situations that require resolution, often expressed as a complicated or hard case, by analogy to which the simpler case is readily resolved. For example, compare the complex first provision of the Laws of Hammurabi with the earlier and simpler first provision of the Laws of Ur-Namma; both provisions involve homicide and serve to establish immediately the state's right to impose the death penalty on a subject:

LU ¶1 If a man commits a homicide, they shall kill that man.

LH ¶1 If a man accuses another man and charges him with homicide but then cannot bring proof against him, his accuser shall be killed.

In formulating LH ¶ 1 in this manner, a number of pieces of information about the legal system are revealed: that a private individual (and not necessarily only an official body or officer) may bring charges against another person; that such charges must be substantiated in some way; and that a false accuser suffers the penalty he sought for his intended victim. We can only infer in the LH that which the LU provision, in its simpler formulation, makes explicit: that homicide demands the death penalty.

The cases dealt with in the Laws of Hammurabi include judicial procedure; theft and robbery; slave sales and matters affecting slaves; agricultural and irrigation work and offenses; pledges, debts, deposits and loans; real estate sales and rentals; marriage, matrimonial property, and sexual offenses; inheritance, adoption and foster care; assault and bodily injuries; rates of hire for equipment, laborers, and craftsmen; failure to complete contracted tasks; renters' and shepherds' liabilities; and goring oxen. The law provisions are marked by the introductory *šumma*, "if."

The epilogue emphasizes the king as military leader who brings peace to his subjects. It explicitly states that these laws were inscribed on a stela and publicly displayed in order to testify to Hammurabi's righteous and just rule, to bring consolation to anyone seeking justice, and to serve as an example for future rulers. It seeks blessings for Hammurabi from his successors and the beneficiaries of his legacy; it blesses them if they treat his stela and laws with respect; and it brings down the terrible curses of the great gods against any who would violate the path Hammurabi opened or who would mutilate or desecrate his monument.

The laws distinguish three principal classes of person: the free person (*awīlu*), including men, women, and minors; the commoner (*muškēnu*), inferior to the *awīlu* in some rights and privileges; and the male and female slave (*wardu* and *amtu*), including slaves belonging to free persons, to commoners, and to the palace. Unless otherwise specified, we assume that the various professionals, craftsmen, laborers, etc., belong to the class of free persons. The laws also take special note of additional groups: tenants or dependents of the palace, including the "soldier" (*rēdû*) and the "fisherman" (*bā'iru*), both of whom are included in the category of persons identified as "state tenants" (*nāši bilti*); classes of priestesses identified as *kulmašītu, nadītu, qadištu, sekretu, šugītu, ugbabtu;* the courtier (*girseqû*) or palace attendant (*muzzaz ekalli*); the merchant (*tamkāru*) and the woman innkeeper (*sābītu*), both of whom function as creditors. Women are included in all categories and classes, and the laws refer to the wife (*aššatu*) of the free person, of the commoner, and of the state tenant, as well as to the "first-ranking" (*ḫīrtu*) wife and to the widow (*almattu*).

About the Sources

The LH is known from numerous manuscripts, copied and recopied over the centuries in the scribal centers of Mesopotamia. The most complete and famous exemplar is the black stone stela, now housed in the Musée du Louvre, Paris, excavated in 1901–1902 by archaeological teams working in the ancient Elamite capital Susa. The stela, one of several that were erected in Babylonian cities, was taken as booty to Susa in the twelfth century B.C.E. by the Elamite ruler Shutruk-Naḫḫunte I, probably from Sippar, from which he also plundered monuments of other Mesopotamian rulers. Fragments of yet a second and possibly a third stela recording Hammurabi's laws were also excavated in the same place, which suggests that the monuments, multiple copies of which were erected in various Babylonian cities, were highly prized plunder.

The Louvre stela, which forms the basis of every edition of the Laws, is a pillar of diorite almost seven and a half feet tall. On the top, covering almost one-third of the stela, is an imposing scene of the sun-god Shamash, god of justice, seated on his throne, and standing before him the king Hammurabi. The precise interpretation of this scene—that the god is dictating the laws to the king, or that the king is offering the laws to the god, or that the king is accepting the rod and ring that are the emblems of temple-building and sovereignty—is debated, but the iconographic message it communicated to even the illiterate must have been clear: King Hammurabi and the god of justice Shamash together protect the people of Babylonia.

The physically imposing Louvre stela, like other monumental inscriptions of its time, is inscribed in an archaic ductus and in the direction employed earlier, before the script was turned ninety degrees counterclockwise; the visual impact of the script and the orientation, along with the archaizing, literary language used in the prologue and epilogue that frame the collection of rules, magnify the authority of the composition. The columns of the text inscribed on the stela are written in bands across the front and then the back of the circumference, beginning immediately below the throne of the god Shamash; the prologue and epilogue each occupy about five columns, and the series of legal provisions occupies about forty-one columns.

We have recovered dozens of duplicates and extracts of the Laws, as well as commentaries, references to the composition in a first-millennium catalogue, and a bilingual Sumerian-Akkadian manuscript, from a variety of sites in Mesopotamia. Some of the manuscripts date to Hammurabi's immediate successors in the First Dynasty of Babylon, while others are copies from a thousand years later. This wide and varied evidence attests to the enduring popularity of the Laws of Hammurabi, which was both an influence on and a reflection of contemporary literary, political, as well as legal thought. The numerous manuscripts suggest more than one original exemplar, and what are sometimes viewed as discrepancies and errors in some manuscripts may be the results of different traditions.

The stela and manuscripts allow us to present almost the entire composition, leaving problematical only the restoration of the gap of seven columns (each with more than eighty lines) in the Louvre stela falling between the last preserved column on the front of the stela, column xvi (which ends in ¶ 65), and the first column on the back, here taken as column xxiv (which begins in the middle of what is traditionally numbered ¶ 100, following the first estimate of the number of lost provisions in the gap [Scheil 1902: 53]). This gap results from a deliberate erasure of the last columns on the bottom of the front of the stela, by the artisans in the Elamite workshop of the ruler Shutruk-Naḫḫunte I, in preparation for a secondary rededication inscription, which was, however, never added. Much of this gap can be filled in by the duplicate manuscripts, and especially with the aid of the recent publication by Donbaz and Sauren (1991) of a piece from the Nippur collection in Istanbul which previously had been only partially and imperfectly known (source t). As a result, some considerations and conventions accepted in the present edition need clarification.

The first problem is the size of the gap (five or seven columns lost) and the consequent numbering of the columns that follow it. Harper (1904) ignored the gap and continued the column numbering without interruption, picking up after the gap directly with "xvii" and continuing through to end with column "xliv"; Harper's edition included only the Louvre stela, and he was not concerned with restoring the gap. (This same numbering convention was used by Deimel 1930, and many others, and is followed by the *CAD*.) Meek (1950a) began column numbers anew after the gap, concluding with "reverse xxviii"; he numbered the restored provisions within the gap in sequence, thus ¶¶ 66, 67, 68, etc. Similar sequential provision numberings for the gap were employed by Laessøe (1950). In their edition, Driver and Miles (1955) identified the columns on the obverse, preceding the gap, as "ia" through "xvia" and those on the reverse, following the gap, as "ib" through "xxviiib"; they used capital letters to identify the provisions in the gap, thus ¶¶ A, B, C, etc. These conventions were accepted by Finet (1973), and by students since. Saporetti (1984: 60-62) mixes numbering conventions, using both numerical (¶ 66, ¶ 67, ¶ 69 ... ¶ 91, etc.) and alphabetical (¶ A, ¶ B, etc.) sigla. In his editions (1963, 1979, and 1982b) Borger accepted a seven-column gap and began the columns on the reverse with "xxiv" but considerately provided the equivalent column number of the reverse; thus, for example, "Kol. XXVI (Rs. III)" (Borger 1979: 24). Furthermore, Borger attempted a new numbering system for the provisions restored in the gap, introducing an alphanumeric system that has the advantage of identifying securely sequenced provisions by the repetition of lower case letters. (Thus, for example, Borger's ¶ 68+c is followed without break by ¶ 69+c, and in turn is followed, after a break, by the uninterrupted run of ¶¶ 69+d, 70+d, 71+d, 72+d.) Another provision numbering system (for the entire composition, and for other Mesopotamian law collections as well) was used by Sauren (1989), in which the laws are grouped by legal and stylistic criteria into eleven groups of approximately twenty provisions each; this system was used in the recent publication of the important large tablet, Ni. 2553+2565 (source t) by Donbaz and Sauren (1991).

Although the numbering system of Sauren and Donbaz has the advantage of trying to account for every provision in the gap, both those recovered and those still lost, it has at least two flaws: first, my examination of Ni. 2553+2565 (source t) from the published copy and photograph has resulted in the decipherment of some additional provisions not in the Donbaz-Sauren edition; and, second, the new numbering system attempts to supplant completely the accepted and conventional numbering of the provisions in all scholarly literature. Nonetheless, Ni. 2553+2565 significantly adds to the reconstruction and restoration of the gap, and demands new sigla at least for those provisions restored within that gap. The present edition of the LH, therefore, attempts to reconcile some of these problems in the following manner: The transcription of the Akkadian identifies the sources that witness the provision. The English translation marks the provisions in the gap serially with lower case Latin letters (¶ a, ¶ b, etc.) and adds at the end of each provision the corresponding identification in three different, widely used systems. Thus, for example, the provision labeled here "gap ¶ t" corresponds to the provision labeled ¶ L in Driver and Miles 1955, to ¶ 70+d in Borger 1979, and to ¶ 5.9 in Donbaz and Sauren 1991.

Three manuscripts from the late Old Babylonian period include subject headings or rubrics at irregular intervals. The manuscripts, sources S, r, and t, include the rubrics: "legal decisions concerning soldier and fisherman" (r iii, before ¶ 26); "legal decisions concerning field, orchard, and house" (r iv, before ¶ 36); "legal decisions concerning contracts of hire and purchase" (t i 1-2, before gap ¶ h; see Donbaz and Sauren 1991: 8); "legal decisions concerning removing property from a house" (S v 28, before ¶ 113); "legal decisions concerning distraint and obligation" (t vii 2-3, before ¶ 117); and "legal decisions concerning [...] and storage" (t vii 21-22) and "legal decisions concerning storage" (S vi 40, both before ¶ 120). No rubrics are included in the complete monumental stela, and their introduction in these three large late Old Babylonian manuscripts suggests a self-reflective scholastic tradition, engaged in organizing and studying the law collection as a whole. Furthermore, the division of the text into law provisions, which is the invention of the first modern editor of the stela (no markings or incised lines divide provisions in the Louvre stela), is clearly marked on some manuscripts in places different from those assumed in early editions, again providing some indication of the traditions current in scribal circles.

For reasons of accessibility and consistency, the Akkadian text is marked throughout by the corresponding column and line numbers of the Louvre stela only; however, for the passages placed in the gap of the stela's columns xvii-xxiii, I indicate all the extant witnesses (see above). As is the practice followed throughout this volume, variants are noted only infrequently.

Prologue

(i 1–26) *īnu Anum ṣīrum šar Anunnakī Enlil bēl šamê u erṣetim šā'im šīmāt mātim ana Marduk mārim rēštîm ša Ea illilūt kiššat nišī išīmušum in Igigī ušarbiušu Bābilam šumšu ṣīram ibbiu in kibrātim ušāterušu ina libbišu šarrūtam dārītam ša kīma šamê u erṣetim išdāša šuršudā ukinnušum*

When the august god Anu, king of the Anunnaku deities, and the god Enlil, lord of heaven and earth, who determines the destinies of the land, allotted supreme power over all peoples to the god Marduk, the firstborn son of the god Ea, exalted him among the Igigu deities, named the city of Babylon with its august name and made it supreme within the regions of the world, and established for him within it eternal kingship whose foundations are as fixed as heaven and earth,

(i 27–49) *inūmišu Ḫammurabi rubâm na'dam pāliḫ ilī jâti mīšaram ina mātim ana šūpîm raggam u ṣēnam ana ḫulluqim dannum enšam ana la ḫabālim kīma Šamaš ana ṣalmāt qaqqadim waṣêmma mātim nuwwurim Anum u Enlil ana šīr nišī ṭubbim šumī ibbû*

at that time, the gods Anu and Enlil, for the enhancement of the well-being of the people, named me by my name: Hammurabi, the pious prince, who venerates the gods, to make justice prevail in the land, to abolish the wicked and the evil, to prevent the strong from oppressing the weak, to rise like the sun-god Shamash over all humankind, to illuminate the land.

(i 50–62) *Ḫammurabi rē'ûm nibīt Enlil anāku mukammer nuḫšim u ṭuḫdim mušaklil mimma šumsu ana Nippur markas šamê u erṣetim zāninum na'dum ša Ekur*

I am Hammurabi, the shepherd, selected by the god Enlil, he who heaps high abundance and plenty, who perfects every possible thing for the city Nippur, (the city known as) band-of-heaven-and-earth, the pious provider of the Ekur temple;

(i 63–ii 1) *šarrum lē'ûm mutīr Eridu ana ašrišu mubbib šuluḫ Eabzu*

the capable king, the restorer of the city Eridu, the purifier of the rites of the Eabzu temple;

(ii 2–12) *tīb kibrāt erbettim mušarbi zikru Bābilim muṭīb libbi Marduk bēlišu ša ūmīšu izzazzu ana Esagil*

the onslaught of the four regions of the world, who magnifies the reputation of the city Babylon, who gladdens the heart of his divine lord Marduk, whose days are devoted to the Esagil temple;

(ii 13–21) *zēr šarrūtim ša Sîn ibniušu munaḫḫiš Urim wašrum muštēmiqum bābil ḫegallim ana Egišnugal*

seed of royalty, he whom the god Sîn created, enricher of the city of Ur, humble and talented, who provides abundance for the Egishnugal temple;

(ii 22–31) *šar tašīmtim šēmû Šamaš dannum mukīn išdī Sippar mušalbiš warqim gigunē Aja muṣīr bīt Ebabbar ša kî šubat šamā'ī*

discerning king, obedient to the god Shamash, the mighty one, who establishes the foundations of the city of Sippar, who drapes the sacred building of the goddess Aja with greenery, who made famous the temple of Ebabbar which is akin to the abode of heaven;

(ii 32–36) *qarrādum gāmil Larsa muddiš Ebabbar ana Šamaš rēṣišu*

the warrior, who shows mercy to the city of Larsa, who renews the Ebabbar temple for the god Shamash his ally;

(ii 37–47) *bēlum muballiṭ Uruk šākin mê nuḫšim ana nišīšu mullî rēš*

the lord who revitalizes the city of Uruk, who provides abundant

Eanna mukammer ḫiṣbim ana Anim u Ištar

waters for its people, who raises high the summit of the Eanna temple, who heaps up bountiful produce for the gods Anu and Ishtar;

(ii 48–54) *ṣulūl mātim mupaḫḫir nišī sapḫātim ša Isin muṭaḫḫid nuḫšim bīt Egalmaḫ*

the protecting canopy of the land, who gathers together the scattered peoples of the city of Isin, who supplies abundance for the temple of Egalmaḫ;

(ii 55–67) *ušumgal šarrī talīm Zababa mušaršid šubat Kiš muštasḫir melimmī Emeteursag mušteṣbî parṣī rabûtim ša Ištar pāqid bītim Ḫursagkalamma*

dragon among kings, beloved brother of the god Zababa, founder of the settlement of Kish, who surrounds the Emeteursag temple with splendor, who arranges the great rites for the goddess Ishtar, who takes charge of the temple of Ḫursagkalamma;

(ii 68–iii 6) *sapar nakirī ša Erra rūšu ušakšidu nizmassu mušāter Kutî murappiš mimma šumšu ana <E>meslam*

the enemy-ensnaring throw-net, whose companion, the god Erra, has allowed him to obtain his heart's desire, who enlarges the city of Kutû, who augments everything for the Emeslam temple;

(iii 7–16) *rīmum kadrum munakkip zā'irī narām Tutu murīš Barsippa na'dum la mupparkûm ana Ezida <šubat> ili šarrī*[1]

the fierce wild bull who gores the enemy, beloved of the god Tutu, the one who makes the city of Borsippa exult, the pious one who does not fail in his duties to the Ezida temple, <the dwelling of> the god of kings;

(iii 17–23) *mudē igigallim mušaddil mēreštim ša Dilbat mugarrin karê ana Uraš gašrim*

the one who is steeped in wisdom, who enlarges the cultivated area of the city of Dilbat, who heaps up the storage bins for the mighty god Urash;

(iii 24–35) *bēlum simat ḫaṭṭim u agêm ša ušaklilušu erištum Mama mukīn*

the lord, worthy recipient of the scepter and crown bestowed upon

uṣurātim ša Keš mudeššī mākalī ellūtim ana Nintu

him by the wise goddess Mama, who devised the plans of the city of Kesh, who provides the pure food offerings for the goddess Nintu;

(iii 36–46) *muštālum gitmālum šā'im mirītim u mašqītim ana Lagaš u Girsîm mukīl nindabê rabûtim ana Eninnu*

the judicious one, the noble one, who allots pasturage and watering place for the cities of Lagash and Girsu, who provides plentiful food-offerings for the Eninnu temple;

(iii 47–54) *mutammeḫ ajābī migir telītim mušaklil tērētim ša Zabala muḫaddi libbi Ištar*

who seizes the enemies, beloved of (the goddess Ishtar) the able one, who perfects the oracles of the city of Zabala, who gladdens the heart of the goddess Ishtar;

(iii 55–64) *rubûm ellum ša nīš qātišu Adad idû munēḫ libbi Adad qurādim ina Karkara muštakkin simātim ina Eudgalgal*

the pure prince, whose prayers the god Adad acknowledges, appeaser of the heart of the god Adad, the hero in the city of Karkara, who installs the proper appointments throughout the Eudgalgal temple;

(iii 65–69) *šarrum nādin napištim ana Adab āšer bīt Emaḫ*

the king who gives life to the city of Adab, who organizes the Emaḫ temple;

(iii 70–iv 6) *etel šarrī qabal la maḫārim šû iqīšu napšatam ana Maškan-šāpir mušešqi nuḫšim ana <E>meslam*

lord of kings, peerless warrior, who granted life to the city of Mashkan-shapir, who gives waters of abundance to the Emeslam temple;

(iv 7–22) *emqum muttabbilum šû ikšudu nagab uršim mušpazzir nišī Malgium ina karašîm mušaršidu šubātišin in nuḫšim ana Enki u Damkina mušarbû šarrūtišu dāriš išīmu zībī ellūtim*

wise one, the organizer, he who has mastered all wisdom, who shelters the people of the city of Malgium in the face of annihilation, who founds their settlements in abundance, who decreed eternal pure food offerings for the gods Enki and Damkina who magnify his kingship;

(iv 23–31) *ašared šarrī mukanniš dadmē Nār Purattim ittum Dagan bānîšu šû igmilu nišī Mera u Tuttul*

leader of kings, who subdues the settlements along the Euphrates River by the oracular command of the god Dagan, his creator, who showed mercy to the people of the cities of Mari and Tuttul;

(iv 32–44) *rubûm na'dum munawwer pani Tišpak šākin mākalī ellūtim ana Ninazu šāṭip nišīšu in pušqim mukinnu išdīšin qerbum Bābilim šulmāniš*

the pious prince, who brightens the countenance of the god Tishpak, who provides pure feasts for the goddess Ninazu, who sustains his people in crisis, who secures their foundations in peace in the midst of the city of Babylon;

(iv 45–52) *rē'ī nišī ša epšētušu eli Ištar ṭābā mukinni Ištar ina Eulmaš qerbum Akkade ribītim*

shepherd of the people, whose deeds are pleasing to the goddess Ishtar, who establishes Ishtar in the Eulmash temple in the midst of Akkad-the-City;

(iv 53–58) *mušēpī kīnātim mušūšer ammi mutīr lamassišu damiqtim ana ālim Aššur*

who proclaims truth, who guides the population properly, who restores its benevolent protective spirit to the city of Assur;

(iv 59–63) *mušeppi nābiḫī šarrum ša ina Ninua ina Emesmes ušūpi'u mê Ištar*

who quells the rebellious, the king who proclaimed the rites for the goddess Ishtar in the city of Nineveh in the Emesmes temple;

(iv 64–v 13) *na'dum muštēmiqum ana ilī rabûtim liplippim ša Sumu-la-el aplum dannum ša Sîn-muballiṭ zērum dārium ša šarrūtim šarrum dannum šamšu Bābilim mušēṣi nūrim ana māt Šumerim u Akkadim šarrum muštešmi kibrāt arba'im migir Ištar anāku*

the pious one, who prays ceaselessly for the great gods, scion of Sumu-la-el, mighty heir of Sîn-muballiṭ, eternal seed of royalty, mighty king, solar disk of the city of Babylon, who spreads light over the lands of Sumer and Akkad, king who makes the four regions obedient, favored of the goddess Ishtar, am I.

(v 14–24) *inūma Marduk ana šutēšur nišī mātim ūsim šūḫuzim uwa'eranni*

When the god Marduk commanded me to provide just ways for the

kittam u mīšaram ina pī mātim aškun šīr nišī uṭīb

people of the land (in order to attain) appropriate behavior, I established truth and justice as the declaration of the land, I enhanced the well-being of the people.

(v 25) *inūmišu*

At that time:

Laws

(v 26–32) *šumma awīlum awīlam ubbirma nērtam elišu iddīma la uktīnšu mubbiršu iddâk*

¶ 1 If a man accuses another man and charges him with homicide but cannot bring proof against him, his accuser shall be killed.

(v 33–56) *šumma awīlum kišpī eli awīlim iddīma la uktīnšu ša elišu kišpū nadû ana Id illak Id išalliamma šumma Id iktašassu mubbiršu bīssu itabbal šumma awīlam šuāti Id ūteb=bibaššuma ištalmam ša elišu kišpī iddû iddâk ša Id išliam bīt mubbirišu itabbal*

¶ 2 If a man charges another man with practicing witchcraft but cannot bring proof against him, he who is charged with witchcraft shall go to the divine River Ordeal, he shall indeed submit to the divine River Ordeal; if the divine River Ordeal should overwhelm him, his accuser shall take full legal possession of his estate; if the divine River Ordeal should clear that man and should he survive, he who made the charge of witchcraft against him shall be killed; he who submitted to the divine River Ordeal shall take full legal possession of his accuser's estate.

(v 57–67) *šumma awīlum ina dīnim ana šībūt sarrātim ūṣiamma awat iqbû la uktīn šumma dīnum šû dīn napištim awīlum šû iddâk*

¶ 3 If a man comes forward to give false testimony in a case but cannot bring evidence for his accusation, if that case involves a capital offense, that man shall be killed.

(v 68–vi 5) *šumma ana šībūt še'im u kaspim ūṣiam aran dīnim šuāti ittanašši*[2]

¶ 4 If he comes forward to give (false) testimony for (a case whose penalty is) grain or silver, he shall be assessed the penalty for that case.

(vi 6–30) *šumma dajānum dīnam idīn purussâm iprus kunukkam ušēzib warkānumma dīnšu īteni dajānam šuāti ina dīn idīnu enêm ukannušuma rugummâm ša ina dīnim šuāti ibbaššû adi 12-šu inaddin u ina puḫrim ina kussī dajānūtišu ušetbûšuma ul itârma itti dajānī ina dīnim ul uššab*

¶ 5 If a judge renders a judgment, gives a verdict, or deposits a sealed opinion, after which he reverses his judgment, they shall charge and convict that judge of having reversed the judgment which he rendered and he shall give twelvefold the claim of that judgment; moreover, they shall unseat him from his judgeship in the assembly, and he shall never again sit in judgment with the judges.

(vi 31–40) *šumma awīlum makkūr ilim u ekallim išriq awīlum šû iddâk u ša šurqam ina qātišu imḫuru iddâk*

¶ 6 If a man steals valuables belonging to the god or to the palace, that man shall be killed, and also he who received the stolen goods from him shall be killed.

(vi 41–56) *šumma awīlum lu kaspam lu ḫurāṣam lu wardam lu amtam lu alpam lu immeram lu imēram ulu mimma šumšu ina qāt mār awīlim ulu warad awīlim balum šībī u riksātim ištām ulu ana maṣṣarūtim imḫur awīlum šû šarrāq iddâk*

¶ 7 If a man should purchase silver, gold, a slave, a slave woman, an ox, a sheep, a donkey, or anything else whatsoever, from a son of a man or from a slave of a man without witnesses or a contract—or if he accepts the goods for safekeeping—that man is a thief, he shall be killed.

(vi 57–69) *šumma awīlum lu alpam lu immeram lu imēram lu šaḫâm ulu elippam išriq šumma ša ilim šumma ša ekallim adi 30-šu inaddin šumma ša muškēnim adi 10-šu iriab šumma šarrāqānum ša nadānim la išu iddâk*

¶ 8 If a man steals an ox, a sheep, a donkey, a pig, or a boat—if it belongs either to the god or to the palace, he shall give thirtyfold; if it belongs to a commoner, he shall replace it tenfold; if the thief does not have anything to give, he shall be killed.

(vi 70–vii 47) *šumma awīlum ša mimmûšu ḫalqu mimmāšu ḫalqam ina qāti*

¶ 9 If a man who claims to have lost property then discovers his lost

awīlim iṣṣabat awīlum ša ḫulqum ina qātišu ṣabtu nādinānummi iddinam maḫar šībīmi ašām iqtabi u bēl ḫulqim šībī mudē ḫulqijami lublam iqtabi šājimānum nādin iddinušum u šībī ša ina maḫrišunu išāmu itbalam u bēl ḫulqim šībī mudē ḫulqišu itbalam dajānū awâtišunu immaruma šībū ša maḫrišunu šīmum iššāmu u šībū mudē ḫulqim mudūssunu maḫar ilim iqabbûma nādinānum šarrāq iddâk bēl ḫulqim ḫuluqšu ileqqe šājimānum ina bīt nādinānim kasap išqulu ileqqe

property in another man's possession, but the man in whose possession the lost property was discovered declares, "A seller sold it to me, I purchased it in the presence of witnesses," and the owner of the lost property declares, "I can bring witnesses who can identify my lost property," (and then if) the buyer produces the seller who sold it to him and the witnesses in whose presence he purchased it, and also the owner of the lost property produces the witnesses who can identify his lost property—the judges shall examine their cases, and the witnesses in whose presence the purchase was made and the witnesses who can identify the lost property shall state the facts known to them before the god, then it is the seller who is the thief, he shall be killed; the owner of the lost property shall take his lost property, and the buyer shall take from the seller's estate the amount of silver that he weighed and delivered.

(vii 48–61) *šumma šājimānum nādinān iddinušum u šībī ša ina maḫrišunu išāmu la itbalam bēl ḫulqimma šībī mudē ḫulqišu itbalam šājimānum šarrāq iddâk bēl ḫulqim ḫuluqšu ileqqe*

¶ **10** If the buyer could not produce the seller who sold (the lost property) to him or the witnesses before whom he made the purchase, but the owner of the lost property could produce witnesses who can identify his lost property, then it is the buyer who is the thief, he shall be killed; the owner of the lost property shall take his lost property.

(vii 62–viii 3) *šumma bēl ḫulqim šībī mudē ḫulqišu la itbalam sār tuššamma iddi*[3] *iddâk*

¶ **11** If the owner of the lost property could not produce witnesses who can identify his lost property, he is a liar, he has indeed spread malicious charges, he shall be killed.

(viii 4–13) *šumma nādinānum ana šīmtim ittalak šājimānum ina bīt nādinānim rugummē dīnim šuāti adi ḫamšīšu ileqqe*

¶ **12** If the seller should go to his fate, the buyer shall take fivefold the claim for that case from the estate of the seller.

(viii 14–24) *šumma awīlum šû šībūšu la qerbu dajānū adannam ana šeššet warḫī išakkanušumma šumma ina šeššet warḫī šībīšu la irdiam awīlum šû sār aran dīnim šuāti ittanašši*

¶ **13** If that man's witnesses are not available, the judges shall grant him an extension until the sixth month, but if he does not bring his witnesses by the sixth month, it is that man who is a liar, he shall be assessed the penalty for that case.

(viii 25–29) *šumma awīlum mār awīlim ṣiḫram ištariq iddâk*

¶ **14** If a man should kidnap the young child of another man, he shall be killed.

(viii 30–36) *šumma awīlum lu warad ekallim lu amat ekallim lu warad muškēnim lu amat muškēnim abullam uštēṣi iddâk*

¶ **15** If a man should enable a palace slave, a palace slave woman, a commoner's slave, or a commoner's slave woman to leave through the main city-gate, he shall be killed.

(viii 37–48) *šumma awīlum lu wardam lu amtam ḫalqam ša ekallim ulu muškēnim ina bītišu irtaqīma ana šisīt nāgirim la uštēṣiam bēl bītim šû iddâk*

¶ **16** If a man should harbor a fugitive slave or slave woman of either the palace or of a commoner in his house and not bring him out at the herald's public proclamation, that householder shall be killed.

(viii 49–58) *šumma awīlum lu wardam lu amtam ḫalqam ina ṣērim iṣbatma ana bēlišu irtediaššu 2 šiqil kaspam bēl wardim inaddiššum*

¶ **17** If a man seizes a fugitive slave or slave woman in the open country and leads him back to his owner, the slave owner shall give him 2 shekels of silver.

(viii 59–67) *šumma wardum šû bēlšu la izzakar ana ekallim ireddīšu warkassu ipparrasma ana bēlišu utaršu*

¶ **18** If that slave should refuse to identify his owner, he shall lead him off to the palace, his circumstances shall be investigated, and they shall return him to his owner.

(viii 68–ix 4) *šumma wardam šuāti ina bītišu iktalāšu warka wardum ina qātišu ittaṣbat awīlum šû iddâk*

¶ **19** If he should detain that slave in his own house and afterward the slave is discovered in his possession, that man shall be killed.

(ix 5–13) *šumma wardum ina qāt ṣābitānišu iḫtaliq awīlum šû ana bēl wardim nīš ilim izakkarma ūtaššar*

¶ **20** If the slave should escape the custody of the one who seized him, that man shall swear an oath by the god to the owner of the slave, and he shall be released.

(ix 14–21) *šumma awīlum bītam ipluš ina pani pilšim šuāti idukkušuma iḫallalušu*

¶ **21** If a man breaks into a house, they shall kill him and hang him in front of that very breach.

(ix 22–27) *šumma awīlum ḫubtam iḫbutma ittaṣbat awīlum šû iddâk*

¶ **22** If a man commits a robbery and is then seized, that man shall be killed.

(ix 28–45) *šumma ḫabbātum la ittaṣbat awīlum ḫabtum mimmâšu ḫalqam maḫar ilim ubârma ālum*[4] *u rabiānum ša ina erṣetišunu u paṭṭišunu ḫubtum iḫḫabtu mimmâšu ḫalqam iriabbušum*[5]

¶ **23** If the robber should not be seized, the man who has been robbed shall establish the extent of his lost property before the god; and the city and the governor in whose territory and district the robbery was committed shall replace his lost property to him.

(ix 46–50) *šumma napištum ālum u rabiānum* 1 *mana kaspam ana nišīšu išaqqalu*

¶ **24** If a life (is lost during the robbery), the city and the governor shall weigh and deliver to his kinsmen 60 shekels of silver.

(ix 51–65) *šumma ina bīt awīlim išātum innapiḫma awīlum ša ana bul=lîm*[6] *illiku ana numāt bēl bītim īnšu iššīma numāt bēl bītim ilteqe awīlum šû ana išātim šuāti innaddi*

¶ **25** If a fire breaks out in a man's house, and a man who came to help put it out covets the household furnishings belonging to the householder, and takes household furnishings belonging to the householder, that man shall be cast into that very fire.

(ix 66–x 12) *šumma lu rēdûm ulu bāʾirum ša ana ḫarrān šarrim alākšu*

¶ **26** If either a soldier or a fisherman who is ordered to go on a royal

qabû la illik ulu agram īgurma pūḫšu iṭṭarad lu rēdûm ulu bāʾirum šû iddâk munaggiršu bīssu itabbal

campaign does not go, or hires and sends a hireling as his substitute, that soldier or fisherman shall be killed; the one who informs against him shall take full legal possession of his estate.

(x 13–29) *šumma lu rēdûm ulu bāʾirum ša ina dannat šarrim turru warkišu eqelšu u kirāšu*[7] *ana šanîm iddinuma ilikšu ittalak šumma ittūramma ālšu iktašdam eqelšu u kirāšu utarrušumma šûma ilikšu illak*

¶ **27** If there is either a soldier or a fisherman who is taken captive while serving in a royal fortress, and they give his field and his orchard to another to succeed to his holdings, and he then performs his service obligation—if he (the soldier or fisherman) should return and get back to his city, they shall return to him his field and orchard and he himself shall perform his service obligation.

(x 30–40) *šumma lu rēdûm ulu bāʾirum ša ina dannat šarrim turru mārušu ilkam alākam ileʾi eqlum u kirûm innaddiššumma ilik abišu illak*

¶ **28** If there is either a soldier or a fisherman who is taken captive while serving in a royal fortress, and his son is able to perform the service obligation, the field and orchard shall be given to him and he shall perform his father's service obligation.

(x 41–50) *šumma mārušu ṣeḫerma ilik abišu alākam la ileʾi šalušti eqlim u kirîm ana ummišu innaddinma ummašu urabbāšu*

¶ **29** If his son is too young and is unable to perform his father's service obligation, one third of the field and orchard shall be given to his mother, and his mother shall raise him.

(x 51–xi 4) *šumma lu rēdûm ulu bāʾirum eqelšu kirāšu u bīssu ina pani ilkim iddīma uddappir šanûm warkišu eqelšu kirāšu u bīssu iṣbatma šalaš šanātim ilikšu ittalak šumma itūramma*[8] *eqelšu kirāšu u bīssu irriš ul innaddiššum ša iṣṣabtuma ilikšu ittalku šûma illak*

¶ **30** If either a soldier or a fisherman abandons his field, orchard, or house because of the service obligation and then absents himself, another person takes possession of his field, orchard, or house to succeed to his holdings and performs the service obligation for three years—if he then returns and claims his field, orchard, or house, it will not be given to him; he who has taken possession of it and has performed his service obligation shall be the one to continue to perform the obligation.

(xi 5–12) *šumma šattam ištiatma uddappirma ittūram eqelšu kirāšu u bīssu innaddiššumma šûma ilikšu illak*

¶ **31** If he should absent himself for only one year and then return, his field, orchard, and house shall be given to him, and he himself shall perform his service obligation.

(xi 13–38) *šumma lu rēdûm ulu bāʾirum ša ina ḫarrān šarrim turru tamkārum ipṭuraššuma ālšu uštakšidaššu šumma ina bītišu ša paṭārim ibašši šûma ramanšu ipaṭṭar šumma ina bītišu ša paṭārišu la ibašši ina bīt ili ālišu ippaṭṭar šumma ina bīt ili ālišu ša paṭārišu la ibašši ekallum ipaṭṭaršu eqelšu kirāšu u bīssu ana ipṭerišu ul innaddin*

¶ **32** If there is either a soldier or a fisherman who is taken captive while on a royal campaign, a merchant redeems him and helps him to get back to his city—if there are sufficient means in his own estate for the redeeming, he himself shall redeem himself; if there are not sufficient means in his estate to redeem him, he shall be redeemed by his city's temple; if there are not sufficient means in his city's temple to redeem him, the palace shall redeem him; but his field, orchard, or house will not be given for his redemption.

(xi 39–50) *šumma lu ša ḫaṭṭātim ulu laputtûm ṣāb nisḫātim*[9] *irtaši ulu ana ḫarrān šarrim agram pūḫam imḫurma irtedi lu ša ḫaṭṭātim ulu laputtûm šû iddâk*

¶ **33** If either a captain or a sergeant should recruit(?) deserters or accepts and leads off a hireling as a substitute on a royal campaign, that captain or sergeant shall be killed.

(xi 51–64) *šumma lu ša ḫaṭṭātim ulu laputtûm numāt rēdîm ilteqe rēdiam iḫtabal rēdiam ana igrim ittadin rēdiam ina dīnim ana dannim ištarak qīšti šarrum ana rēdîm iddinu ilteqe*[10] *lu ša ḫaṭṭātim ulu laputtûm šû iddâk*

¶ **34** If either a captain or a sergeant should take a soldier's household furnishings, oppress a soldier, hire out a soldier, deliver a soldier into the power of an influential person in a law case, or take a gift that the king gave to a soldier, that captain or sergeant shall be killed.

(xi 65–xii 4) *šumma awīlum liātim u ṣēnī ša šarrum ana rēdîm iddinu ina qāti rēdîm ištām ina kaspišu ītelli*

¶ **35** If a man should purchase from a soldier either the cattle or the sheep and goats which the king gave to the soldier, he shall forfeit his silver.

(xii 5–9) *eqlum kirûm u bītum ša rēdîm bā'irim u nāši biltim ana kaspim ul innaddin*

¶ **36** (Furthermore), the field, orchard, or house of a soldier, fisherman, or a state tenant will not be sold.

(xii 10–21) *šumma awīlum eqlam kirâm u bītam ša rēdîm bā'irim u nāši biltim ištām ṭuppašu iḫḫeppe u ina kaspišu ītelli eqlum kirûm u bītum ana bēlišu itâr*

¶ **37** If a man should purchase a field, orchard, or house of a soldier, fisherman, or a state tenant, his deed shall be invalidated and he shall forfeit his silver; the field, orchard, or house shall revert to its owner.

(xii 22–30) *rēdûm bā'irum u nāši biltim ina eqlim kirîm u bītim ša ilkišu ana aššatišu u mārtišu ul išaṭṭar u ana e'iltišu ul inaddin*

¶ **38** (Furthermore), a soldier, fisherman, or a state tenant will not assign in writing to his wife or daughter any part of a field, orchard, or house attached to his service obligation, nor will he give it to meet any outstanding obligation.

(xii 31–38) *ina eqlim kirîm u bītim ša išammuma iraššû ana aššatišu u mārtišu išaṭṭar u ana e'iltišu inaddin*

¶ **39** He shall assign in writing to his wife or daughter or give to meet an outstanding obligation only a field, orchard, or house which he himself acquires by purchase.

(xii 39–48) *nadītum tamkārum u ilkum aḫûm eqelšu kirāšu u bīssu ana kaspim inaddin šājimānum ilik eqlim kirîm u bītim ša išammu illak*

¶ **40** (However), a *nadītu*, a merchant, or any holder of a field with a special service obligation may sell her or his field, orchard, or house; the buyer shall perform the service obligation on the field, orchard, or house which he purchases.

(xii 49–62) *šumma awīlum eqlam kirâm u bītam ša rēdîm bā'irim u nāši*

¶ **41** If a man accepts a field, orchard, or house of a soldier, fish-

biltim upīḫ u niplātim iddin rēdûm bā'irum u nāši biltim ana eqlišu kirîšu u bītišu itâr u niplātim ša innadnušum itabbal

erman, or state tenant in an exchange and gives him a compensatory payment (for the difference in value), the soldier, fisherman, or state tenant shall reclaim his field, orchard, or house and shall also keep full legal possession of the compensatory payment which was given to him.

(xii 63–xiii 5) *šumma awīlum eqlam ana errēšūtim ušēṣīma ina eqlim še'am la uštabši ina eqlim šiprim la epēšim ukannušuma še'am kīma itēšu ana bēl eqlim inaddin*

¶ **42** If a man rents a field in tenancy but does not plant any grain, they shall charge and convict him of not performing the required work in the field, and he shall give to the owner of the field grain in accordance with his neighbor's yield.

(xiii 6–16) *šumma eqlam la īrišma ittadi še'am kīma itēšu ana bēl eqlim inaddin u eqlam ša iddû majārī imaḫḫaṣ išakkakma*[11] *ana bēl eqlim utâr*

¶ **43** If he does not cultivate the field at all but leaves it fallow, he shall give to the owner of the field grain in accordance with his neighbor's yield, and he shall plow and harrow the field which he left fallow and return it to the owner of the field.

(xiii 17–34) *šumma awīlum kankallam ana šalaš šanātim ana teptītim ušēṣīma aḫšu iddīma eqlam la iptete ina rebûtim šattim eqlam majārī imaḫḫaṣ imarrar u išakkakma ana bēl eqlim utâr u ana* 1 *burum* 10 *kur še'am imaddad*

¶ **44** If a man rents a previously uncultivated field for a three-year term with the intention of opening it for cultivation but he is negligent and does not open the field, in the fourth year he shall plow, hoe, and harrow the field and return it to the owner of the field; and in addition he shall measure and deliver 3,000 silas of grain per 18 ikus (of field).

(xiii 35–46) *šumma awīlum eqelšu ana biltim ana errēšim*[12] *iddinma u bilat eqlišu imtaḫar warka eqlam Adad irtaḫiṣ ulu bibbulum itbal bitiqtum ša errēšimma*

¶ **45** If a man leases his field to a cultivator and receives the rent for his field, and afterwards the storm-god Adad devastates the field or a flood sweeps away the crops, the loss is the cultivator's alone.

(xiii 47–57) *šumma bilat eqlišu la imtaḫar ulu ana mišlāni ulu ana šaluš eqlam iddin še'am ša ina eqlim ibbaššû errēšum u bēl eqlim ana apšītêm izuzzu*

¶ **46** If he (the owner) should not receive the rent for his field (before the catastrophe destroys the field) or he leases out the field on terms of a half share or a third share (of the yield), the cultivator and the owner of the field shall divide whatever grain there is remaining in the agreed proportions.

(xiii 58–70) *šumma errēšum aššum ina šattim maḫrītim mānaḫātišu la ilqû eqlam erēšam iqtabi bēl eqlim ul uppas errēssuma eqelšu irrišma ina ebūrim kīma riksātišu še'am ileqqe*

¶ **47** If the cultivator should declare his intention to cultivate the field (in the next year) because in the previous year he did not recover his expenses, the owner of the field will not object; his same cultivator shall cultivate his field and he shall take (his share of) the grain at the harvest in accordance with his contract.

(xiii 71–xiv 17) *šumma awīlum ḫubullum elišu ibaššīma eqelšu Adad irtaḫiṣ ulu bibbulum itbal ulu ina la mê še'um ina eqlim la ittabši ina šattim šuāti še'am ana bēl ḫubullišu ul utâr ṭuppašu uraṭṭab u ṣibtam ša šattim šuāti ul inaddin*

¶ **48** If a man has a debt lodged against him, and the storm-god Adad devastates his field or a flood sweeps away the crops, or there is no grain grown in the field due to insufficient water—in that year he will not repay grain to his creditor; he shall suspend performance of his contract and he will not give interest payments for that year.

(xiv 18–44) *šumma awīlum kaspam itti tamkārim ilqēma eqel epšētim ša še'im ulu šamaššammī ana tamkārim iddin eqlam erišma še'am ulu šamaššammī ša ibbaššû esip tabal iqbīšum šumma errēšum ina eqlim še'am ulu šamaššammī uštabši ina ebūrim še'am u šamaššammī ša ina eqlim ibbaššû bēl eqlimma ileqqēma še'am ša kaspišu u ṣibassu ša itti tamkārim ilqû u mānaḫāt erēšim ana tamkārim inaddin*

¶ **49** If a man borrows silver from a merchant and gives the merchant a field prepared for planting with either grain or sesame[13] (as a pledge for the loan) and declares to him, "You cultivate the field and collect and take away as much grain or sesame as will be grown"—if the cultivator should produce either grain or sesame in the field, at the harvest it is only the owner of the field who shall take the grain or sesame that is grown in the field, and he shall give to the merchant the grain equivalent to his silver which he borrowed from the merchant and the interest on it and also the expenses of the cultivation.

(xiv 45–55) *šumma eqel <še'im> eršam ulu eqel šamaššammī eršam iddin še'am ulu šamaššammī ša ina eqlim ibbaššû bēl eqlimma ileqqēma kaspam u ṣibassu ana tamkārim utâr*

¶ **50** If he gives (to the merchant as a pledge for the loan) a field already plowed and sown with either <grain> or sesame, (at the harvest) it is only the owner of the field who shall take the grain or sesame that is grown in the field and he shall repay the silver and the interest on it to the merchant.

(xiv 56–66) *šumma kaspam ana turrim la išu <še'am ulu> šamaššammī ana maḫīrātišunu ša kaspišu u ṣibtišu ša itti tamkārim ilqû ana pī ṣimdat šarrim ana tamkārim inaddin*

¶ **51** If he does not have silver to repay, he shall give to the merchant, in accordance with the royal edict, <either grain or> sesame according to their market value for his silver borrowed from the merchant and the interest on it.

(xv 1–6) *šumma errēšum ina eqlim še'am ulu šamaššammī la uštabši riksātišu ul inni*

¶ **52** If the cultivator should not produce grain or sesame in the field, he will not alter his agreement.

(xv 7–20) *šumma awīlum ana kār eqlišu dunnunim aḫšu iddīma kāršu la udanninma ina kārišu pītum ittepte u ugāram mê uštābil awīlum ša ina kārišu pītum ippetû še'am ša uḫalliqu iriab*

¶ **53** If a man neglects to reinforce the embankment of (the irrigation canal of) his field and does not reinforce its embankment, and then a breach opens in its embankment and allows the water to carry away the common irrigated area, the man in whose embankment the breach opened shall replace the grain whose loss he caused.

(xv 21–30) *šumma še'am riābam la ile'i šuāti u bīšašu ana kaspim inaddinuma mārū ugārim ša še'šunu mû ublū izuzzu*

¶ **54** If he cannot replace the grain, they shall sell him and his property, and the residents of the common irrigated area whose grain crops the water carried away shall divide (the proceeds).

(xv 31–38) *šumma awīlum atappašu ana šiqītim ipte aḫšu iddīma eqel itēšu mê uštābil še'am kīma itēšu imaddad*

¶ **55** If a man opens his branch of the canal for irrigation and negligently allows the water to carry away his neighbor's field, he shall measure and deliver grain in accordance with his neighbor's yield.

(xv 39–45) *šumma awīlum mê iptēma epšētim ša eqel itēšu mê uštābil ana* 1 *burum* 10 *kur še'am imaddad*

¶ **56** If a man opens (an irrigation gate and releases) waters and thereby he allows the water to carry away whatever work has been done in his neighbor's field, he shall measure and deliver 3,000 silas of grain per 18 ikus (of field).

(xv 46–64) *šumma rē'ûm ana šammī ṣēnim šūkulim itti bēl eqlim la imtagarma balum bēl eqlim eqlam ṣēnam uštākil bēl eqlim eqelšu iṣṣid rē'ûm ša ina balum bēl eqlim eqlam ṣēnam ušākilu elēnumma ana* 1 *burum* 20 *kur še'am ana bēl eqlim inaddin*

¶ **57** If a shepherd does not make an agreement with the owner of the field to graze sheep and goats, and without the permission of the owner of the field grazes sheep and goats on the field, the owner of the field shall harvest his field and the shepherd who grazed sheep and goats on the field without the permission of the owner of the field shall give in addition 6,000 silas of grain per 18 ikus (of field) to the owner of the field.

(xv 65–xvi 3) *šumma ištu ṣēnum ina ugārim īteliānim kannu gamartim ina abullim ittaḫlalu rē'ûm ṣēnam ana eqlim iddīma eqlam ṣēnam uštākil rē'ûm eqel ušākilu inaṣṣarma ina ebūrim ana* 1 *burum* 60 *kur še'am ana bēl eqlim imaddad*

¶ **58** If, after the sheep and goats come up from the common irrigated area when the pennants announcing the termination of pasturing are wound around the main city-gate, the shepherd releases the sheep and goats into a field and allows the sheep and goats to graze in the field—the shepherd shall guard the field in which he allowed them to graze and at the harvest he shall measure and deliver to the owner of the field 18,000 silas of grain per 18 ikus (of field).

(xvi 4–9) *šumma awīlum balum bēl kirîm ina kirī awīlim iṣam ikkis ½ mana kaspam išaqqal*

¶ **59** If a man cuts down a tree in another man's date orchard without the permission of the owner of the orchard, he shall weigh and deliver 30 shekels of silver.

(xvi 10–26) *šumma awīlum eqlam ana kirîm zaqāpim ana nukaribbim iddin nukaribbum kiriam izqup erbe šanātim kiriam urabba ina ḫamuštim šattim bēl kirîm u nukaribbum mitḫāriš izuzzu bēl kirîm zittašu inassaqma ileqqe*

¶ **60** If a man gives a field to a gardener to plant as a date orchard and the gardener plants the orchard, he shall cultivate the orchard for four years; in the fifth year, the owner of the orchard and the gardener shall divide the yield in equal shares; the owner of the orchard shall select and take his share first.

(xvi 27–33) *šumma nukaribbum eqlam ina zaqāpim la igmurma nidītam īzib nidītam ana libbi zittišu išakkanušum*

¶ **61** If the gardener does not complete the planting of (the date orchard in) the field, but leaves an uncultivated area, they shall include the uncultivated area in his share.

(xvi 34–47) *šumma eqlam ša innadnušum ana kirîm la izqup šumma šer'um bilat eqlim ša šanātim ša innadû nukaribbum ana bēl eqlim kīma itēšu imaddad u eqlam šipram ippešma ana bēl eqlim utâr*

¶ **62** If he does not plant as a date orchard the field which was given to him—if it is arable land, the gardener shall measure and deliver to the owner of the field the estimated yield of the field for the years it is left fallow in accordance with his neighbor's yield; furthermore he shall perform the required work on the field and return it to the owner of the field.

(xvi 48–57) *šumma kankallum eqlam šipram ippešma ana bēl eqlim utâr u ana 1 burum 10 kur še'am ša šattim ištiat imaddad*

¶ **63** If it is uncultivated land, he shall perform the required work on the field and return it to the owner of the field, and in addition he shall measure and deliver 3,000 silas of grain per 18 ikus (of field) per year.

(xvi 58–70) *šumma awīlum kirāšu ana nukaribbim ana rukkubim iddin nukaribbum adi kirâm ṣabtu ina bilat kirîm šittīn ana bēl kirîm inaddin šaluštam šû ileqqe*

¶ 64 If a man gives his orchard to a gardener to pollinate (the date palms), as long as the gardener is in possession of the orchard, he shall give to the owner of the orchard two thirds of the yield of the orchard, and he himself shall take one third.

(xvi 71–xvii 1) *šumma nukaribbum kirâm la urakkibma biltam umtaṭṭi nukaribbum bilat kirîm ana* <*bēl kirîm kīma*> *itēšu* [*imaddad* (...)]

¶ 65 If the gardener does not pollinate the (date palms in the) orchard and thus diminishes the yield, the gardener [shall measure and deliver] a yield for the orchard to <the owner of the orchard in accordance with> his neighbor's yields.

(P ii 1–18; Q iii 1–27) *šumma awīlum kaspam itti tamkārim ilqēma tamkāršu īsiršuma mimma ša nadānim la ibaššīšum kirâšu ištu tarkibtim ana tamkārim iddinma suluppī mala ina kirîm ibbaššû ana kaspika tabal iqbīšum tamkārum šû ul immaggar suluppī ša ina kirîm ibbaššû bēl kirîmma ileqqēma kaspam u ṣibassu ša pī ṭuppišu tamkāram ippalma suluppī watrūtim ša ina kirîm ibbaššû bēl kirîmma ile*[*qqe*]

gap ¶ a If a man borrows silver from a merchant and his merchant presses him for payment but he has nothing to give in repayment, and therefore he gives his orchard after pollination to the merchant and declares to him, "Take away as many dates as will be grown in the orchard as payment for your silver"—the merchant will not agree; the owner of the orchard himself shall take the dates that are grown in the orchard, he shall satisfy the merchant with silver and the interest on it in accordance with the terms of his contract, and only the owner of the orchard shall take the dates that are grown in the orchard in excess (of the debt).

(¶ A, ¶ 66)

(P ii 19–23) *šumma aw*[*īlum*] *bītam ip*[*pešma*] *ṭēḫušu* [...] *ša* [...] *x* [...]

gap ¶ b If a man intends to build a house and his neighbor [...]

(¶ B, ¶ 67)

(P i 1–6 and b 1–8; Q iv 1–15) [*šumma* ...] *ana šīm*[*im* ...] *ul*

gap ¶ c [If ...] he will not give to him [...] for a price; if he intends to

i[nad]diššum šumma še'am kaspam u bīšam ana bīt ilkim ša bīt itēšu ša išammu inaddin ina mimma ša iddinu ītelli bītum ana [bēli]šu itâr šumma bītum šū ilkam la išu išâm ana bītim šuāti še'am kaspam u bīšam inaddin

give grain, silver, or any other commodity for a house encumbered by a service obligation and belonging to the estate of his neighbor which he wishes to buy, he shall forfeit whatever he gave; it shall return to its owner. If that house is not encumbered by a service obligation, he may buy it; he may give grain, silver, or any other commodity for that house.

(¶ C, ¶ 67+a)

(Q iv 16–21) *šumma awī[lum] ni[dītam] balum i[tēšu] īt[epuš] ina bīt* [...] *itē[šu* ...] *ana* [...]

gap ¶ d If a man should work his neighbor's uncultivated plot without his neighbor's permission, in the house [...] his neighbor [...]

(¶ D, ¶ 68+a)

(P iii 1–9; R i 1–12) [*šumma* ...] *nabalkattaka dunnin ištu bītika ibbalakkatunim ana bēl nidītim nidītka epuš* [*iš*]*tu nidītika* [*bīt*]*ī ipallašunim* [*iq*]*bi* [*šī*]*bī iškun* [*šumma*] *ina nabalkattim* [*šarr*]*āqum*(?) [...] [*mimma ša ina*] *naba*[*lkattim ḫalqu*] *bēl* [...] *šumma x* [...] *bēl* [...] *mimma* [...] *iri*[*ab*] *šumma* [...] *ú-x* [...]

gap ¶ e [If ... a man] declares [to the owner of a rundown house], "Reinforce your scalable wall; they could scale over the wall to here from your house," or to the owner of an uncultivated plot, "Work your uncultivated plot; they could break into my house from your uncultivated plot," and he secures witnesses—if a thief [breaks in] by scaling the wall, the owner [of the rundown house shall replace anything which is lost by] the scaling; if [a thief breaks in by access through the uncultivated plot], the owner [of the uncultivated plot] shall replace anything [which was lost ...]; if [...]

(¶¶ H, G, ¶ 68+b)

(R ii 1–4) [*šumma* ...] *ina* [...] *bītum* [...] *i-*[...]

gap ¶ f [If ...] house [...]

(¶ J_1, ¶ 68+c)

(P ii 1–18; R ii 5–13; s rev.) *š*[*umma awīlum* ...] *i*[*na* ...] *x* [...] *awīlum*

gap ¶ g If [a man rents a house ... and] the tenant gives the full

ašbumm[a] kasap kiṣri[šu] gamram ša šana[t] ana bēl [bītim] iddi[nma] bēl bītim ana waššābi[m] ina ūmī[šu] la malûtim waṣâ[m] iqtab[i] bēl bītim aš[šum] waššā[bam] ina ūmī[šu] la malû[tim] ina bītišu u[šēṣû] ina kaspim ša waššāb[um] idd[inušum īt]el[li]

amount of the silver for his annual rent to the owner of the house, but the owner of the house then orders the tenant to leave before the expiration of the full term of his lease, the owner of the house, because he evicted the tenant from his house before the expiration of the full term of his lease, shall forfeit the silver that the tenant gave him.

(¶¶ J_2, E, ¶ 69+c)

(t i 3–15) *[šumma waš]bum [bīt muškēnim] išā[m …] kiṣrim ša ippušu [ana b]īt muškēnim šâmim [… š]a išakkanu […] x išakkanšu […]-ú šumma rūqim […] ša muškēnim […] šumma ul išāmma [ina kaspim ša] ilqû [ītellī]ma [bīt muškēnim ana bēl]išu [itâ]r*

gap ¶ h [If] a tenant intends to purchase [the house of a commoner, …] the rent obligation which he shall perform, in order to purchase the house of a commoner, […] which he shall place […] he shall place it […]; if he is abroad(?) […] of the commoner; if he does not purchase (the house) [he shall forfeit the silver that] he took and [the house of the commoner shall revert to] its owner.

(¶ 4.12)[14]

(t i 16–?) […]

gap ¶¶ i, j, k […]

(¶¶ 4.13, 4.14, 5.1)

(t i ?–ii 5) *[šumma awīlum … i]na ebūrim kasapšu u ṣibassu [išaqqal] šumma a<na> nadānim ul [išu] mimmûšu bīšam u še᾿am [inaddinšum] šumma ana nadānim x išu […]*

gap ¶ l [If a man borrows silver …] he shall weigh and deliver his silver and the interest on it at the harvest; if he has nothing to give, [he shall give to him] any of his property, any commodity or grain; if he has … to give, […]

(¶ 5.2)

(t ii 6–13) *šumma tamkārum ša ana […] it-ta-x ša ana […] ú-na-x-x-x […] x ana 5 šiqil kaspim […] kunukkišu la išṭuršum […] ma-ḫar(-)šu-ú-x-ma x x mār awīlim la ki tu x x x šuāti idu[kkušu]*

gap ¶ m If a merchant who for […] … for 5 shekels of silver […] he did not write for him a sealed document […] … the son of a man … that one … they shall kill him.

(¶ 5.3)

(t ii 14–18) *šumma warad awīlim* [...] 1/3 *mana kaspam išaqqal u wardum šû* [... *g*]*amram ra*(?)-*ni*(?)-*a*-[...] *ša*(?) *idû iddâk*

gap ¶ n If a man's slave [...] he shall weigh and deliver 20 shekels of silver, and that slave [...] complete ... he shall be killed.

(t ii 19–26) [*šumma*] *awīlum awīlam* ... [...]-*ma* [...] *kaspum* [...]

gap ¶ o [If] a man [...] another man [...] silver [...]

(¶ 5.4)

(t ii 27–iii 5) [...]

gap ¶¶ p, q [...]

(¶¶ 5.5, 5.6)

(t iii 6–23) [*šumma* ...] *ú*-[...] *ana* [...] *idī* [...] *kaspam x* [...] *šumma awīlum šuā*[*ti*] *ša a-x* [...] *la ú*-[...] *ina*(?) *kaspim ša iddinu*(?) *ītelli*

gap ¶ r [If ...] to [...] wages [...] silver [...]; if that man who [...] does not [...] he shall forfeit the silver that he gave.

(¶ 5.7)

(S i 1'–3'; t iii 24–34) *šumma* [*lu*] *wardum lu* [*amtum* ...] *ana bē*[*lišu utarrušu*] *šumma* [...] *itarrakaššu* [... *ana bēli*]*šu ul utarrušum*

gap ¶ s If either a male slave or [a female slave ..., they shall return him] to [his] master; if [...] he beats(?) him, they will not return him [to] his [master].

(¶ K, ¶ 69+d, ¶ 5.8)

(S i 4'–12'; t iii 35–40) *šumma tamkārum še'am u kaspam ana ḫubullim iddin ana 1 kurrum 1 pān 4 sūt še'am ṣibtam ileqqe šumma kaspam ana ḫubullim iddin ana 1 šiqil kaspim* IGI.6.GÁL *u 6 uṭṭet ṣibtam ileqqe*

gap ¶ t If a merchant gives grain or silver as an interest-bearing loan, he shall take 100 silas of grain per kur as interest (= 33%); if he gives silver as an interest-bearing loan, he shall take 36 barleycorns per shekel of silver as interest (= 20%).

(¶ L, ¶ 70+d, ¶ 5.9)

(S i 14'–27'; t iii 41–iv 7) *šumma awīlum*[15] *ša ḫubullam iršû kaspam ana turrim la išu*[16] *še'am u kaspam kīma ṣimdat šarrim u ṣibassu 1 kurrum še'am 1 pān ana šattim*(?) *ileqqe šumma tamkārum ṣibat ḫubulli* [...] *ana 1 kur* [...] IGI.6.GÁL *6 uṭṭet* [...] *uwatterma ilqe ina m*[*imma*] *ša iddinu īt*[*elli*]

gap ¶ u If a man who has an interest-bearing loan does not have silver with which to repay it, he (the merchant) shall take grain and silver in accordance with the royal edict and the interest on it at the annual rate of 60 silas per 1 kur (= 20%); if the merchant should attempt to increase and collect the interest on the (silver) loan [up to the grain interest rate of 100 silas of grain] per 1 kur (= 33%), [or in any other way beyond] 36 barleycorns [per shekel (= 20%) of silver], he shall forfeit whatever he had given.

(¶ M, ¶ 71+d, ¶ 5.10)

(S i 29'–35'; t iv 8–19) *šumma tamkārum še*ʾ*[am u kaspa]m ana ṣibtim [iddinm]a ṣibtam ma[la qaqqadi]šu še*ʾ*am kaspam* [...] *ilteqēma* [...] *x* [...] *še*ʾ*um u ka[spum qaqqada]šu u ṣib[assu* ...] *ṭuppi rik[istišu iḫḫeppe]*

gap ¶ v If a merchant gives grain or silver at interest and he then takes [...] grain or silver as interest according to the amount of his capital sum, [...] the grain and silver, his capital and interest [...], the tablet recording [his debt obligation shall be broken].

(¶ N, ¶ 72+d, ¶ 5.11)

(S ii 1'–8'; t iv 20–39) *šumma tamkār[um* ...] *ana* [...] *ṣibtam* [...] *ilteqēma* [...] *ulu še*ʾ*am [ulu kaspam] mala [imḫuru ulu] la uštaḫriṣma ṭuppam eššam(?) la išṭur ulu ṣibātim ana qaqqadim uṭṭeḫḫi tamkārum šû še*ʾ*am mala ilqû uštašannāma utâr*

gap ¶ w If a merchant [...] should take [...] interest and [...], then does not deduct the payments of either grain [or silver] as much as [he received, or] does not write a new tablet, or adds the interest payments to the capital sum, that merchant shall return two-fold as much grain as he received.

(¶ O, ¶ 72+e, ¶ 5.12)

(S ii 10'–21') *šumma tamkārum še*ʾ*am u kaspam ana ḫubullim iddinma inūma ana ḫubullim iddinu kaspam ina abnim maṭītim u še*ʾ*am ina sūtim maṭītim iddin u inūma imḫuru kaspam ina abnim [rabītim] še*ʾ*am ina sūtim rabītim imḫur [tamkārum šû] ina [mimma ša iddinu] ī[telli]*

gap ¶ x If a merchant gives grain or silver as an interest-bearing loan and when he gives it as an interest-bearing loan he gives the silver according to the small weight or the grain according to the small seah-measure but when he receives payment he receives the silver according to the large weight or the grain according to the large seah-measure, [that merchant] shall forfeit [anything that he gave].

(¶ P, ¶ 73+e, ¶ 5.13)

(S ii 23'–28') *šumma [tamkārum ...] ana ḫub[ullim ...] iddin ina mimma [ša] iddinu ītelli*

gap ¶ y If [a merchant] gives [...] as an interest-bearing loan, [...] he shall forfeit anything that he gave.
(¶ Q, ¶ 74+e, <¶ 5.14>)

(P rev. i 1–13; S ii 30'–40') *šumma awīlum še'am u kaspam itti tamkārim ilqēma še'am u kaspam ana turrim la išu bīšamma išu mimma ša ina qātišu ibaššû maḫar šībī kīma ubbalu ana tamkārišu inaddin tamkārum ul uppas imaḫḫar*

gap ¶ z If a man borrows grain or silver from a merchant and does not have grain or silver with which to repay but does have other goods, he shall give to his merchant in the presence of witnesses whatever he has at hand, in amounts according to the exchange value; the merchant will not object; he shall accept it.
(¶ R, ¶ 75+e, ¶ 5.15)

(T rev. i 1'–3') *[šumma awīlum ...] i-si-[...] kīma [...] x [...]*

gap ¶ aa [If a man ...] like [...]
(¶ S, ¶ 76+e, ¶ 5.16)

(S iii 1') *[šumma ...] iddâk*

gap ¶ bb [If ...] he shall be killed.
(¶ T, ¶ 76+f)

(S iii 3'–7') *šumma awīlum ana awīlim kaspam ana tappûtim iddin nēmelam u butuqqâm ša ibbaššû maḫar ilim mitḫāriš izuzzu*

gap ¶ cc If a man gives silver to another man for investment in a partnership venture, before the god they shall equally divide the profit or loss.
(¶ U, ¶ 77+f)

(S iii 8'–21'; xxiv 1–7) *šumma tamkārum ana šamallêm kaspam ana [nad]ā[nim u maḫā]rim id[di]nma ana ḫarrānim iṭrussu šamallûm ina ḫarrānim [...] šumma ašar illiku [nēmelam] ītamar ṣibāt kaspim mala ilqû isaddarma ūmīšu imannūma tamkāršu ippal*

¶ 100 If a merchant gives silver to a trading agent for conducting business transactions and sends him off on a business trip, the trading agent [shall ...] while on the business trip; if he should realize [a profit] where he went, he shall calculate the total interest, per transaction and time elapsed, on as much silver as he took, and he shall satisfy his merchant.
(¶ V = ¶ 100, ¶ 78+f)

(xxiv 8–14) *šumma ašar illiku nēmelam la ītamar kasap ilqû uštašannāma šamallûm ana tamkārim inaddin*

¶ **101** If he should realize no profit where he went, the trading agent shall give to the merchant twofold the silver he took.

(xxiv 15–23) *šumma tamkārum ana šamallîm kaspam ana tadmiqtim ittadinma ašar illiku bitiqtam ītamar qaqqad kaspim ana tamkārim utâr*

¶ **102** If a merchant should give silver to a trading agent for an investment venture, and he incurs a loss on his journeys, he shall return silver to the merchant in the amount of the capital sum.

(xxiv 24–31) *šumma ḫarrānam ina alākišu nakrum mimma ša našû uštaddīšu šamallûm nīš ilim izakkarma ūtaššar*

¶ **103** If enemy forces should make him abandon whatever goods he is transporting while on his business trip, the trading agent shall swear an oath by the god and shall be released.

(xxiv 32–45) *šumma tamkārum ana šamallîm še'am šipātim šamnam u mimma bīšam ana pašārim iddin šamallûm kaspam isaddarma ana tamkārim utâr šamallûm kanīk kaspim ša ana tamkārim inaddinu ileqqe*

¶ **104** If a merchant gives a trading agent grain, wool, oil, or any other commodity for local transactions, the trading agent shall return to the merchant the silver for each transaction; the trading agent shall collect a sealed receipt for (each payment in) silver that he gives to the merchant.

(xxiv 46–54) *šumma šamallûm ītegīma kanīk kaspim ša ana tamkārim iddinu la ilteqe kasap la kanīkim ana nikkassim ul iššakkan*

¶ **105** If the trading agent should be negligent and not take a sealed receipt for (each payment in) silver that he gives to the merchant, any silver that is not documented in a sealed receipt will not be included in the final accounting.

(xxiv 55–67) *šumma šamallûm kaspam itti tamkārim ilqēma tamkāršu ittakir tamkārum šû ina maḫar ilim u šībī ina kaspim leqêm šamallâm ukânma šamallûm kaspam mala ilqû adi 3-šu ana tamkārim inaddin*

¶ **106** If the trading agent takes silver from the merchant but then denies the claim of his merchant, that merchant shall bring charges and proof before the god and witnesses against the trading agent concerning the silver taken, and the trading agent shall give to the merchant threefold the amount of silver that he took.

(xxiv 68–xxv 14) *šumma tamkārum kaspam šamallâm iqīpma šamallûm mimma ša tamkārum iddinušum ana tamkārišu uttēr tamkārum mimma ša šamallûm iddinušum ittakiršu šamallûm šû ina maḫar ilim u šībī tamkāram ukânma tamkārum aššum šamallâšu ikkiru mimma ša ilqû adi 6-šu ana šamallêm inaddin*

¶ **107** If a merchant entrusts silver to a trading agent and the trading agent then returns to his merchant everything that the merchant had given him but the merchant denies (having received) everything that the trading agent had given him, that trading agent shall bring charges and proof before the god and witnesses against the merchant, and because he denied the account of his trading agent, the merchant shall give to the trading agent sixfold the amount that he took.

(xxv 15–25) *šumma sābītum ana šīm šikarim še᾿am la imtaḫar ina abnim rabītim kaspam imtaḫar u maḫīr šikarim ana maḫīr še᾿im umtaṭṭi sābītam šuāti ukannušima*[17] *ana mê inaddûši*

¶ **108** If a woman innkeeper should refuse to accept grain for the price of beer but accepts (only) silver measured by the large weight, thereby reducing the value of beer in relation to the value of grain, they shall charge and convict that woman innkeeper and they shall cast her into the water.

(xxv 26–35) *šumma sābītum sarrūtum ina bītiša ittarkasuma sarrūtim šunūti la iṣṣabtamma ana ekallim la irdiam sābītum šî iddâk*

¶ **109** If there should be a woman innkeeper in whose house criminals congregate, and she does not seize those criminals and lead them off to the palace authorities, that woman innkeeper shall be killed.

(xxv 36–44) *šumma nadītum ugbabtum ša ina gagîm la wašbat bīt sībim iptete ulu ana šikarim ana bīt sībim īterub awīltam šuāti iqallûši*

¶ **110** If a *nadītu* or[18] an *ugbabtu* who does not reside within the cloister should open (the door to?) a tavern or enter a tavern for some beer, they shall burn that woman.

(xxv 45–49) *šumma sābītum ištēn pīḫam ana qīptim iddin ina ebūrim 5 sūt šeʾam ileqqe*

¶ **111** If a woman innkeeper gives one vat of beer as a loan(?), she shall take 50 silas of grain at the harvest.

(xxv 50–74) *šumma awīlum ina ḫarrānim wašibma kaspam ḫurāṣam abnam u bīš qātišu ana awīlim iddinma ana šēbultim ušābilšu awīlum šû mimma ša šūbulu ašar šūbulu la iddinma itbal bēl šēbultim awīlam šuāti ina mimma ša šūbuluma la iddinu ukânšuma*[19] *awīlum šû adi 5-šu mimma ša innadnušum ana bēl šēbultim inaddin*

¶ **112** If a man is engaged in a trading expedition and gives silver, gold, precious stones, or any other goods to another under consignment for transportation, and the latter man does not deliver that which was consigned to him where it was to be consigned but appropriates it, the owner of the consigned property shall charge and convict that man of whatever consignment he failed to deliver, and that man shall give to the owner of the consigned property fivefold the property that had been given to him.

(xxv 75–xxvi 16) *šumma awīlum eli awīlim šeʾam u kaspam išūma ina balum bēl šeʾim ina našpakim ulu ina maškanim šeʾam ilteqe awīlam šuāti ina balum bēl šeʾim ina našpakim ulu ina maškanim ina šeʾim leqêm ukannušuma šeʾam mala ilqû utâr u ina mimma šumšu mala iddinu ītelli*

¶ **113** If a man has a claim of grain or silver against another man and takes grain from the granary or from the threshing floor without obtaining permission from the owner of the grain, they shall charge and convict that man of taking grain from the granary or from the threshing floor without the permission of the owner of the grain, and he shall return as much grain as he took; moreover, he shall forfeit whatever he originally gave as the loan.

(xxvi 17–25) *šumma awīlum eli awīlim šeʾam u kaspam la išūma nipûssu ittepe ana nipûtim ištiat ⅓ mana kaspam išaqqal*

¶ **114** If a man does not have a claim of grain or silver against another man but distrains a member of his household, he shall weigh and deliver 20 shekels of silver for each distrainee.

(xxvi 26–37) *šumma awīlum eli awīlim še᾽am u kaspam išūma nipûssu ippēma nipûtum ina bīt nēpīša ina šīmātiša imtūt dīnum šû rugummâm ul išu*

¶ **115** If a man has a claim of grain or silver against another man, distrains a member of his household, and the distrainee dies a natural death while in the house of her or his[20] distrainer, that case has no basis for a claim.

(xxvi 38–53) *šumma nipûtum ina bīt nēpīša ina maḫāṣim ulu ina uššušim imtūt bēl nipûtim tamkāršu ukânma šumma mār awīlim mārašu idukku šumma warad awīlim ⅓ mana kaspam išaqqal u ina mimma šumšu mala iddinu ītelli*

¶ **116** If the distrainee should die from the effects of a beating or other physical abuse while in the house of her or his distrainer, the owner of the distrainee shall charge and convict his merchant, and if (the distrainee is) the man's son,[21] they shall kill his (the distrainer's) son; if the man's slave, he shall weigh and deliver 20 shekels of silver; moreover, he shall forfeit whatever he originally gave as the loan.

(xxvi 54–67) *šumma awīlam e᾽iltum iṣbassuma aššassu mārašu u mārassu ana kaspim iddin ulu ana kiššātim ittandin šalaš šanātim bīt šājimānišunu u kāšišišunu ippešu ina rebûtim šattim andurāršunu iššakkan*

¶ **117** If an obligation is outstanding against a man and he sells or gives into debt service his wife, his son, or his daughter, they shall perform service in the house of their buyer or of the one who holds them in debt service for three years; their release shall be secured in the fourth year.

(xxvi 68–73) *šumma wardam ulu amtam ana kiššātim ittandin tamkārum ušetteq ana kaspim inaddin ul ibbaqqar*

¶ **118** If he should give a male or female slave into debt service, the merchant may extend the term (beyond the three years), he may sell him; there are no grounds for a claim.

(xxvi 74–xxvii 3) *šumma awīlam e᾽iltum iṣbassuma amassu ša mārī uldušum ana kaspim ittadin kasap tamkārum išqulu bēl amtim išaqqalma amassu ipaṭṭar*

¶ **119** If an obligation is outstanding against a man and he therefore sells his slave woman who has borne him children, the owner of the slave woman shall weigh and deliver the silver which the merchant weighed and delivered (as the loan) and he shall thereby redeem his slave woman.

(xxvii 4–23) *šumma awīlum še'ašu ana našpakūtim ina bīt awīlim išpukma ina qarītim ibbûm ittabši ulu bēl bītim našpakam iptēma še'am ilqe ulu še'am ša ina bītišu iššapku ana gamrim ittakir*[22] *bēl še'im maḫar ilim še'ašu ubârma bēl bītim še'am ša ilqû uštašannāma ana bēl še'im inaddin*

¶ **120** If a man stores his grain in another man's house, and a loss occurs in the storage bin or the householder opens the granary and takes the grain or he completely denies receiving the grain that was stored in his house—the owner of the grain shall establish his grain before the god, and the householder shall give to the owner of the grain twofold the grain that he took (in storage).

(xxvii 24–30) *šumma awīlum ina bīt awīlim še'am išpuk ina šanat ana* 1 *kur še'im* 5 *qa še'am idī našpakim inaddin*[23]

¶ **121** If a man stores grain in another man's house, he shall give 5 silas of grain per kur (i.e., per 300 silas) of grain as annual rent of the granary.

(xxvii 31–43) *šumma awīlum ana awīlim kaspam ḫurāṣam u mimma šumšu ana maṣṣarūtim inaddin mimma mala inaddinu šībī ukallam riksātim išakkanma ana maṣṣarūtim inaddin*

¶ **122** If a man intends to give silver, gold, or anything else to another man for safekeeping, he shall exhibit before witnesses anything which he intends to give, he shall draw up a written contract, and (in this manner) he shall give goods for safekeeping.

(xxvii 44–52) *šumma balum šībī u riksātim ana maṣṣarūtim iddinma ašar iddinu ittakrušu dīnum šû rugummâm ul išu*

¶ **123** If he gives goods for safekeeping without witnesses or a written contract, and they deny that he gave anything, that case has no basis for a claim.

(xxvii 53–65) *šumma awīlum ana awīlim kaspam ḫurāṣam u mimma šumšu maḫar šībī ana maṣṣarūtim iddinma ittakiršu awīlam šuāti ukannušuma mimma ša ikkiru uštašannāma inaddin*

¶ **124** If a man gives silver, gold, or anything else before witnesses to another man for safekeeping and he denies it, they shall charge and convict that man, and he shall give twofold that which he denied.

(xxvii 66–xxviii 7) *šumma awīlum mimmâšu ana maṣṣarūtim iddinma ašar iddinu ulu ina pilšim ulu ina nabalkattim mimmûšu itti mimmê bēl bītim iḫtaliq bēl bītim ša īgūma mimma ša ana maṣṣarūtim iddinušumma uḫalliqu ušallamma ana bēl makkūrim iriab bēl bītim mimmâšu ḫalqam ištene'īma itti šarrāqānišu ileqqe*

¶ **125** If a man gives his property for safekeeping and his property together with the householder's property is lost either by (theft achieved through) a breach or by scaling over a wall, the householder who was careless shall make restitution and shall restore to the owner of the property that which was given to him for safekeeping and which he allowed to be lost; the householder shall continue to search for his own lost property, and he shall take it from the one who stole it from him.

(xxviii 8–24) *šumma awīlum mimmûšu la ḫal*[*iq*]*ma mimmê ḫaliq iqtabi babtašu ūtebbir kīma mimmûšu la ḫalqu babtašu ina maḫar ilim ubâršuma mimma ša irgumu uštašannāma ana babtišu inaddin*

¶ **126** If a man whose property is not lost should declare, "My property is lost," and accuse his city quarter, his city quarter shall establish against him before the god that no property of his is lost, and he shall give to his city quarter twofold whatever he claimed.

(xxviii 25–34) *šumma awīlum eli ugbabtim u aššat awīlim ubānam ušatriṣma la uktīn awīlam šuāti maḫar dajānī inaṭṭûšu u muttassu ugallabu*

¶ **127** If a man causes a finger to be pointed in accusation against an *ugbabtu* or against a man's wife but cannot bring proof, they shall flog that man before the judges[24] and they shall shave off half of his hair.

(xxviii 35–41) *šumma awīlum aššatam īḫuzma riksātiša la iškun sinništum šî ul aššat*

¶ **128** If a man marries a wife but does not draw up a formal contract for her, that woman is not a wife.

(xxviii 42–53) *šumma aššat awīlim itti zikarim šanîm ina itūlim ittaṣbat ikassûšunūtima ana mê inaddûšunūti šumma bēl aššatim aššassu uballaṭ u šarrum warassu uballaṭ*

¶ **129** If a man's wife should be seized lying with another male, they shall bind them and cast them into the water; if the wife's master allows his wife to live, then the king shall allow his subject (i.e., the other male) to live.

(xxviii 54–67) *šumma awīlum aššat awīlim ša zikaram la idûma ina bīt abiša wašbat ukabbilšima ina sūniša ittatīlma iṣṣabtušu awīlum šû iddâk sinništum šî ūtaššar*

¶ **130** If a man pins down another man's virgin wife who is still residing in her father's house, and they seize him lying with her, that man shall be killed; that woman shall be released.

(xxviii 68–76) *šumma aššat awīlim mussa ubbiršima itti zikarim šanîm ina utūlim la iṣṣabit nīš ilim izakkarma ana bītiša itâr*

¶ **131** If her husband accuses his own wife (of adultery), although she has not been seized lying with another male, she shall swear (to her innocence by) an oath by the god, and return to her house.

(xxviii 77–xxix 6) *šumma aššat awīlim aššum zikarim šanîm ubānum eliša ittariṣma itti zikarim šanîm ina utūlim la ittaṣbat ana mutiša Id išalli*

¶ **132** If a man's wife should have a finger pointed against her in accusation involving another male, although she has not been seized lying with another male, she shall submit to the divine River Ordeal for her husband.

(xxix 7–17) *šumma awīlum iššalilma ina bītišu šà akālim ibašši [aš]assu [...]-ša [... ana bīt šanîm ul ir]rub*

¶ **133a** If a man should be captured and there are sufficient provisions in his house, his wife [..., she will not] enter [another's house].

(xxix 18–26) *šu[mma] sinništum šî [pa]garša la iṣṣurma ana bīt šanîm īterub sinništam šuāti ukannušima ana mê inaddûši*

¶ **133b** If that woman does not keep herself chaste but enters another's house, they shall charge and convict that woman and cast her into the water.

(xxix 27–36) *šumma awīlum iššalilma ina bītišu ša akālim la ibašši aššassu ana bīt šanîm irrub sinništum šî arnam ul išu*

¶ **134** If a man should be captured and there are not sufficient provisions in his house, his wife may enter another's house; that woman will not be subject to any penalty.

(xxix 37–56) *šumma awīlum iššalilma ina bītišu ša akālim la ibašši ana panīšu aššassu ana bīt šanîm īterubma mārī ittalad ina warka mussa ittūramma ālšu iktaš-*

¶ **135** If a man should be captured and there are not sufficient provisions in his house, before his return his wife enters another's house and bears children, and afterwards her

dam sinništum šî ana ḫāwiriša itâr mārū warki abišunu illaku

husband returns and gets back to his city, that woman shall return to her first husband; the children shall inherit from their father.

(xxix 57–73) *šumma awīlum ālšu iddīma ittābit warkišu aššassu ana bīt šanîm īterub šumma awīlum šû ittūramma aššassu iṣṣabat aššum ālšu izēruma innabitu aššat munnabtim ana mutiša ul itâr*

¶ **136** If a man deserts his city and flees, and after his departure his wife enters another's house—if that man then should return and seize his wife, because he repudiated his city and fled, the wife of the deserter will not return to her husband.

(xxix 74–xxx 13) *šumma awīlum ana šugītim ša mārī uldušum ulu nadītim ša mārī ušaršûšu ezēbim panīšu ištakan ana sinništim šuāti šeriktaša utarrušim u muttat eqlim kirîm u bīšim inaddinušimma mārīša urabba ištu mārīša urtabbû ina mimma ša ana mārīša innadnu zittam kīma aplim ištēn inaddinušimma mutu libbiša iḫḫassi*

¶ **137** If a man should decide to divorce a *šugītu* who bore him children, or a *nadītu* who provided him with children, they shall return to that woman her dowry and they shall give her one half of (her husband's) field, orchard, and property, and she shall raise her children; after she has raised her children, they shall give her a share comparable in value to that of one heir from whatever properties are given to her sons, and a husband of her choice may marry her.

(xxx 14–24) *šumma awīlum ḫīrtašu ša mārī la uldušum izzib kaspam mala terḫatiša inaddiššim u šeriktam ša ištu bīt abiša ublam ušallamšimma izzibši*

¶ **138** If a man intends to divorce his first-ranking wife who did not bear him children, he shall give her silver as much as was her bridewealth and restore to her the dowry that she brought from her father's house, and he shall divorce her.

(xxx 25–29) *šumma terḫatum la ibašši 1 mana kaspam ana uzubbêm inaddiššim*

¶ **139** If there is no bridewealth, he shall give her 60 shekels of silver as a divorce settlement.

(xxx 30–32) *šumma muškēnum ⅓ mana kaspam inaddiššim*

¶ **140** If he is a commoner, he shall give her 20 shekels of silver.

(xxx 33–59) *šumma aššat awīlim ša ina bīt awīlim wašbat ana waṣêm*

¶ **141** If the wife of a man who is residing in the man's house should

panīša ištakanma sikiltam isakkil bīssa usappaḫ mussa ušamṭa ukan-nušima šumma mussa ezēbša iqtabi izzibši ḫarrānša uzubbûša mimma ul innaddiššim šumma mussa la ezēbša iqtabi mussa sinništam šanītam iḫḫaz sinništum šî kīma amtim ina bīt mutiša uššab

decide to leave, and she appropriates goods, squanders her household possessions, or disparages her husband, they shall charge and convict her; and if her husband should declare his intention to divorce her, then he shall divorce her; neither her travel expenses, nor her divorce settlement, nor anything else shall be given to her. If her husband should declare his intention to not divorce her, then her husband may marry another woman and that (first) woman shall reside in her husband's house as a slave woman.

(xxx 60–xxxi 5) *šumma sinništum mussa izērma ul taḫḫazanni iqtabi warkassa ina bābtiša ipparrasma šumma naṣratma ḫiṭītam la išu u mussa waṣīma magal ušamṭāši sin-ništum šî arnam ul išu šeriktaša ileq-qēma ana bīt abiša ittallak*

¶ **142** If a woman repudiates her husband, and declares, "You will not have marital relations with me"—her circumstances shall be investigated by the authorities of her city quarter, and if she is circumspect and without fault, but her husband is wayward and disparages her greatly, that woman will not be subject to any penalty; she shall take her dowry and she shall depart for her father's house.

(xxxi 6–12) *šumma la naṣratma waṣiat bīssa usappaḫ mussa ušamṭa sinništam šuāti ana mê inaddûši*

¶ **143** If she is not circumspect but is wayward, squanders her household possessions, and disparages her husband, they shall cast that woman into the water.

(xxxi 13–27) *šumma awīlum nadītam īḫuzma nadītum šî amtam ana mutiša iddinma mārī uštabši awīlum šû ana šugītim aḫāzim panīšu ištakan awīlam šuāti ul imaggarušu šugītam ul iḫḫaz*

¶ **144** If a man marries a *nadītu,* and that *nadītu* gives a slave woman to her husband, and thus she provides children, but that man then decides to marry a *šugītu,* they will not permit that man to do so, he will not marry the *šugītu.*

(xxxi 28–42) *šumma awīlum nadītam īḫuzma mārī la ušaršīšuma ana šugītim aḫāzim panīšu ištakan awīlum šû šugītam iḫḫaz ana bītišu ušerrebši šugītum šî itti nadītim ul uštamaḫḫar*

¶ **145** If a man marries a *nadītu,* and she does not provide him with children, and that man then decides to marry a *šugītu,* that man may marry the *šugītu* and bring her into his house; that *šugītu* should not aspire to equal status with the *nadītu.*

(xxxi 43–59) *šumma awīlum nadītam īḫuzma amtam ana mutiša iddinma mārī ittalad warkānum amtum šî itti bēltiša uštatamḫir aššum mārī uldu bēlessa ana kaspim ul inaddiššī abbuttam išakkanšimma itti amātim imannūši*

¶ **146** If a man marries a *nadītu,* and she gives a slave woman to her husband, and she (the slave) then bears children, after which that slave woman aspires to equal status with her mistress—because she bore children, her mistress will not sell her; she shall place upon her the slave-hairlock, and she shall reckon her with the slave women.

(xxxi 60–64) *šumma mārī la ūlid bēlessa ana kaspim inaddišši*

¶ **147** If she does not bear children, her mistress shall sell her.

(xxxi 65–81) *šumma awīlum aššatam īḫuzma la'bum iṣṣabassi ana šanītim aḫāzim panīšu ištakkan iḫḫaz aššassu ša la'bum iṣbatu ul izzibši ina bīt īpušu uššamma adi balṭat ittanaššīši*

¶ **148** If a man marries a woman, and later *la'bum*-disease[25] seizes her and he decides to marry another woman, he may marry, he will not divorce his wife whom *la'bum*-disease seized; she shall reside in quarters he constructs and he shall continue to support her as long as she lives.

(xxxii 1–9) *šumma sinništum šî ina bīt mutiša wašābam la imtagar šeriktaša ša ištu bīt abiša ublam ušallamšimma ittallak*

¶ **149** If that woman should not agree to reside in her husband's house, he shall restore to her her dowry that she brought from her father's house, and she shall depart.

(xxxii 10–25) *šumma awīlum ana aššatišu eqlam kirâm bītam u bīšam išrukšim kunukkam īzibšim warki mutiša mārūša ul ipaqqarūši ummum warkassa ana māriša ša irammu inaddin ana aḫîm ul inaddin*

¶ **150** If a man awards to his wife a field, orchard, house, or movable property, and makes out a sealed document for her, after her husband's death her children will not bring a claim against her; the mother shall give her estate to whichever of her children she loves, but she will not give it to an outsider.

(xxxii 26–51) *šumma sinništum ša ina bīt awīlim wašbat aššum bēl ḫubullim ša mutiša la ṣabātiša mussa urtakkis ṭuppam uštēzib šumma awīlum šû lāma sinništam šuāti iḫḫazu ḫubullum elišu ibašši bēl ḫubullīšu aššassu ul iṣabbatu u šumma sinništum šî lāma ana bīt awīlim irrubu ḫubullum eliša ibašši bēl ḫubullīša mussa ul iṣabbatu*

¶ **151** If a woman who is residing in a man's house should have her husband agree by binding contract that no creditor of her husband shall seize her (for his debts)—if that man has a debt incurred before marrying that woman, his creditors will not seize his wife; and if that woman has a debt incurred before entering the man's house, her creditors will not seize her husband.

(xxxii 52–60) *šumma ištu sinništum šî ana bīt awīlim īrubu elišunu ḫubullum ittabši kilallāšunu tamkāram ippalu*

¶ **152** If a debt should be incurred by them after that woman enters the man's house, both of them shall satisfy the merchant.

(xxxii 61–66) *šumma aššat awīlim aššum zikarim šanîm mussa ušdīk sinništam šuāti ina gašīšim išakkanuši*

¶ **153** If a man's wife has her husband killed on account of (her relationship with) another male, they shall impale that woman.

(xxxii 67–71) *šumma awīlum mārassu iltamad awīlam šuāti ālam ušeṣṣûšu*

¶ **154** If a man should carnally know his daughter, they shall banish that man from the city.

(xxxii 72–xxxiii 1) *šumma awīlum ana mārišu kallatam iḫīrma mārušu ilmassi šû warkānumma ina sūniša ittatīlma iṣṣabtušu awīlam šuāti ikassûšuma ana mê inaddûšu*[26]

¶ **155** If a man selects a bride for his son and his son carnally knows her, after which he himself then lies with her and they seize him in the act, they shall bind that man and cast him into the water.

(xxxiii 2–17) *šumma awīlum ana mārišu kallatam iḫīrma mārušu la ilmassima šû ina sūniša ittatīl ½ mana kaspam išaqqalšimma u mimma ša ištu bīt abiša ublam ušallamšimma mutu libbiša iḫḫassi*

¶ **156** If a man selects a bride for his son and his son does not yet carnally know her, and he himself then lies with her, he shall weigh and deliver to her 30 shekels of silver; moreover, he shall restore to her whatever she brought from her father's house, and a husband of her choice shall marry her.

(xxxiii 18–23) *šumma awīlum warki abišu ina sūn ummišu ittatīl kilallīšunu iqallûšunūti*

¶ **157** If a man, after his father's death, should lie with his mother, they shall burn them both.

(xxxiii 24–32) *šumma awīlum warki abišu ina sūn rabītišu*[27] *ša mārī waldat ittaṣbat awīlum šû ina bīt abim innassaḫ*

¶ **158** If a man, after his father's death, should be discovered in the lap of his (the father's) principal wife who had borne children, that man shall be disinherited from the paternal estate.

(xxxiii 33–46) *šumma awīlum ša ana bīt emišu biblam ušābilu terḫatam iddinu ana sinništim šanītim uptallisma ana emišu māratka ul aḫḫaz iqtabi abi mārtim mimma ša ibbablušum itabbal*

¶ **159** If a man who has the ceremonial marriage prestation brought to the house of his father-in-law, and who gives the bridewealth, should have his attention diverted to another woman and declare to his father-in-law, "I will not marry your daughter," the father of the daughter shall take full legal possession of whatever had been brought to him.

(xxxiii 47–59) *šumma awīlum ana bīt emim biblam ušābil terḫatam iddinma abi mārtim mārtī ul anaddikkum iqtabi mimma mala ibbablušum uštašannāma utâr*

¶ **160** If a man has the ceremonial marriage prestation brought to the house of his father-in-law and gives the bridewealth, and the father of the daughter then declares, "I will not give my daughter to you," he shall return twofold everything that had been brought to him.

(xxxiii 60–77) *šumma awīlum ana bīt emišu biblam ušābil terḫatam iddinma ibiršu uktarrissu emušu ana bēl aššatim mārtī ul taḫḫaz iqtabi mimma mala ibbablušum uštašannāma utâr u aššassu ibiršu ul iḫḫaz*

¶ **161** If a man has the ceremonial marriage prestation brought to the house of his father-in-law and gives the bridewealth, and then his comrade slanders him (with the result that) his father-in-law declares to the one entitled to the wife, "You will not marry my daughter," he shall return twofold everything that had been brought to him; moreover, his comrade will not marry his (intended) wife.

(xxxiii 78–xxxiv 6) *šumma awīlum aššatam īḫuz mārī ūlissumma sinništum šī ana šīmtim ittalak ana šeriktiša abuša ul iraggum šeriktaša ša mārīšama*

¶ **162** If a man marries a wife, she bears him children, and that woman then goes to her fate, her father shall have no claim to her dowry; her dowry belongs only to her children.

(xxxiv 7–23) *šumma awīlum aššatam īḫuzma mārī la ušaršīšu sinništum šī ana šīmtim ittalak šumma terḫatam ša awīlum šû ana bīt emišu ublu emušu uttēršum ana šerikti sinništim šuāti mussa ul iraggum šeriktaša ša bīt abišama*

¶ **163** If a man marries a wife but she does not provide him with children, and that woman goes to her fate—if his father-in-law then returns to him the bridewealth that that man brought to his father-in-law's house, her husband will have no claim to that woman's dowry; her dowry belongs only to her father's house.

(xxxiv 24–32) *šumma emušu terḫatam la uttēršum ina šeriktiša mala terḫatiša iḫarraṣma šeriktaša ana bīt abiša utâr*

¶ **164** If his father-in-law should not return to him the bridewealth, he shall deduct the value of her bridewealth from her dowry and restore (the balance of) her dowry to her father's house.

(xxxiv 33–50) *šumma awīlum ana aplišu ša īnšu maḫru eqlam kirâm u bītam išruk kunukkam išṭuršum warka abum ana šīmtim ittalku inūma aḫḫū izuzzu qīšti abum iddinušum ileqqēma elēnumma ina makkūr bīt abim mitḫāriš izuzzu*

¶ **165** If a man awards by sealed contract a field, orchard, or house to his favorite heir, when the brothers divide the estate after the father goes to his fate, he (the favorite son) shall take the gift which the father gave to him and apart from that gift they shall equally divide the property of the paternal estate.

(xxxiv 51–73) *šumma awīlum ana mārīšu*[28] *ša irbû* (text: *iršû*) *aššātim īḫuz ana mārišu ṣiḫrim aššatam la īḫuz warka abum ana šīmtim ittalku inūma aḫḫū izuzzu ina makkūr bīt abim ana aḫišunu ṣiḫrim ša aššatam*

¶ **166** If a man provides wives for his eligible sons but does not provide a wife for his youngest son, when the brothers divide the estate after the father goes to his fate, they shall establish the silver

la aḫzu eliāt zittišu kasap terḫatim išakkanušumma aššatam ušaḫḫazušu

value of the bridewealth for their young unmarried brother from the property of the paternal estate, in addition to his inheritance share, and thereby enable him to obtain a wife.

(xxxiv 74–xxxv 8) *šumma awīlum aššatam īḫuzma mārī ūlissum sinništum šī ana šīmtim ittalak warkiša sinništam šanītam ītaḫazma mārī ittalad warkānum abum ana šīmtim ittalku mārū ana ummātim ul izuzzu šerikti ummātišunu ileqqûma makkūr bīt abim mitḫāriš izuzzu*

¶ **167** If a man marries a wife and she bears him children, and later that woman goes to her fate, and after her death he marries another woman and she bears children, after which the father then goes to his fate, the children will not divide the estate according to the mothers; they shall take the dowries of their respective mothers and then equally divide the property of the paternal estate.

(xxxv 9–24) *šumma awīlum ana mārišu nasāḫim panam ištakan ana dajānī mārī anassaḫ iqtabi dajānū warkassu iparrasuma šumma mārum arnam kabtam ša ina aplūtim nasāḫim la ublam abum mārašu ina aplūtim ul inassaḫ*

¶ **168** If a man should decide to disinherit his son and declares to the judges, "I will disinherit my son," the judges shall investigate his case and if the son is not guilty of a grave offense deserving the penalty of disinheritance, the father may not disinherit his son.

(xxxv 25–36) *šumma arnam kabtam ša ina aplūtim nasāḫim ana abišu itbalam ana ištiššu panīšu ubbalu šumma arnam kabtam adi šinīšu itbalam abum mārašu ina aplūtim inassaḫ*

¶ **169** If he should be guilty of a grave offense deserving the penalty of disinheritance by his father, they shall pardon him for his first one; if he should commit a grave offense a second time, the father may disinherit his son.

(xxxv 37–59) *šumma awīlum ḫīrtašu mārī ūlissum u amassu mārī ūlissum abum ina bulṭišu ana mārī ša amtum uldušum mārūa iqtabi itti mārī ḫīrtim imtanūšunūti warka abum ana šīmtim ittalku ina makkūr bīt abim mārū ḫīrtim u mārū amtim*[29] *mitḫāriš*

¶ **170** If a man's first-ranking wife bears him children and his slave woman bears him children, and the father during his lifetime then declares to (or: concerning) the children whom the slave woman bore to him, "My children," and he

izuzzu aplum mār ḫīrtim ina zittim inassaqma ileqqe

reckons them with the children of the first-ranking wife—after the father goes to his fate, the children of the first-ranking wife and the children of the slave woman shall equally divide the property of the paternal estate; the preferred heir is a son of the first-ranking wife, he shall select and take a share first.

(xxxv 60–xxxvi 5) *u šumma abum ina bulṭišu ana mārī ša amtum uldušum*[30] *mārūja la iqtabi warka abum ana šīmtim ittalku ina makkūr bīt abim mārū amtim itti mārī ḫīrtim ul izuzzu andurār amtim u mārīša iššakkan mārū ḫīrtim ana mārī amtim ana wardūtim ul iraggumu ḫīrtum šeriktaša u nudunnâm ša mussa iddinušim ina ṭuppim išṭurušim ileqqēma ina šubat mutiša uššab adi balṭat ikkal ana kaspim ul inaddin warkassa ša mārīšama*

¶ **171** But if the father during his lifetime should not declare to (or: concerning) the children whom the slave woman bore to him, "My children," after the father goes to his fate, the children of the slave woman will not divide the property of the paternal estate with the children of the first-ranking wife. The release of the slave woman and of her children shall be secured; the children of the first-ranking wife will not make claims of slavery against the children of the slave woman. The first-ranking wife shall take her dowry and the marriage settlement which her husband awarded to her in writing, and she shall continue to reside in her husband's dwelling; as long as she is alive she shall enjoy the use of it, but she may not sell it; her own estate shall belong (as inheritance) only to her own children.

(xxxvi 6–40) *šumma mussa nudunnâm la iddiššim šeriktaša ušallamušimma ina makkūr bīt mutiša zittam kīma aplim ištēn ileqqe šumma mārūša aššum ina bītim šūṣîm usaḫḫamuši dajānū warkassa iparrasuma mārī arnam immidu sinništum šî ina bīt mutiša ul uṣṣi šumma sinništum šî ana waṣêm panīša ištakan*

¶ **172** If her husband does not make a marriage settlement in her favor, they shall restore to her in full her dowry, and she shall take a share of the property of her husband's estate comparable in value to that of one heir. If her children pressure her in order to coerce her to depart from the house, the judges shall

nudunnâm ša mussa iddinušim ana mārīša izzib šeriktam ša bīt abiša ileqqēma mut libbiša iḫḫassi

investigate her case and shall impose a penalty on the children; that woman will not depart from her husband's house. If that woman should decide on her own to depart, she shall leave for her children the marriage settlement which her husband gave to her; she shall take the dowry brought from her father's house and a husband of her choice shall marry her.

(xxxvi 41–50) *šumma sinništum šî ašar īrubu ana mutiša warkîm mārī ittalad warka sinništum šî imtūt šeriktaša mārū maḫrûtum u warkûtum izuzzu*

¶ **173** If that woman should bear children to her latter husband into whose house she entered, after that woman dies, her former and latter children shall equally divide her dowry.

(xxxvi 51–56) *šumma ana mutiša warkîm mārī la ittalad šeriktaša mārū ḫāwirišama ileqqû*

¶ **174** If she does not bear children to her latter husband, only the children of her first husband shall take her dowry.

(xxxvi 57–68) *šumma lu warad ekallim ulu warad muškēnim mārat awīlim īḫuzma mārī ittalad bēl wardim ana mārī mārat awīlim ana wardūtim ul iraggum*

¶ **175** If a slave of the palace or a slave of a commoner marries a woman of the *awīlu*-class and she then bears children, the owner of the slave will have no claims of slavery against the children of the woman of the *awīlu*-class.

(xxxvi 69–xxxvii 9) *u šumma warad ekallim ulu warad muškēnim mārat awīlim īḫuzma inūma īḫuzuši qadum šeriktim ša bīt abiša ana bīt warad ekallim ulu warad muškēnim*[31] *īrubma ištu innemdū bītam īpušu bīšam iršû*[32] *warkānumma lu warad ekallim ulu warad muškēnim ana šīmtim ittalak mārat awīlim šeriktaša ileqqe*[33] *u mimma ša mussa u šî ištu innemdū iršû ana šinīšu izuzzuma mišlam bēl wardim ileqqe mišlam mārat awīlim ana mārīša ileqqe*

¶ **176a** And if either a slave of the palace or a slave of a commoner marries a woman of the *awīlu*-class, and when he marries her she enters the house of the slave of the palace or of the slave of the commoner together with the dowry brought from her father's house, and subsequent to the time that they move in together they establish a household and accumulate possessions, after which either the slave of the palace or the slave of the commoner should go to his fate—the woman of the *awīlu*-class shall take her dowry; furthermore, they shall divide into two parts everything that her husband and she accumulated subsequent to the time that they moved in together, and the slave's owner shall take half and the woman of the *awīlu*-class shall take half for her children.

(xxxvii 10–21) *šumma mārat awīlim šeriktam la išu mimma ša mussa u šî ištu innemdū iršû ana šinīšu izuzzuma mišlam bēl wardim ileqqe mišlam mārat awīlim ana mārīša ileqqe*

¶ **176b** If the woman of the *awīlu*-class does not have a dowry, they shall divide into two parts everything that her husband and she accumulated subsequent to the time that they moved in together, and the slave's owner shall take half and the woman of the *awīlu*-class shall take half for her children.

(xxxvii 22–60) *šumma almattum ša mārūša ṣeḫḫeru ana bīt šanîm erēbim panīša ištakan balum dajānī ul irrub inūma ana bīt šanîm irrubu dajānū warkat bīt mutiša panîm iparrasuma bītam ša mutiša panîm ana mutiša warkîm u sinništim šuāti ipaqqiduma ṭuppam ušezzebušunūti bītam inaṣṣaru u ṣeḫḫerūtim urabbû uniātim ana kaspim ul inaddinu šājimānum ša unūt mārī almattim išammu ina kaspišu ītelli makkūrum ana bēlišu itâr*

¶ **177** If a widow whose children are still young should decide to enter another's house, she will not enter without (the prior approval of) the judges. When she enters another's house, the judges shall investigate the estate of her former husband, and they shall entrust the estate of her former husband to her later husband and to that woman, and they shall have them record a tablet (inventorying the estate). They shall safeguard the estate and they shall raise the young children; they will not sell the household goods. Any buyer who buys the household goods of the children of a widow shall forfeit his silver; the property shall revert to its owner.

(xxxvii 61–xxxviii 19) *šumma ugbabtum nadītum ulu sekretum ša abuša šeriktam išrukušim ṭuppam išṭurušim ina ṭuppim ša išṭurušim warkassa ēma eliša ṭābu nadānamma la išṭuršimma mala libbiša la ušamṣīši warka abum ana šīmtim ittalku eqelša u kirāša aḫḫūša ileqqûma kīma emūq zittiša ipram piššatam u lubūšam inaddinušimma libbaša uṭabbu šumma aḫḫūša kīma emūq zittiša ipram piššatam u lubūšam la ittadnušimma libbaša la uṭṭibbu eqelša u kirāša ana errēšim ša eliša ṭābu inaddinma errēssa ittanaššīši eqlam kirâm*[34] *u mimma ša abuša iddinušim*[35] *adi balṭat ikkal ana kaspim ul inaddin šaniam ul uppal aplūssa ša aḫḫīšama*

¶ **178** If there is an *ugbabtu*, a *nadītu*, or a *sekretu* whose father awards to her a dowry and records it in a tablet for her, but in the tablet that he records for her he does not grant her written authority to give her estate to whomever she pleases and does not give her full discretion—after the father goes to his fate, her brothers shall take her field and her orchard and they shall give to her food, oil, and clothing allowances in accordance with the value of her inheritance share, and they shall thereby satisfy her. If her brothers should not give to her food, oil, and clothing allowances in accordance with the value of her inheritance share and thus do not satisfy her, she shall give her field and her orchard to any agricultural tenant she pleases, and her agricultural tenant shall support her. As long as she lives, she shall enjoy the use of the field, orchard, and anything else which her father gave to her, but she will not sell it and she will not satisfy another person's obligations with it; her inheritance belongs only to her brothers.

(xxxviii 20–42) *šumma ugbabtum nadītum*[36] *ulu sekretum ša abuša šeriktam išrukušim kunukkam išṭurušim ina ṭuppim ša išṭurušim warkassa ēma eliša ṭābu nadānam išṭuršimma mala libbiša uštamṣīši warka abum ana šīmtim ittalku warkassa ēma eliša ṭābu inaddin aḫḫūša ul ipaqqaruši*

¶ **179** If there is an *ugbabtu*, a *nadītu*, or a *sekretu* whose father awards to her a dowry and records it for her in a sealed document, and in the tablet that he records for her he grants her written authority to give her estate to whomever she pleases and gives her full discretion—after the father goes to his fate, she shall give her estate to whomever she pleases; her brothers will not raise a claim against her.

(xxxviii 43–59) *šumma abum ana mārtišu nadīt gagîm*[37] *ulu sekretim šeriktam la iš<r>ukšim warka abum ana šīmtim ittalku ina makkūr bīt abim zittam kīma aplim ištēn izâzma adi balṭat ikkal warkassa ša aḫḫīšama*

¶ **180** If a father does not award a dowry to his daughter who is a cloistered *nadītu* or a *sekretu*, after the father goes to his fate, she shall have a share of the property of the paternal estate comparable in value to that of one heir; as long as she lives she shall enjoy its use; her estate belongs only to her brothers.

(xxxviii 60–75) *šumma abum nadītam qadištam ulu kulmašītam ana ilim iššīma šeriktam la išrukšim warka abum ana šīmtim ittalku ina makkūr bīt abim šalušti aplūtiša izâzma adi balṭat ikkal warkassa ša aḫḫīšama*

¶ **181** If a father dedicates (his daughter) to the deity as a *nadītu*, a *qadištu*, or a *kulmašītu* but does not award to her a dowry, after the father goes to his fate she shall take her one-third share[38] from the property of the paternal estate as her inheritance, and as long as she lives she shall enjoy its use; her estate belongs only to her brothers.

(xxxviii 76–xxxix 1) *šumma abum ana mārtišu nadīt Marduk ša Bābilim šeriktam la išrukšim kunukkam la išṭuršim warka abum ana šīmtim ittalku ina makkūr bīt abim šalušti aplūtiša itti aḫḫīša izâzma ilkam ul illak nadīt Marduk warkassa ēma eliša ṭābu inaddin*

¶ **182** If a father does not award a dowry to his daughter who is a *nadītu* dedicated to the god Marduk of the city of Babylon or does not record it for her in a sealed document, after the father goes to his fate, she shall take with her brothers her one-third share[39] from the property of the paternal estate as her inheritance, but she will not perform any service obligations; a *nadītu* dedicated to the god Marduk shall give her estate as she pleases.

(xxxix 2–14) *šumma abum ana mārtišu šugītim šeriktam išrukšim ana mutim iddišši kunukkam išṭuršim warka abum ana šīmtim ittalku ina makkūr bīt abim ul izâz*

¶ **183** If a father awards a dowry to his daughter who is a *šugītu*, gives her to a husband, and records it for her in a sealed document, after the father goes to his fate, she will not have a share of the property of the paternal estate.

(xxxix 15–30) *šumma awīlum ana mārtišu šugītim šeriktam la išrukšim ana mutim la iddiššši warka abum ana šīmtim ittalku aḫḫūša kīma emūq bīt abim šeriktam išarrakušimma ana mutim inaddinuši*

¶ **184** If a man does not award a dowry to his daughter who is a *šugītu*, and does not give her to a husband, after the father goes to his fate, her brothers shall award to her a dowry proportionate to the value of the paternal estate, and they shall give her to a husband.

(xxxix 31–38) *šumma awīlum ṣiḫram ina mêšu ana mārūtim ilqēma urtabbīšu tarbītum šî ul ibbaqqar*

¶ **185** If a man takes in adoption a young child at birth and then rears him, that rearling will not be reclaimed.

(xxxix 39–49) *šumma awīlum ṣiḫram ana mārūtim ilqe inūma ilqûšu abašu u ummašu iḫiaṭ tarbītum šî ana bīt abišu itâr*

¶ **186** If a man takes in adoption a young child, and when he takes him, he (the child?) is seeking his father and mother, that rearling shall return to his father's house.

(xxxix 50–53) *mār girseqîm muzzaz ekallim u mār sekretim ul ibbaqqar*

¶ **187** A child of (i.e., reared by) a courtier who is a palace attendant or a child of (i.e., reared by) a *sekretu* will not be reclaimed.

(xxxix 54–59) *šumma mār ummânim ṣiḫram ana tarbītim ilqēma šipir qātišu uštāḫissu ul ibbaqqar*

¶ **188** If a craftsman takes a young child to rear and then teaches him his craft, he will not be reclaimed.

(xxxix 60–64) *šumma šipir qātišu la uštāḫissu tarbītum šî ana bīt abišu itâr*

¶ **189** If he should not teach him his craft, that rearling shall return to his father's house.

(xxxix 65–74) *šumma awīlum ṣiḫram ša ana mārūtišu ilqûšuma urabbûšu itti mārīšu la imtanūšu tarbītum šî ana bīt abišu itâr*

¶ **190** If a man should not reckon the young child whom he took and raised in adoption as equal with his children, that rearling shall return to his father's house.

(xxxix 75–95) *šumma awīlum ṣiḫram ša ana mārūtišu ilqûšuma urabbûšu bīssu īpuš warka mārī irtašīma ana tarbītim nasāḫim panam ištakan ṣiḫrum šû rēqūssu ul ittallak abum*

¶ **191** If a man establishes his household (by reckoning as equal with any future children) the young child whom he took and raised in adoption, but afterwards he has

murabbīšu ina makkūrišu šalušti aplūtišu inaddiššumma ittallak ina eqlim kirîm u bītim ul inaddiššum

children (of his own) and then decides to disinherit the rearling, that young child will not depart empty-handed; the father who raised him shall give him a one-third share[40] of his property as his inheritance and he shall depart; he will not give him any property from field, orchard, or house.

(xxxix 96–xl 9) *šumma mār girseqîm ulu mār sekretim ana abim murabbīšu u ummim murabbītišu ul abī atta ul ummī atti iqtabi lišānšu inakkisu*

¶ **192** If the child of (i.e., reared by) a courtier or the child of (i.e., reared by) a *sekretu* should say to the father who raised him or to the mother who raised him, "You are not my father," or "You are not my mother," they shall cut out his tongue.

(xl 10–22) *šumma mār girseqîm ulu mār sekretim bīt abišu uweddīma abam murabbīšu u ummam murabbīssu izīrma ana bīt abišu itta= lak īnšu inassaḫu*

¶ **193** If the child of (i.e., reared by) a courtier or the child of (i.e., reared by) a *sekrētu* identifies with his father's house and repudiates the father who raised him or the mother who raised him and departs for his father's house, they shall pluck out his eye.

(xl 23–40) *šumma awīlum mārašu ana mušēniqtim iddinma ṣiḫrum šû ina qāt mušēniqtim imtūt mušēniqtum balum abišu u ummišu ṣiḫram šani= amma irtakas ukannušima aššum balum abišu u ummišu ṣiḫram šaniam irkusu tulāša inakkisu*

¶ **194** If a man gives his son to a wet nurse and that child then dies while in the care of the wet nurse, and the wet nurse then contracts for another child without the knowledge of his father and mother, they shall charge and convict her, and, because she contracted for another child without the consent of his father and mother, they shall cut off her breast.

(xl 41–44) *šumma mārum abašu imtaḫaṣ rittašu inakkisu*

¶ **195** If a child should strike his father, they shall cut off his hand.

(xl 45–49) *šumma awīlum īn mār awīlim uḫtappid īnšu uḫappadu*

¶ **196** If an *awīlu* should blind the eye of another *awīlu*, they shall blind his eye.

(xl 50–53) *šumma eṣemti awīlim ište-bir eṣemtašu išebbiru*

¶ **197** If he should break the bone of another *awīlu*, they shall break his bone.

(xl 54–59) *šumma īn muškēnim uḫ-tappid ulu eṣemti muškēnim ištebir* 1 *mana kaspam išaqqal*

¶ **198** If he should blind the eye of a commoner or break the bone of a commoner, he shall weigh and deliver 60 shekels of silver.

(xl 60–65) *šumma īn warad awīlim uḫtappid ulu eṣemti warad awīlim ište-bir mišil šīmišu išaqqal*

¶ **199** If he should blind the eye of an *awīlu*'s slave or break the bone of an *awīlu*'s slave, he shall weigh and deliver one-half of his value (in silver).

(xl 66–70) *šumma awīlum šinni awīlim meḫrišu ittadi šinnašu inaddû*

¶ **200** If an *awīlu* should knock out the tooth of another *awīlu* of his own rank, they shall knock out his tooth.

(xl 71–74) *šumma šinni muškēnim ittadi* 1⁄3 *mana kaspam išaqqal*

¶ **201** If he should knock out the tooth of a commoner, he shall weigh and deliver 20 shekels of silver.

(xl 75–81) *šumma awīlum lēt awīlim ša elišu rabû imtaḫaṣ ina puḫrim ina qinnaz alpim* 1 *šūši immaḫḫaṣ*

¶ **202** If an *awīlu* should strike the cheek of an *awīlu* who is of status higher than his own, he shall be flogged in the public assembly with 60 stripes of an ox whip.

(xl 82–87) *šumma mār awīlim lēt mār awīlim ša kīma šuāti imtaḫaṣ* 1 *mana kaspam išaqqal*

¶ **203** If a member of the *awīlu*-class should strike the cheek of another member of the *awīlu*-class who is his equal, he shall weigh and deliver 60 shekels of silver.

(xl 88–91) *šumma muškēnum lēt muškēnim imtaḫaṣ* 10 *šiqil kaspam išaqqal*

¶ **204** If a commoner should strike the cheek of another commoner, he shall weigh and deliver 10 shekels of silver.

(xl 92–xli 3) *šumma warad awīlim lēt mār awīlim imtaḫaṣ uzunšu inakkisu*

¶ **205** If an *awīlu*'s slave should strike the cheek of a member of the *awīlu*-class, they shall cut off his ear.

(xli 4–13) *šumma awīlum awīlam ina risbatim imtaḫaṣma simmam ištakanšu awīlum šû ina idû la amḫaṣu itamma u asâm ippal*

¶ **206** If an *awīlu* should strike another *awīlu* during a brawl and inflict upon him a wound, that *awīlu* shall swear, "I did not strike intentionally," and he shall satisfy the physician (i.e., pay his fees).

(xli 14–19) *šumma ina maḫāṣišu imtūt itammāma šumma mār awīlim ½ mana kaspam išaqqal*

¶ **207** If he should die from his beating, he shall also swear ("I did not strike him intentionally"); if he (the victim) is a member of the *awīlu*-class, he shall weigh and deliver 30 shekels of silver.

(xli 20–22) *šumma mār muškēnim ⅓ mana kaspam išaqqal*

¶ **208** If he (the victim) is a member of the commoner-class, he shall weigh and deliver 20 shekels of silver.

(xli 23–30) *šumma awīlum mārat awīlim imḫaṣma ša libbiša uštaddīši 10 šiqil kaspam ana ša libbiša išaqqal*

¶ **209** If an *awīlu* strikes a woman of the *awīlu*-class and thereby causes her to miscarry her fetus, he shall weigh and deliver 10 shekels of silver for her fetus.

(xli 31–34) *šumma sinništum šî imtūt mārassu idukku*

¶ **210** If that woman should die, they shall kill his daughter.

(xli 35–40) *šumma mārat muškēnim ina maḫāṣim ša libbiša uštaddīši 5 šiqil kaspam išaqqal*

¶ **211** If he should cause a woman of the commoner-class to miscarry her fetus by the beating, he shall weigh and deliver 5 shekels of silver.

(xli 41–44) *šumma sinništum šî imtūt ½ mana kaspam išaqqal*

¶ **212** If that woman should die, he shall weigh and deliver 30 shekels of silver.

(xli 45–50) *šumma amat awīlim imḫaṣma ša libbiša uštaddīši 2 šiqil kaspam išaqqal*

¶ **213** If he strikes an *awīlu*'s slave woman and thereby causes her to miscarry her fetus, he shall weigh and deliver 2 shekels of silver.

(xli 51–54) *šumma amtum šī imtūt* ⅓ *mana kaspam išaqqal*

¶ **214** If that slave woman should die, he shall weigh and deliver 20 shekels of silver.

(xli 55–66) *šumma asûm awīlam sim⸗mam kabtam ina karzilli siparrim īpušma awīlam ubtalliṭ ulu nakkapti awīlim ina karzilli siparrim iptēma īn awīlim ubtalliṭ 10 šiqil kaspam ileqqe*

¶ **215** If a physician performs major surgery with a bronze lancet upon an *awīlu* and thus heals the *awīlu*, or opens an *awīlu*'s temple with a bronze lancet and thus heals the *awīlu*'s eye, he shall take 10 shekels of silver (as his fee).

(xli 67–69) *šumma mār muškēnim 5 šiqil kaspam ileqqe*

¶ **216** If he (the patient) is a member of the commoner-class, he shall take 5 shekels of silver (as his fee).

(xli 70–73) *šumma warad awīlim bēl wardim ana asîm 2 šiqil kaspam inaddin*

¶ **217** If he (the patient) is an *awīlu*'s slave, the slave's master shall give to the physician 2 shekels of silver.

(xli 74–83) *šumma asûm awīlam sim⸗mam kabtam ina karzilli siparrim īpušma awīlam uštamīt ulu nakkapti awīlim ina karzilli siparrim iptēma īn awīlim uḫtappid rittašu inakkisu*

¶ **218** If a physician performs major surgery with a bronze lancet upon an *awīlu* and thus causes the *awīlu*'s death, or opens an *awīlu*'s temple with a bronze lancet and thus blinds the *awīlu*'s eye, they shall cut off his hand.

(xli 84–88) *šumma asûm simmam kabtam warad muškēnim ina karzilli siparrim īpušma uštamīt wardam kīma wardim iriab*

¶ **219** If a physician performs major surgery with a bronze lancet upon a slave of a commoner and thus causes the slave's death, he shall replace the slave with a slave of comparable value.

(xli 89–94) *šumma nakkaptašu ina karzilli siparrim iptēma īnšu uḫtappid kaspam mišil šīmišu išaqqal*

¶ **220** If he opens his (the commoner's slave's) temple with a bronze lancet and thus blinds his eye, he shall weigh and deliver silver equal to half his value.

(xli 95–xlii 9) *šumma asûm eṣemti awīlim šebirtam uštallim ulu šer᾽ānam marṣam ubtalliṭ bēl simmim ana asîm 5 šiqil kaspam inaddin*

¶ **221** If a physician should set an *awīlu*'s broken bone or heal an injured muscle, the patient shall give the physician 5 shekels of silver.

(xlii 10–12) *šumma mār muškēnim 3 šiqil kaspam inaddin*

¶ **222** If he (the patient) is a member of the commoner-class, he shall give 3 shekels of silver.

(xlii 13–17) *šumma warad awīlim bēl wardim ana asîm 2 šiqil kaspam inaddin*

¶ **223** If he (the patient) is an *awīlu*'s slave, the slave's master shall give the physician 2 shekels of silver.

(xlii 18–28) *šumma asî alpim ulu imērim lu alpam ulu imēram simmam kabtam īpušma ubtalliṭ bēl alpim ulu imērim* IGI.6.GÁL *kaspam ana asîm idīšu inaddin*

¶ **224** If a veterinarian performs major surgery upon an ox or a donkey and thus heals it, the owner of the ox or of the donkey shall give the physician as his fee one sixth (of a shekel, i.e., 30 barleycorns) of silver.

(xlii 29–35) *šumma alpam ulu imēram simmam kabtam īpušma uštamīt* IGI.4(?).GÁL *šīmišu ana bēl alpim ulu imērim inaddin*

¶ **225** If he performs major surgery upon an ox or a donkey and thus causes its death, he shall give one quarter(?)[41] of its value to the owner of the ox or donkey.

(xlii 36–42) *šumma gallābum balum bēl wardim abbutti wardim la šêm ugallib ritti gallābim šuāti inakkisu*

¶ **226** If a barber shaves off the slave-hairlock of a slave not belonging to him without the consent of the slave's owner, they shall cut off that barber's hand.

(xlii 43–55) *šumma awīlum gallābam idāṣma abbutti wardim la šêm ugdallib awīlam šuāti idukkušuma ina bābišu iḫallalušu gallābum ina idû la ugallibu itammāma ūtaššar*

¶ **227** If a man misinforms a barber so that he then shaves off the slave-hairlock of a slave not belonging to him, they shall kill that man and hang him in his own doorway; the barber shall swear, "I did not knowingly shave it off," and he shall be released.

(xlii 56–63) *šumma itinnum bītam ana awīlim īpušma ušaklilšum ana 1 musar bītim 2 šiqil kaspam ana qīštišu inaddiššum*

¶ **228** If a builder constructs a house for a man to his satisfaction, he shall give him 2 shekels of silver for each sar of house as his compensation.

(xlii 64–72) *šumma itinnum ana awīlim bītam īpušma šipiršu la udan= ninma bīt īpušu imqutma bēl bītim uštamīt itinnum šû iddâk*

¶ **229** If a builder constructs a house for a man but does not make his work sound, and the house that he constructs collapses and causes the death of the householder, that builder shall be killed.

(xlii 73–76) *šumma mār bēl bītim uštamīt mār itinnim šuāti idukku*[42]

¶ **230** If it should cause the death of a son of the householder, they shall kill a son of that builder.

(xlii 77–81) *šumma warad bēl bītim uštamīt wardam kīma wardim ana bēl bītim inaddin*

¶ **231** If it should cause the death of a slave of the householder, he shall give to the householder a slave of comparable value for the slave.

(xlii 82–92) *šumma makkūram uḫ= talliq mimma ša uḫalliqu iriab u aššum bīt īpušu la udanninuma imqutu ina makkūr ramanišu bīt imqutu ippeš*

¶ **232** If it should cause the loss of property, he shall replace anything that is lost; moreover, because he did not make sound the house which he constructed and it collapsed, he shall construct (anew) the house which collapsed at his own expense.

(xlii 93–xliii 3) *šumma itinnum bītam ana awīlim īpušma šipiršu la ušteṣbīma igārum iqtūp itinnum šû ina kasap ramanišu igāram šuāti udannan*

¶ **233** If a builder constructs a house for a man but does not make it conform to specifications so that a wall then buckles, that builder shall make that wall sound using his own silver.

(xliii 4–9) *šumma malāḫum elip 60 kur ana awīlim ipḫi 2 šiqil kaspam ana qīštišu inaddiššum*

¶ **234** If a boatman caulks a boat of 60-kur capacity for a man, he shall give him 2 shekels of silver as his compensation.

(xliii 10–26) *šumma malāḫum elip= pam ana awīlim ipḫīma šipiršu la*

¶ **235** If a boatman caulks a boat for a man but does not satisfactorily

utakkilma ina šattimma šuāti elippum šî iṣṣabar ḫiṭītam irtaši malāḫum elippam šuāti inaqqarma ina makkūr ramanišu udannanma elippam dannatam ana bēl elippim inaddin

complete his work and within that very year the boat founders or reveals a structural defect, the boatman shall dismantle that boat and make it sound at his own expense, and he shall give the sound boat to the owner of the boat.

(xliii 27–37) *šumma awīlum elippašu ana malāḫim ana igrim iddinma malāḫum īgīma elippam uṭṭebbi ulu uḫtalliq malāḫum elippam ana bēl elippim iriab*

¶ **236** If a man gives his boat to a boatman for hire, and the boatman is negligent and causes the boat to sink or to become lost, the boatman shall replace the boat for the owner of the boat.

(xliii 38–55) *šumma awīlum malāḫam u elippam īgurma še'am šipātim šamnam suluppī u mimma šumšu ša ṣênim iṣēnši malāḫum šû īgīma elippam uṭṭebbi u ša libbiša uḫtalliq malāḫum elippam ša uṭebbû u mimma ša ina libbiša uḫalliqu iriab*

¶ **237** If a man hires a boatman and a boat and loads it with grain, wool, oil, dates, or any other lading, and that boatman is negligent and thereby causes the boat to sink or its cargo to become lost, the boatman shall replace the boat which he sank and any of its cargo which he lost.

(xliii 56–61) *šumma malāḫum elip awīlim uṭṭebbīma uštēliašši kaspam mišil šīmiša inaddin*

¶ **238** If a boatman should cause a man's boat to sink and he raises it, he shall give silver equal to half of its value.

(xliii 62–66) *šumma awīlum malāḫam* [*īgur*] 6 [*kur še'am*] *ina šan*[*at*] *inaddiš*[*šum*]

¶ **239** If a man hires a boatman, he shall give him 1,800 silas of grain per year.

(xliii 67–80) *šumma elip ša māḫirtim elip ša muqqelpītim imḫaṣma uṭṭebbi bēl elippim ša elippašu ṭebiat mimma ša ina elippišu ḫalqu ina maḫar ilim ubârma ša māḫirtim ša elip ša muqqelpītim uṭebbû elippašu u mimmašu ḫalqam iriabšum*

¶ **240** If a boat under the command of the master of an upstream-boat collides with a boat under the command of the master of a downstream-boat and thus sinks it, the owner of the sunken boat shall establish before the god the property that is lost from his boat, and the master of the upstream-boat who sinks the boat of the master of the downstream-boat shall replace to him his boat and his lost property.

(xliii 81–84) *šumma awīlum alpam ana nipûtim ittepe 1/3 mana kaspam išaqqal*

¶ **241** If a man should distrain an ox, he shall weigh and deliver 20 shekels of silver.

(xliii 85–91) *šumma awīlum ana šattim ištiat īgur idī alpim ša warka 4 kur še'am idī alpim ša qabla 3 kur še'am ana bēlišu inaddin*

¶ **242/243** If a man rents it for one year, he shall give to its owner 1,200 silas of grain as the hire of an ox for the rear (of the team), and 900 silas of grain as the hire of an ox for the middle (of the team).

(xliv 1–5) *šumma awīlum alpam imēram īgurma ina ṣērim nēšum iddūkšu ana bēlišuma*

¶ **244** If a man rents an ox or a donkey and a lion kills it in the open country, it is the owner's loss.

(xliv 6–13) *šumma awīlum alpam īgurma ina mēgûtim ulu ina maḫāṣim uštamīt alpam kīma alpim ana bēl alpim iriab*

¶ **245** If a man rents an ox and causes its death either by negligence or by physical abuse, he shall replace the ox with an ox of comparable value for the owner of the ox.

(xliv 14–21) *šumma awīlum alpam īgurma šēpšu ištebir ulu labiānšu ittakis*[43] *alpam kīma alpim ana bēl alpim iriab*

¶ **246** If a man rents an ox and breaks its leg or cuts its neck tendon, he shall replace the ox with an ox of comparable value for the owner of the ox.

(xliv 22–27) *šumma awīlum alpam īgurma īnšu uḫtappid kaspam ½ šīmišu ana bēl alpim inaddin*

¶ **247** If a man rents an ox and blinds its eye, he shall give silver equal to half of its value to the owner of the ox.

(xliv 28–35) *šumma awīlum alpam īgurma qaranšu iš<te>bir zibbassu ittakis ulu šašallašu ittasak kaspam* IGI.4(?).GÁL *šīmišu inaddin*

¶ **248** If a man rents an ox and breaks its horn, cuts off its tail, or injures its hoof tendon, he shall give silver equal to one quarter of its value.

(xliv 36–43) *šumma awīlum alpam īgurma ilum imḫassuma imtūt awīlum ša alpam īguru nīš ilim izakkarma ūtaššar*

¶ **249** If a man rents an ox, and a god strikes it down dead, the man who rented the ox shall swear an oath by the god and he shall be released.

(xliv 44–51) *šumma alpum sūqam ina alākišu awīlam ikkipma uštamīt dīnum šû rugummâm ul išu*

¶ **250** If an ox gores to death a man while it is passing through the streets, that case has no basis for a claim.

(xliv 52–65) *šumma alap awīlim nakkāpīma kīma nakkāpû bābtašu ušēdīšumma qarnīšu la ušarrim alapšu la usanniqma alpum šû mār awīlim ikkipma uštamīt ½ mana kas*= *pam inaddin*

¶ **251** If a man's ox is a known gorer, and the authorities of his city quarter notify him that it is a known gorer, but he does not blunt(?) its horns or control his ox, and that ox gores to death a member of the *awīlu*-class, he (the owner) shall give 30 shekels of silver.

(xliv 66–68) *šumma warad awīlim* ⅓ *mana kaspam inaddin*

¶ **252** If it is a man's slave (who is fatally gored), he shall give 20 shekels of silver.

(xliv 69–82) *šumma awīlum awīlam ana panī eqlišu uzuzzim īgurma aldâm iqīpšu liātim ipqissum [ana] eqlim erēšim urakkissu šumma awīlum šû zēram ulu ukullâm išriqma ina qātišu ittaṣbat rittašu inakkisu*

¶ **253** If a man hires another man to care for his field, that is, he entrusts to him the stored grain, hands over to him care of the cattle, and contracts with him for the cultivation of the field—if that man steals the seed or fodder and it is then discovered in his possession, they shall cut off his hand.

(xliv 83–87) *šumma aldâm ilqēma liātim ūtenniš tašna še᾽am ša imḫuru iriab*

¶ **254** If he takes the stored grain and thus weakens the cattle, he shall replace twofold the grain which he received.

(xliv 88–96) *šumma liāt awīlim ana igrim ittadin ulu zēram išriqma ina eqlim la uštabši awīlam šuāti ukan*= *nušuma ina ebūrim ana 1 burum 60 kur še᾽am imaddad*

¶ **255** If he should hire out the man's cattle, or he steals seed and thus does not produce crops in the field, they shall charge and convict that man, and at the harvest he shall measure and deliver 18,000 silas of grain for every 18 ikus of land.

(xliv 97–100) *šumma pīḫassu apālam la ile'i ina eqlim šuāti ina liātim*[44] *imtanaššarušu*

¶ **256** If he is not able to satisfy his obligation, they shall have him dragged around[45] through that field by the cattle.

(xliv 101–xlv 4) *šumma awīlum ikkaram īgur* 8 *kur še'am ina šattim ištiat inaddiššum*

¶ **257** If a man hires an agricultural laborer, he shall give him 2,400 silas of grain per year.

(xlv 5–9) *šumma awīlum kullizam īgur* 6 *kur še'am ina šattim ištiat inaddiššum*

¶ **258** If a man hires an ox driver, he shall give him 1,800 silas of grain per year.

(xlv 10–15) *šumma awīlum epinnam ina ugārim išriq* 5 *šiqil kaspam ana bēl epinnim inaddin*

¶ **259** If a man steals a plow from the common irrigated area, he shall give 5 shekels of silver to the owner of the plow.

(xlv 16–20) *šumma ḫarbam ulu maškakātim ištariq* 3 *šiqil kaspam inaddin*

¶ **260** If he should steal a clod-breaking plow or a harrow, he shall give 3 shekels of silver.

(xlv 21–27) *šumma awīlum nāqidam ana liātim u ṣēnim re'îm īgur* 8 *kur še'am ina šattim ištiat inaddiššum*

¶ **261** If a man hires a herdsman to herd the cattle or the sheep and goats, he shall give him 2,400 silas of grain per year.

(xlv 28–36) *šumma awīlum alpam ulu immeram ana* [*nāqidim* ...]

¶ **262** If a man [gives] an ox or a sheep to a [herdsman ...]

(xlv 37–43) *šumma* [*alpam*] *ulu* [*immeram*] *ša innadnušum uḫtalliq alpam kīma* [*alpim*] *immeram kīma* [*immerim*] *ana bēli*[*šu*] *iriab*

¶ **263** If he should cause the loss of the ox or sheep which were given to him, he shall replace the ox with an ox of comparable value or the sheep with a sheep of comparable value for its owner.

(xlv 44–60) *šumma* [*rē'ûm*] *ša liātum ulu ṣēnum ana re'îm innadnušum idīšu gamrātim maḫir libbašu ṭāb liātim uṣṣaḫḫir ṣēnam uṣṣaḫḫir tālit=*

¶ **264** If a shepherd, to whom cattle or sheep and goats were given for shepherding, is in receipt of his complete hire to his satisfaction,

tam umtaṭṭi ana pī riksātišu tālittam u biltam inaddin

then allows the number of cattle to decrease, or the number of sheep and goats to decrease, or the number of offspring to diminish, he shall give for the (loss of) offspring and by-products in accordance with the terms of his contract.

(xlv 61–75) *šumma rē᾽ûm ša liātum ulu ṣēnum ana re᾽îm innadnušum usarrirma šimtam uttakkir u ana kaspim ittadin ukannušuma adi 10-šu ša išriqu liātim u ṣēnam ana bēlišunu iriab*

¶ **265** If a shepherd, to whom cattle or sheep and goats were given for shepherding, acts criminally and alters the brand and sells them, they shall charge and convict him and he shall replace for their owner cattle or sheep and goats tenfold that which he stole.

(xlv 76–81) *šumma ina tarbaṣim lipit ilim ittabši ulu nēšum iddūk rē᾽ûm maḫar ilim ubbamma miqitti tarbaṣim bēl tarbaṣim imaḫḫaršu*

¶ **266** If, in the enclosure, an epidemic[46] should break out or a lion make a kill, the shepherd shall clear himself before the god, and the owner of the enclosure shall accept responsibility for him for the loss sustained in the enclosure.

(xlv 82–89) *šumma rē᾽ûm īgūma ina tarbaṣim pissatam uštabši rē᾽ûm ḫiṭīt pissatim ša ina tarbaṣim ušabšû liātim u ṣēnam ušallamma ana bēlišunu inaddin*

¶ **267** If the shepherd is negligent and allows mange(?) to spread in the enclosure, the shepherd shall make restitution—in cattle or in sheep and goats—for the damage caused by the mange(?) which he allowed to spread in the enclosure, and give it to their owner.

(xlv 90–92) *šumma awīlum alpam ana diāšim īgur 2 sūt še᾽um idūšu*

¶ **268** If a man rents an ox for threshing, 20 silas of grain is its hire.

(xlv 93–95) *šumma imēram ana diāšim īgur 1 sūt še᾽um idūšu*

¶ **269** If he rents a donkey for threshing, 10 silas of grain is its hire.

(xlv 96–98) *šumma urīṣam ana diāšim īgur 1 qa še᾽um idūšu*

¶ **270** If he rents a goat for threshing, 1 sila of grain is its hire.

(xlv 99–xlvi 2) *šumma awīlum liātim ereqqam u murteddīša īgur ina ūmim ištēn 3 parsikat še'am inaddin*

¶ **271** If a man rents cattle, a wagon, and its driver, he shall give 180 silas of grain per day.

(xlvi 3–7) *šumma awīlum ereqqamma ana ramaniša īgur ina ūmim ištēn 4 sūt še'am inaddin*

¶ **272** If a man rents only the wagon, he shall give 40 silas of grain per day.

(xlvi 8–19) *šumma awīlum agram īgur ištu rēš šattim adi ḫamšim warḫim 6 uṭṭet kaspam ina ūmim ištēn inaddin ištu šiššim warḫim adi taqtīt šattim 5 uṭṭet kaspam ina ūmim ištēn inaddin*

¶ **273** If a man hires a hireling, he shall give 6 barleycorns of silver per day from the beginning of the year until (the end of) the fifth month, and 5 barleycorns of silver per day from the sixth month until the end of the year.

(xlvi 20–44) *šumma awīlum mār ummânim iggar idī* LÚ.[x] *5 uṭṭet kaspam idī kāmidim 5 uṭṭet kaspam* [*idī*] *ša kitîm*(?) [x *uṭṭet*] *kaspam* [*idī*] *purkullim* [x *uṭṭet ka*]*spam* [*idī*] *sasinnim*(?) [x *uṭṭet kas*]*pam* [*idī nap*]*pāḫim* [x *uṭṭet kas*]*pam* [*idī*] *naggārim* 4(?) *uṭṭet kaspam idī aškāpim* [x] *uṭṭet kaspam idī atkuppim* [x *uṭ*]*tet kaspam* [*idī*] *itinnim* [x *uṭṭet kas*]*pam* [*ina ūmim*] *ištēn* [*inadd*]*in*

¶ **274** If a man intends to hire a craftsman, he shall give, per [day]: as the hire of a ..., 5 barleycorns of silver; as the hire of a woven-textile worker, 5 barleycorns of silver; as the hire of a linen-worker(?), [x barleycorns] of silver; as the hire of a stone-cutter, [x barleycorns] of silver; as the hire of a bow-maker,[47] [x barleycorns of] silver; as the hire of a smith, [x barleycorns of] silver; as the hire of a carpenter, 4(?) barleycorns of silver; as the hire of a leatherworker, [x] barleycorns of silver; as the hire of a reedworker, [x] barleycorns of silver; as the hire of a builder, [x barleycorns of] silver.

(xlvi 45–48) [*šumma aw*]*īlum* [...] *īgur ina ūmim ištēn 3 uṭṭet kaspum idūša*

¶ **275** If a man rents a [...-boat], 3 barleycorns of silver per day is its hire.

(xlvi 49–52) *šumma māḫirtam īgur 2½ uṭṭet kaspam idīša ina ūmim ištēn inaddin*

¶ **276** If a man rents a boat for traveling upstream, he shall give 2½ barleycorns of silver as its hire per day.

(xlvi 53–57) *šumma awīlum elip šūšim īgur ina ūmim ištēn* IGI.6.GÁL *kaspam idīša inaddin*

¶ **277** If a man rents a boat of 60-kur capacity, he shall give one sixth (of a shekel, i.e., 30 barleycorns) of silver per day as its hire.

(xlvi 58–66) *šumma awīlum wardam amtam išāmma warahšu la imlāma benni elišu imtaqut ana nādinānišu utârma šājimānum kasap išqulu ileqqe*

¶ **278**[48] If a man purchases a slave or slave woman and within his one-month period epilepsy then befalls him, he shall return him to his seller and the buyer shall take back the silver that he weighed and delivered.

(xlvi 67–71) *šumma awīlum wardam amtam išāmma baqrī irtaši nādinānšu baqrī ippal*

¶ **279** If a man purchases a slave or slave woman and then claims arise, his seller shall satisfy the claims.

(xlvi 72–87) *šumma awīlum ina māt nukurtim wardam amtam ša awīlim ištām inūma ina libbū mātim ittal-kamma bēl wardim ulu amtim lu warassu ulu amassu ūteddi šumma wardum u amtum šunu mārū mātim balum kaspimma andurāršunu iššakkan*

¶ **280** If a man should purchase another man's slave or slave woman in a foreign country, and while he is traveling about within the (i.e., his own) country the owner of the slave or slave woman identifies his slave or slave woman—if they, the slave and slave woman, are natives of the country, their release shall be secured without any payment.

(xlvi 88–96) *šumma mārū mātim šanītim šājimānum ina mahar ilim kasap išqulu iqabbīma bēl wardim ulu amtim kasap išqulu ana tamkārim inaddinma lu warassu lu amassu ipaṭṭar*

¶ **281** If they are natives of another country, the buyer shall declare before the god the amount of silver that he weighed, and the owner of the slave or slave woman shall give to the merchant the amount of silver that he paid, and thus he shall redeem his slave or slavewoman.

(xlvi 97–102) *šumma wardum ana bēlišu ul bēlī atta iqtabi kīma warassu ukânšuma bēlšu uzunšu inakkis*

¶ **282** If a slave should declare to his master, "You are not my master," he (the master) shall bring charge and proof against him that he is indeed his slave, and his master shall cut off his ear.

Epilogue

(xlvii 1–8) *dīnāt mīšarim ša Ḫammurabi šarrum lēʾûm ukinnuma mātam ussam kīnam u rīdam damqam ušaṣbitu*

These are the just decisions which Hammurabi, the able king, has established and thereby has directed the land along the course of truth and the correct way of life.

(xlvii 9–58) *Ḫammurabi šarrum gitmālum anāku ana ṣalmāt qaqqadim ša Enlil išrukam rēʾûssina Marduk iddinam ul ēgu aḫī ul addi ašrī šulmim ešteʾīšināšim pušqī waštūtim upetti nūram ušēṣišināšim ina kakkim dannim ša Zababa u Ištar ušatlimūnim ina igigallim ša Ea išīmam ina lēʾûtim ša Marduk iddinam nakrī eliš u šapliš assuḫ qablātim ubelli šīr mātim uṭīb nišī dadmī aburrī ušarbiṣ mugallitam ul ušaršīšināti ilū rabûtum ibbûninnima anākuma rēʾûm mušallimum ša ḫaṭṭašu išarat ṣillī ṭābum ana ālija tariṣ ina utlija nišī māt Šumerim u Akkadîm ukīl ina lamassija iḫbiša ina šulmim attabbalšināti ina nēmeqija uštapziršināti*

I am Hammurabi, noble king. I have not been careless or negligent toward humankind, granted to my care by the god Enlil, and with whose shepherding the god Marduk charged me. I have sought for them peaceful places, I removed serious difficulties, I spread light over them. With the mighty weapon which the gods Zababa and Ishtar bestowed upon me, with the wisdom which the god Ea allotted to me, with the ability which the god Marduk gave me, I annihilated enemies everywhere, I put an end to wars, I enhanced the well-being of the land, I made the people of all settlements lie in safe pastures, I did not tolerate anyone intimidating them. The great gods having chosen me, I am indeed the shepherd who brings peace, whose scepter is just. My benevolent shade is spread over my city, I held the people of the lands of Sumer and Akkad safely on my lap. They prospered under my protective spirit, I maintained them in peace, with my skillful wisdom I sheltered them.

(xlvii 59–78) *dannum enšam ana la ḫabālim ekūtam almattam šutēšurim ina Bābilim ālim ša Anum u Enlil rēšīšu ullû ina Esagil bītim ša kīma šamê u erṣetim išdāšu kīnā dīn mātim*

In order that the mighty not wrong the weak, to provide just ways for the waif and the widow, I have inscribed my precious pronouncements upon my stela and set it up

ana diānim purussê mātim ana parāsim ḫablim šutēšurim awâtija šūqurātim ina narîja ašṭurma ina maḫar ṣalmija šar mīšarim ukīn

before the statue of me, the king of justice,[49] in the city of Babylon, the city which the gods Anu and Enlil have elevated, within the Esagil, the temple whose foundations are fixed as are heaven and earth, in order to render the judgments of the land, to give the verdicts of the land, and to provide just ways for the wronged.

(xlvii 79–xlviii 2) *šarrum ša in šarrī šūturu anāku awâtūa nasqā lē'ûtī šāninam ul išû ina qibīt Šamaš dajānim rabîm ša šamê u erṣetim mīšarī ina mātim lištēpi ina awat Marduk bēlija uṣurātūa mušassikam aj iršia ina Esagil ša arammu šumī ina damiqtim ana dār lizzakir*

I am the king preeminent among kings. My pronouncements are choice, my ability is unrivaled. By the command of the god Shamash, the great judge of heaven and earth, may my justice prevail in the land. By the order of the god Marduk, my lord, may my engraved image not be confronted by someone who would remove it. May my name always be remembered favorably in the Esagil temple which I love.

(xlviii 3–19) *awīlum ḫablum ša awatam iraššû ana maḫar ṣalmija šar mīšarim lillikma narî šaṭram lištassīma awâtija šūqurātim lišmēma narî awatam likallimšu dīnšu līmur libbašu linappišma*

Let any wronged man who has a lawsuit come before the statue of me, the king of justice, and let him have my inscribed stela read aloud to him, thus may he hear my precious pronouncements and let my stela reveal the lawsuit for him; may he examine his case, may he calm his (troubled) heart, (and may he praise me), saying:

(xlviii 20–38) *Ḫammurabimi bēlum ša kīma abim wālidim ana nišī ibaššû ana awat Marduk bēlišu uštaktitma irnitti Marduk eliš u šapliš ikšud libbi Marduk bēlišu uṭīb u šīram ṭābam ana nišī ana dār išīm u mātam uštēšer*

"Hammurabi, the lord, who is like a father and begetter to his people, submitted himself to the command of the god Marduk, his lord, and achieved victory for the god Marduk everywhere. He gladdened the heart of the god Marduk, his lord, and he secured the eternal well-being of the people and provided just ways for the land."

(xlviii 39–58) *annītam liqbīma ina maḫar Marduk bēlija Zarpānītum bēltija ina libbišu gamrim likrubam šēdum lamassum ilū ēribūt Esagil libitti Esagil igirrê ūmišam ina maḫar Marduk bēlija Zarpānītum bēltija lidammiqu*

May he say thus, and may he pray for me with his whole heart before the gods Marduk, my lord, and Zarpanitu, my lady. May the protective spirits, the gods who enter the Esagil temple, and the very brickwork of the Esagil temple, make my daily portents auspicious before the gods Marduk, my lord, and Zarpanitu, my lady.

(xlviii 59–94) *ana warkiāt ūmī ana matima šarrum ša ina mātim ibbaššû awât mīšarim ša ina narîja ašṭuru liṣṣur dīn mātim ša adīnu purussē mātim ša aprusu aj unakkir uṣurātija aj ušassik šumma awīlum šû tašīmtam išūma mâssu šutēšuram ile'i ana awâtim ša ina narîja ašṭuru liqūlma kibsam rīdam dīn mātim ša adīnu purussē mātim ša aprusu narûm šû likallimšuma ṣalmāt qaqqadišu lištēšer dīnšina lidīn purussāšina liprus ina mātišu raggam u ṣēnam lissuḫ šīr nišīšu liṭīb*

May any king who will appear in the land in the future, at any time, observe the pronouncements of justice that I inscribed upon my stela. May he not alter the judgments that I rendered and the verdicts that I gave, nor remove my engraved image. If that man has discernment, and is capable of providing just ways for his land, may he heed the pronouncements I have inscribed upon my stela, may that stela reveal for him the traditions, the proper conduct, the judgments of the land that I rendered, the verdicts of the land that I gave and may he, too, provide just ways for all humankind in his care. May he render their judgments, may he give their verdicts, may he eradicate the wicked and the evil from his land, may he enhance the well-being of his people.

(xlviii 95–xlix 17) *Ḫammurabi šar mīšarim ša Šamaš kīnātim išrukušum anāku awâtūa nasqā epšētūa šāninam ul išâ ela ana la ḫassim rēqa ana emqim ana tanādātim šūṣâ šumma awīlum šû ana awâtija*

I am Hammurabi, king of justice, to whom the god Shamash has granted (insight into) the truth. My pronouncements are choice, and my achievements are unrivaled; they are meaningless only to the

ša ina narîja ašṭuru iqūlma dīnī la ušassik awâtija la uštepīl uṣurātija la unakkir awīlum šû kīma jâti šar mīšarim Šamaš ḫaṭṭašu lirrik nišīšu ina mīšarim lirī

fool, but to the wise they are praiseworthy. If that man (a future ruler) heeds my pronouncements which I have inscribed upon my stela, and does not reject my judgments, change my pronouncements, or alter my engraved image, then may the god Shamash lengthen his reign, just as (he has done) for me, the king of justice, and so may he shepherd his people with justice.

(xlix 18–44) *šumma awīlum šû ana awâtija ša ina narîja ašṭuru la iqūlma errētija imēšma errēt ilī la īdurma dīn adīnu uptassis awâtija uštepīl uṣurātija uttakkir šumī šaṭram ipšiṭma šumšu ištaṭar aššum errētim šināti šaniamma uštāḫiz awīlum šû lu šarrum lu bēlum*[50] *lu iššiakkum ulu awīlūtum ša šumam nabiat*

(But) should that man not heed my pronouncements, which I have inscribed upon my stela, and should he slight my curses and not fear the curses of the gods, and thus overturn the judgments that I rendered, change my pronouncements, alter my engraved image, erase my inscribed name and inscribe his own name (in its place)—or should he, because of fear of these curses, have someone else do so—that man, whether he is a king, a lord, or a governor, or any person at all,

(xlix 45–52) *Anum rabûm abu ilī nābû palêja melimmī šarrūtim līṭeršu ḫaṭṭašu lišbir šīmātišu līrur*

may the great god Anu, father of the gods, who has proclaimed my reign, deprive him of the sheen of royalty, smash his scepter, and curse his destiny.

(xlix 53–80) *Enlil bēlum mušīm šīmātim ša qibīssu la uttakkaru mušarbû šarrūtija tēšî la šubbîm gabaraḫ ḫalāqišu ina šubtišu lišappiḫaššum*[51] *palê tānēḫim ūmī īṣūtim šanāt ḫušaḫḫim iklet la nawārim mūt niṭil īnim ana šīmtim lišīmšum ḫalāq ālišu naspuḫ nišīšu*

May the god Enlil, the lord, who determines destinies, whose utterance cannot be countermanded, who magnifies my kingship, incite against him even in his own residence disorder that cannot be quelled and a rebellion that will result in his obliteration; may he

šarrūssu šupēlam šumšu u zikiršu ina mātim la šubšâm ina pīšu kabtim liqbi

cast as his fate a reign of groaning, of few days, of years of famine, of darkness without illumination, and of sudden death; may he declare with his venerable speech the obliteration of his city, the dispersion of his people, the supplanting of his dynasty, and the blotting out of his name and his memory from the land.

(xlix 81–97) *Ninlil ummum rabītum ša qibīssa ina Ekur kabtat bēltum mudammiqat igirrēja ašar šipṭim u purussêm ina maḫar Enlil awassu lilemmin šulput mātišu ḫalāq nišīšu tabāk napištišu kīma mê ina pī Enlil šarrim lišaškin*

May the goddess Ninlil, the great mother, whose utterance is honored in the Ekur temple, the mistress who makes my portents auspicious, denounce his case before the god Enlil at the place of litigation and verdict; may she induce the divine king Enlil to pronounce the destruction of his land, the obliteration of his people,[52] and the spilling of his life force like water.

(xlix 98–l 13) *Ea rubûm rabium ša šīmātušu ina maḫra illakā apkal ilī mudē mimma šumšu mušāriku ūm balāṭija uznam u nēmeqam līteršuma ina mīšītim littarrūšu nārātišu ina nagbim liskir ina erṣetišu ašnan napišti nišī aj ušabši*

May the god Ea, the great prince, whose destinies take precedence, the sage among the gods, all-knowing, who lengthens the days of my life, deprive him of all understanding and wisdom, and may he lead him into confusion; may he dam up his rivers at the source; may he not allow any life-sustaining grain in his land.

(l 14–40) *Šamaš dajānum rabium ša šamê u erṣetim muštēšer šaknat napištim bēlum tukultī šarrūssu liskip dīnšu aj idīn uruḫšu līši išdī ummānišu lišḫelṣi ina bīrišu šīram lemnam ša nasāḫ išdī šarrūtišu u ḫalāq mātišu liškunšum awatum maruštum ša Šamaš arḫiš likšussu*

May the god Shamash, the great judge of heaven and earth, who provides just ways for all living creatures, the lord, my trust, overturn his kingship; may he not render his judgments, may he confuse his path and undermine the morale of his army; when divination is per-

eliš ina balṭūtim lissuḫšu šapliš ina erṣetim eṭemmašu mê lišaṣmi

formed for him, may he provide an inauspicious omen portending the uprooting of the foundations of his kingship and the obliteration of his land; may the malevolent word of the god Shamash swiftly overtake him, may he uproot him from among the living above and make his ghost thirst for water below in the nether world.

(l 41–63) *Sîn bēl šamê ilum bānî ša têressu*[53] *ina ilī šūpât agâm kussiam ša šarrūtim līṭeršu arnam kabtam šēressu rabītam ša ina zumrišu la iḫalliqu līmussuma ūmī warḫī šanāt palēšu ina tānēḫim u dimmatim lišaqti kammāl šarrūtim lišaṭṭilšu balāṭam ša itti mūtim šitannu ana šīmtim lišīmšum*

May the god Sîn, my creator, whose oracular decision prevails among the gods, deprive him of the crown and throne of kingship, and impose upon him an onerous punishment, a great penalty for him, which will not depart from his body; may he conclude every day, month, and year of his reign with groaning and mourning; may he unveil before him a contender for the kingship; may he decree for him a life that is no better than death.

(l 64–80) *Adad bēl ḫegallim gugal šamê u erṣetim rēṣūa zunnī ina šamê mīlam ina nagbim līṭeršu mātsu ina ḫušaḫḫim u bubūtim liḫalliq eli ālišu ezziš lissīma mātsu ana til abūbim litēr*

May the god Adad, lord of abundance, the canal-inspector of heaven and earth, my helper, deprive him of the benefits of rain from heaven and flood from the springs, and may he obliterate his land through destitution and famine; may he roar fiercely over his city, and may he turn his land into the abandoned hills left by flood.

(l 81–91) *Zababa qarrādum rabium mārum rēštûm ša Ekur āliku imnija ašar tamḫārim kakkašu lišbir ūmam ana mūšim litēršumma nakiršu elišu lišziz*

May the god Zababa, the great warrior, the firstborn son of the Ekur temple, who travels at my right side, smash his weapon upon the field of battle; may he turn day into night for him, and make his enemy triumph over him.

(l 92–li 23) *Ištar bēlet tāḫazim u qablim pātiat kakkija lamassī damiq-tum rā'imat palêja ina libbiša aggim ina uzzātiša rabiātim šarrūssu līrur damqātišu ana lemnētim litēr*[54] *ašar tāḫazim u qablim kakkašu lišbir*[55] *išītam saḫmaštam liškunšum qarrādīšu lišamqit damīšunu erṣetam lišqi gurun šalmāt ummānātišu ina ṣērim littaddi ummānšu rēmam ajušarši šuāti ana qāt nakrīšu limallīšuma ana māt nukurtišu kamîš līrūšu*

May the goddess Ishtar, mistress of battle and warfare, who bares my weapon, my benevolent protective spirit, who loves my reign, curse his kingship with her angry heart and great fury; may she turn his auspicious omens into calamities; may she smash his weapon on the field of war and battle, plunge him into confusion and rebellion, strike down his warriors, drench the earth with their blood, make a heap of the corpses of his soldiers upon the plain, and may she show his soldiers no mercy; as for him, may she deliver him into the hand of his enemies, and may she lead him bound captive to the land of his enemy.

(li 24–39) *Nergal dannum ina ilī qabal la maḫār mušakšidu irnittija ina kašūšišu rabîm kīma išātim ezze-tim ša apim nišīšu liqmi ina kakkišu dannim lišaṭṭīšuma biniātišu kīma ṣalam ṭiddim liḫbuš*

May the god Nergal, the mighty one among the gods, the irresistible onslaught, who enables me to achieve my triumphs, burn his people with his great overpowering weapon like a raging fire in a reed thicket; may he have him beaten with his mighty weapon, and shatter his limbs like (those of) a clay figure.

(li 40–49) *Nintu bēltum ṣīrtum ša mātātim ummum bānītī aplam līṭeršuma šumam aj ušaršīšu ina qerbīt nišīšu zēr awīlūtim aj ibni*

May the goddess Nintu, august mistress of the lands, the mother, my creator, deprive him of an heir and give him no offspring; may she not allow a human child to be born among his people.

(li 50–69) *Ninkarrak mārat Anim qābiat dumqija ina Ekur murṣam kab-*

May the goddess Ninkarrak, daughter of the god Anu, who pro-

tam asakkam lemnam simmam marṣam ša la ipaššeḫu asûm qerebšu la ilammadu ina ṣimdi la unaḫḫušu kīma nišik mūtim la innassaḫu ina biniātišu lišāṣiaššumma adi napištašu ibellû ana eṭlūtišu liddammam

motes my cause in the Ekur temple, cause a grievous malady to break out upon his limbs, an evil demonic disease, a serious carbuncle which cannot be soothed, which a physician cannot diagnose, which he cannot ease with bandages, which, like the bite of death, cannot be expunged;[56] may he bewail his lost virility until his life comes to an end.

(li 70–83) *ilū rabûtum ša šamê u erṣetim Anunnakū ina napḫarišunu šēd bītim libitti Ebabbara šuāti zērašu māssu ṣābašu nišīšu u ummānšu erretam maruštam līruru*

May the great gods of heaven and earth, all the Anunnaku deities together, the protective spirit of the temple, the very brickwork of the Ebabbar temple, curse that one, his seed, his land, his troops, his people, and his army with a terrible curse.

(li 84–91) *errētim anniātim*[57] *Enlil ina pīšu ša la uttakkaru līruršuma arḫiš likšudašu*

May the god Enlil, whose command cannot be countermanded, curse him with these curses and may they swiftly overtake him.

Notes

1. The emendation inserting *šubat*, "the dwelling of" (and following three variants with the genitive *ili* against the stela's nominative *ilu*) follows Reiner 1970: 73, but see the reservations in Borger 1971: 22 n. 5, and see also Ries 1983: 47-48; here, however, I include *mudē igigallim* (iii 17) with the following section dealing with Dilbat and as an epithet of Hammurabi, rather than as a further qualification of the god Tutu of the Ezida temple. Although it is difficult to accept as epithet of Hammurabi *ilu šarrī*, "god among kings" (so, e.g., Borger 1982: 42, and passim in translations; but see *AHw* 372 s.v. *illu(m)* I, already in 1962 expressing doubts about the force of the epithet, and compare the still grandiose but not blasphemous *etel šarrī* [iii 70] and *ašared šarrī* [iv 23]), the emendation of the passage still presents difficulties.

2. Var. *rugummānē [dīnim šuā]ti ippal*, "he shall satisfy the claims for that case."

3. Texts *id*-KI and *iq-bi*, "he has spoken (malicious ...)."

4. Var. possibly *puḫrum*, "the assembly (and the governor ...)," but Borger (1979: 13) prefers reading URU[ki] (*ālum*) to UNKIN (Finkelstein 1967: 45, 47).

5. Error for *iribbušum*, see Gelb 1955: 111.

6. Var. *ana išāti bullîm*, "to put out the fire."

7. Var. *[eqelšu kirāšu] u bītišu ana šanûmma iddinuma*, "they give [his field, his orchard] and his house to another and ..."

8. Text gives the perfect *it-tu-ra-am-ma*.

9. Var. *ṣābē ana nisiḫtim*, "(should recruit(?) [or: induce(?)]) troops for desertion(?)."

10. Var. *ina qāti rēdîm ilteqe*, "or take from the soldier (the gift that ...)."

11. Var. *imaḫḫaṣ imarrar [u i]šakkakma*, "he shall plow, hoe, and harrow."

12. Var. *ana errēšūtim*, "for cultivation."

13. Or "linseed"; see the discussion and literature cited in *CAD* Š/1 306f. s.v. *šamaššammū*.

14. Taken by Donbaz and Sauren (1991: 8-13) as a variant of the preceding provision presented here separately as gap ¶ g.

15. Var. adds *kasapšu*, "(has) his silver (as an interest-bearing loan)."

16. Var. adds *še'amma išu*, "but he has grain."

17. Var. *ikassûšima*, "they shall bind her in fetters and (cast her ...)."

18. Or: "If a *nadītu* who is an *ugbabtu* ..."

19. Text *ukannušuma*, "they shall charge and convict him and ..."

20. The Akkadian *nipûtu* is fem., hence the feminine pronoun, but the person or animal given in distress could be male or female.

21. Or: "(if the distress is) a member of the *awīlu*-class."

22. Var. *šapku ana gamrimma ittadin* (error).

23. Var. *ileqqe*, "he (the owner of the granary) shall take."

24. Others suggest the verb *nadû* (*inaddûšu*), thus "they shall drag that man into the presence of (or: before) the judges," but for that sense (not well attested) the text should have *ana pani dajānī* ...

25. The disease or illness *la'bu* might refer to a contagious skin disease; see Stol 1993b: 143 with literature.

26. Text *inaddûši*, "they shall cast her," var. *inaddûši inaddûšu*, "they shall cast her, they shall cast him."

27. Some emend to <*mu*>*rabbītišu*, "the woman who raised him (i.e., his father's wife)" (so *CAD* M/2 216 s.v., and cf. MAL A ¶ 51 cited *CAD* s.v. *rabû* A mng. 5a-1'), but with Cardascia (1980: 12-13 with n. 22) I prefer the sense obtained from the feminine adjective, without emending the manuscripts.

28. Var. *ana mārī*, "for the (eligible) sons."

29. Var. reverses the order: *mārū amtim u mārū ḫīrtim* ..., "the children of the slave woman and the children of the first-ranking wife (shall divide ...)."

30. Var. omits "during his lifetime" (*šumma abum ana [mārī] ša amtum ul[dušum ...]*).

31. Var. *ulu warad awīlim*, "(she enters the house of the slave of the palace) or of the slave of an *awīlum*."

32. Var. *ikšudu*, "they attain (possessions)."

33. Var. *elēnumma ileqqe*, "she shall take in addition."

34. Var. adds *bītam*, "(the usufruct of the field, orchard,) house (or anything ...)."

35. Var. *išṭurušim*, "(which her father) wrote for her."

36. Var. *kulmašītum*.

37. Stol 1979 suggests a third class of priestess, reading É.GI$_4$.A (*kallatum*, usually "bride" or "daughter-in-law") rather than GÁ.GI$_4$.A (*gagûm*, "cloistered").

38. That is, not the preferential (double) inheritance share of a primary heir, but

the single share of any other heir; the terminology derives from the paradigmatic case of two heirs in which the estate is divided into three parts.

39. See note at ¶ 181.

40. See note at ¶ 181.

41. Or IGI.5.GÁL, "one fifth."

42. Var. *iddâk*, "(the son of the builder) shall be killed."

43. Var. *šēpšu ištebir ulu gilissu ištaḫaṭ*, "breaks its leg or flays its hide."

44. Var. *ina alpim*, "by an ox."

45. Akkadian expresses this in the active voice ("they shall drag him around ...").

46. Literally, "a plague (or touch) of the god."

47. Or *zadimmu*, "lapidary."

48. See Stol 1993b, especially pp. 133ff.

49. The understanding of *šar mīšarim*, "king of justice," as an epithet of Hammurabi here (xlvii 77) and below (xlviii 7) agrees with that put forth in *CAD* N/1 364a s.v. *narû* A mng. 1, and is supported by the repetition of the phrase elsewhere in the epilogue (xlviii 96 and xlix 13), where it clearly is a royal epithet in apposition to a proper noun or a pronoun.

50. EN, read *bēlum*, "lord," or *ēnum*, "high priest."

51. See *CAD* Š/3 s.v. *šuppuḫu*.

52. Var. "his city."

53. Emended, with *CAD* A/2 203b; text *še-re-sú*.

54. *li-te-er* mistakenly repeated in the last line of column l and the first line of column li.

55. Variant (source w) provides a bilingual Sumerian-Akkadian version from here (li 5) through li 75.

56. Bilingual var. reads [...] su-ni-šè (error for -ta) na-an-zi-zi : *ina šīrišu la itebbû*, "which cannot rise up(?) from his flesh"; see the comments in Sjöberg 1991: 223.

57. Text DA-*ni-a-tim*.

9

Neo-Babylonian Laws (LNB) (ca. 700 B.C.E., Sippar)

From the middle of the second millennium, after the weakening and ultimately the demise of the Old Babylonian dynasty of Hammurabi, the military supremacy of the Assyrian empire held most of the ancient Near East, including Babylonia, under its domination. But toward the end of the seventh century B.C.E., when Babylonian and Median forces decisively defeated the Assyrians and the Neo-Babylonian (or Chaldean) dynasty (625–539 B.C.E.) became the political and military successor to the Sargonid kings of the Neo-Assyrian empire, Babylonia had regained a position of economic and military strength. During the reigns of the first of the Neo-Babylonian kings, Nabopolassar and Nebuchadnezzar, there were conscious attempts to emulate the achievements of Hammurabi's dynasty more than a millennium earlier, in temple and public building projects, social reforms, scientific (especially astronomical) and literary enterprises, legal and bureaucratic organizations, etc. This is the Babylon of political and cultural sophistication that, with its ziggurat temple tower and hanging gardens, entered the popular imagination and found expression in biblical and classical writings. By the end of the sixth century B.C.E., however, the expanding Persian state under Cyrus the Great swept through Babylonia. Cyrus incorporated Babylonia into his empire as a satrapy, ending independent native rule in Mesopotamia.

About the Laws

Fifteen law provisions are preserved. There is no recognizable prologue or epilogue. The tablet is a copy of a damaged original, or records a collection assembled from incomplete sources, as is demonstrated by the brief two-line notation (written in the middle of an otherwise blank space with room for approximately ten lines) that follows ¶ 7. The preserved laws cover topics including agriculture and irrigation, purchase by proxy, slave sales, unauthorized performance of a magic or ritual act, marriage, marital property, and inheritance.

The protases of all the extant provisions (except ¶ 13) begin *amēlu* (etc.) *ša*, "a man (or woman, wife, etc.) who ...," constructed with preterite subjunctive forms (translated as presents) to express the points of the case. Each provision is marked off and concluded with a horizontal ruling on the tablet.

The laws are concerned only with the class of free person (*amēlu*); the slave (*amēluttu*) is mentioned as personal property, but is not the subject of any law.

About the Source

One tablet in the British Museum, London, possibly from Sippar, preserves the remains of three columns on each side and originally recorded between fifteen and eighteen laws. The left side of the tablet, with columns i and vi, is eroded, and thus the damaged opening and concluding lines, where one might expect to find a heading or colophon, are of little help in determining the composition's date or an attribution to a particular ruler; on internal evidence, the tablet is to be dated to the early part of the Neo-Babylonian period, i.e., to the early seventh century B.C.E. (see Roth 1989a: 29 n. 89).

The author's collations made in the summer of 1978 and again in the summer of 1993 confirm in most details those reported by Borger 1982d: 92–93 n. a.

(i 1–20) [...]-*ma* [...]-*ru* [...]-*tam-mu* [...] ⌈*i-tu*⌉-*ru* [...] *ina pani bēl eqli* [...]-*tu x* [...] *ina pani bēl eqli x* [...]-*x-ru* [...]-*x-x-tam-mu* [...] *x bēl eqli* [...]-*din* [...] KÁM [...] *ta-din-nu* [...] *x* [...]-*il*?-*ma*-[...]-*x* [...] *x x x* [...] *išṭuru* [...] MU.2.KÁM [...]-*a*? LUGAL *x x x* [...] *x x x* [...]-*x-x-x-a-ti*

¶ 1 [...] in the presence of the owner of the field [...] in the presence of the owner of the field [...] the owner of the field [...] they wrote [...] year 2 [...] the king [...]

(i 21–34) [*amēlu ša* ...] *x-e-nu* [...] *eqli* [...]-*ma* [...]-*du-ma* [... *ir*]*ʾû* [... *ir*]*ʾû* [...].MEŠ [...] *mukinnūssu* [(*ša*) *ina*]*ššû* [...]-*id rit-ti ša eqli* [...] *kî itê* [*ana*] *bēl*

¶ 2 [A man who ...] field [...] pastures [...] he pastures [...] the testimony which he will provide ... of the field [...], he shall give [grain] in

eqli inandin [...] MAN-[... *mala ina eq*]*li ir'û* [*k*]*î itê uṭṭata inandin*

accordance with the (yields of his) neighbor to the owner of the field; [... as much as] he pastured, he shall give grain in accordance with the (yields of his) neighbor.

(i 35–41) [*amēlu ša*] *būrašu ana mašqītu* [*ipt*]*û la udanninuma* [...] *x ibtuquma* [*eqel it*]*êšu* [*uṭab*]*bû* [*uṭṭata kî*] *itê* [*ana bēl eqli*] *inandin*

¶ **3** [A man who opens] his well to the irrigation outlet but does not reinforce it, and who thus causes a breach and thereby [floods] his neighbor's field, shall give [grain in accordance with the (yields of his)] neighbor [to the owner of the field].

(i 42–ii 3) [...] *parû* [...]-*tum* [...] *x kî mi-i-x* [...]-*qu u*(-)*še-eb*(-) [...]-*x inandin*

¶ **4** [...] an onager [...] he shall give.

(ii 4–14) *amēlu ša ṭuppi ša bēl eqli u bīti ana šumi ša mamma*[1] *iknukuma riksu ša našpartu ana muḫḫi la irkusu u gabarî ṭuppi la ilqû amēlu ša ṭuppa u u'ilti ana šumišu šaṭrū eqla lu bīta šuāti ileqqe*

¶ **5** A man who seals a tablet as owner of (i.e., who bought) a field or a house in another's name, but does not make out a contract of proxy for the matter or does not take a copy of the tablet–it is the man in whose name the tablet and sale document are written who shall take the field or house.

(ii 15–23) *amēlu ša amēlutti ana kaspi iddinuma paqāru ina muḫḫi ibšûma abkati nādinānu kaspa kî pī u'ilti ina qaqqadišu ana māḫirānu inandin kî mārē tuldu ina ištēn ½ šiqil kaspa inandin*

¶ **6** A man who sells a slave woman against whom a claim arises so that she is taken away–the seller shall give to the buyer the silver (of the purchase price) in its capital amount according to the sale document. Should she bear children (while in the possession of the buyer), he shall give half a shekel of silver for each.

(ii 24–45) *amēltu ša nēpešu lu takpirtu ina eqel amēli*[2] <<*x x x*>> *lu ina* [*elip*]*pi lu ina utūni lu ina mimma šumšu*[3] *tukappiru iṣṣī ša* [*ina lib*]*bi*

¶ **7**[7] A woman who performs a magic act or a ritual purification against(?) (i.e., in order to affect?) a man's field, or a boat, or an oven, or

tukappiru bilassu ištēn adi 3 ana bēl eqli tanandin šumma ina elippi[4] *ina utūni u mimma šumšu tukappiru miṭīti ša ina eqli taššakkanu ištēn adi*[5] *3 tanandin kî ina bāb [bīt] amēli x x [...]-x*[6] *ṣabtatu taddâ[ku]*

anything whatsoever—(if it is a field, then concerning) the trees (or: wood) among which(?) she performs the ritual, she shall give to the owner of the field threefold its yield. If she performs the purification against(?) (i.e., in order to affect?) a boat, or an oven, or anything else, she shall give threefold the losses caused to the property (text: field). Should she be seized [performing the purification] against(?) (i.e., in order to affect?) the door of a man's [house], she shall be killed.

(iii 1–2) *dīnšu ul qati u ul šaṭir*

Its case[8] is not complete and is not written (here).

(iii 3–22) *amēlu ša mārassu ana mār amēli iddinuma abu mimma ina ṭuppišu ušēdûma ana mārišu iddinu u emu nudunnû ša mārtišu ušēdûma ṭuppī itti aḫāmeš išṭuru ṭuppašunu ul innû abi nušurrû ina mimma ša ana mārišu ina ṭuppi išṭuruma ana emišu ukallimu ul išakkan kīma abu aššassu šīmti ublu*[9] *aššati arkīti ītaḫzuma mārē ittaldušu šalšu ina rēḫet nikkassīšu mārū arkīti ileqqû*

¶ **8** A man who gives his daughter in marriage to a member of the *amēlu*-class, and the father (of the groom) commits certain properties in his tablet and awards them to his son, and the father-in-law commits the dowry of his daughter, and they write the tablets in mutual agreement—they will not alter the commitments of their respective tablets. The father will not make any reduction to the properties as written in the tablet to his son's benefit which he showed to his in-law. Even should the father, whose wife fate carries away, then marry a second wife and should she then bear him sons, the sons of the second woman shall take one third[10] of the balance of his estate.

(iii 23–31) *amēlu ša nudunnû ana mārtišu iqbûma lu ṭuppi išṭurušu u arki nikkassīšu imṭû akî nikkassīšu ša rēḫi nudunnû ana mārtišu inandin eme u ḫatanu aḫāmeš ul innû*

¶ **9** A man who makes an oral promise of the dowry for his daughter, or writes it on a tablet for her, and whose estate later decreases—he shall give to his daughter a dowry in accordance with the remaining assets of his estate; the father-in-law (i.e., the bride's father) and the groom will not by mutual agreement alter the commitments.

(iii 32–36) *amēlu ša nudunnû ana mārtišu iddinuma māra u mārta la tišû u šīmti ubluš nudunnāšu ana bīt abišu itâri*[11]

¶ **10** A man who gives a dowry to his daughter, and she has no son or daughter, and fate carries her away—her dowry shall revert to her paternal estate.

(iv 1–8) [*aššatu ša*...] *ana* [...] *šī*[*mti ubluš* (...)] *ana muḫḫi māri x x nudunnāšu ana mutišu u ana mamma ša panīšu maḫru tanandin*

¶ **11** [A wife who ...] fate [carries her away (...)] to a son [...]—she shall give her dowry to her husband or to whomever she wishes.

(iv 9–25) *aššatu ša nudunnāšu mussu ilqû māra u mārta la tišû u mussu šīmti ublu ina nikkassī ša mutišu nudunnû mala nudunnû innandinšu šumma mussu širiktu ištarakšu širikti ša mutišu itti nudunnêšu taleqqēma aplat šumma nudunnû la tiši dajānu nikkassī ša mutišu imma*[*r*]*ma kî nikkassī ša mutišu mimma inandinšu*

¶ **12** A wife whose husband takes her dowry, and who has no son or daughter, and whose husband fate carries away—a dowry equivalent to the dowry (which her husband had received) shall be given to her from her husband's estate. If her husband should award to her a marriage gift, she shall take her husband's marriage gift together with her dowry, and thus her claim is satisfied. If she has no dowry, a judge shall assess the value of her husband's estate, and shall give to her some property in accordance with the value of her husband's estate.

(iv 26–v 4) *amēlu aššata īḫuzma mārē ulissu arki amēlu šuāti šīmti ubilšuma amēltu šuāti ana bīt šanî erēbi panīšu iltakan nudunnâ ša ultu bīt abišu tublu u mimma ša mussu išrukušu ileqqēma muti libbišu iḫḫassi adi ūmē balṭatu akalu itti aḫ*[*āmeš*] *ina libbi ikk*[*alu*] *šumma ana mu*[*tišu*]

¶ **13** A man marries a wife, and she bears him sons, and later on fate carries away that man, and that woman then decides to enter another man's house—she shall take (from her first husband's estate) the dowry that she brought from her father's house and any-

mārē it[taldu] arkišu mārū [arkī] u mārū maḫ[rī] nudun[nāšu] aḫāti [šunu][12] [...]

thing that her husband awarded to her, and the husband she chooses shall marry her; as long as she lives, they shall have the joint use of the properties. If she should bear sons to her (second) husband, after her death the sons of the second and first (husbands) shall have equal shares in her dowry. [...]

(v 5–31) [...]-*x-x-šú* [...] *mutišu* [...] *x taleqqû* [...]-*ab ina muḫḫi abišu u* [...][13]

¶ **14** [...] her husband [...] she shall take [...] to her father [...]

(v 32–44, vi 1ff.) *amēlu ša aššata īḫuzuma mārē uldušuma aššassu šīmti ublu aššati šanīti īḫuzuma mārē uldušu arki abu ana šīmtu ittalku ina nikkassī ša bīt abi* 2.TA *qātāti mārē maḫrīti u šalšu mārē arkīti ileqqû aḫḫātišunu ša ina bīt abi ašbāma* (vi 1ff.) [...]

¶ **15** A man who marries a wife who bears him sons, and whose wife fate carries away, and who marries a second wife who bears him sons, and later on the father goes to his fate–the sons of the first woman shall take two-thirds of the paternal estate, and the sons of the second shall take one-third. Their sisters, who are still residing in the paternal home [...]

Colophon

(vi x+1-2) [...]-*a*? [(...) *šar*] *Bābili*

[... king of] the city of Babylon.

Notes

1. Written (here in ii 5 and again in ¶ 11, iv 7) MAN-*ma*, possibly to be read *šanîma*.
2. The beginning of ii 27, reading *ina* A.ŠÀ LÚ, is clear and the wedges are incised deeply on the tablet; in contrast, the wedges that follow are faint and partially obscured by the signs of the lines both above and below. The readings for these wedges proposed by previous editors are all unsatisfactory, and I conclude that the final signs simply were incompletely erased by the scribe.
3. Text: *šum-ma* (error).
4. The copy's line 36 (reading *tu-kap-pi-ru*) is not on the tablet.
5. Read *ištēn adi*, although the first signs are represented as the ligature 1+*en*.
6. The entire line (ii 43) is damaged, and no satisfactory reading can be provided.

7. The difficult provision deals with a case in which a woman sought to undermine the basis of a man's livelihood—exemplified by the selection of the essentials of three common professions: a farmer's field, a boatman's boat, and a baker's or potter's kiln—for which, in the first and second apodoses, she is to compensate the man threefold for his loss. One of the many obstacles to a full understanding of the provision is the sense of the preposition *ina* which is most commonly used as a locative preposition ("in"), but also can be a causative or an instrumental. My understanding of the provision takes *ina* as a causative, thus "... performed a magic act ... *in order to cause harm* to a man's field ..." But it is also possible to understand *ina* as an instrumental particle, thus the woman would be using a model or figurine representing the profession (a model of a tree, a boat, or a kiln) in her act of magic, or as the common locative, thus the woman would be performing her magic within the field, boat, oven, etc. In any case, at least one scribal error appears and an emendation is necessary: "... caused to the property (text: field)." The third and final case is damaged, but the protasis presents a variant situation in which she appears to be performing the act of magic against a man's private residence, thus bringing harm to his entire household, for which the apodosis calls for the woman's death.

8. The Akkadian word *dīnu* is translatable as "case," "decision," or "judgment," and refers both to the entire proceedings of a suit or trial and to the decision rendered by the officiating judge; this is the term used in the LH, for example, at the beginning of the epilogue, in order to characterize the preceding law provisions as Hammurabi's "just decisions." The antecedent of "its" is not clear; the reference could be, for example, to a defective original examplar from which this tablet was copied, or to a court case that has not yet been decided.

9. Only the first sign of the word is clear in iii 17 (= iii 24 in Borger 1982d: 92–93 n. a), and none of the expected readings can be confirmed.

10. I.e., not the preferential or double share; see n. 38 to LH ¶ 181.

11. There is an incised line at the bottom of column iii, marking the end of the provision.

12. There is no line incised at the bottom of column iv, thus indicating that the provision continued into the first lines of the next column.

13. There may be more than one provision lost in the breaks of these fragmentary lines.

Translations

C. Assyrian

10

Middle Assyrian Laws (MAL) (ca. 1076 B.C.E., Assur)

By the mid-fourteenth century, political and military control of the Near East was in the hands of the Hittites in Anatolia, the Egyptians in the Mediterranean coastal areas, the Assyrians in northern Mesopotamia, and the Kassites in southern Mesopotamia. The Assyrian king Ashur-uballiṭ I (r. 1363–1328 B.C.E.) challenged the dominance of the Hittite New Kingdom; Tukultī-Ninurta I (r. 1243–1207 B.C.E.) captured Babylon; by the time of Tiglath-pileser I (r. 1114–1076 B.C.E.), both Kassite Babylonia and Hittite Anatolia were no longer forces in the region, and Assyria was established as the unrivaled political power in the region.

About the Laws

Each "tablet" (A through O) of the Middle Assyrian Laws is represented by only one source, with the exception of MAL A, which does have a late but fragmentary duplicate, and the duplication of provisions in MAL B and MAL O. Thus, we have a series of tablets with law provisions, rather than a single systematic, reconstructed, composition. Some of the tablets appear to record laws dealing with one or more related concerns, most prominently the well-preserved MAL A, which deals almost exclusively with laws in which women figure as victims or principals. The specific situations in the fifty-nine provisions of MAL A, however, range throughout the legal realm, and include theft, blasphemy, deposit, bodily injury and assault, sexual assault and sexual offenses, homicide, false accusations, inheritance, marriage and matrimonial property, veiling, witchcraft, pledges and debts, and abortion. The twenty provisions in MAL B include situations dealing with inheritance, and with agriculture and irrigation. MAL C+G has eleven provisions, generally dealing with pledges and deposits. In the remaining tablets, all smaller and less well preserved, some topics covered are: theft, herders' responsibilities, maritime traffic rules, blasphemy, false accusations, inheritance, irrigation.

Almost all the paragraphs begin with *šumma* and are clearly marked on the cuneiform tablets by single incised horizontal lines. The rationale for such divisions is not, however, always clear; some separate provisions are variations or alternative situations which should be considered together as one legal situation, and in other cases longer paragraphs include multiple subparagraphs that might logically be separated. To facilitate the translations of these longer, sometimes rambling, paragraphs, line numbers are occasionally presented with the beginning of a new situation or variation, usually introduced by Akkadian *šumma*, "if."

The laws in the MAL consider two principal classes of person, the free person (*a'īlu*, "man"), and the male and female slave (*urdu* and *amtu*).[1] MAL A, which is concerned with regulations involving women of the *a'īlu*-class, refers to wives, widows, and devotees of the *qadiltu*-class.

About the Sources

The provisions are found on a number of tablets, almost all of which are eleventh century B.C.E. copies of earlier fourteenth-century originals, excavated in the Assyrian capital Assur.[2] One later Neo-Assyrian fragment is a fragmentary piece from Nineveh which duplicates some of the first paragraphs of MAL A. The only preserved date formula, on the Middle Assyrian copy of MAL A, refers to an official named Sagiu, during the reign of Tiglath-pileser I (r. 1114–1076 B.C.E. or, with Freydank 1991, of Ninurta-apil-ekur, r. 1191–1179 B.C.E.). Although the tablets were written and the collection assembled probably during the reign of that Assyrian monarch, it is uncertain whether the recovered texts were compiled for his royal library (Weidner 1952/53b) or for later scribes' personal libraries (Lambert 1976: 85-86 n. 2).

The provision numbers used here conform to those in the standard editions; the reader must be aware, however, that there are gaps at the beginnings and ends of columns or surfaces in which an unknown number of provisions might be lost, and that these gaps are not reflected in the sequence of provision numbers. Thus, for example, in MAL B the entire first and last columns are lost, and undetermined portions of the beginnings and ends of columns are missing, but the provision numbering is sequential without gaps; MAL N is known from a fragment with one surface preserving only the left edge (but not the beginning) and portions of two provisions. Thus, although provision numbers within each Tablet begin with "1," the first preserved provision might not have been the first on the complete tablet.

MAL A

(a i 1–13; b 1–4) *šumma sinniltu lu aššat aʾīle u lu mār[at] aʾīle [ana] bēt ile tētarab ina bēt ile mimma [ša eš]rēte t[alti]riq [ina qātēša] iṣṣabi[t]*[3] *u lu ubtaʾeruši lu uktaʾinu[ši] bārûta* [...] *ila išaʾ[ulu] u kî ša ilu [ana epāše iq]ab[biuni] eppušuši*

A ¶ 1 If a woman,[4] either a man's wife or a man's daughter, should enter into a temple and steal something from the sanctuary in the temple[5] and either it is discovered in her possession or they prove the charges against her and find her guilty, [they shall perform(?)] a divination(?), they shall inquire of the deity; they shall treat her as the deity instructs them.

(a i 14–22; b 5–7) *šumma sinniltu lu aššat aʾīle u lu mārat aʾīle šillata taqṭibi lu miqit pê tartiši sinniltu šīt aranša tanašši ana mutiša mārēša mārāteša la iqarribu*

A ¶ 2 If a woman,[6] either a man's wife or a man's daughter, should speak something disgraceful or utter a blasphemy, that woman alone bears responsibility for her offense; they shall have no claim against her husband, her sons, or her daughters.

(a i 23–45; b 8–10) *šumma aʾīlu lu mariṣ lu mēt aššassu ina bētišu mimma taltiriq lu ana aʾīle lu ana sinnilte u lu ana mamma šanêmma tattidin aššat aʾīle u māḫirānūtema idukkušunu* (a i 32) *u šumma aššat aʾīle ša mussa balṭuni ina bēt mutiša taltiriq lu ana aʾīle lu ana sinnilte u lu ana mamma šanêmma tattidin aʾīlu aššassu ubaʾar u ḫīṭa emmed u māḫirānu ša ina qāt aššat aʾīle imḫuruni šurqa iddan u ḫīṭa kî ša aʾīlu aššassu ēmiduni māḫirāna emmidu*

A ¶ 3 If a man is either ill or dead, and his wife should steal something from his house and give it either to a man, or to a woman, or to anyone else, they shall kill the man's wife as well as the receivers (of the stolen goods). (a i 32) And if a man's wife, whose husband is healthy, should steal from her husband's house and give it either to a man, or to a woman, or to anyone else, the man shall prove the charges against his wife and shall impose a punishment; the receiver who received (the stolen goods) from the man's wife shall hand over the stolen goods, and they shall impose a punishment on the receiver identical to that which the man imposed on his wife.

(i 46–56[7]) *šumma lu urdu lu amtu ina qāt aššat a᾿īle mimma imtaḫru ša urde u amte appēšunu uznēšunu unakkusu šurqa umallû a᾿īlu ša aššiti[šu] uznēša unakkas u šumma aššassu uššer [uz]nēša la unakkis ša urde u amte la unakkusuma šurqa la umallû*

A ¶ 4 If either a slave or a slave woman should receive something from a man's wife, they shall cut off the slave's or slave woman's nose and ears; they shall restore the stolen goods; the man shall cut off his own wife's ears. But if he releases his wife and does not cut off her ears, they shall not cut off (the nose and ears) of the slave or slave woman, and they shall not restore the stolen goods.

(i 57–69) *šumma aššat a᾿īle ina bēt a᾿īle šanêmma mimma taltiriq ana qāt 5 mana anneke tūtatter bēl šurqe itamma mā šumma ušāḫizušini mā ina bētija širqī* (i 63) *šumma mussa magir šurqa iddan u ipaṭṭarši uznēša unakkas šumma mussa ana paṭāriša la imaggur bēl šurqe ilaqqēši u appaša inakkis*

A ¶ 5 If a man's wife should steal something with a value greater than 300 shekels of lead[8] from the house of another man, the owner of the stolen goods shall take an oath, saying, "I did not incite her, saying, 'Commit a theft in my house.'" (i 63) If her husband is in agreement, he (her husband) shall hand over the stolen goods and he shall ransom her; he shall cut off her ears. If her husband does not agree to her ransom, the owner of the stolen goods shall take her and he shall cut off her nose.

(i 70–73) *šumma aššat a᾿īle maškatta ina kīde taltakan māḫirānu šurqa inašši*

A ¶ 6 If a man's wife should place goods for safekeeping outside of the family, the receiver of the goods shall bear liability for stolen property.

(i 74–77) *šumma sinniltu qāta ana a᾿īle tattabal ubta᾿eruši 30 mana annaka taddan 20 ina ḫaṭṭāte imaḫḫuṣuši*

A ¶ 7 If a woman should lay a hand upon a man and they prove the charges against her, she shall pay 1,800 shekels of lead; they shall strike her 20 blows with rods.

(i 78–87) *šumma sinniltu ina ṣalte iška ša a᾿īle taḫtepi 1 ubānša inakkisu u šumma asû urtakkisma išku šanītu*

A ¶ 8 If a woman should crush a man's testicle during a quarrel, they shall cut off one of her fin-

iltešama tattalpat [*x*]*-ri-im-ma tartiši* [*u*] *lu ina ṣalte* [*iš*]*ka šanīta taḫtepi* [....M]EŠ-*ša kilallūn inappulu*

gers. And even if the physician should bandage it, but the second testicle then becomes infected(?) along with it and becomes ...,[9] or if she should crush the second testicle during the quarrel—they shall gouge out both her [...]-s.[10]

(i 88–96) [*šumma*] *a'īlu qāta ana aššat a'īle* [*u*]*bil kî būre ēpussi* [*ub*]*ta'eruš* [*uk*]*ta'inuš* [1] *ubānšu inakkisu* [*šumm*]*a ittišiqši* [*ša*]*passu šaplīta* [*ana p*]*an erimte ša pāše* [*iša*]*ddudu inakkisu*

A ¶ 9 If a man lays a hand upon a woman, attacking her like a rutting bull(?), and they prove the charges against him and find him guilty, they shall cut off one of his fingers. If he should kiss her, they shall draw his lower lip across the blade(?) of an ax and cut it off.

(i 97–ii 6) [*šumma l*]*u a'īlu lu sinniltu* [*ana bēt a'īle*] *ērubuma* [*lu a'īla l*]*u sinnilta idūku* [*ana bēl bēte*] *dā'ikānūte* [*iddunu*] *panūšuma* [*idukk*]*ušunu* [*panūšuma imma*]*ggar* [*mimmâšunu*] *ilaqqe* (ii 1) [*u šumma ina bē*]*t dā'i*[*kānūte*] *mimm*[*a ša tadāne laššu*] *lu mā*[*ra lu mārta* ...] *im* [...]

A ¶ 10 [If either] a man or a woman enters [another man's] house and kills [either a man] or a woman, [they shall hand over] the manslayers [to the head of the household]; if he so chooses, he shall kill them, or if he chooses to come to an accommodation, he shall take [their property]; and if there is [nothing of value to give from the house] of the manslayers, either a son [or a daughter ...]

(ii 7-13) [*šumma* ...] *ši*-[...] *ša* [*x x*] *x pa-a-*[...]*-li*

A ¶ 11 [If ...]

(ii 14–24) *šumma aššat a'īle ina rebēte tētetiq a'īlu iṣṣabassu lanīkkime iqṭibiašše la tamaggur tattanaṣṣar emūqamma iṣṣabassi ittiakši lu ina muḫḫi aššat a'īle ikšuduš u lu kî sinnilta inīkuni šēbūtu ubta'eruš a'īla idukku ša sinnilte ḫīṭu laššu*

A ¶ 12 If a wife of a man should walk along the main thoroughfare and should a man seize her and say to her, "I want to have sex with you!"[11]—she shall not consent but she shall protect herself; should he seize her by force and fornicate with her—whether they discover him upon the woman or witnesses later prove the charges against him that he fornicated with the woman—they shall kill the man; there is no punishment for the woman.

(ii 25–29) *šumma aššat aʾīle ištu bētiša tattiṣīma ana muḫḫi aʾīle ašar usbuni tattalak ittiakši kî aššat aʾīlenni īde aʾīla u aššata idukku*

A ¶ 13 If the wife of a man should go out of her own house, and go to another man where he resides, and should he fornicate with her knowing that she is the wife of a man, they shall kill the man and the wife.

(ii 30–40) *šumma aššat aʾīle aʾīlu lu ina bēt altamme lu ina rebēte kî aššat aʾīlenni ide ittiakši kî aʾīlu ša aššassu ana epāše iqabbiuni nāʾikāna eppušu šumma kî aššat aʾīlenni la īde ittiakši nāʾikānu zaku aʾīlu aššassu ubâr kî libbišu eppassi*

A ¶ 14 If a man should fornicate with another man's wife either in an inn or in the main thoroughfare, knowing that she is the wife of a man, they shall treat the fornicator as the man declares he wishes his wife to be treated. If he should fornicate with her without knowing that she is the wife of a man, the fornicator is clear; the man shall prove the charges against his wife and he shall treat her as he wishes.

(ii 41–57) *šumma aʾīlu ištu aššitišu aʾīla iṣṣabat ubtaʾeruš uktaʾinuš kilallēšunuma idukkušunu aranšu laššu šumma iṣṣabta lu ana muḫḫi šarre lu ana muḫḫi dajānī ittabla ubtaʾeruš uktaʾinuš šumma mut sinnilte aššassu iduak u aʾīla iduakma šumma appa ša aššitišu inakkis aʾīla ana ša rēšēn utâr u panīšu gabba inaqquru u šumma aššass[u uššar] aʾīla u[ššar]*

A ¶ 15 If a man should seize another man upon his wife and they prove the charges against him and find him guilty, they shall kill both of them; there is no liability for him (i.e., the husband). If he should seize him and bring him either before the king or the judges, and they prove the charges against him and find him guilty—if the woman's husband kills his wife, then he shall also kill the man; if he cuts off his wife's nose, he shall turn the man into a eunuch and they shall lacerate his entire face; but if [he wishes to release] his wife, he shall [release] the man.

(ii 58–66) *šumma aʾīlu aššat [aʾīle ...] pīša [...] ḫīṭu ša aʾīle laššu aʾīlu aššassu ḫīṭa kî libbišu emmid šumma*

A ¶ 16 If a man [should fornicate] with the wife of a man [... by] her invitation, there is no punishment

emūqamma ittiakši ubtaʾeruš uktaʾinuš ḫīṭašu kî ša aššat aʾīlemma

for the man; the man (i.e., husband) shall impose whatever punishment he chooses upon his wife. If he should fornicate with her by force and they prove the charges against him and find him guilty, his punishment shall be identical to that of the wife of the man.

(ii 67–71) *šumma aʾīlu ana aʾīle iqtibi mā aššatka ittinikku šēbūtu laššu riksāte išakkunu ana Id illuku*

A ¶ 17 If a man should say to another man, "Everyone has sex with[12] your wife," but there are no witnesses, they shall draw up a binding agreement, they shall undergo the divine River Ordeal.

(ii 72-81) *šumma aʾīlu ana tappāʾišu lu ina puzre lu ina ṣalte iqbi mā aššatka ittinikku mā anāku ubâr baʾura la ilaʾe la ubaʾer aʾīla šuātu* 40 *ina ḫaṭṭāte imaḫḫuṣuš iltēn uraḫ ūmāte šipar šarre eppaš igaddimuš u* 1 *bilat annaka iddan*

A ¶ 18 If a man says to his comrade, either in private or in a public quarrel, "Everyone has sex with[13] your wife," and further, "I can prove the charges," but he is unable to prove the charges and does not prove the charges, they shall strike that man 40 blows with rods; he shall perform the king's service for one full month; they shall cut off his hair;[14] moreover, he shall pay 3,600 shekels of lead.

(ii 82–92) *šumma aʾīlu ina puzre ina muḫḫi tappāʾišu abata iškun mā ittinikkuš lu ina ṣalte ana pani ṣābē iqbiaššu mā ittinikkuka mā ubârka baʾura la ilaʾe la ubaʾer aʾīla šuātu* 50 *ina ḫaṭṭāte imaḫḫuṣuš iltēn uraḫ ūmāte šipar šarre eppaš igaddimuš u* 1 *bilat annaka iddan*

A ¶ 19 If a man furtively spreads rumors about his comrade, saying, "Everyone sodomizes him,"[15] or in a quarrel in public says to him, "Everyone sodomizes you," and further, "I can prove the charges against you," but he is unable to prove the charges and does not prove the charges, they shall strike that man 50 blows with rods; he shall perform the king's service for one full month; they shall cut off his hair;[16] moreover, he shall pay 3,600 shekels of lead.

(ii 93–97) *šumma a'īlu tappâšu inīk ubta'eruš ukta'inuš inikkuš ana ša rēšēn utarruš*

A ¶ 20 If a man sodomizes[17] his comrade and they prove the charges against him and find him guilty, they shall sodomize him and they shall turn him into a eunuch.

(ii 98–104) *šumma a'īlu mārat a'īle imḫaṣma ša libbiša ultaṣlēš ubta'eruš ukta'inuš 2 bilat 30 mana annaka iddan 50 ina ḫaṭṭāte imaḫḫuṣuš iltēn uraḫ ūmāte šipar šarre eppaš*

A ¶ 21 If a man strikes a woman of the *a'īlu*-class thereby causing her to abort her fetus, and they prove the charges against him and find him guilty—he shall pay 9,000 shekels of lead; they shall strike him 50 blows with rods; he shall perform the king's service for one full month.

(ii 105–iii 13) *šumma aššat a'īle la abuša la aḫuša la māruša a'īlu šani=umma ḫarrāna ultaṣbissi u kî aššat a'īlenni la īde itamma u 2 bilat anna=ka ana mut sinnilte iddan [šu]mma kî [aššat a'īlenni īde b]itqāte idd[anma itamma m]ā šumma anī[kušini] u šumma aššat [a'īle taqṭibi m]ā ittīkanni [kî a']īlu bitqāte [ana] a'īle iddinuni [ana] Id illak [rik]sātušu laššu šumma ina Id ittūra kî mut sin=nilte aššassu eppušuni ana šuāšu eppušuš*

A ¶ 22 If an unrelated man—neither her father, nor her brother, nor her son—should arrange to have a man's wife travel with him, then he shall swear an oath to the effect that he did not know that she is the wife of a man and he shall pay 7,200 shekels of lead to the woman's husband. If [he knows that she is the wife of a man], he shall pay damages and he shall swear, saying, "I did not fornicate with her." But if the man's wife should declare, "He did fornicate with me," since the man has already paid damages to the man (i.e., husband), he shall undergo the divine River Ordeal; there is no binding agreement. If he should refuse to undergo the divine River Ordeal, they shall treat him as the woman's husband treats his wife.

(iii 14–40) *šumma aššat a'īle aššat a'īlimma ana bētiša talteqe ana a'īle ana niāke tattidinši u a'īlu kî aššat a'īlenni īde kî ša aššat a'īle inīkuni*

A ¶ 23 If a man's wife should take another man's wife into her house and give her to a man for purposes of fornication, and the man knows

eppušuš u kî ša mut sinnilte aššassu nīkta eppušuni mummerta eppušu u šumma mut sinnilte aššassu nīkta mimma la eppaš nā'ikāna u mummerta mimma la eppušu uššurušunu u šumma aššat a'īle la tīde u sinniltu ša ana bētiša talqeušini kî pīge a'īla ana muḫḫiša tultērib u ittiakši šumma ištu bēte ina uṣāiša kî nīkutuni taqṭibi sinnilta uššuru zakuat nā'ikāna u mummerta idukku u šumma sinniltu la taqṭibi a'īlu aššassu ḫīṭa kî libbišu emmid nā'ikāna u mummerta idukku

that she is the wife of a man, they shall treat him as one who has fornicated with the wife of another man; and they treat the female procurer just as the woman's husband treats his fornicating wife. And if the woman's husband intends to do nothing to his fornicating wife, they shall do nothing to the fornicator or to the female procurer; they shall release them. But if the man's wife does not know (what was intended), and the woman who takes her into her house brings the man in to her by deceit(?), and he then fornicates with her—if, as soon as she leaves the house, she should declare that she has been the victim of fornication, they shall release the woman, she is clear; they shall kill the fornicator and the female procurer. But if the woman should not so declare, the man shall impose whatever punishment on his wife he wishes; they shall kill the fornicator and the female procurer.

(iii 41–81) *šumma aššat a'īle ina pani mutiša ramanša taltadad lu ina libbi āle ammiemma lu ina ālāni qurbūte ašar bēta uddûšenni ana bēt Aššuraje tētarab ištu bēlet bēte usbat 3-šu 4-šu bēdat bēl bēte kî aššat a'īle ina bētišu usbutuni la īde ina urkette sinniltu šī<t> tattaṣbat bēl bēte ša aššassu [ina pa]nīšu ramanša [tald]uduni aššassu [unakkasma la*[18]*] ilaqqe [ašša]t a'īle ša aššassu ilteša usbutuni uznēša unakkusu ḫadīma mussa* 3 *bilat* 30 *mana annaka šīmša iddan u ḫadīma aššassu ilaqqeu* (iii 61) *u šumma bēl bēte kî aššat a'īle ina bētišu ištu ašši[tišu] usbutuni ī[de]*

A ¶ 24 If a man's wife should withdraw herself from her husband and enter into the house of (another) Assyrian, either in that city[19] or in any of the nearby towns, to a house which he assigns to her, residing with the mistress of the household, staying overnight three or four nights, and the householder is not aware that it is the wife of a man who is residing in his house, and later that woman is seized, the householder whose wife withdrew herself from him shall [mutilate] his wife and [not] take her back. As for the man's wife with whom his

šalšāte iddan u šumma itteker la īdema iqabbi ana Id illuku (iii 68) *u šumma a'īlu ša aššat a'īle ina bētišu usbutuni ina Id ittūra šalšāte iddan šumma a'īlu ša aššassu ina panīšu ramanša talduduni ina Id ittūra zaku gimrī ša Id umalla u šumma a'īlu ša aššassu ina panīšu ramanša taldu-duni aššassu la unakkis aššassu ilaqqe emittu mimma laššu*

wife resided, they shall cut off her ears; if he pleases, her husband shall give 12,600 shekels of lead as her value, and, if he pleases, he shall take back his wife. (iii 61) However, if the householder knows that it is a man's wife who is residing in his house with his wife, he shall give "triple."[20] And if he should deny (that he knew of her status), he shall declare, "I did not know," they shall undergo the divine River Ordeal. (iii 68) And if the man in whose house the wife of a man resided should refuse to undergo the divine River Ordeal, he shall give "triple"; if it is the man whose wife withdrew herself from him who should refuse to undergo the divine River Ordeal, he (in whose house she resided) is clear; he shall bear the expenses of the divine River Ordeal. However, if the man whose wife withdrew herself from him does not mutilate his wife, he shall take back his wife; no sanctions are imposed.

(iii 82–94) *šumma sinniltu ina bēt abišama usbat u mussa mēt aḫḫū mutiša la zēzu u māruša laššu mimma dumāqē ša mussa ina muḫ-ḫiša iškununi la ḫalquni aḫḫū mutiša la zīzūtu ilaqqeu ana rīḫāte ilāni ušet-tuqu ubarru ilaqqeu ana Id u māmīte la iṣṣabbutu*

A ¶ 25 If a woman is residing in her own father's house and her husband is dead, her husband's brothers have not yet divided their inheritance, and she has no son—her husband's brothers who have not yet received their inheritance shares shall take whatever valuables her husband bestowed upon her that are not missing. As for the rest (of the property), they shall resort to a verdict by the gods, they shall provide proof, and they shall take the property; they shall not be seized for (the settlement of any dispute by) the divine River Ordeal or the oath.

(iii 95–102) *šumma sinniltu ina bēt abišama usbat u mussa mēt mimma dumāqē ša mussa iškunušini šumma mārū mutiša ibašši ilaqqeu šumma mārū mutiša laššu šītma talaqqe*

A ¶ 26 If a woman is residing in her own father's house and her husband is dead, if there are sons of her husband, it is they who shall take whatever valuables her husband bestowed upon her; if there are no sons of her husband, she herself shall take the valuables.

(iii 103–108) *šumma sinniltu ina bēt abišama usbat mussa ētanarrab mimma nudunnâ ša mussa iddinaššenni šuamma ilaqqe ana ša bēt abiša la iqarrib*

A ¶ 27 If a woman is residing in her own father's house and her husband visits her regularly, he himself shall take back any marriage settlement which he, her husband, gave to her; he shall have no claim to anything belonging to her father's house.

(iv 1–10) *šumma almattu ana bēt aʾīle tētarab u mārаša ḫurda ilteša naṣṣat ina bēt āḫizāniša irtibi u ṭuppu ša mārūtišu la šaṭrat zitta ina bēt murabbiānišu la ilaqqe ḫubullē la inašši ina bēt ālidānišu zitta kî qātišu ilaqqe*

A ¶ 28 If a widow should enter a man's house and she is carrying her dead husband's surviving son with her (in her womb), he grows up in the house of the man who married her but no tablet of his adoption is written, he will not take an inheritance share from the estate of the one who raised him, and he will not be responsible for its debts; he shall take an inheritance share from the estate of his begetter in accordance with his portion.

(iv 11–19) *šumma sinniltu ana bēt mutiša tētarab širkīša u mimma ša ištu bēt abiša naṣṣutuni u lu ša emuša ina erābiša iddinaššenni ana mārēša zaku mārū emeša la iqarribu u šumma mussa ipūagši ana mārēšu ša libbišu iddan*

A ¶ 29 If a woman should enter her husband's house, her dowry and whatever she brings with her from her father's house, and also whatever her father-in-law gave her upon her entering, are clear for her sons; her father-in-law's sons shall have no valid claim. But if her husband intends to take control of her,[21] he shall give it to whichever of his sons he wishes.

(iv 20–39) *šumma abu ana bēt eme ša mārišu bibla ittabal <zubullâ> izzibil sinniltu ana mārišu la tadnat u mārušu šaniu ša aššassu ina bēt abiša usbutuni mēt aššat mārišu mēte ana mārišu šanāʾije ša ana bēt emešu izbiluni ana aḫuzzete iddanši šumma bēl mārte ša zubullâ imtaḫḫuruni mārassu ana tadāne la imaggur ḫadīma abu ša zubullâ izbiluni kallassu ilaqqea ana mārišu iddan u ḫadīma ammar izbiluni annaka ṣarpa ḫurāṣa ša la akāle qaqqadamma ilaqqe ana ša akāle la iqarrib*

A ¶ 30 If a father should bring the ceremonial marriage prestation and present <the bridal gift> to the house of his son's father-in-law, and the woman is not yet given to his son, and another son of his, whose wife is residing in her own father's house, is dead, he shall give the wife of his deceased son into the protection of the household[22] of his second son to whose father-in-law's house he has presented (the ceremonial marriage prestation). If the master of the daughter who is receiving the bridal gift decides not to agree to give his daughter (in these altered circumstances), if the father who presented the bridal gift so pleases, he shall take his daughter-in-law (i.e., the wife of his deceased son) and give her in marriage to his (second) son. And if he so pleases, as much as he presented—lead, silver, gold, and anything not edible—he shall take back in the quantities originally given; he shall have no claim to anything edible.

(iv 40–49) *šumma aʾīlu ana bēt emišu zubullâ izbil u aššassu mētat mārāt emišu ibašši ḫadīma «emu» mārat emišu kî aššitišu mette iḫḫaz u ḫadīma kaspa ša iddinuni ilaqqe lu šeʾam lu immerē lu mimma ša akāle la iddununeššu kaspamma imaḫḫar*

A ¶ 31 If a man presents the bridal gift to his father-in-law's house, and although his wife is dead there are other daughters of his father-in-law, if he so pleases, he[23] shall marry a daughter of his father-in-law in lieu of his deceased wife. Or, if he so pleases, he shall take back the silver that he gave; they shall not give back to him grain, sheep, or anything edible; he shall receive only the silver.

(iv 50–55) *šumma sinniltu ina bēt abišama usbat* [...]-*ša tadnat lu ana bēt emiša laqiat lu la laqiat ḫubullē arna u ḫīṭa ša mutiša tanašši*

A ¶ 32 If a woman is residing in her own father's house and her [...] is given, whether or not she has been taken into her father-in-law's house, she shall be responsible for her husband's debts, transgression, or punishment.

(iv 56–70) [*šumma*] *sinniltu ina bēt abišama usbat mussa mēt u mārū ibašši* [...(59–64 broken)] *u* [*ḫadīma*] *ana emiša ana aḫuzzete iddanši šumma mussa u emuša mētuma u māruša laššu almattu šīt ašar ḫadi*= [*ut*]*uni tallak*

A ¶ 33 If a woman is residing in her own father's house, her husband is dead, and she has sons [...], or [if he so pleases], he shall give her into the protection of the household of her father-in-law. If her husband and her father-in-law are both dead, and she has no son, she is indeed a widow; she shall go wherever she pleases.

(iv 71–74) *šumma aʾīlu almattu ēta*= *ḫaz rikassa la rakis 2 šanāte ina bētišu usbat aššutu šīt la tuṣṣa*

A ¶ 34 If a man should marry a widow without her formal binding agreement and she resides in his house for two years, she is a wife; she shall not leave.

(iv 75–81) *šumma almattu ana bēt aʾīle tētarab mimma ammar naṣṣatuni gabbu ša mutiša u šumma aʾīlu ana muḫḫi sinnilte ētarab mimma ammar naṣṣuni gabbu ša sinnilte*

A ¶ 35 If a widow should enter into a man's house, whatever she brings with her belongs to her (new) husband; and if a man should enter into a woman's house, whatever he brings with him belongs to the woman.

(iv 82–v 14) *šumma sinniltu ina bēt abiša usbat lu mussa bēta ana batte ušēšibši u mussa ana eqle ittalak la šamna la šapāte la lubulta la ukullâ la mimma ēzibašše la mimma šūbulta ištu eqle ušēbilašše sinniltu šīt 5 šanāte pani mutiša tadaggal ana mute la tuššab* (iv 93) *šumma mārūša*

A ¶ 36 If a woman is residing in her father's house, or her husband settles her in a house elsewhere, and her husband then travels abroad but does not leave her any oil, wool, clothing, or provisions, or anything else, and sends her no provisions from abroad—that

ibašši innagguru u ekkulu sinniltu mussa tuqa'a ana mute la tuššab (iv 97) *šumma mārūša laššu 5 šanāte mussa tuqa'a 6 šanāte ina kabāse ana mut libbiša tuššab mussa ina alāke la iqarribašše ana mutiša urkie zakuat* (iv 103) *šumma ana qāt 5 šanāte uḫḫeranni ina raminišu la ikkaluni lu qa-a-li iṣbassuma innabi[t] lu kî sar[te] ṣabitma ūtaḫ[ḫer] ina alāke ubâr sinnilta ša kî aššitišu iddan u aššassu ilaqqe* (v 4) *u šumma šarru ana māte šanītemma iltaparšu ana qāt 5 šanāte ūtaḫḫera aššassu tuqa'ašu ana mute la tuššab* (v 8) *u šumma ina pani 5 šanāte ana mute tattašab u tattalad mussa ina alāke aššum riksa la tuqa'iuni u tannaḫizuni ana šuāša u līdānišama ilaqqēšunu*

woman shall still remain (the exclusive object of rights) for her husband for five years, she shall not reside with another husband. (iv 93) If she has sons, they shall be hired out and provide for their own sustenance; the woman shall wait for her husband, she shall not reside with another husband. (iv 97) If she has no sons, she shall wait for her husband for five years; at the onset of(?) six years, she shall reside with the husband of her choice; her (first) husband, upon returning, shall have no valid claim to her; she is clear for her second husband. (iv 103) If he is delayed beyond the five years but is not detained of his own intention, whether because a ... seized him and he fled or because he was falsely arrested[24] and therefore he was detained, upon returning he shall so prove, he shall give a woman comparable to his wife (to her second husband) and take his wife. (v 4) And if the king should send him to another country and he is delayed beyond the five years, his wife shall wait for him (indefinitely); she shall not go to reside with another husband. (v 8) And furthermore, if she should reside with another husband before the five years are completed and should she bear children (to the second husband), because she did not wait in accordance with the agreement, but was taken in marriage (by another), her (first) husband, upon returning, shall take her and also her offspring.

(v 15–19) *šumma a'īlu aššassu ezzib*

A ¶ 37 If a man intends to divorce

libbušuma mimma iddanašše la lib⸗ bušuma mimma la iddanašše rāqū⸗ teša tuṣṣa

his wife, if it is his wish, he shall give her something; if that is not his wish, he shall not give her anything, and she shall leave empty-handed.

(v 20–25) *šumma sinniltu ina bēt abi⸗ šama usbat u mussa ētezibši dumāqē ša šūtma iškunušenni ilaqqe ana ter⸗ ḫete ša ubluni la iqarrib ana sinnilte zaku*

A ¶ 38 If a woman is residing in her own father's house and her husband divorces her, he shall take the valuables which he himself bestowed upon her; he shall have no claim to the bridewealth which he brought (to her father's house), it is clear for the woman.

(v 26–41) *šumma a'īlu la mārassu ana mute ittidin šumma panīma abuša ḫabbul kî šaparte šēšubat ummiānu paniu ittalka ina muḫḫi tādināne ša sinnilte šīm sinnilte išallim šumma ana tadāne laššu tādināna ilaqqe u šumma ina lumne balluṭat ana mubal⸗ liṭāniša zakuat u šumma āḫizā[nu š]a sinnilte lu ṭuppa ul-ta-[x-(x)]-ú-šu*[25] *u lu rugu[mmān]â irtišiuneššu šīm sinnilte ú-[x-x-x] u tādinānu [x-x-x-x]*

A ¶ 39 If a man should give one who is not his own daughter in marriage to a husband—if (this situation arose because) previously her father had been in debt and she had been made to reside as a pledge—and a prior creditor should come forward, he (i.e., the prior creditor) shall receive the value of the woman, in full, from the one who gives the woman in marriage; if he has nothing to give, he (i.e., the prior creditor) shall take the one who gives the woman in marriage. However, if she had been saved from a catastrophe, she is clear for the one who saved her. And if the one who marries the woman either causes a tablet to be ... for him or they have a claim in place against him, he shall [...] the value of the woman, and the one who gives (the woman) [...]

(v 42–106) *lu aššāt a'īle lu [alma⸗ nātu] u lu sinnišātu [Aššurajātu] ša ana rebēte u[ṣṣâni] qaqqassina [la pattu] mārāt a'īle [...] lu* TÚG *ša ri-[...] lu ṣubātī lu [...] paṣ[ṣuna] qaqqassina*

A ¶ 40 Wives of a man, or [widows], or any [Assyrian] women who go out into the main thoroughfare [shall not have] their heads [bare]. Daughters of a man [... with] either

[...] *lu* [...] *lu* [...]*-aṣ-ṣa-*[...] *ina ūme ina rebēte e-*[...] *illakāni uptaṣṣa*[*namma*] *esirtu ša ištu bēlti*[*ša*] *ina rebēte tallukuni paṣṣunat qadiltu ša mutu aḫzušini ina rebēte paṣṣunatma ša mutu la aḫzušini ina rebēte qaqqassa pattu la tuptaṣṣan ḫarīmtu la tuptaṣṣan qaqqassa pattu* (v 68) *ša ḫarīmta paṣṣunta ētamruni i<ṣa>bbassi šēbūte išakkan ana pī ekalle ubbalašši šukuttaša la ilaqqeu lubultaša ṣābitānša ilaqqe* 50 *ina ḫaṭṭāte imaḫ<ḫu>ṣuši qīra ana qaqqidiša itabbuku* (v 77) *u šumma aʾīlu ḫarīmta paṣṣunta ētamarma ūtaššer ana pī ekalle la ublašši aʾīlu šuātu* 50 *ina ḫaṭṭāte imaḫḫuṣuš bātiqānšu lubultušu ilaqqe uznēšu upallušu ina eble išakkuku ina kutallišu irakkusu iltēn uraḫ ūmāte šipar šarre eppaš* (v 88) *amātu la uptaṣṣanama ša amta paṣṣunta ētamruni iṣabbatašši ana pī ekalle ubbalašši uznēša unakkusu ṣābitānša lubultaša ilaqqe* (v 94) *šumma aʾīlu amta paṣṣunta ētamaršima ūtaššer la iṣṣabtašši ana pī ekalle la ublašši ubtaʾeruš uktaʾinuš* 50 *ina ḫaṭṭāte imaḫḫuṣuš uznēšu upallušu ina eble išakkuku* [*ina kut*]*allišu irakkusu* [*bāti*]*qānšu lubultušu ilaqqe iltēn uraḫ ūmāte šipar* [*šarre*] *eppaš*

a ...-cloth or garments or [...] shall be veiled, [...] their heads [... (gap of ca. 6 lines) ...] When they go about [...] in the main thoroughfare during the daytime, they shall be veiled. A concubine who goes about in the main thoroughfare with her mistress is to be veiled. A married *qadiltu*-woman is to be veiled (when she goes about) in the main thoroughfare, but an unmarried one is to leave her head bare in the main thoroughfare, she shall not veil herself. A prostitute shall not be veiled, her head shall be bare. (v 68) Whoever sees a veiled prostitute shall seize her, secure witnesses, and bring her to the palace entrance. They shall not take away her jewelry, but he who has seized her takes her clothing; they shall strike her 50 blows with rods; they shall pour hot pitch over her head. (v 77) And if a man should see a veiled prostitute and release her, and does not bring her to the palace entrance, they shall strike that man 50 blows with rods; the one who informs against him shall take his clothing; they shall pierce his ears, thread them on a cord, tie it at his back; he shall perform the king's service for one full month. (v 88) Slave women shall not be veiled, and he who should see a veiled slave woman shall seize her and bring her to the palace entrance; they shall cut off her ears; he who seizes her shall take her clothing. (v 94) If a man should see a veiled slave woman but release her and not seize her, and does not bring her to the palace entrance, and they then prove the charges against him and find him guilty, they shall strike him 50 blows with rods; they shall pierce his ears, thread them on a cord, tie it at his back; the one who informs against him shall take his garments; he shall perform the king's service for one full month.

(vi 1–13) *šumma aʾīlu esirtušu upaṣṣan 5 6 tappaʾēšu ušeššab ana panīšunu upaṣṣanši mā aššitī šīt iqabbi aššassu šīt esirtu ša ana pani ṣābē la paṣṣunutuni mussa la iqbiuni mā aššitī šīt la aššat esirtumma šīt šumma aʾīlu mēt mārū aššitišu paṣṣunte laššu mārū esrāte mārū šunu zitta ilaqqeu*

A ¶ 41 If a man intends to veil his concubine, he shall assemble five or six of his comrades, and he shall veil her in their presence, he shall declare, "She is my *aššutu*-wife"; she is his *aššutu*-wife. A concubine who is not veiled in the presence of people, whose husband did not declare, "She is my *aššutu*-wife," she is not an *aššutu*-wife, she is indeed a concubine. If a man is dead and there are no sons of his veiled wife, the sons of the concubines are indeed sons; they shall (each) take an inheritance share.

(vi 14–18) *šumma aʾīlu ina ūme rāqe šamna ana qaqqad mārat aʾīle itbuk lu ina šākulte ḫuruppāte ubil tūrta la utarru*

A ¶ 42 If a man pours oil on the head of a woman of the *aʾīlu*-class on the occasion of a holiday, or brings dishes on the occasion of a banquet, no return (of gifts) shall be made.

(vi 19–39) *šumma aʾīlu lu šamna ana qaqqade itbuk lu ḫuruppāte ubil māru ša aššata uddiuneššunni lu mēt lu innabit ina mārēšu rīḫāte ištu muḫḫi māre rabê adi muḫḫi māre ṣeḫre ša 10 šanātušuni ana ša ḫadiuni iddan šumma abu mēt u māru ša aššata uddiuniššunni mētma mār māre mēte ša 10 šanātušuni ibašši eḫḫazma (vi 31) šumma ana qāt 10 šanāte mārū māre ṣeḫḫeru abu ša mārte ḫadīma mārassu iddan u ḫadīma tūrta ana*

A ¶ 43 If a man either pours oil on her head or brings (dishes for) the banquet, (after which) the son to whom he assigned the wife either dies or flees, he shall give her in marriage to whichever of his remaining sons he wishes, from the oldest to the youngest of at least ten years of age. If the father is dead and the son to whom he assigned the wife is also dead, a son of the deceased son who is at

mitḫār utâr šumma māru laššu ammar imḫuruni abna u mimma ša la akāle qaqqadamma utâr u ša akāle la utâr

least ten years old shall marry her. (vi 31) If the sons of the (dead) son are less than ten years old, if the father of the daughter wishes, he shall give his daughter (to one of them), but if he wishes he shall make a full and equal return (of gifts given). If there is no son, he shall return as much as he received, precious stones or anything not edible, in its full amount; but he shall not return anything edible.

(vi 40–45) *šumma Aššurajau u šumma Aššurajītu ša kî šaparte ammar šīmišu ina bēt a'īle usbuni ana šīm gamer laqeuni inaṭṭu ibaqqan uznēšu uḫappa upallaš*

A ¶ 44 If there is an Assyrian man or an Assyrian woman who is residing in a man's house as a pledge for a debt, for as much as his value, and he is taken for the full value (i.e., his value as pledge does not exceed that of the debt), he (the pledge holder) shall whip (the pledge), pluck out (the pledge's) hair, (or) mutilate or pierce (the pledge's) ears.

(vi 46–88) [*šumm*]*a sinniltu tadnat* [*u*] *mussa nakru ilteqe emuša u māruša laššu 2 šanāte pani muteša tadaggal ina 2 šanāte annâte šumma ša akāle laššu tallakamma taqabbi* [*šumma*] *ālājītu ša ekalle šīt* [*ab*]*uša*(?) *ušakkalši* [*u šip*]*aršu teppaš* [*šumma aššutu š*]*a ḫupše šīt* [... *ušakk*]*alši* [*šiparšu teppaš*] (vi 58) *u* [*šumma aššat a'īle*(?) *šīt ša*] *eqla u* [*bēta* ...] *tallaka*[*mma ana dajānē taqabbi*] *mā ana akā*[*le laššu*] *dajānū ḫaziāna rabiūte ša āle iša'ulu kî eqla ina āle šuātu illukuni eqla u bēta ana ukullāiša ša 2 šanāte uppušu iddununešše usbat u ṭuppaša išaṭṭuru 2 šanāte tumalla ana mut libbiša tuššab ṭuppaša kî almattemma išaṭṭuru* (vi 72) *šumma ina arkât ūmē mussa*

A ¶ 45[26] If a woman is given in marriage and the enemy then takes her husband prisoner, and she has neither father-in-law nor son (to support her), she shall remain (the exclusive object of rights) for her husband for two years. During these two years, if she has no provisions, she shall come forward and so declare. If she is a resident of the community dependent upon the palace, her [father(?)] shall provide for her and she shall do work for him. If she is a wife of a *ḫupšu*-soldier, [...] shall provide for her [and she shall do work for him]. (vi 58) But [if she is a wife of a man(?) whose] field and [house are not sufficient to support her(?)], she

ḫalqu ana māte ittūra aššassu ša ana kīde aḫzutuni ilaqqeašši ana mārē ša ana mutiša urkie ulduṭuni la iqarrib mussama urkiu ilaqqe eqlu u bētu ša kî ukullāiša ana šīm gamer ana kīde taddinuni šumma ana dannat šarre la ērub kî tadnunima iddan u ilaqqe (vi 85) *u šumma la ittūra ina māte šanī⸗temma mēt eqelšu u bēssu ašar šarru iddununi iddan*

shall come forward and declare before the judges, "[I have nothing] to eat"; the judges shall question the mayor and the noblemen of the city to determine the current market rate(?) of a field in that city; they shall assign and give the field and house for her, for her provisioning for two years; she shall be resident (in that house), and they shall write a tablet for her (permitting her to stay for the two years). She shall allow two full years to pass, and then she may go to reside with the husband of her own choice; they shall write a tablet for her as if for a widow. (vi 72) If later her lost husband should return to the country, he shall take back his wife who married outside the family; he shall have no claim to the sons she bore to her later husband, it is her later husband who shall take them. As for the field and house that she gave for full price outside the family for her provisioning, if it is not entered into the royal holdings(?),[27] he shall give as much as was given, and he shall take it back. (vi 85) But if he should not return but dies in another country, the king shall give his field and house wherever he chooses to give.

(vi 89–112) *šumma sinniltu ša mussa mētuni mussa ina muāte ištu bētiša la tuṣṣâ šumma mussa mimma la ilṭu⸗rašše ina bēt mārēša ašar panūšani tuššab mārū mutiša ušakkuluši ukul⸗lāša u maltīssa kî kallete ša ira'u⸗mūšini irakkusunešše* (vi 99) *šumma urkittu šīt mārūša laššu ištu iltēn tuššab ana puḫrišunu ušakkuluši*

A ¶ 46 If a woman whose husband is dead does not move out of her house upon the death of her husband, if her husband (while alive) does not deed her anything in writing, she shall reside in the house of (one of) her own sons, wherever she chooses; her husband's sons shall provide for her, they shall

(vi 108) *šumma mārūša ibašši mārū panīte ana šākuliša la imagguru ina bēt mārē raminiša ašar panūšani tuššab mārū raminišama ušakkuluši u šiparšunu teppaš u šumma ina mārē mutišama ša eḫḫuzušini i[baš]ši [... mārūšama l]a ušakkuluši*

draw up an agreement to supply her with provisions and drink as for an in-law whom they love. (vi 99) If she is a second wife and has no sons of her own, she shall reside with one (of her husband's sons) and they shall provide for her in common. (vi 103) If she does have sons, and the sons of a prior wife do not agree to provide for her, she shall reside in the house of (one of) her own sons, wherever she chooses; her own sons shall provide for her, and she shall do service for them. And if there is one among her husband's sons who is willing to marry her, [it is he who shall provide for her; her own sons] shall not provide for her.

(vii 1–31) *šumma lu a'īlu lu sinniltu kišpī uppišuma ina qātēšunu iṣṣabtu ubta'erušunu ukta'inušunu muppišāna ša kišpē idukku a'īlu ša kišpē epāša ēmuruni ina pī āmerāne ša kišpē išme'uni mā anāku ātamar iqbiaššunni šāme'ānu illaka ana šarre iqabbi* (vii 14) *šumma āmerānu ša ana šarre iqbiuni itteker ana pani* ᵈGUD.DUMU.ᵈUTU *iqabbi mā šumma la iqbianni zaku āmerānu ša iqbiuni u ikkeruni šarru kî ila'uni iltana'alšu u kutallušu emmar āšipu ina ūme ullulūni a'īla ušaqba u šūt iqabbi mā māmīta ša ana šarre u mārišu tam'ātani la ipaššarakkunu kî pī ṭuppimma ša ana šarre u mārišu tam'ātani tam'āta*

A ¶ 47 If either a man or a woman should be discovered practicing witchcraft, and should they prove the charges against them and find them guilty, they shall kill the practitioner of witchcraft. A man who heard from an eyewitness to the witchcraft that he witnessed the practice of the witchcraft, who said to him, "I myself saw it," that hearsay-witness shall go and inform the king. (vii 14) If the eyewitness should deny what he (i.e., the hearsay-witness) reports to the king, he (i.e., the hearsay-witness) shall declare before the divine Bull-the-Son-of-the-Sun-God, "He surely told me"—and thus he is clear. As for the eyewitness who spoke (of witnessing the deed to his comrade) and then denied (it to the king), the king shall interrogate him as he sees fit, in order to determine his intentions; an exorcist shall have the man make a declaration when they make a purification, and then he himself (i.e., the exorcist) shall say as follows, "No one shall release any of you from the oath you swore by the king and by his son; you are bound by oath to the stipulations of the agreement to which you swore by the king and by his son."

(vii 32–52) *šumma aʾīlu mārat ḫabbulišu ša kî ḫubulle ina bētišu usbutuni* <...> *abuša išaʾal ana mute iddanši šumma abuša la mager la iddan šumma abuša mēt iltēn ina aḫḫēša išaʾal u šūt ana aḫḫēša iqabbi šumma aḫu iqabbi mā aḫātī adi iltēn uraḫ ūmāte apaṭṭar šumma adi iltēn uraḫ ūmāte la iptaṭar bēl kaspe ḫadīma uzakkašši ana mute iddanši* [... *kî*] *pī* [... *id*]*danši* [...]-*šu-nu* [...]-*šu-nu* [...]-*šu*

A ¶ 48 If a man <wants to give in marriage> his debtor's daughter who is residing in his house as a pledge, he shall ask permission of her father[28] and then he shall give her to a husband. If her father does not agree, he shall not give her. If her father is dead, he shall ask permission of one of her brothers and the latter shall consult with her (other) brothers. If one brother so desires he shall declare, "I will redeem my sister within one month"; if he should not redeem her within one month, the creditor, if he so pleases, shall clear her of encumbrances and shall give her to a husband. [...] according to [...] he shall give her [...]

(vii 53–62) [...] *kî aḫe* [...] *u šumma ḫarīmtu mētat* [*aš*]*šum aḫḫūša iqabbiūni* [*x*] *ša kî* [*x*] *aḫe zitte* [*x x*] *aḫḫē* [*um*:]*mišunu* [*izu*]*zzu*

A ¶ 49 [...] like a brother [...]. And if the prostitute is dead, because(?) her brothers so declare, ... they shall divide shares [with(?)] the brothers of their mother(?).

(vii 63–81) [*šumma aʾīlu aššat aʾīli*[29] *i*]*mḫaṣma* [*ša libbiša ušaṣlī*]*ši* [... *aššā*]*t aʾīle š*[*a* ...]-*ni u* [*kî ša ēpuš*]*ušini eppu*[*šušu kīmū š*]*a libbiša napšāte umalla u šumma sinniltu šīt mētat aʾīla idukku kīmū ša libbiša napšāte umalla u šumma ša mut sin*=

A ¶ 50 [If a man] strikes [another man's wife thereby causing her to abort her fetus, ...] a man's wife [...] and they shall treat him as he treated her; he shall make full payment of a life for her fetus. And if that woman dies, they shall kill

nilte šiāte mārušu laššu aššassu imḫuṣuma ša libbiša taṣli kīmū ša libbiša māḫiṣāna idukku šumma ša libbiša ṣuḫārtu napšātemma umalla

that man; he shall make full payment of a life for her fetus. And if there is no son of that woman's husband, and his wife whom he struck aborted her fetus, they shall kill the assailant for her fetus. If her fetus was a female, he shall make full payment of a life only.

(vii 82–86) *šumma a'īlu aššat a'īle la murabbīta imḫaṣma ša libbiša ušaṣlīši ḫīṭu anniu 2 bilat annaka iddan*

A ¶ **51** If a man strikes another man's wife who does not raise her child, causing her to abort her fetus, it is a punishable offense; he shall give 7,200 shekels of lead.

(vii 87–91) *šumma a'īlu ḫarīmta imḫaṣma ša libbiša ušaṣlīši miḫṣī kî miḫṣī išakkunuš napšāte umalla*

A ¶ **52** If a man strikes a prostitute causing her to abort her fetus, they shall assess him blow for blow, he shall make full payment of a life.

(vii 92–108) *šumma sinniltu ina raminiša ša libbiša taṣṣili ubta'eruši ukta'inuši ina iṣṣē izaqqupuši la iqabberuši šumma ša libbiša ina ṣalê mētat ina iṣṣē izaqqupuši la iqabberuši šumma sinnilta šīt kî ša libbiša taṣliuni [uptazz]eruši* [...] *iqbiu* [...]*-x-me* [...]*-te* [...]

A ¶ **53** If a woman aborts her fetus by her own action and they then prove the charges against her and find her guilty, they shall impale her, they shall not bury her. If she dies as a result of aborting her fetus,[30] they shall impale her, they shall not bury her. If any persons should hide that woman because she aborted her fetus [...]

(vii 109–viii 5) [*šumma* ...] *laššu* [...].MEŠ [...]*-ú-ni* [... *l*]*u amāte* [...]*-aṣ*

A ¶ **54** [If ...] or slave women [...]

(viii 6–41) [*šumma a'ī*]*lu batulta* [*ša ina bēt a*]*biša* [*usbu*]*tuni* [...] *ša la ūtarrišuni* [*puš*]*qa*(?) *la patteatuni la aḫzatuni u rugummānâ ana bēt abiša la iršiuni a'īlu lu ina libbi āle lu ina ṣēre lu ina mūše ina rebēte lu ina bēt qarīte lu ina isinni āle a'īlu kî da'āne batulta iṣbatma umanzi'ši abu ša*

A ¶ **55** If a man forcibly seizes and rapes a maiden who is residing in her father's house, [...] who is not betrothed(?),[31] whose [womb(?)] is not opened, who is not married, and against whose father's house there is no outstanding claim—whether within the city or in the

batulte aššat nā'ikāna ša batulte ilaqqe ana manzu'e iddanši ana mutiša la utâršī ilaqqēši abu mārassu nīkta ana nā'ikāniša kî aḫuzzete iddanši (viii 33) *šumma aššassu laššu šalšāte kaspe šīm batulte nā'ikānu ana abiša iddan nā'ikānša iḫḫassi la isammakši šumma abu la ḫadi kaspa šalšāte ša batulte imaḫḫar mārassu ana ša ḫadiuni iddan*

countryside, or at night whether in the main thoroughfare, or in a granary, or during the city festival—the father of the maiden shall take the wife of the fornicator of the maiden and hand her over to be raped; he shall not return her to her husband, but he shall take (and keep?) her; the father shall give his daughter who is the victim of fornication into the protection of the household of her fornicator. (viii 33) If he (the fornicator) has no wife, the fornicator shall give "triple" the silver as the value of the maiden to her father; her fornicator shall marry her; he shall not reject(?) her. If the father does not desire it so, he shall receive "triple" silver for the maiden, and he shall give his daughter in marriage to whomever he chooses.

(viii 42–49) *šumma batultu ramanša ana a'īle tattidin a'īlu itamma ana aššitišu la iqarribu šalšāte kaspe šīm batulte nā'ikānu iddan abu māras*[*su*] *kî ḫadiuni epp*[*aš*]

A ¶ 56 If a maiden should willingly give herself to a man, the man shall so swear; they shall have no claim to his wife; the fornicator shall pay "triple" the silver as the value of the maiden; the father shall treat his daughter in whatever manner he chooses.

(viii 50–53) *lu maḫāṣu lu* [... *ša ašš*]*at a'ī*[*li* ... *ša ina ṭup*]*pe šaṭru*[*ni* ...]

A ¶ 57 Whether it is a beating or [... for] a man's wife [... that is (specifically)] written on the tablet [...]

(viii 54–57) *ina ḫīṭāni gab*[*bi* ...] *nakāse* [...] *u gallule de-e-*[...] *kî ša* [...]

A ¶ 58 For all punishable offenses [...] cutting off [...] and ...[32] [...]

(viii 58–62) *uššer ḫīṭāni ša* [*aššat a'īle*] *ša ina ṭuppe* [*šaṭruni*] *a'īlu aššassu* [*inaṭṭu*] *ibaqqan u*[*znēša*] *uḫappa ul*[*appat*] *aranšu laššu*[33]

A ¶ 59 In addition to the punishments for [a man's wife] that are [written] on the tablet, a man may [whip] his wife, pluck out her hair, mutilate her ears, or strike her, with impunity.

(viii 64–65) *uraḫ ša-sarrāte ūm* 2.KAM *līmu Sa*[*gi*]*u*

Month II, day 2, eponymy of Sagiu.

MAL B

(break of undetermined size)

(ii 1–14) [*šumma aḫḫū bēt abišunu izūzu ki*]*râte* [*u būrāte in*]*a qaqqere* [... *māru rab*]*û* 2 *qātā*[*te*] *inassaq* [*i*]*laqqe u aḫḫūšu urki aḫāʾiš inassuqu ilaqqeu ina eqle šiluḫlē mimma u mānaḫāte gabbe māru ṣeḫru ussaq māru rabû* 1 *qāta inassaq ilaqqe u ša šanīte qātišu ištu aḫḫēšu pūršu iṣalli*

B ¶ 1[34] [If brothers divide the estate of their father], orchards [and wells] in the plot of land [...], the oldest son shall select and take a double share, and his brothers shall select and take shares one after the other; the youngest son is the one who apportions whatever *šiluḫlu*-personnel there are and all the associated equipment in the field; the oldest son shall select and take one share, and for his second share he shall cast lots with his brothers.

(ii 15–21) *šumma aʾīlu ina aḫḫē la zēzūte napšāte igmur ana bēl napšāte iddunuš panūšuma bēl napšāte iduakšu u panūšuma immaggar* [*u*] *zittašu ilaqqe*

B ¶ 2 If a man, who has not yet received his inheritance share, takes a life, they shall hand him over to the next-of-kin.[35] Should the next-of-kin so choose, he shall kill him, or, if he chooses to come to an accommodation, then he shall take his inheritance share.

(ii 22–26) [*šumm*]*a aʾīlu ina aḫḫē* [*l*]*a zēzūte lu šillata*[36] [*iq*]*bi u lu innabit* [*u*] *zittašu šarru* [*k*]*î libbišu*

B ¶ 3 If a man, who has not yet received his inheritance share, speaks treason or flees, the disposition of his inheritance share shall be determined by the king.

(ii 27–38) [*šumma*] *aḫḫū ina eqle la zēze* [*iltēn*] *aḫu ina libbišunu* [...] *zēra izru* [...] *eqla ēruš* [*aḫu šaniu*]*mma ittalka* [*zēr mēr*]*eše ša aḫišu* [... *ina*]

B ¶ 4 If there are brothers in possession of an undivided field, and one brother among them [...] sows seed [...] cultivates the field, [and a

šanūtešu [ilqe ub]ta'eruš [ukta]'inuš [ina ūme šūt ill]akanni [aḫu ša eqla] ērušuni [zittašu] ilaqqe

second brother] then comes and for a second time [takes the seed of] his brother's cultivation [...], and they prove the charges against him and find him guilty—[on the day that he himself] comes forward, [the brother] who cultivated [the field] shall take [his inheritance share].

(ii 39–46) *[šumma aḫḫū ina eqle la] zēze [iltēn aḫu ina libbi]šunu* [...]*-aṣ* [...]*-x-ma* [...]*-ka* [...]*-li* [...]*-ni* [...]

B ¶ 5 [If there are brothers in possession of] an undivided [field, and one brother] among them [...]

(gap)

(iii 1–51) [...]*-la*?*-a ana kaspe* [(...) *ilaq*]*qe udīni eq*[*la u*] *bēta ana kaspe la* [*ilaq*]*qeuni iltēn uraḫ ūmāte nāgira 3-šu ina libbi Āl-Aššur usassa 3-šu-ma ina libbi āl eqle u bēte ša ilaqqeuni usassa mā eqla u bēta ša annanna mār annanna ina ugār āle annie ana* [*kaspe*] *alaqqe ša* [*la*]*qāšunu u* [*da*]*bābšunu ibaššiūni ṭuppātešunu lušēlianemma ana pani qēpūte liškunu lidbubu luzakkiuma lilqeu ša ina uraḫ ūmāte annâte udīni edānu la mašāe ṭuppātešunu ittablūnenni*[37] *ana pani qēpūte iltaknūni a'īlu ana sīr eqlišu išallim ilaqqe* (iii 28) *ina ūme nāgiru ina libbi Āl-Aššur isassiuni iltēn ina sukkallē ša pani šarre ṭupšar āle nāgiru u qēpūtu ša šarre izzazzu ša āl eqle u bēte ilaqqeuni ḫaziānu 3 rabiūte ša āle izzazzu nāgiramma usassû ṭuppātešunu išaṭṭuru iddunu mā ina iltēn uraḫ ūmāte annâte 3-šu nāgiru issisi ša ina iltēn uraḫ ūmāte annâte ṭuppušu la ittablanni ana pani qēpūte la iltaknuni ina eqle u bēte qāssu elli ana musassiāne ša nāgire zaku 3 ṭuppāte ša sassu nāgire ša dajānū išaṭṭurū* 1 [*ṭuppa qēp*]*ūtu* [...]

B ¶ 6 [If ...] intends to purchase [a field or house ...]; before he purchases the field or house, he shall have the herald make a proclamation three times during the course of one full month within the City of Assur, and he shall also have him make a proclamation three times within the city of the field or house which he intends to purchase, as follows: "I intend to purchase the field or house, within the common irrigated area of this city, belonging to so-and-so, son of so-and-so. Let all who have a right to acquire (the property) or a contest (against this transfer) bring forth their tablets and present them before the officials, let them thus contest (the purchase), let them clear (the property of other claims), and let them take it. Of those who, during the course of this full month, bring their tablets without fail by the due date and present them before the officials, the man (whose claim is successful) shall take full possession of the extent of his field."

(iii 28) When the herald makes his proclamation in the City of Assur, one of the royal court officials, the city scribe, the herald, and the royal officials are to be present; representing the city of the field or house that he intends to purchase, the mayor and three noblemen of the city are to be present; they also shall have the herald make his proclamation; they shall write their tablets and give (them to the purchaser, saying) as follows: "The herald has made proclamations three times during the course of this full month. He who during the course of this full month has not brought his tablet and has not presented it before the officials forfeits (any claims to) the field or house; it is cleared for the benefit of the person who had the herald make the proclamation." Three tablets that the judges will write (attesting to the fact) of having the herald make a proclamation, one [tablet] the officials [...]

(gap)

(iv 1–10) *ammar* [...] *ira*[*ggumuni* ...] *ana x-x-*[...] *u šīm bē*[*te* ...] *iqqurun*[*i* ...] *2-šu ina šīm bēte* [... *a*]*na bēl bēte id*[*dan*] *ana iltēn bilat anneke* 5 [*ina ḫaṭṭāte*] *imaḫḫuṣuš iltēn ur*[*aḫ ūmāte*] *šipar šarre epp*[*aš*]

B ¶ 7 [...] as much as [...] he shall claim [...] and the price of the house [...] he demolished [...; he shall give] the owner of the house [...] twofold from the value of the house. For 3,600 shekels of lead they shall strike him 5 blows with rods; he shall perform the king's service for one full month.

(iv 11–19) *šumma aʾīlu taḫūma rabia ša tappāʾišu ussammeḫ ubtaʾeruš uktaʾinuš eqla ammar usammeḫuni šalšāte iddan* 1 *ubānšu inakkisu* 1

B ¶ 8 If a man should incorporate a large border area of his comrade's (property into his own) and they prove the charges against him and

meat ina ḫaṭṭāte imaḫḫuṣuš iltēn uraḫ ūmāte šipar šarre eppaš

find him guilty, he shall give a field "triple" that which he had incorporated; they shall cut off one of his fingers; they shall strike him 100 blows with rods; he shall perform the king's service for one full month.

(iv 20–28) *šumma aʾīlu taḫūma ṣeḫra ša pūrāni usbalkit ubtaʾeruš uktaʾinuš iltēn bilat annaka iddan eqla ammar usammeḫuni šalšāte*[38] *iddan* 50 *ina ḫaṭṭāte imaḫḫuṣuš iltēn uraḫ ūmāte šipar šarre eppaš*

B ¶ 9 If a man transfers a small border area of the lots and they prove the charges against him and find him guilty, he shall give 3,600 shekels of lead; he shall give a field "triple" that which he had incorporated; they shall strike him 50 blows with rods; he shall perform the king's service for one full month.

(iv 29–46) *šumma aʾīlu ina la eqlišu būrta iḫri dunna ēpu[š] ina būrtišu dunni[šu] qāssu elli* 30 *ina ḫa[ṭṭāte] imaḫḫuṣu[š]* 20 *ūmāte šipar šarre [eppaš] sum-ma ḫu-ú-ga-a-x-[...] i-na ma-áš-šu-ú-te [...] dunna [...] itamma mā [...] mā šumma [...] būrta la [...] u du[nna la ...] bēl eqle [...] ka-x-[...] ina [...] būrta [...] x [...]*

B ¶ 10 If a man digs a well and builds a permanent structure in a field not his own, he shall forfeit his claim to his well and his permanent structure; they shall strike him 30 blows with rods; he shall perform the king's service for 20 days. ... [...] ... [...] the permanent structure [...] he shall swear, "[...]," and further, "I have indeed [dug] the well, I have [indeed built] a permanent structure." The owner of the field [...] ... the well [...]

(gap)

(v 1–12) *x [...] u [...] ummi[ānu...] ana x [...] ù lu-ú [...] ummiān[u ...] ṭuppātu [...] mānaḫta [...] ana ēpi[še ...]* A.ŠÀ *ši-in-[...] ana ummiāne [...] inad[din]*

B ¶ 11 [...] creditor [...] creditor [...] tablets [...] improvements [...] to the worker [...] the field ... [...] he shall give to the creditor.

(v 13–18) *šumma aʾīlu ina eqle ša [tappāʾišu] kiria iddi būrta [iḫri] iṣṣē urab[bi] bēl eqle idaggal la [...] kiriu*

B ¶ 12 If a man plants an orchard, digs a well, or raises trees in a field belonging to [his comrade], and the

ana nādiāne za[ku] eqla kî eqle ana bēl kirî ina[ddin]

owner of the field notices it but does not [object], the orchard is clear for the benefit of the planter; he shall give another field in lieu of the field to the owner of the orchard.

(v 19–25) *šumma aʾīlu ina la qaqqirišu lu kiria iddi lu būrta iḫri lu urqē lu iṣṣē urabbi ubtaʾeruš uktaʾinuš ina ūme bēl eqle illakanni kiria adi mānihātišu ilaqqe*

B ¶ 13 If a man either plants an orchard, or digs a well, or raises vegetables or trees in a plot not his own, and they prove the charges against him and find him guilty, when the owner of the field comes forward, he shall take the orchard together with its (new) installations.

(v 26–33) *šumma aʾīlu ina la qaqqirišu iglušuma libitta ilbin ubtaʾeruš uktaʾinuš qaqqara šalšāte iddan libnātišu ilaqqeu* ⸢50?⸣ *ina ḫaṭṭāte imaḫḫuṣuš* [x *ūmāt*]*e šipar šarre eppaš*

B ¶ 14 If a man digs(? a pit) and makes bricks in a plot not his own and they prove the charges against him and find him guilty, he shall give "triple" the plot; they shall take his bricks; they shall strike him 50(?) blows with rods; he shall perform the king's service for [x days].

(v 34–38) [*šumma aʾīlu ina*] *la qaqqirišu* [...] *libitta ilbin* [*libnātišu il*]*aqqeu* [x *ina ḫaṭṭāte imaḫḫu*]*ṣuš* [x *ūmāte šipar šarre*] *eppa*[*š*]

B ¶ 15 [If a man ...] and makes bricks in a plot not his own, they shall take [his bricks; they shall] strike him [x blows with rods]; he shall perform [the king's service for x days.]

(gap)

(vi 1) [...] *la-a* [...]

B ¶ 16 [If ...] will not [...]

(vi 2–20) [*šumma ina ug*]*āre ina libbi b*[*ūrāte māʾū ša a*]*na šīqe* [*ana ša*]*kāne* [*ill*]*ukūni ibašši* [*bēl*]*ū eqlāte ištu aḫāʾiš* [*iz*]*zazzu aʾīlu ana sīr eqlišu šipra eppaš eqelšu išaqqi u šumma ina libbišunu la magrūtu*

B ¶ 17[39] If there is sufficient water for irrigation available in the common irrigated area in the wells, the owners of the fields shall act together; each man shall perform the work in accordance with the

ibašši magru ša libbišunu dajānē išaʾal ṭuppa ša dajānē iṣabbat u šipra eppaš māʾē šunātunu ana raminišu ilaqqe eqelšu išaqqi mamma šaniumma la išaqqi

extent of his field, and shall irrigate his field. But if there are some among them who are not amenable to an agreement, the one among them who is amenable to an agreement shall appeal to the judges; he shall obtain a tablet (with the decision) of the judges, and perform the work; he shall take those waters for himself, and irrigate his own field; no one else may irrigate (with the waters).

(vi 21–vii 3) *šumma māʾū ša Adad ša ana šīqe ana šakāne illukūni ibašši bēlū eqlāte ištu aḫāʾiš izzazzu aʾīlu ana sīr eqlišu šipra eppaš eqelšu išaqqi u šumma ina libbišunu la magrūtu ibašši u magru ša libbišunu ṭuppa ša dajānē ana muḫḫi la magrūte ilaqqe [ḫaziānu] u 5 rabiūtu [ša āle izzazzu* ... (gap)] (vii 1) [...] *x* [x *ina ḫaṭṭāte imaḫḫuṣ]uš* [x *ūmāte šipar šarre] eppaš*

B ¶ 18 If there is sufficient rainwater for irrigation available, the owners of the fields shall act together; each man shall perform the work in accordance with the extent of his field, and shall irrigate his field. But if there are some among them who are not amenable to an agreement, then the one among them who is amenable to an agreement shall take the tablet (with the decision) of the judges before those who are not amenable to an agreement; the mayor and five noblemen [of the city shall be present ... (gap) ... they shall strike] him [x blows with rods]; he shall perform [the king's service for x days].

(vii 4–17) [*šumma aʾīlu eqe*]*l tappāʾišu* [*e*]*rraš* [...]-*ú iklāšu* [...] *nīš šarre* [*izkur*]*aššumma ēruṣ* [*šumma* ...]-*x ittalkanni* [*ēri*]*šānu ša eqle* [*ina t*]*urēze* [*šeʾa eṣ*]*ṣid ušrâq*[40] [*šeʾa*] *ana bēt ḫašīme itabbak* [...] *ana kurdišše utâr* [*kî*] *bilat eqle ša āle* [2 *na*]*ppaltēn* [*ana bēl e*]*qle inaddin*

B ¶ 19[41] If a man intends to cultivate the field of his comrade, [and ...] prevented(?) him, [... he swore for] him an oath by the king and he cultivated it. [If ...] he should come forth, the cultivator of the field shall harvest and thresh [the grain] at harvest time, he shall store [the grain] in the storage facility, [... and] he shall return the [straw(?)] to the barn; in accordance with the yield of a field of the city, he shall give two shares [to the owner] of the field.

(vii 18–25) [*šumma aʾī*]*lu ina la eqlišu* [...]-*x-ša itruḫ* [*taḫ*]*ūma ilbi* [*kudur*]*ra ukaddir* [...]-*x-me iqbi* [*ubtaʾe*]*ruš* [*uktaʾin*]*uš* [...]

B ¶ 20 If a man digs [...] in a field not belonging to him, surrounds it with a border, sets up a boundary stone, and says, ["...,"] and they prove the charges against him and find him guilty, [...]

(remainder broken)

MAL C+G

(break of undetermined size)

(obv. 1–7) [...] *bēlšunu* [...]-*nu u šumma lāqiānu* [*iqabbi mā* ...] *x ša apṭuranni mi*-[... *urda ana* x] *bilat anneke amta ana* 4 *bilat anneke* [...] *u šumma māḫirānu iqabbi mā* [...] *ana pani ile itamma u ammar ina* [...] *ilaqqe* [...]

C ¶ 1 [...] their owner [...] and if the buyer [declares, "...] which I redeemed [...," he shall give a slave for x] shekels of lead and a slave woman for 14,400 shekels of lead [...]; and if the one who receives should declare, ["..."]; he shall swear an oath before the god and as much as [...] he shall take [...]

(8–13) [*šumma aʾīlu lu mār aʾīle*] *u lu mārat aʾīle ša kî kaspe u kî* [*šaparte ina bētišu us*]*buni ana kaspe ana aʾīle šanîmma* [*iddin u mamma šaniam*]*ma ša ina bētišu usbuni id*[*din ubta*-*ʾerušu*] *ina kaspišu qāssu el*[*li* ...]-*x-šu ana bēl mimmû idd*[*an* x *ina ḫaṭṭāte im*]*aḫḫuṣušu* 20 *ūmāte šipar šarre eppaš*

C ¶ 2 [If a man] sells to another man [either a man's son] or a man's daughter who is residing [in his house] either for a silver (debt?) or as [a pledge], or sells [anyone else] who is residing in his house, [and they prove the charges against him], he shall forfeit his silver; [...] he shall give his/its [...] to the owner of the property; they shall strike him [x blows with rods]; he shall perform the king's service for 20 days.

(14–21) [*šumma aʾīlu lu mār aʾīle*] *u lu mārat aʾīle ša kî kaspe u kî šaparte* [*ina bētišu usbuni*] *ana māte šanīte*

C ¶ 3 [If a man] sells into a foreign land [either a man's son] or a man's daughter who [is residing in his

ana kaspe iddin [ubtaʾerušu ukt]aʾinušu ina kaspišu qāssu elli [...-x-šu ana bē]l mimmû iddan [x ina ḫaṭṭāte i]maḫḫuṣušu 40 ūmāte šipar šarre eppaš [u šumma aʾīlu ša iddinu]ni ina māte šanīte mēt [napšāte umal]la Aššurajau u Aššurajītu [ša ana šīm gam]er laqeuni ana māt šanīte [inad]din

house] either for a silver (debt?) or as a pledge, and they prove the charges against him and find him guilty, he shall forfeit his silver; [...] he shall give his/its [...] to the owner of the property; they shall strike him [x blows with rods]; he shall perform the king's service for 40 days. But if the man whom he sells dies in the foreign land, he shall make full payment for a life. He may sell into a foreign land an Assyrian man or an Assyrian woman who had been taken for full value (i.e., the value as pledge does not exceed that of the debt).

(22–27) *[šumma aʾīlu lu alpa lu] emāra lu sīsâ u lu mimma la u[māmšu ša kî šaparte ina] bētišu usbuni ana kaspe id[din ... umāma id]dan kaspa la utâr šumma u[māma la iddin ina kaspišu qās]su elli bēl mimmû ša [umāmšu ina bēt aʾīle us]buni umāmšu iṣabbat mā[ḫirānu ša um]āme kasapšu ina muḫḫi tādinā[ne ...]*

C ¶ 4 [If a man] sells [an ox, or] a donkey, or a horse, or any other animal not his own, that is staying in his house as a pledge, [...] he shall give [another animal], he shall not return the silver. If [he does not give another animal], he shall forfeit his silver. The owner of the property [whose animal had been in the man's house] shall seize his animal; the purchaser of the animal [shall ...] his silver from the seller [...]

(28–32) *[šumma aʾīlu ištu u]šallimma lu alpa lu emāra lu sī[sâ u lu mimma la umāmšu ištari]q(?)*[42] *kî šīme tarṣe ana a[ʾīle iddin u māḫir]ānu la īde šīma [tarṣa ana aʾīle id]din šurqa ammar e-*[...] (32)[43] *[tādin]ānu um[alla]*

C ¶ 5 [If a man should steal(?) from] a meadow either an ox, or a donkey, or a horse, or any other animal not his own, and then sells it to another man at the prevailing price, and the purchaser is not aware (that it is stolen property) and he gives the man the prevailing price, the seller shall restore the stolen goods, as much as [...]

(33–43) *[šumma aʾīlu ...]-x-ta lu umāma u l[u ...] u aʾīlū šībūt[u ...] bēl*

C ¶ 6a [If a man ...-s a ...] ... or an animal or [...] and witnesses [...] the

mimma annê [...]*-ad-di iṣṣabbat u aʾīlu* [... *b*]*ēl mimmû mimmûšu* [...] *x x* [... *ina muḫḫ*]*i tādināne ilaqqēma* [... *ša*] *x ilqeuni u ina qātišu* [...] *x ina muḫḫi aʾīle ša iddinašš*[*uni* ... *t*]*ādinānu ḫalāq mimmûšu la* [...] *x-x-ni ubar*[*ru* ...] TA [...]

owner of all this [...] shall be seized, and the man [...] the owner of the property his property [...] he shall take from the seller and [... which] he has taken, and in his hand [...] against the man who gave it to him [...] the seller shall not [...] the loss of his property [...] he shall prove the charges [...]

(gap)

(G rev. 1–6) [*šumma* ...] *ša id-*[...] *ilaqqe u lāqiā*[*nu* ...] *ša ana kaspe x* [...] 2(?) *urīṣē*(?) *ana bēl kaspe* [...] *x ittalkamma mimma ša* [...] *x ina muḫḫišu la ila*[*qqe* ...]

C ¶ 6b [If ...] he shall take and the purchaser [...] for silver [...] two(?) goats(?) to the owner of the silver [...] he shall come and something which [...] he shall not take against him [...]

(G rev. 7–13 + C rev. 1–2) [*šumma* ...] *u lu mimma ša kî šaparte* [... *ina bēt Aššu*]*rajae usbuni u edannu ēt*[*iquni* ...]*-x-ú-ni šumma kaspu ammar šīmišu ik*[*tašad* ...] *x la-qé šumma kaspu ammar šīmišu la ik*[*tašad* ...] *uppašma ilaqqe* [...] *x ušaddi qaqqad kaspimma x* [...] *laššu* [...]

C ¶ 7 [If ...] or anything else that is staying in the house of an Assyrian as a pledge [...] and the term (of the loan) elapses [...]; if the silver (owed) amounts to as much as its/his value [...]; if the silver (owed) does not amount to as much as its/his value [...] he shall acquire and he shall take [...] he made abandon, the capital sum of the silver [...] there is not [...]

(C rev. 3–9) [*šumma aʾīlu* ...] *lu umāma u lu mimma šanâmma* [*ištariq ubt*]*aʾerušu uktaʾinu*[*šu šurq*]*a*(?) *iddan* 50 *ina ḫaṭṭāte imaḫḫuṣu*[*šu* x *ūmāte šipar šarre*] *eppaš dēna annia dajānū x*[44] [*idinnu u šumma* ...] *iktaldamma šurqa ammar išr*[*iquni ana šīm gam*]*er ēṣi u mādma* [*utâr ḫīṭa ša*] *šarre kî libbišu emmid*[*uš*]

C ¶ 8 [If a man should steal] either [...], or an animal, or anything else, and they prove the charges against him and find him guilty, he shall repay [the stolen goods]; they shall strike him 50 blows with rods; he shall perform [the king's service for x days]; the judges ... shall render this judgment. [But if ...] he/it should "reach" [... (in value?)], he shall return the stolen goods, as much as he stole, to the full value, as much as it may be; they shall impose upon him the punishment determined by the king.

(rev. 10–15) [*šumma aššat* (or: *mār, mārat?*) *a'īle*] *u lu urdu mimma šumšu gabba qīp*[*ta* ...] *ana maškatte ina kīde šaknat* [*u a'īlu* (...) *š*]*a maškattu ina bētišu šaknutu*[*ni ana bēl* ...] *ša bēssu qīpuni la iq*[*bi mimmû ina qā*]*tišu ittaṣbat* [*bēlšu ilaqqēš*]*u a'īlu šūt šurqa inaš*[*ši*]

C ¶ 9 [If a man's wife (or: son, or: daughter?)] or a slave [...-s] anything of value as trust [...] it is deposited outside of the family [and the man] in whose house the goods are deposited does not notify [the owner of (the property)] that was entrusted to his house, and the property is then seized in his possession, [its owner shall take it]; that man shall be liable for theft.

(rev. 16–19) [*šumma a'īlu qīpta*] *ša tappāišu ūtattir* [... *ubta'er*]*ušu ukta'inušu* [*šarrāqu*] *šūt u ḫīṭa ša šarre* [*kî libbišu*] *emmiduš*

C ¶ 10 If a man should inflate the value of his comrade's [goods left in trust, ...] and they prove the charges against him and find him guilty, that man is [a thief]; and they shall impose upon him the punishment determined by the king.

(rev. 20–26) [*šumma a'īlu* ...] *ūtattir iltaṭar* [...] *ummiānāte šēlue* [*ubta'erušu*] *ukta'inušu* [... *ša* ...]*-a-ti ilṭurni* [... x *ina*] *ḫaṭṭāte imaḫḫuṣušu* [...] *ina qāt ummiā*[*nāte* ...] *ṭupšarru*(?) [...]

C ¶ 11 If a man should inflate (the value) and record (the inflated value) [...] the creditors are debited, and [they prove the charges against him] and find him guilty, [... which] he has recorded; they shall strike him [x blows with] rods; [...] the possession of the creditors [...] scribe(?) [...]

(remainder broken)

MAL D

(break of undetermined size)

(1–6) [...] *x bu* [...] *ana x* LÚ.GAL KÁ[45] [... *i*]*qabbiaššu*(?) [...] *x-ri-iṣ alāka la i-*[...]*-x-nu aḫišu iqabbi* [...] *ina dēnišu abi* [...]

D ¶ 1 [If ...] to the official in charge of the gate [...] shall declare to him [...] ... not [...] ... his brother shall declare [...] in his judgment, the father [...]

(7–8) [*šumma* ...]-*x šarru id*-[...] *x x* [...]

D ¶ 2 [If ...] the king [...]

(remainder broken)

MAL E

(break of undetermined size)

(1–10) [*šumma* ... *ubta'eru*]*š ukta'inu*[*š ša* ...]-*x-ši ubbuluni x*-[... x *ina ḫaṭṭāte i*]*maḫḫuṣuš ištu x*-[...] *x* 30 *mana anneke x*-[...]-*ma rīḫāte* 14 *mana* [...]-*x mārū šarre dajānū* [...]-*ni ubbuluni kî ša šar*[*ru* ... *š*]*a*[46] *kīde ana muḫḫi mār x* [...] *šarrumma* [...]

E ¶ 1 [If ... and they prove the charges] against him and find him guilty, [... which ...] he shall bring [...]; they shall strike him [x blows with rods]; from [...] 1,800 shekels of lead [...] the remainder, 840 shekels [...] the princes, the judges [...] he shall bring, according to the king [...] outside of the family against the son [...] the king himself [...].

(11–rev. 3) [*šumma* ...]-*bu-šu imḫaṣ ub-x*-[...]-*x ana rēš x*-[... (gap) ...] (rev. 1) [...] *ša* [...] x[47] *mana x* [...]-*x-ku-su-uš* [...]

E ¶ 2 [If ...] his [...] he strikes [...] to the head(?) [... (gap) ...] shekels [...]

(rev. 4–9) [*šumma* ...] *gabbu ammar qi-x*-[...] *limḫur u šumma išt*[*u* ...] *iṣbat u ši-ip*-[...]-*x-qi la i-pa-an-ni-x*-[...] *igrīšu la i-ṣa-x*-[...] *bēl šipre* [...]

E ¶ 3 [If ...] all, as much as [...] he shall receive and if from [...] he seizes and [...] he shall not [...] his hire he shall not [...] the official in charge of the work [...]

(rev. 10–15) [*šumma* ...]-*x-qi ki-ip ēpiš* [...] *išakkunu x* [... *um*]*miāne pani* [...] *x ummiāne* [...] *u x* [...] *x i*-[...]

E ¶ 4 [If ...] ... the one who performs [...] they shall do [...] the previous creditor [...] the creditor [...]

(remainder broken)

MAL F

(break of undetermined size)

(col. i, fragmentary ends of about 8 lines)

[*šumma* ...] (ii 1–8) *ana* [...] *immeru ša x* [...] *x* [...] *u šumma* [...] *x x x x* [...] *ina pitqe ša tappāišu x* [...] *ušašnīma šûma ša-*[...] *nāšiāna ša immere* 1 *meat in*[*a ḫaṭṭāte imaḫ-ḫuṣuš*] *ibaqqunuš iltēn uraḫ ūmāte šip*[*ar šarre eppaš*] *u šurqa ša immere i*[*našši*]

F ¶ 1 [If ...] a sheep of [...] and if [...] in his comrade's sheepfold [...] he changes ... [... they shall strike] the one who carried off the sheep 100 blows [with rods], and they shall tear out his hair; he shall perform service for the king for one full month; and he shall be liable for the theft of the sheep.

(ii 9–14) *rēʾi sugulle ša sīs*[*āʾē* ...] *balu bēlišu šâle lu ana kaspe* [*lu ana* ...] *la iddan ina qātišu la* [... *rē*]*ʾi sugulle u māḫirā*[*na* ...] *umāma ša iddi*[*nuni* ...]*-x-šu inaqquru*

F ¶ 2 The horse herder who [tends] horses shall not give [a horse] for silver [or for ...] without obtaining the permission of its owner.[49] [...] shall not [...] from him. The horse herder and the buyer [...] the animal which he sold [...] they shall lacerate his [entire face(?)].

(ii 15–17) [*šumma* ...] *ša ekalle* [...]*-x-x-*[...] TA [...]

F ¶ 3 [If ...] of the palace [...]

(remainder broken)

MAL J

(break of undetermined size)

(obv. 1) [... *il*]*aqqeu*

J ¶ 1 [If ...] they shall take.

(2–3) [*šumma* ... *i*]*šaqqe* [... *i*]*šaqqe*

J ¶ 2 [If ...] he shall irrigate, [...] he shall irrigate.

(4–7) [*šumma* ...] 3[50] *aʾīlū* 1 *aʾīlu* [...] *ša āle ma-e-ni* [... *la*]*ššu ina ūme kesēra* [...] *x ēpušu ušallumu*

J ¶ 3 [If ...] three(?) men one man [...] of the city ... [...] there is not [...] when the (irrigation canal?) is blocked(?) [...] they have performed, they shall make restitution.

(8–13) *[šumma ...] ēpušu ana iltêt šattišunu [... iba]ššiuni [...]-aš-tu ki* 2[a] *qatinnu [... ša š]arre izzazzu [... ana š]ipirti šarre [... uša]llumu*

J ¶ 4 [If ...] they perform, for their one year [...] there is [...] ... two *qatinnu*-personnel [...] of the king shall be present [... for] the royal assignment [...] they shall make restitution.

(rev. 1–4) *[šumma ...] ušēṣûni [...] ušēṣû[ni ...]-x-ru-šu-nu [...]-x ušeppušušunu*

J ¶ 5 [If ...] they lease [...] they lease [...] ... [...] they shall have them perform.

(rev. 5–7) *[šumma ...]-šu ukalluni [...]-a-ar [...]*

J ¶ 6 [If ...]

(remainder broken)

MAL K

(break of undetermined size)

(1–2) [...] *x ù x* [...] *x ù šūt ki-x-*[...]

K ¶ 1 [...]

(3–6) *[šumma ...] x ša šarre la t[alaqqe ... qā]tāte kaspe ina muḫḫi [... qātāt]e la talaqqe qātā[te ... qātāt]e la talaqqe qātāte [...]*

K ¶ 2 [If ...] of the king she shall not take [...] shares of the silver charged against [...] she shall not take [shares], shares [...] she shall not take [shares], shares [...]

(7–9) *[šumma ...] kaspu lu šēlu mimma qājipānu x [...] šanāte(?) lišḫut lu ša* [... M]EŠ *annâte kaspa u mitḫaršu [...]*

K ¶ 3 [If ...] the silver is produced; whatever the creditor [...] years(?) let him cast off either [...] these [...] the silver and its equivalent [...]

(remainder broken)

MAL L

(break of undetermined size)

(1–4) *[šumma ...] x [...] x [... in]a muḫḫišu x [...]-ti la talaqq[e ...]*

L ¶ 1 [If ...] against him [...] she shall not take [...]

(5–6) *[šumma ...] x ana* LÚ *ubre [...] x x x ša šaknuni [...]*

L ¶ 2 [If ...] to a foreigner [...] which is placed [...]

(7–9) *[šumma ... mā]r mātišu ultataʾidma*[52] *i-[...] x ubtaʾeruš uktaʾinu[š ...] x ina ku si igammaršu u [...]*

L ¶ 3 [If ...] a native of his country [...] ... [...] and they prove the charges against him and find him guilty [...] ... he shall settle with him [...]

(10–12) *[šumma ...] x dajānu ḫabbulaššu ana bēt[išu ... da]jānu ḫabbulu la eppal šumma [...] ša bēl dēnišu e-[...]*

L ¶ 4 [If ...] the judge [shall ...] his indebtedness to/for his house [...] the judge, he is indebted, he shall not satisfy; if [...] of his adversary in court [...]

(13–15) *[šumma ...] x ukalluni [...] šulmān[u ...] an[a ...]*

L ¶ 5 [If ...] he shall hold [...] the gratuity [...]

(remainder broken)

MAL M

(obv. 1–7) *[šumma ...] ina raminiš[u x ...] ... mā pušran[i elip]pu(?) x-it-x-[x]-ša-ru-ša*[53] *lu iṭbu lu innie [eli]ppa adi mānihāteša lu rabiu [ša i]špurušuni u lu šūtma ša elippa [ut]taeranni*[54] *umallû malaḫḫu [ša n]īš šarre la izkurūneššuni la iturra*

M ¶ 1 [If a boat drifts(?)] by itself [and the captain(?) calls a warning], saying, "Clear (a passage) for me," the boat(?) ... whether it sinks or capsizes(?)[55]—either the commander(?) who dispatched him or he who steered(?) the boat shall restore the boat together with all its equipment. The boatman against whom they do not swear an oath by the life of the king (accusing him of negligence) shall not turn back (from taking the oath?).

(8–14) *[šumm]a elippu lu ištu eliš iqqalpua [u l]u ištu ebertān ēbera ina šaḫāt [(x) nā]bili lu elippa malīta imḫaṣma u[ṭebbi u lu eli]ppa rāqtamma imḫa[ṣma uṭebbi] mimma mānihāte ammar iḫall[iquni ... elip]pu maḫiltu [...] x x [...]*

M ¶ 2a If a boat either drifts down from upstream or crosses over from the opposite bank, and either rams and sinks a fully laden boat or rams and [sinks] an empty boat moored at the bank, whatever equipment is lost [...] the rammed boat [...]

(gap)

(rev. 1–3) [...] *x x* [...] *x x*.ḪI.A [...][56]

M ¶ 2b [...]

(rev. 4–13) [*šumma aʾīlu* ...] *ṣubātē adi muḫḫi ša ḫarr*[*āne* ... *ana a*]*šlāke ana masāe iddin*[*aššu* ...] *ḫalaqme iqbi mimm*[*a ša* ... *ḫalq*]*uni qaqqadamma ana x* [*x umalla*] *u šumma kî ana kaspe iddinuni*[57] [...] *ittašme* [*ubtaʾeruš*] *uktaʾinuš* [...] *iṣṣabtu ša aʾīle* [...] *x šurqa x* [... (one or two lines lost)]

M ¶ 3 [If a man] gives [...] garments to the cleaner for washing while he is off on a journey, [... and] the cleaner declares, "They are lost," [he shall restore to him garments equal to those] lost, up to the original value. But if it is known [...] that he sold them [and they prove the charges against him] and find him guilty, [...] they are seized, of the man [...] the theft [...]

MAL N

(break of undetermined size)

(1–4) [*šumm*]*a aʾīlu ina ṣalte ana aʾīle* [... *iqbi*] *mā šillata ta*[*qbi* ...] *u bēt ile tuḫtammiṣ x* [...] 40 *ina ḫaṭṭāte imaḫḫuṣuš* [x *ūmāte šipar šarre eppaš*]

N ¶ 1 If a man [says ...] to another man in a quarrel, "You have spoken blasphemy, [...] and furthermore you have pilfered the temple," [...] they shall strike him 40 blows with rods; [he shall perform the king's service for x days].

(5–10) *šumma aʾīlu ina ṣalte ana* [*aʾīle*(?) ... *iqbi*] *mā šillata* [*taqbi* ...] *u bēt ile tuḫt*[*ammiṣ* ...] *baʾura l*[*a ilaʾe la ubaʾer*] *aʾīla šuā*[*tu* x *ina ḫaṭṭāte imaḫḫuṣuš*] *iltēn ur*[*aḫ ūmāte šipar šarre eppaš*]

N ¶ 2 If a man [says ...] to [another man(?)] in a quarrel, "You have spoken blasphemy, [...] and furthermore you have pilfered the temple," [...] but he is unable to prove the charges and does not prove the charges, [they shall strike] that man [x blows with rods; he shall perform the king's service] for one full month.

(remainder broken)

MAL O

(obv. col. i 1–2) [*šumma aʾīlu šīmat* ... *ana m*]*ārēšu išīm* [...] *x x x eppušu*

O ¶ 1 [If a man] determines [the disposition of his estate in favor of] his sons [...] they shall perform.

(obv. col. i 3–9) *[šumma a'īlu ...]-x-zu-ma ṭēmšu šanīšu [... u šīmat] bētišu la išiam [...] x x x eppušuni [...]-lu-ku [...]-ur [...] x [...]*

O ¶ 2a [If a man ...] ... and he is incompetent [... and] he does not determine the [disposition] of his household [...] which they make [...]

(gap)

[šumma ...] (col. ii 1–7) *ina ūmāte x x [...] bētāte ša x [...] urdē izuzz[u ...] u kirâte [...] urki annê x [...] ṭuppāte ša x [...] u šēbūte amma[r ...]*

O ¶ 2b [If ...] days [...] houses which [...] slaves they shall divide [...] and orchards [...] later these [...] tablets which [...] and as many witnesses [...]

(obv. col. ii 8–13) *[šumm]a aḫḫū bēt abi[šunu izūzu kir]âte u būrāte [ina qaqqere ... māru rabû 2 qāt]āte in[assaq ilaqqe u aḫḫūšu urki a]ḫā'iš in[assuqu ilaqqeu ina eqel šiluḫlē mimma u] māna[ḫāte gabbe māru ṣeḫru ussaq ...]*

O ¶ 3[58] If brothers [divide] the estate of their father, orchards and wells [in the plot of land ..., the oldest son shall select and take a double] share, [and his brothers shall select and take] shares one after the other; [the youngest son is the one who apportions whatever *šiluḫlu*-personnel there are and all the associated] equipment [in the field (to be divided) ...]

(gap)

(rev. col. i 1–3) *šumma bēl [...] mêšina x [...] ubarrû u id[dinu ...]*

O ¶ 4 If the owner of [...] their water [...] they claim and they give [...]

(rev. col. i 4–11) *[šu]mma ina ugāre ina libbi [būrāte mā'u ša ana šīqe ana šakāne illukūni] ibašši bēlū [eqlāte ištu aḫā'iš izzazzu a'īlu ana sīr eqlišu] šipra eppaš eqelšu i[šaqqi u šumma ina libbišunu] la magrūtu iba[šši magru ša libbišunu dajānē] iša'al ṭuppa ša d[ajānē iṣabbat u šipra eppaš] mā'e šunātunu ana ra[minišu ilaqqe eqelšu išaqqi mamma šaniumma la išaqqi]*

O ¶ 5[59] If there is sufficient water for irrigation available in the common irrigated area in the wells, the owners of the fields shall act together; each man shall perform the work in accordance with the extent of his field, and shall irrigate his field. But if there are some among them who are not amenable to an agreement, the one among them who is amenable to an agreement shall appeal to the judges; he shall obtain a tablet (with the decision) of the judges, and perform the work; [he shall take] those waters for himself [and irrigate his own field; no one else may irrigate (with the waters)].

(gap)

(rev. col. ii 1–9) [*šumma* ...] *x x x uššurašu* [...]-*ki ibtuq iltēn mana ṣarpa iddan* [... x *m*]*ana ṣarpa iddan* [(x) ...] *bilat annaka idd*[*an* (*x*) ...] *šurqa*[60] *idd*[*an* (*x*) ...]-*x-x-ab-bu-šu ina ki-x* [...] ... *ilaqqeu*

O ¶ 6 [If ...] his release [...] he accuses, he shall give 60 shekels of silver, [...] he shall give [x] shekels of silver, [...] he shall give [x] talents of lead, [...] he shall give [...] the theft [...] ... [...] they shall take.

Notes

1. Some literature refers to a third class, the "Assyrian (man or woman)" (*aššuraju* or *aššuraʾītu*), and suggests that persons so designated were members of a class socially, legally, or economically inferior to the *aʾīlu* (see Driver and Miles 1935: 284–86). However, the distinction is not borne out in the provisions in the MAL that refer to the *aššuraju* (especially A ¶ 44 and C ¶ 3; see also A ¶¶ 24 and 40 and C ¶ 7), or in other contemporary Middle Assyrian texts (*KAJ* 2 and 167 [= *ARU* 5 and 7] are cited in the arguments). The distinguishing point in MAL C ¶ 3 (the key provision in the arguments) is whether or not the value of the person as pledge exceeds the amount of the debt, and not whether the person is an "Assyrian."

2. David 1939: 121 n. 4 argued that Schroeder 1920: no. 144 ("MAL H") is a fragment of a ritual and not of a law collection; see further Saporetti 1979: 134 with n. 91.

3. Lines 5–6 differently restored by Otto 1993: 157; see p. 158 n. 49.

4. Var. omits *sinniltu*, "a woman."

5. Var. omits "from the sanctuary."

6. Var. omits *sinniltu*, "a woman."

7. Only source a preserved from here on.

8. AN.NA (*annuku*) is translated "lead" (rather than "tin"), following the arguments presented by Freydank 1982: 74–75 n. 27 and Müller 1982.

9. Restoration [*e*]-*ri-im-ma*, "became inflamed(?), atrophied(?)," remains uncertain; see *CAD* E 295 s.v. *erimu* discussion section.

10. Possible restorations include "eyes" and "breasts"; see Paul 1990: 337–38 with notes.

11. Literally, "I want to fornicate with you"; the verb *nâku* is used of initiating illicit sexual intercourse.

12. See the note at MAL A ¶ 12.

13. See the note at MAL A ¶ 12.

14. Or "beard."

15. The implication of sodomy is obtained from the context, and not from the verb *nâku*, which refers to fornication; see also the note at MAL A ¶ 12.

16. Or "beard."

17. See the note at MAL A ¶ 19.

18. Otto 1993: 146 restores in line 55 [*ú-na-ka-áš la-a*]; *CAD* Š/1 s.v. *šadādu* mng. 3c restores [*ana bētišu*], thus "... takes his wife back to his house." The restoration here follows Driver and Miles 1935, Borger 1982c: 84, etc., seeing a form of *nakāsu* (see *CAD* N/1 s.v., mng. 6b) and presenting the opposite solution to that foreseen in the final clause of the provision.

19. Or, reading (albeit without the geographical determinative) the proper noun *Libbi-āle*, thus "either in the Inner City (i.e., Assur) itself or in any of the nearby towns."

20. See *CAD* Š/1 288 s.v. *šaluštu* A mng. 2b; written 3-*a-te* (in MAL A ¶¶ 24, 55, 56, and B ¶ 14), 3.TA.ÀM-*a-te* (in MAL B ¶ 8) and 3-*ti* (in MAL B ¶ 9). The amount and nature of the compensation indicated by *šalšāte*, "one-third" or "triple," of what commodity it consists, and to whom it is paid, all remain obscure.

21. The full legal implications of this action are unclear.

22. See *CAD* A/1 217 s.v. *aḫūzatu*, understanding a "marriage-like relationship of dependency and protection between an unprotected female and the head of a household."

23. Text: "the father-in-law" (error).

24. Or, restoring *kī sar*[*re*] *ṣabitma*, "he was arrested as a criminal."

25. Restoring a II/2 or III/2 of *šaṭāru* (so Driver and Miles 1935, Cardascia 1969, Borger 1982, etc.) not certain.

26. Problems in restoration and interpretation of A ¶ 45 are discussed by Postgate 1971: 502–8 and Aynard and Durand 1980: 9–13.

27. The clause (*šumma ana dannat šarre la ērub*) is usually translated with the sense "if he (the husband) does not enter royal military service" (e.g., *CAD* E 264 s.v. *erēbu* mng. 1b–2', Cardascia 1969: 218, etc.), with parallels drawn to LH ¶¶ 27–28, but this fails to explain the import of the clause here. Perhaps the clause includes an elliptical allusion to the *ṭuppu dannutu*, "binding tablet" of MA real estate transfers which receives royal sanction and provides final and irrevocable proof of purchase (see Postgate 1971: 514–17; also Aynard and Durand 1980: 12-13); thus here the sense would be that if the sale were not yet registered by a binding tablet, the original owner could reclaim the house and field by payment of the sum realized from the sale.

28. Text: "Her father will ask ..."

29. The break may rather have room for only [*šumma aʾīlu sinnilta im*]*ḫaṣma*, "If a man strikes a woman ..."

30. Or "If the fetus dies as a result of the (attempted) abortion, ..."(?).

31. *ūtarrišuni* (viii 9) is taken, following von Soden (*AHw*. s.v. *urrušu* II), as a II/2 of *erēšu* (B) "to ask, request."

32. Borger 1982: 92: "des Blendens," cf. *CAD* G s.v. **gullulu* adj.; perhaps *gullulu* v. "to commit a sin"?

33. ¶ 59 concludes, following line 63, with double incised partition lines, following which there are five sections before the date formula which begins in line 64. The first and largest section is a completely blank space the size of about 15 lines concluded by a single incised line; the second is a space with traces of 10 erased lines, concluded by double lines, within which there is a drawing of a bisected

triangle; the third, fourth, and fifth, each concluded by double lines, show traces of four erased lines, four erased lines, and three erased lines, respectively.

34. See O ¶ 3.

35. Lit., "owner of life."

36. Reading *lu ši*(text PI)*-la-ta*, see *CAD* Š/2 446 s.v. *šillatu* mng. 1b.

37. Reading with Weidner 1937/39: 50.

38. Copy *a-ti*, emended to 3*-ti* with Weidner 1937/39: 50.

39. See O ¶ 5.

40. Text: *ut*(error for *uš*)*-ra-a-aq*, following Cardascia 1969: 290 n. b.

41. Restorations are conjectural; see the various restorations and interpretations proposed in Landsberger 1949: 291; Driver and Miles 1935; Cardascia 1969; Saporetti 1979; and Aynard and Durand 1980: 32–33 n. 41.

42. So with Saporetti 1979 ([... *iš-ta-r*]*i-iq*); copy [...]*-x-ḫu-ḫi*.

43. G obv. joins C here, and provides most or all of the following ¶ 6a; G rev. 1–6 = ¶ 6b; G rev. 7–13 (the last two lines joining C rev. 1–2) = ¶ 7; and G rev. 14 restores some of the first line of ¶ 8. (For consistency, the line numbering of C is continued through the obverse, and resumed at ¶ 8; the line numbers of G rev. are used only for ¶¶ 6b and 7.)

44. Reading KUR, "(the judges of) the land" is not certain.

45. So Weidner 1937/39: 50.

46. Reading follows Weidner 1937/39: 50.

47. Possibly read: [...] 1 MA.NA "[...] one mina (= 60 shekels)."

48. Line 15 is the final line of the provision.

49. Or: "his master."

50. The sign is partially broken, and could also be "7."

51. Saporetti 1979: 177 reads [... *qe-p*]*u-tu ù*! 1 LÚ ...

52. See *CAD* N/1 6 s.v. *na'ādu* mng. 7b.

53. Saporetti 1979 reads in line 3, [GIŠ.M]Á *š*[*i*]-⸢*i*⸣*-it p*[*u-uš*?]*-ša-ru-ša*, etc., translating the passage, "q[ue]sta(?) barca x [x] x x x."

54. Taking a II/3 from *âru*, see the references *CAD* A/2 323 s.v. *âru* mng. 5 and compare *CAD* A/2 315 s.v. *arû* A mng. 2b (I/3).

55. See Cardascia 1969: 330.

56. The gap between the end of the preserved obverse and the beginning of the preserved reverse is probably much too large to permit including these lines within the previous provision.

57. Reading *id-di-nu-ni*(copy *-uš*) follows David 1939: 132.

58. See B ¶ 1.

59. See B ¶ 17.

60. Weidner 1937/39: 54, followed by Cardascia 1969: 338, reads 4 SILA; *šur-qa* here follows Sapporetti 1979: 146.

Middle Assyrian Palace Decrees (MAPD) (ca. 1076 B.C.E., Assur)

About the Laws

The Middle Assyrian Palace Decrees (also known as the "Harem Edicts") is a collection of regulations dealing with the internal activities and behavior of the palace personnel, and in particular of the palace women (the "harem") and those male officials who interact with them. The decrees were issued by the Assyrian kings, who were personally concerned with maintaining the order and inviolability of the "Inner Quarters" in which the royal women resided. The collection as we have it includes decrees issued by nine kings and was assembled in the time of Tiglath-pileser I (r. 1114-1076 B.C.E.), four of whose palace decrees conclude the collection. The Assyrian practice of dating years by eponyms—sequential reference to named high officials—allows us to assign the eponym in the colophon of Source A to an official of the reign of Tiglath-pileser I, placing the scribal effort that assembled the collection within the first quarter of the eleventh century.

There are few precedents for such decrees, but one unusual text suggests that royal involvement in the daily affairs of the palace household was not unique to the Middle Assyrian kings. An edict (*šūdūtu*) from fourteenth-century B.C.E. Nuzi (roughly contemporary with the earliest of the Assyrian rulers whose decrees are included in the MAPD) dictates internal palace behavior. The Nuzi edict (Pfeiffer and Speiser 1936: No. 51) reads:

> This is the old edict concerning the personnel, the palace slaves and the palace retainers. Thus says [the king]:
>
> No one, whether palace slave or palace retainer, shall force his daughter into homeless destitution or into prostitution without the permission of the king. Whosoever, whether palace slave <or palace retainer>, has forced his daughter into homeless destitution or into prostitution without the permission of the king, or has ...-ed his daughter into homeless destitution or into

prostitution—they shall take him into the palace and they shall moreover(?) take into the palace as a gift (dedicated to palace service) a second daughter of his in lieu of (the daughter lost to the palace); and as for him, they shall impose a replacement-fine upon him.

They shall proclaim this tablet in their (the palace personnel's) presence every three or four years, lest it be forgotten.

Although the precise subject matter with which the Nuzi edict is concerned does not appear in the extant MAPD, there are several illuminating similarities between the two documents.[1] First, of course, is the Nuzi and Assur palaces' efforts to secure the women in their charge or to whom they have a claim. Second, the Nuzi text's self-identification as an "old" edict parallels the MAPD's assembly and reporting of the decrees of previous kings and the continuing relevance of these earlier pronouncements for palace life. Third, the Nuzi edict is to be proclaimed periodically as a reminder for the relevant personnel, clarifying the sense of the largely broken subscript in the MAPD. Other, similar palace edicts or decrees may have been common elsewhere, too, in the middle of the second millennium.

About the Sources

Each decree (Akkadian *riksu*) in the MAPD is marked off on the tablets by a single horizontal line, and a shift to the decrees of a subsequent king is marked by a double horizontal line (source G, exceptionally, has a double line also before ¶ 17). The reconstruction of the sequence of decrees within the compilation is generally secure, resulting in a composition with twenty-three decrees of nine rulers whose reigns spanned almost three centuries, from 1363 to 1076 B.C.E.[2] The cumulative nature of the compilation reveals an overlap and repetition of decrees from one ruler to another and suggests that the final compilation may have served as a reference work rather than as (or in addition to) a set of immediately practical rules.

The nine fragmentary sources of the MAPD are all Middle Assyrian in date and from the capital city Assur. Eight (now in Berlin) were excavated in Assur and published together, with the first edition of the composition, by Weidner 1954/56; a ninth (at Yale), from a purchased collection without documented provenience, was published by Beckman and Foster 1988.

¶ 1. Ashur-uballiṭ I (r. 1363–1328 B.C.E.)

(1–12 [A 1–12, B 1–11, C 1–2]) [*Aššur-uballiṭ uklu mār Erība-Adad uklemma riksa ana … irkus*]

¶ 1 [Ashur-uballiṭ, overseer, son of Erība-Adad, himself also overseer, issued a decree for …:]

[*šumma* ...] *sikkāte ša pan ṣābē ekalle* [...] *la uššab sikkāte* [...] *u ki-i(-)mu(-) še-im-ma epšu* [... *l*]*u mār mamma ša kalze ekalle* [... *ša*] *errubu emmurušunu* [...] *sikkāte balut rab ekalle* [*ša'āle* ...]*-ni bēl pāḫite ana* [...]*-te ūr ekalle iserru* [... *ša ana ūr eka*]*lle ētelliuni ḫīṭa inašši* [...]*-bu kî qāt gišḫurāte* [...] *sabsūtu u qadiltu* [...] *la irraba la uṣṣâ*

[If ...] the locks(?) which are before the palace personnel [...] he shall not reside; the locks(?) [...] and ... is made [...] or anyone from the palace area [... who] enters and sees them, [...] the locks(?), without asking the permission of the palace commander [...] the provincial governor to the [...]; they shall plaster the roof of the palace; [... he who] goes up to the roof of the palace is held responsible for a punishable offense [...] according to the building plans [...] the midwife and the *qadiltu*-woman [...] shall not go in or go out.

¶ 2. Enlil-nārārī (r. 1327–1318 B.C.E.)

(13–21 [A 13–21, B 12–20, C 3–11, D 1–9]) *Enlil-nārārī uklu* [*mār Aššur-uballiṭ uklemma riksa ana ... irk*]*us*

¶ **2** Enlil-nārārī, overseer, [son of Ashur-uballiṭ, himself also overseer,] issued [a decree for ...:]

ilu lu la iqabbi šumma lu mār šarre lu aḫi šarre [...] *ša aššāt šarre ina kīde mēt u lu* [...] *gabbu ša sinnišāte ša ekalle mēt šumma šarru ina Libbi-*[*āle uššab ... ša*] *ibbaššûni illaka ana ukal ekalle iqabbi u ukal ek*[*alle ana šarre iqabbi* ...]

God forbid, if either the king's son, or the king's brother, [or ... one] of the wives of the king dies outside of the palace, or [... one of] any of the palace women dies, if the king is residing in the Inner City, [... any official] who is available shall go and report to the palace overseer, and the palace overseer shall report to the king ...]

u šumma šarru ina 2 bēr eqle uššab ukal ekalle ana muḫḫi [*šarre išappar* ...]

However, if the king is residing within a distance of two double-hours[3] (travel time from the palace), the palace overseer [shall send written tablets] to [the king ...]

[... *šumm*]*a šarru aqqāt 2 bēr eqle* [*uššab*] *ṭuppāte ana muḫḫi šarre la iša*[*ppar ... sinnišātu ša ekalle*] *kī pī rikse ša šarre ibakkia*

[... If] the king [is residing] farther away than two double-hours (travel time from the palace), he shall not send written tablets to the king; [...

the palace women] shall perform the mourning rites according to the king's decree.

šumma balut ukal ekal[le ša'āle ... an]a ṣābē ša ekalle iqtibi ubarrušu [... appušu uznēšu] inakkisu

If, without asking the permission of the palace overseer, he (the official) should report (the death directly) to the palace personnel, they shall prove the charge against him, [...] they shall cut off [his nose and ears(?).]

¶ 3. Adad-nārārī I (r. 1305–1274 B.C.E.)

(22–27 [B 21–22, C 12–17, D 10–15]) *Adad-nārārī uklu mār Ar[ik-dēn-ili uklemma riksa ana ... irkus ...]*

¶ 3 Adad-nārārī, overseer, son of Arik-[dēn-ili, himself also overseer, issued a decree for ... :]

[sinnišātu ... ša] kīdânu aḫḫuzāni ina bēt mutēšina us[bāni ...] lu [ina] ūme rāqe balut šarre ša'ā[le la ... šumma ... ša ina Libbi-āl]e usbuni la iš'aluni [... us]buni atû [... l]u ša rēš šarre lu mazz[iz pane ...]

[Women ... (working in the palace) who are] married to men from outside of it and who are residing in their husbands' houses [shall not ... either during ...] or on the day of a holiday, without asking permission of the king; [if ... who] resides within the Inner City does not ask permission, [... who] resides, the doorkeepers [...], or a royal eunuch, or a court attendant [...]

¶¶ 4–5. Shalmaneser I (r. 1273–1244 B.C.E.)

(28–32 [D 16–19, E 1–3]) *Šulmā[nu-ašarid uk]lu [mār Adad-nārārī uklemma riksa ana ... irkus]*

¶ 4 Shalmaneser, overseer, [son of Adad-nārārī, himself also overseer, issued a decree for ... :]

[...] *a[na ḫarr]āne* [...] *x* [...] *tu* [...] *x* [...]

[...] on a journey [...]

(33–37 [E 4–8, I 1–5]) *Šulmānu-ašarid uklu mār Adad-nārārī uklemma riksa ana ṣā[bē ša ekalle irk]us*

¶ 5 Shalmaneser, overseer, son of Adad-nārārī, himself also overseer, issued a decree for the [palace] personnel:

sinniltu ša ek[alle] lu ḫurāṣa lu ṣarpa u lu abna ana urad ekalle la [taddan ... ēpiš] šipre la ú-te-[... šumma ...] u rab ekalle ultēṣi sinnilta ša ekalle la uššuru [šumma ... lu] urad ekalle lu [...] appušu uznēšu inakkisu ēpiš šipre [ša lu ḫurāṣa lu ṣarpa u lu abna ina qāt urad ekalle ...] imtaḫruni šipra x [... a'īlu ša] ana šarre la ibtatquni utaḫḫuḫušu [...] mārūšu ana ekalle i[t-...]

A palace woman shall not [give] gold, silver, or precious stones to a palace slave; [...] a craftsman shall not [...; if the ...] and the palace commander should allow (him/her) to leave, they shall not release the palace woman; [if ... either] a palace slave or [a ...] they shall cut off his nose and ears. A craftsman [who] has received [gold, silver, or precious stones from a palace slave shall ...], the work [...]; they shall douse (with hot oil?) [the person who] has not denounced (the craftsman) to the king; [...] his sons shall [be enslaved(?)] to the palace.

¶¶ 6–8. Tukultī-Ninurta I (r. 1243–1207 B.C.E.)

(38–45 [E 9–16, F 1–8, I 6–13]) *Tukultī-Ninurta uklu mār Šulmānu-ašarid uklemma riksa an[a ... irkus]*

¶ **6** Tukultī-Ninurta, overseer, son of Shalmaneser, himself also overseer, [issued] a decree for the [...:]

kî šarru ištu Libbi-āle i-x-[...] ṣābū ša ekalle ša ištu šarre ana ḫarrāne illakūni bētāssunu [...]-x-ub-bu lu dumāqē lu lubu[lte lu šapāte] u lu šamnē ša ṣābē ekalle ša ištu šarre illakūni rab ek[allemma] ipatte e-šar ú-še-ṣ[u-ú(?) ...] ša balut rab ekalle lu ina mūše lu ina kal ūme mamma mimma [uš]ēṣiuni idukkuš

When the king [leaves] the Inner City, the palace personnel who travel with the king on the journey [shall bring] their containers(?) [into the palace; only] the palace commander shall open (the containers holding) the jewelry, the clothing, [the wool], and the oil rations of the palace personnel who travel with the king; they shall remove(?) in proper manner(?) [...]; they shall kill anyone who removes anything, either at night or anytime during the day, without the permission of the palace commander.

[šumma šarru] lu ina bīt lušme lu ina bīt nāre lu ina ekallāte ša li[bīt] Libbi-āle uššab sinniltu ša ekal[le] la tašap-paramma ištu muḫḫi ṣubāte ša qable

[If the king] should reside either in the Lushmu House or in the River House or in any of the other palaces within the environs of the

lēdē paṣiūte ṣubāte ša ḫarrā[ne ...] šuḫuppāte u mim[ma šumšu] balut šarre u rab ekalle ša'āle la tašapparamma ištu ek[all]e la ušēṣû ina ūme a[na ...] tuṣṣûni lubultaša rab ekalle u atû emmuru la ikallû[ši]

Inner City, a palace woman shall not send for anything; she shall not send for a skirt, white wraps, a travel cloak, [...], leather boots, or anything else, without asking permission of the king or of the palace commander, and they shall remove nothing from the palace (without permission). On the day that she leaves (the palace) to [meet the king(?)], the palace commander and the door keepers shall inspect her wardrobe but they shall not detain her (or: withhold it).

(46–47 [E 17–18, F 9–10, G 1–2, I 14–15]) *Tukultī-Ninurta uklu mār Šulmānu-ašarid uklemma riksa ana ṣābē ša ekalle irkus*

¶ 7 Tukultī-Ninurta, overseer, son of Shalmaneser, himself also overseer, issued a decree for the palace personnel:

ištu niqiāte kašāde sinniltu ša ekalle ša la qarābšani ana pan šarre la terrab

When the time for making sacrifices draws near, a palace woman who is menstruating (lit.: unapproachable) shall not enter into the presence of the king.

(48–51 [E 19, F 11–14, G 3–6, I 16]) *Tukultī-Ninurta uklu mār Šulmānu-ašarid uklemma ana mazziz panūte riksa irkus*

¶ **8** Tukultī-Ninurta, overseer, son of Shalmaneser, himself also overseer, issued a decree for the court attendants:

ina ūm il ḫarrāne kî ana ekalle errabuni ša muḫḫi ekalle nāgir ekalle rab zāriqē asû ša bētānu kî mazziz panūte iḫirrūni lu ša rēš šarre lu mazziz pane ša la marruruni iqabbiu ša šanuttešu ana mazziz panutte iddunuš šumma qēpūtu annûtu la iqtibiu ḫīṭa inaššiu

On the day of the God-of-the-Journey,[4] when he (the statue of the deity) enters the palace, and when the palace administrator, the palace herald, the chief of the water-sprinklers (of the Processional Residence[5]), and the physician of the Inner Quarters inspect the court attendants, they shall report any royal eunuch or court attendant who is not castrated (lit.: who is not checked) and they shall hand him over to be made into a (castrated) court attendant for a second time. If these officials should not make a report, they are held responsible for a punishable offense.

¶¶ 9–17. Ninurta-apil-Ekur (r. 1191–1179 B.C.E.)

(52–55 [F 15–18, G 7–10]) [*Ninurta-api*]*l-Ekur uklu mār Erība-Adad uklemma riksa ana ekallišu irkus*

¶ 9 Ninurta-apil-Ekur, overseer, son of Erība-Adad, himself also overseer, issued a decree for his palace:

šumma šarru ša rēš šarre ina kal ūme ana muḫḫi [*sinnišāte ša ekalle*] *išappar šumma ina āle balut rab ekalle ša āle ana ekall*[*e ad*]*i*(?) *maškan-itḫuru šaknuni* [*la errab ana rab*] *ekalle iqabbi adi errabuni uṣṣâni rab ekalle ina pī x*-[(*x*)]-*sa-te izzaz*

If the king intends to send a royal eunuch during the daytime to [the quarters of the palace women]—if (the women are) in the city, [he (the royal eunuch) shall not enter] into the palace, without the permission of the palace commander of the city, as long as(?) the tent of the *itḫuru*-standard is erected. He shall (first) report to the palace commander. As long as he enters (and stays inside), the women shall leave and the palace commander shall stand at the entrance to the [...]

šumma ina ḫūle [*balut rab ek*]*alle u rab zāriqē la errab šumma ša rēš šarre balut qēp*[*ūte*] *annûte ētarab ḫīṭa inašši*

If (the women are) in the Processional Residence,[6] he shall not enter (their quarters) without the permission of the palace commander and of the chief of the water sprinklers. If the royal eunuch enters without the permission of these officials, he is held responsible for a punishable offense.

(56–59 [F 19–22, G 11–13]) [*Ninurta-apil-Ekur uklu*] *mār Erība-Adad uklemma riksa ana ekallišu irk*[*us*]

¶ 10 [Ninurta-apil-Ekur, overseer,] son of Erība-Adad, himself also overseer, issued a decree for his palace:

lu aššāt šarre lu sinnišātu mādātu [*ša ekalle ša* ...] *aḫā'iš idūkāni ina*

(Any royal women), either the king's wives or other women [of

ṣaltišina šu[m il]e ana masikte tazzakrūni [... (la) e]rrab napšāte ša Aššur it-[...] inakkisu ina ṣaltišina [...]-ki ana pi-x-[x-x]-x la tappal

the palace, who ...] fight among themselves and in their quarrel blasphemously swear by the name of the god, [...] he shall [(not)] enter; they shall cut the throat of the one who has [cursed(?)] the god Ashur; in their quarrel [...] ... [...] she shall not satisfy the claim.

(60–63 [F 23–26, G 14]) [*Ninurta-apil-Ekur uklu mār Erība-Adad uklemma*] *riksa irkus*

¶ **11** [Ninurta-apil-Ekur, overseer, son of Erība-Adad, himself also overseer,] issued a decree:

[*šumma* ...] *napšāteja ana la kitte* [... *šu*]*m šarre ina ṣalte la* [*izakkar šu*]*m ile lu la izakkar* [...] ... [...] *šum ile ana la kitte* [...] ... [...] *la uballuṭuši*

[If ... says: "...] my life," for improper purposes [...; he shall] not [swear] by the name of the king in a quarrel; and even more so indeed he shall not swear by the name of the god. [... They shall kill a palace woman who swears] by the name of the god for improper purposes [...], they shall not spare her life.

(64–66 [F 27–29]) [*Ninurta-apil-Ekur uklu mār Erība-Adad uklemma riksa ana ... irkus*]

¶ **12** [Ninurta-apil-Ekur, overseer, son of Erība-Adad, himself also overseer, issued a decree for ... :]

[...] *aššat šarre* [...]-*šu* [...]-*ši-na* [...] *izzakar* [... (*la*) *tap*]*pal*

[...] a wife of the king [...] his [...] their (fem.) [...] he has sworn [... she shall (not)] satisfy the claim.

(67–69 [F 30–32]) [*Ninurta-apil-Ekur uklu mār Erība-Adad uklemma riksa ana* ...] *irkus*

¶ **13** [Ninurta-apil-Ekur, overseer, son of Erība-Adad, himself also overseer,] issued a [decree for ... :]

šumma [...]-*ta-at* [...] *sinniltu ša ekal*[*le* ...]-*ni* [...] *x* [...]-*ru*

If [...] a palace woman [...]

(70–72 [F 33–35, H 1–2]) [*Ninurta-apil-Ekur uklu mār Erība-Adad uklemma riksa ana* ...]-*šu irkus*

¶ **14** [Ninurta-apil-Ekur, overseer, son of Erība-Adad, himself also overseer, issued a decree for] his [...:]

šumma [... *ma*]*šikta* [...]-*ma taqṭibi kinat*[*tu* ...] *x* [...]-*ru-ni tašmeuni la* [...]

If [...] she should [...] or utter a blasphemy, a woman of equal status [... that she ...] saw or heard, [she shall] not [...]

(73–75 [F 36–38, G rev. 1, H 3–5]) [*Ninurta-apil-Ekur uklu mār Erība-Adad uklemma riksa ana*] *ṣābē ša ekalli*[*šu irkus*]

¶ **15** [Ninurta-apil-Ekur, overseer, son of Erība-Adad, himself also overseer, issued a decree for] the personnel of [his] palace:

[...] *ḫaliqta* [...] *adi šarru iqabbiašš*[*enni* ...] *šarru* [(...)] *la iqbiaššenni* [...]

[...] a fugitive woman [...] until the king reports it to her [...] the king [(...)] did not report it to her [...]

(76–77 [F rev. 1–2, G rev. 2, H 6–7]) [*Ninurta-apil-Ekur uklu mār Erība-Adad uklem*]*ma riksa ana ekallišu irkus*

¶ **16** [Ninurta-apil-Ekur, overseer, son of Erība-Adad,] himself also [overseer,] issued a decree for his palace:

[*šumma sinniltu ša ekal*]*le* [...] *ekalle ta-x-*[...] *i-*[*x*]-*x-qu*

[If a palace woman ... (the ... of)] the palace [...]

(78–81 [F rev. 3–6, G rev. 3–5, H 8–10]) [*Ninurta-apil-Ekur uklu mār Erība-Adad uklem*]*ma riksa ana ekallišu irkus*

¶ **17** [Ninurta-apil-Ekur, overseer, son of Erība-Adad,] himself also [overseer,] issued a decree for his palace:

[*šumma sinniltu ša*] *ekalle* [...] *tātarar lu mār Tukultī-Ninurta* [*lu* ... *lu ša bē*]*te ša šarre ša majā*[*le* ... *lu*] *ša litte* [... *tātarar lu sinnilta*] *ša šaplānuša tātarar lemniš* [...] *x-na našāʾenni sinniltu ša* [*ekalle a*]*ppaša ipallušu* [30(?) *ina ḫaṭṭāte*] *imaḫḫuṣuši*

[If a] palace [woman] should curse [...], or [should she curse] either a descendant of Tukultī-Ninurta, [or another member of the royal household, or an official of the] royal bedroom, [...] or an official of the stool,[7] or if she should spitefully curse any woman who is beneath her in station, [...] carrying (a child?); they shall pierce the nose of the palace woman; they shall strike her [30(?) blows with rods].

¶ 18. Ashur-dan I (r. 1178–1133 B.C.E.)

(82–90 [F rev. 7–15, G rev. 6–12]) [*Aššur-dan uklu mār Ninurta-apil-*

¶ **18** [Ashur-dan, overseer, son of Ninurta-apil-Ekur,] himself also

Ek]ur uklemma riksa ana ṣābē ša ekall[išu irkus]

overseer, issued a decree for his palace personnel:

[l]u aššat šarre [lu sinniltu ša ekalle šumma amassa lu ḫīṭa ana bēltiša taḫṭia lu ...] lu sarta mimma tētapaš lu [aššat šarre lu] sinniltu ša [ekalle ša am]assa ḫīṭa taḫṭiaššini 30 ina ḫaṭṭāte tamaḫḫassi

Either a wife of the king [or any other palace woman—if her slave woman] commits [a punishable offense against her mistress, or ...-s a ...], or should commit any misdeed, either [the wife of the king or] the palace woman whose slave woman committed a punishable offense against her shall strike her 30 blows with rods.

[... šumma amtu] naṭītu tu-ur-[... lu ḫī]ṭa ana bēltiša taḫṭi[a lu ... lu s]arta tētapaš bēltuša ana [muḫḫi šarre tušerr]ab pan šarre ḫīṭa š[a libb]išu emmid[uši ...] šanītamma ana bēltiša iddan

[... If the slave woman] who was beaten (by her mistress for her first offense) [...] commits a (second) punishable offense against her mistress, [or ...-s a (second) ..., or] commits a (second) misdeed, her mistress shall bring her [before the king]; in the presence of the king, they shall impose upon her the punishment which he shall determine; [...] a second time he shall give (the slave woman back) to her mistress.

šumma sinniltu [ša ekall]e ša pī ri[kse ša šarre ... ša amassa] tattuṭu ina ḫaṭṭāte mētat lu ana muḫ[ḫi ... sinniltu ša ekal]le ša amassa taddūkuni ana šillitiša [...] ḫīṭa ša šarre ta[našši]

If the palace woman [whose slave woman] she beat in accordance with [the royal decree ... is excessive and the slave] dies from the blows, or to [..., the palace woman] who has killed her slave woman [shall suffer] for her insolence; she [is held responsible for] a punishable offense against the king.

¶ 19. Ashur-rēsha-ishi I (r. 1132–1115 B.C.E.)

(91–94 [F rev. 16–19, G rev. 13–16]) *[Aššur-rēša-iši šar māt Aššur mār] Mutakkil-Nusku šar māt Aššurma riksa ana ekallišu irkus*

¶ **19** [Ashur-rēsha-ishi, king of Assyria, son of] Mutakkil-Nusku, himself also king of Assyria, issued a decree for his palace:

šumma sinniltu ša ekall[e ...]-si udīšunu izzazzu šaššu iltešunu laššu lu namutta [...] idukkušunu

If a palace woman [and a ... (man)] are standing by themselves, with no third person with them, whether [they are behaving] in a flirtatious manner [or in a serious manner(?)], they shall kill them.

šumma lu mazziz pane lu sinnišat kinattēša ša tāmurušini [...]-a-x ana bēliša katmat lu sinnilta lu a'īla āmerāna ana libbi utūne ikarrurušunu

If a court attendant or a woman of her own status who sees her [does not inform the king(?), ...]; she is veiled for her master; they shall throw the eyewitness, whether a woman or a man, into the oven.

¶¶ 20–23. Tiglath-pileser I (r. 1114–1076 B.C.E.)

(95–101 [F rev. 20–26, G rev. 17–22]) *[Tukultī-apil]-ešarra šar kiššete šar māt Aššur mār Aššur-rēša-iši šar māt Aššurma riksa ana rab ekalle ša Libbi-āle nāgir ekalle [rab] zāriqē ša ḫūle asue ša bētānu u ša muḫḫi ekallāte ša šiddi māte gabba irkus*

¶ 20 Tiglath-pileser, king of the universe, king of Assyria, son of Ashur-rēsha-ishi, himself also king of Assyria, issued a decree for the palace commander of the Inner City, the palace herald, the chief of the water sprinklers of the Processional Residence, the physician of the Inner Quarters, and the administrator of all the palaces of the entire extent of the country:

lu mazziz panūte ša šarre u lu širkū ša ṣābē ekalle ša ana ekalle errabūni balut ḫiāre [an]a ekalle la errab šumma la marrur ša šanuttešu ana mazziz panutte utarrušu

Royal court attendants or dedicatees of the palace personnel who have access to the palace shall not enter the palace without an inspection; if he is not (properly) castrated, they shall turn him into a (castrated) court attendant for a second time.

šumma lu rab ekalle ša Libbi-āle lu nāgir ekalle lu rab zāriqē ša ḫūle lu asû ša bētānu u lu ša muḫḫi ekallāte ša šiddi māte gabbu mazziz pane la marrura ana ekalle ultēribu urkiš

If either the palace commander of the Inner City, or the palace herald, or the chief of the water sprinklers of the Processional Residence, or the physician of the Inner Quar-

ētamru ša qēpūte annûte iltēnâ[8] *šēpēšunu ubattuqu*

ters, or the administrator of all the palaces of the entire expanse of the country allows an uncastrated court attendant to enter into the palace, and he is later discovered, they shall amputate one foot of each of these officials.

(102–112 [E rev. 1–7, F rev. 27–37]) *Tukultī-apil-ešarra šar kiššete šar māt Aššur mār Aššur-rēša-iši šar māt Aššurma riksa ana mazziz panūte irkus*

¶ **21** Tiglath-pileser, king of the universe, king of Assyria, son of Ashur-rēsha-ishi, himself also king of Assyria, issued a decree for the court attendants:

lu ša-rēš-šarrānu lu mazziz panūte u lu širkū šumma sinniltu ša ekalle lu tazammur u lu ṣalta ištu meḫertiša gar'at u šūt izzaz iltanamme 100 *immaḫḫaṣ* 1 *uzanšu inakkisu*

Either royal eunuchs or court attendants or dedicatees—if a palace woman either sings, or quarrels with her colleague, and he stands by and eavesdrops, he shall be struck 100 blows, they shall cut off one of his ears.

[*šumm*]*a sinnišat ekalle naglabāša pattua kindabašše la kattumat ana ma*[*zziz*] *pane tartugum* [*mā* ... *al*]*ka lašpurka u šūt iltuḫur ilteša idabbub* 100 [*immaḫḫ*]*aṣ āmerānšu* [*kuz*]*ippēšu ilaqqe u šua sāga qablīšu irakkusu*

If a woman of the palace has bared her shoulders and is not covered with even a *kindabašše*-garment, and she summons a court attendant, [saying: "..., come] hither, I wish to give you an order," and he tarries to speak with her—he shall be struck 100 blows. The eyewitness who denounces him shall take his clothing; and as for him, they shall tie (only) sackcloth around his waist.

šumma mazzi[*z pane*] *ištu sinnišat ekalle* [*i*]*dabbub* 7 *eberta*^{MEŠ} *ana muḫḫiša la iqarrib*

If a court attendant wishes to speak with a palace woman, he shall approach no closer to her than seven paces.

ša riksa annia ē[*tiq*]*uni u rab ekalle išmiuni ḫīṭa la ēmidušuni rab ekalle ḫīṭa inašši šumma ša* [*rab ek*]*alle*

Whoever violates this decree, and the palace commander hears of it and does not impose a punishment upon him, the palace commander

qēpūtušu ana šiddi ekalle la iṭṭulu ḫīṭāni la utta'eruneššu urkiš šarru [ḫī]ṭa ilteme gabbi ḫīṭāni rab ekalle emmid[ušu]

shall be held responsible for a punishable offense. Even if the officials of the palace commander do not carefully inspect the entire palace area, and do not inform him of any punishable offenses—later should the king hear of a punishable offense, they shall impose all the appropriate punishments upon the palace commander.

šumma zāriqū ina qabal ekalle šipra ana epāše u sinnišātu ša ekalle ina pī ḫūlišunu ana r[ab ekalle] iqabbiu ištu pī ḫūle upaṭ[ṭarši]na

If the water sprinklers have a task to perform within the palace and the palace women are at the entrance to their (masc.) Processional Residence, they shall report it to the palace commander; (only) he shall clear them from the entrance to the Processional Residence.

(113–121 [D rev. 1–6, E rev. 8–16, F rev. 38–39]) *Tukultī-apil-ešarra šar kiššete šar māt Aššur mār Aš[šur-rēša-iši šar māt Aššur]ma riksa ana ekalli[šu irkus]*

¶ **22** Tiglath-pileser, king of the universe, king of Assyria, son of Ashur-[rēsha-ishi, himself also king of Assyria, issued] a decree for his palace:

[...] *lu širku lu nuāru mā ṣābē ekalle* [...] *šumma ṣābē ekalle ištu ekal šarre ana* [...] *š[a-rēš]-šarrāne mazziz panūte u širkē* [...] *ša akelē u šikerē ana ekalle* [...] *ša* [...]*-ni la iptete* [...] *lu ummi [šarre l]u aššat šarre* [...] *upaṭṭar* [...] *lu ekurr[e* ...] *usbat* [...] *ša rēš šarre* [...]

[If ...] either a dedicatee or a musician [speaks to ...], saying, "The palace personnel [... ," ...] If the palace personnel [leave] the royal palace to [go to ... of(?)] the royal eunuchs, the court attendants, and the dedicatees [...] who [bring(?)] food and beer to the palace [...] ... he has not opened [...] either the king's mother or the king's wife [...] he shall clear [...] either the temple [...] she is residing [...] the royal eunuch [...]

(122–136 [A rev. 1–2, D rev. 7–21, E rev. 17]) *Tukultī-apil-ešarra [šar*

¶ **23** Tiglath-pileser, [king of the universe, king of Assyria, son of

kiššete šar māt Aššur mār Aššur-rēša-iši šar māt Aššurma riksa ana ...] irkus mā

Ashur-rēsha-ishi, himself also king of Assyria,] issued [a decree for ...,] saying:

mamma [...] *ša ekal Aššur-nādin-aḫḫē* [...] 2 *šāqû* 1 *nuḫatimmu* [...] *ša qātišunu ṣābē ek*[*alle* ...] *innammuru lu pan* [...] *ana ṣābē ekalle ana* [...] *la amārišu atû* [...] *rāqūtu ša* [...] *ina ekal Aššur-nādin-aḫḫē* [...] *ištu atuʾē* [...] *napḫarma* 19 *mazziz* [*panūte* ...] *mazziz pa*[*ne* ...] *mazz*[*iz pa*[*ne* ...] (A rev. 1–2) [...]-*ši*

Anyone [who ...] of the palace of Ashur-nādin-ahhē[9] [...] two butlers, one baker, [...] whose hands the palace personnel [...] are discovered, or before [...] to the palace personnel to [...] without his seeing, the door keepers [...] empty [...] in the palace of Ashur-nādin-ahhē [...] with the door keepers [...] a total of 19 court attendants [...] a court attendant [...] a court attendant [...]

Colophon

(A rev. 3–5) [...] *širkē* [... *ḫīṭa*] *inašši* [...] *isassiu*

[If any one of the court attendants, eunuchs, ... (palace officials),] dedicatees, [... violates any of these decrees,] he is held responsible [for a punishable offense.] They shall proclaim [these decrees ... every x years(?).]

(A rev. 6) [*uraḫ* ... *ūm* ... *līmu Sî*]*n-apla-iddina*[10]

[Month ..., day ..., eponymy of] Sîn-apla-iddina.

Notes

1. In the first publication of the MAPD, Weidner (1954/56: 257–58) also drew parallels to Hittite palace instructions.

2. Source A preserves the top edge, presenting the first decree, but there could have been additional decrees of Tiglath-pileser at the end. Note also that there could have been more than the two decrees (¶¶ 4 and 5) attributed here (with Weidner 1954/56) to Shalmaneser: Source D preserves a first decree of Shalmaneser (preceded by a double horizontal line), and source E preserves a decree—perhaps the first but also perhaps a subsequent one—and the final decree of Shalmaneser (followed by a double horizontal line). Furthermore, the sources for ¶ 4 (D and E) do not duplicate at any point. Thus what is taken as ¶ 4 could be two separate decrees, perhaps also with one or more additional decrees between.

3. The "double-hour" (*bēru*) is the distance that can be covered in a twelfth part of a full day, approximately six miles.

4. This probably refers to the chief god, Ashur; see Weidner 1954/56: 277.

5. See n. 6 below.

6. *ḫūlu* generally is taken as "road, track, processional way" (thus: "If the women are on the road ...") but the context of the references in the MAPD, and especially of the final clause of ¶ 21, suggests rather a residence or private quarters; in the MAPD, the duties of the "water sprinklers" are associated with the *ḫūlu*.

7. Probably references to two groups of ranking officials, with access to the king's bedchamber and permitted to sit in the presence of the king.

8. 1.TA.ÀM, both the Akkadian reading and the sense of the distributive are uncertain; W. Farber suggests "they shall cut off the feet of one of these officials."

9. Predecessor of the father of Ashur-uballiṭ I, the first king whose palace decree is included in this collection.

10. For the eponym, see Weidner 1957/58: 347 n. 21.

Translations

D. Hittite

12

Hittite Laws

Introduction

The Hittite People

The Hittites were one of a small number of groups speaking languages belonging to the Indo-European family who migrated into the Anatolian peninsula–corresponding roughly to the present republic of Turkey–from the north. The date of their immigration is unknown but is generally set in the final quarter of the third millennium. The Hittites established themselves as a political power during the seventeenth century and continued to dominate central Anatolia until the beginning of the twelfth century.

Although at the peak of its power the Hittite empire included subordinate states as far west as the Aegean coast and as far southeast as Damascus in Syria, its heartland was the central plateau of Anatolia, represented by the basin of the great river known in modern Turkey as the Kızıl Irmak (English "Red River"), which lies to the east of the Turkish capital city, Ankara.

The Hittites left behind in the ruins of their capital city, Hattusha, thousands of baked clay tablets inscribed with cuneiform characters. Among these tablets can be found historical narratives, treaties with foreign powers, literary compositions (myths, hymns, collections of proverbs), descriptions of religious ceremonies, and administrative records (inventories and censuses). Of great interest is a collection of laws the earliest copies of which date to the Old Hittite period (ca. 1650–1500).

Origin and Revision of the Laws

The Hittite laws were first written down in the early Old Kingdom (ca. 1650–1500). Four of the many copies of the laws are Old Hittite (henceforth abbreviated OH), and the remainder are copies made during the Middle Hittite (MH) or New Hittite (NH) periods (ca. 1500–1180). The OH copies are characterized by a more archaic form of the language and by a form of cuneiform writing that is typical of the Hittite Old Kingdom.

Only one NH copy actually attempts to revise the law. The others are content to modernize the language of the OH copies. The NH revising text is called the Late Parallel Version,[1] abbreviated PT for "Parallel Text." It contains forty-one sections, customarily numbered with roman numerals by modern scholars. Although in Hrozný 1922: 78–99 and Friedrich 1959: 48–61 this parallel version was presented separately, it has been decided here to interleave the Late Parallel Version with the Main Version of Series One in the manner of Goetze 1969. In order to distinguish it more clearly from the copies of the main recension I have indented the translation of paragraphs from this Late Parallel Version. NH copies other than PT differ from the earlier OH ones only in minor details and together with the OH ones are assigned to the Main Version.

Even the OH copies occasionally indicate a process of revising an earlier form of the laws that has not come down to us. These notations are worded thus: "Formerly they did such-and-such, but now he shall do such-and-such," with the second ruling differing significantly from the former. Since the Main Version itself dates from the Old Kingdom, the earlier formulations marked by the word "formerly" (Hittite *karū*) must belong to a very early stage of the Old Kingdom, perhaps to the reigns of the very first monarchs, Labarna I and Ḫattušili I (first half of the seventeenth century). I date the Main Version to the reign of King Telipinu, since in other respects he is attested as reforming the laws of royal succession and has left behind a lengthy royal edict pertaining to that reform.[2] At the end of King Telipinu's edict (see p. 237 below) there are even rulings on murder and sorcery, the former being a notable omission from the main law collection. Von Schuler (1982: 96) considers the king referred to in law ¶ 55 as the "father of the king" to be the one responsible for this first revision of the laws.

The revisions follow a pattern. Some corporal punishments were replaced by fines (compare ¶¶ 92 and 121). There is also a general reduction in the amounts of the fines. In several cases it is stated that this reduction results from abolishing the palace's share of the fine (¶ 9; see also ¶ 25). Although other cases in which a 50 percent reduction in the fine has occurred may likewise be due to the king forfeiting his share, other ratios of reduction warn us against assuming that forfeiture of the royal share was the cause of each reduction. The main recension sometimes reformed an earlier ruling by adding further specifications, such as differentiating between free persons and slaves (¶¶ 94–95). Another noticeable characteristic of the reform was a reduction of the number of exemptions from required public services, see ¶¶ 51, 54–55.

Form of the Laws

Scope and Organization

The laws were grouped in two series, each named after its opening words. The Hittite scribes designated Series One, consisting of laws 1–100, "If a man," and Series Two, consisting of laws 101–200, "If a vine."

Most scholars agree that the technical term "code" is inappropriate for the collections from Mesopotamia and Anatolia. Clearly, not every type of legal case is represented in the collection of laws. For example, the Hittite corpus does not include a ruling on premeditated homicide of an ordinary person, although the special case of the merchant is included. From the Telipinu Proclamation ¶ 49 (see p. 237 below), it is known that "Whoever commits murder, whatever the heir of the murdered man says (will be done): if he says: 'Let him die,' he shall die; if he says 'Let him make compensation,' he shall make compensation. The king shall have no role in the decision."[3] If the main version of the law corpus was introduced during the reign of Telipinu, it is possible that premeditated homicide (murder) was omitted because it was already described in the Telipinu Proclamation. Inheritance law is involved only marginally in ¶ 171, which is so specifically worded that it almost certainly derives from a precedent case, and possibly in ¶ 192, alternate version (see note 62). There is much to be said for the idea that the Hittite laws represent a collection of cases that served originally as precedents. Such a theory can explain, for instance, the occurrence of irrelevant details in some laws, which look like remnants of the precedent cases (see ¶¶ 43 and 44).

A certain degree of organization can be seen in the arrangement of the individual cases: homicide (¶¶ 1–6, 42–44), assault (¶¶ 7–18), stolen and runaway slaves (¶¶ 19–24), marriage (¶¶ 26–36), land tenure (¶¶ 39–41, 46–56), lost property (¶ 45), theft of or injury to animals (¶¶ 57–92), unlawful entry (¶¶ 93–97), arson (¶¶ 98–100), theft of or damage to plants (¶¶ 101–120), theft of or damage to implements (¶¶ 121–144), wages, hire, and fees (¶¶ 150–161), prices (¶¶ 176–186), and sexual offences (¶¶ 187–200). Individual laws are sandwiched between the above-mentioned categories, but it is clear that the collection aimed at some organization. Within some of the categories, individual laws are arranged according to a gradation of penalties, from the more to the less severe.

In a number of cases the fines are graded according to the social status or gender of the victim or the offender. Fines in cases involving slaves are often half that of cases involving free persons (see ¶¶ 7–8, 13–18); and those involving free women half that of free men (see ¶ II[= ¶¶ 3–4], IV [= 6], XVI [= 17]). Similarly, the wages of women are usually half that of men (¶¶ 24, 158). Yet the price of an unskilled man or woman is the same (¶ 177), and fines expressed in terms of slaves are often indifferent as to biological gender, as though male and female slaves were of equal value (e.g., ¶¶ 1–2).

Formulation

The laws are formulated in what is known as "case law." The condition—"if a person does such-and-such a thing"—is followed by a statement of the ruling: "he shall pay ... shekels of silver," "he shall be put to death," "they shall ... him," or something similar. This manner of formulation is one of several types of formulation found in the laws of the Hebrew Bible and the Mesopotamian law collections. No laws in the Hittite collection are expressed in the second person, that is, "you shall (not) do such-and-such," although such a formulation can be found in texts of a legal nature outside the law corpus, such as treaties or loyalty oaths.

Conventions Employed in the Presentation of the Text

Unlike previous published translations of the laws, this one uses the Old Hittite manuscripts (ca. 1650–1500), as the primary source, even if a New Hittite manuscript (ca. 1400–1180)[4] is better preserved in that passage. Reasons behind this decision will be given in my forthcoming full edition of the Hittite laws. A transliteration of the Hittite text has not been provided for this translation because of the complexity of the source material, which can be presented more adequately in my new edition.

Restorations of broken portions of the text stand in square brackets [ ]. Alternative translations have been inserted in the main text, following the format: "a dog trainer (or: hunter)." Other words not actually in the Hittite text but supplied for clarity also appear in the main text in parentheses. An ellipsis (...) represents either an unrestorable lacuna or an untranslatable term not discussed in the glossary.

Unknown words designating plants, animals, personnel, institutions, and so forth, are represented as "*eya*-tree," "*ḫipparaš*-man," "TUKUL-obligation." Hittite units of measure, so far as they are known, have been converted into modern metrical equivalents. Exceptions are the shekel and mina, used for weighing silver. When these units are used simply to indicate size or weight of objects (¶ 157), we have converted them to metrical equivalents. We have not done so when they represent standard units of universal exchange (i.e., shekels of silver). Paragraphs are numbered following Hrozný 1922. Subdivided paragraphs (i.e., those with numbers like ¶ 19a and ¶ 19b) appear in separate paragraphs only when they occur this way in the base manuscript being used at that point in the translation.

At the request of the series editor I have included in the translations clarifying words not actually found in the original. These additions are not indicated by parentheses. No transliterated Hittite text accompanies this translation, by means of which readers with some knowledge of Hittite could see what those additions are. Therefore, scholars planning to use my translations in discussions of ancient society and law are referred to my 1997 edition of the Hittite text for details.

Text of the Laws

¶ 1 [If] anyone kills [a man] or a woman in a [quarr]el, he shall [bring him] for burial and shall give 4 persons, male or female respectively. He shall look [to his house for it.][5]

¶ 2 [If] anyone kills [a male] or female slave in a quarrel, he shall bring him for burial [and] shall give [2] persons (lit., heads), male or female respectively. He shall look to his house for it.

¶ 3 [If] anyone strikes a free [man] or woman so that he dies, but it is an accident, he shall bring him for burial and shall give 2 persons. He shall look to his house for it.

¶ 4 If anyone strikes a male or female slave so that he dies, but it is an accident, he shall bring him for burial and shall give one person. He shall look to his house for it.

> ¶ II (= late version of ¶¶ 3–4) [If anyone] strikes [a (free) man,] so that he dies, but it is an accident, [he shall pay ... shekels of silver.] If it is a free woman or a female slave, he shall pay 80 shekels of silver.[6]

¶ 5 If anyone kills a merchant[6a] (in a foreign land), he shall pay 4,000 shekels of silver. He shall look to his house for it. If it is in the lands of Luwiya or Pala, he shall pay the 4,000 shekels of silver and also replace his goods. If it is in the land of Hatti, he shall also bring the merchant himself for burial.

> ¶ III (= late version of ¶ 5) [If] anyone kills a Hittite [merchant] in the midst of his goods, he shall pay [... shekels of silver], and he shall pay three times the value of his goods. But [if] the merchant has no goods with him, and someone kills him in a quarrel, he shall pay 240 shekels of silver. If it is only an accident, he shall pay 80 shekels of silver.

¶ 6 If a person, man or woman, is killed in another city, the victim's heir shall deduct 12,000 square meters[7] from the land of the person on whose property the person was killed and shall take it for himself.

¶ IV (= late version of ¶ 6) If a free man is found dead on another's property, the property owner shall give his property, house, and 60 shekels of silver. If the dead person is a woman, the property owner shall give (no property, but) 120 shekels of silver. If the place where the dead person was found is not private property, but uncultivated open country, they shall measure 3 miles in all directions, and the dead person's heir shall take those same payments from whatever village is found to lie within that radius.[8] If there is no village within that radius, the heir shall forfeit his claim.

¶ 7 If anyone blinds a free person or knocks out his tooth,[9] they used to pay 40 shekels of silver. But now he shall pay 20 shekels of silver. He shall look to his house for it.

¶ V (=late version of ¶ 7) If anyone blinds a free man in a quarrel, he shall pay 40 shekels of silver. If it is an accident, he shall pay 20 shekels of silver.

¶ 8 If anyone blinds a male or female slave or knocks out his tooth, he shall pay 10 shekels of silver. He shall look to his house for it.

¶ VI (= late version of ¶ 8) If anyone blinds a male slave in a quarrel, he shall pay 20 shekels of silver. If it is an accident, he shall pay 10 shekels of silver.

¶ VII (= late version of ¶¶ 7–8) If anyone knocks out a free man's tooth—if he knocks out 2 or 3 teeth—he shall pay 12 shekels of silver. If the injured party is a slave, his assailant shall pay 6 shekels of silver.

¶ 9 If anyone injures a person's head, they used to pay 6 shekels of silver: the injured party took 3 shekels of silver, and they used to take 3 shekels of silver for the palace. But now the king has waived the palace share, so that only the injured party takes 3 shekels of silver.

¶ VIII (= late version of ¶ 9) If anyone injures a free man's head, the injured man shall take 3 shekels of silver.

¶ 10 If anyone injures a person and temporarily incapacitates him, he shall provide medical care for him. In his place he shall provide a person to work on his estate until he recovers. When he recovers, his assailant shall pay him 6 shekels of silver and shall pay the physician's fee as well.

¶ IX (= late version of ¶ 10) If anyone injures a free man's head, he shall provide medical care for him. In his place he shall provide a person to work on his estate until he recovers. When he recovers, his assailant shall pay him 10 shekels of silver and shall pay the 3-shekel physician's fee as well. If it is a slave, he shall pay 2 shekels of silver.

¶ 11 If anyone breaks a free person's arm or leg, he shall pay him 20 shekels of silver. He shall look to his house for it.

¶ X (= late version of ¶ 11) If anyone breaks a free man's arm or leg, if the injured man is permanently disabled(?), he shall pay him 20 shekels of silver. If he is not permanently disabled(?), he shall pay him 10 shekels of silver.

¶ 12 If anyone breaks a male or female slave's arm or leg, he shall pay 10 shekels[9a] of silver. He shall look to his house for it.

¶ XI (= late version of ¶ 12) If anyone breaks a slave's arm or leg, if he is permanently disabled(?), he shall pay him 10 shekels of silver. If he is not permanently disabled(?), he shall pay him 5 shekels of silver.

¶ 13 If anyone bites off the nose of a free person, he shall pay 40 shekels of silver. He shall look to his house for it.

¶ XII (=late version of ¶ 13) If anyone bites off the nose of a free man, he shall pay 1,200 shekels[10] of silver. He shall look to his house for it.

¶ 14 If anyone bites off the nose of a male or female slave, he shall pay 3 shekels of silver. He shall look to his house for it.

¶ XIII (=late version of ¶ 14) If anyone bites off the nose of a male or female slave, he shall pay 600 shekels[11] of silver.

¶ 15 If anyone tears off the ear of a free person, he shall pay 12 shekels of silver. He shall look to his house for it.

¶ XIV (=late version of ¶ 15) If anyone tears off the ear of a free man, he shall pay 12 shekels of silver.

¶ 16 If anyone tears off the ear of a male or female slave, he shall pay him 3 shekels of silver.

¶ XV (=late version of ¶ 16) If anyone tears off the ear of a male or female slave, he shall pay 6 shekels of silver.

¶ 17 If anyone causes a free woman to miscarry, [if] it is her tenth month,[12] he shall pay 10 shekels of silver, if it is her fifth month, he shall pay 5 shekels of silver. He shall look to his house for it.

¶ XVI (=late version of ¶ 17) If anyone causes a free woman to miscarry, he shall pay 20 shekels of silver.

¶ 18 If anyone causes a female slave to miscarry,[13] if it is her tenth month, he shall pay 5 shekels of silver.

¶ XVII (=late version of ¶ 18) If anyone causes a female slave to miscarry, he shall pay 10 shekels of silver. [...]

¶ 19a If a Luwian abducts a free person, man or woman, from the land of Hatti, and leads him away to the land of Luwiya/Arzawa, and subsequently the abducted person's owner[14] recognizes him, the abductor shall bring (i.e., forfeit) his entire house.[14a]

¶ 19b If a Hittite abducts a Luwian man in the land of Hatti itself, and leads him away to the land of Luwiya, formerly they gave 12 persons, but now he shall give 6 persons. He shall look to his house for it.

¶ 20 If a Hittite man abducts a Hittite male slave from the land of Luwiya, and leads him here to the land of Hatti, and subsequently the abducted person's owner recognizes him, the abductor shall pay him 12 shekels of silver. He shall look to his house for it.

¶ 21 If anyone abducts the male slave of a Luwian man from the land of Luwiya and brings him to the land of Hatti, and his owner later recognizes him, the owner shall only take back his own slave: there shall be no compensation.

¶ 22a If a male slave runs away, and someone brings him back, if he seizes him nearby, his owner shall give shoes to the finder. ¶ 22b If he seizes him on the near side of the river, he shall pay 2 shekels of silver. If on the far side of the river, he shall pay him 3 shekels of silver.

¶ 23a If a male slave runs away and goes to the land of Luwiya, his owner shall pay 6 shekels of silver to whomever brings him back. ¶ 23b If a male slave runs away and goes into an enemy country, whoever brings him back shall keep him for himself.

¶ 24 If a male or female slave runs away, the one at whose hearth the slave-owner finds him/her shall pay one month's wages: 12 shekels of silver for a man, 6 shekels of silver for a woman.[15]

¶ 25a [If] a person is impure in a vessel or a vat,[16] they used to pay 6 shekels of silver: the one who is impure pays 3 shekels of silver,[17] and they used to take 3 shekels for the [king]'s house.[18] ¶ 25b But now the king has [waived] the palace's share. The one who is impure only pays 3 shekels of silver.[19] The claimant shall look to his/her house for it.

¶ 26a If a woman re[fuses][20] a man, [the man] shall give [her ...], and [the woman shall take] a wage for her seed.[21] But the man [shall take the land] and the children. [...]

¶ 26b But if a man divor[ces] a woman, [and she ...s, he shall] s[ell her.] Whoever buys her [shall] pa[y him] 12 shekels of silver.

¶ 27 If a man takes his wife and leads [her] away to his house, he shall carry her dowry to his house. If the woman [dies] th[ere], they shall burn her personal possessions, and the man shall take her dowry. If she dies in her father's house, and there [are] children,[21a] the man shall not [take] her dowry.

¶ 28a If a daughter has been promised to a man, but another man runs off with her, he who runs off with her shall give to the first man whatever he paid and shall compensate him.[22] The father and mother (of the woman) shall not make compensation. 28b If her father and mother give her to another man, the father and mother shall make compensation (to the first man). 28c If the father and mother refuse to do so,[23] they shall separate her from him.

¶ XX (=late version of ¶ 28) [Too broken for connected translation.]

¶ XXI [Too broken for connected translation.]

¶ 29 If a daughter has been betrothed to a man, and he pays a brideprice for her, but afterwards the father and mother contest the agreement, they shall separate her from the man, but they[24] shall restore the brideprice double.

¶ XXII (=late version of ¶ 29) [Too broken for connected translation.]

¶ 30 But if before a man has taken the daughter in marriage he refuses her, he shall forfeit the brideprice which he has paid.

¶ XXIII (=late version of ¶ 30) If a man [...s] a young woman, the brideprice which [he paid, [25]].

¶ 31 If a free man and a female slave are lovers and live together, and he takes her as his wife, and they make a house and children, but afterwards either they become estranged or they each find a new marriage partner, they shall divide the house equally, and the man shall take the children, with the woman taking one child.

¶ XXIV (=late version of ¶ 31) [Too broken for connected translation.]

¶ 32 If a male slave [takes] a [free] woman in marriage, [and they make a home and children, when they divide their house], they shall divide their possessions [equally, and the free woman shall take] most of [the children,] with [the male slave taking] one child.

¶ 33 If a male slave takes a female slave in marriage, [and they have children,] when they divide their house, they shall divide their possessions equally. [The slave woman shall take] mos[t of the children,] with the male slave [taking] one child.

¶ 34 If a male slave pays a brideprice for a woman and takes her as his wife, no one shall free her from slavery.

¶ XXVI (=late version of ¶ 32 or ¶ 34) If a male slave [..., and takes] her [in] ma[rriage...]

¶ 35 If a herdsman[26] [takes] a free woman [in marriage], she will become a slave for (only) 3 years.[26a]

¶ 36 If a slave pays a brideprice for a free young man and acquires him as a son-in-law, no one shall free him from slavery.

¶ 37 If anyone elopes with a woman, and a group of supporters goes after them, if 3 or 2 men are killed, there shall be no compensation: "You (singular) have become a wolf."

¶ 38 If persons are engaged in a lawsuit, and some supporter goes to them, if a litigant becomes furious and strikes the supporter, so that he dies, there shall be no compensation.

¶ XXXII (=late version of ¶ 38) If a person [...], and if/when [a supporter(?) ...] and he/she becomes angry [...], and he/she dies, [if(?) ...], and he/she dies, [...].

¶ 39 But if a person holds another's land, he shall perform the *šaḫḫan*-services entailed by it. [But if] he refuses(?)[27] [the *šaḫḫan*-services,] he shall relinquish the land: he shall not sell it.

¶ XXXIII (=late version of ¶ 39) If [anyone holds] vacated [land], he shall work [it,] and not [...]

¶ 40 If a man who has a TUKUL-obligation defaults, and a man owing *šaḫḫan*-services has taken his place, the man owing *šaḫḫan*-services shall say: "This is my TUKUL-obligation, and this other is my obligation for *šaḫḫan*-services." He shall secure for himself a sealed deed concerning the land of the man having the TUKUL-obligation, he shall hold the TUKUL-obligation and perform the *šaḫḫan*-services. But if he refuses the TUKUL-obligation, they will declare the land to be that of a man having a TUKUL-obligation who has defaulted,[28] and the men of the village will work it.[29] If the king gives an *arnuwalaš*-man, they will give him the land, and he will become a TUKUL-(man).

¶ XXX (=late version of ¶ 40) If a free man [defaults], and a man owing *šaḫḫan*-services [has taken his place, the man owing *šaḫḫan*-services shall declare: "This is my ...], and this other is [my] obligation for *šaḫḫan*-services." He shall secure for himself a sealed deed concerning [the land of the man having the ...-obligation, he shall ... the ...-obligation] and perform [the *šaḫḫan*-services. But if he refuses the ...-obligation, they will declare the land] vacated, [and the men of the village will work it.] If the king [gives an *arnuwalaš*-man,] they will give [him the land, and he will become a ... -(man).]

¶ 41 If a man owing *šaḫḫan*-services defaults, and a man having a TUKUL-obligation has stepped in his place, the man having the TUKUL-obligation shall say: "This is my TUKUL-obligation, and this other is my obligation for *šaḫḫan*-services." He shall secure for himself a sealed deed concerning the land of the man owing *šaḫḫan*-services. He shall hold the TUKUL-obligation and perform the *šaḫḫan*-services. But if he refuses to perform the *šaḫḫan*-services, they will take for the palace the land of the man owing *šaḫḫan*-services. And the obligation for *šaḫḫan*-services shall cease.

¶ XXXI (=late version of ¶ 41) *[See ¶ 41 for probable translation.]*

¶ 42 If anyone hires a person, and that person goes on a military campaign[29a] and is killed, if the hire has been paid, there shall be no compensation. But if the hire has not been paid, the hirer shall give one slave.[30]

¶ 43 If a man is crossing a river with his ox, and another man pushes him off (the ox's tail), seizes the tail of the ox, and crosses the river, but the river carries off the owner of the ox, the dead man's heirs shall take that man who pushes him off.

¶ 44a If anyone makes a man fall into a fire, so that he dies, he shall give a son in return.

¶ 44b If anyone performs a purification ritual on a person, he shall dispose of the remnants (of the ritual) in the incineration dumps. But if he disposes of them in someone's house,[31] it is sorcery and a case for the king.

¶ XXXIV (=late version of ¶ 44b?) ... and he shall make it ritually pure again. If in the house anything goes wrong, he shall make it pure again. And he shall make compensation for whatever is lost.

¶ 45 If anyone finds implements, [he shall bring] them back to their owner. He (the owner) will reward him. But if the finder does not give them (back), he shall be considered a thief.

¶ XXXV (=late version of ¶¶ 45 and 71) If anyone finds implements or an ox, a sheep, a horse, or an ass, he shall drive it back to its owner, and the owner will lead it away. But if he cannot find its owner, he shall secure witnesses (that he is only maintaining custody). Afterwards when its owner finds it, he shall carry off in full what was lost. But if he does not secure witnesses, and afterwards its owner finds it (in his possession), he shall be considered a thief, and he shall make threefold compensation.

¶ 46 If in a village someone holds fields as an inheritance share, if the [larger part of] the fields has been given to him, he shall render the *luzzi*-services. But if the sm[aller part] (of) the fields [has been given] to him, he shall not render the *luzzi*-services: they shall render them from the house of his father.[32] If an heir cuts out for himself idle land, or the men of the village give land to him in addition to his inheritance, he shall render the *luzzi*-services on the idle land.

¶ XXXVIII (=late version of ¶ 46) If anyone holds land and obligation to perform *šaḫḫan*-services as an inheritance share in a village, if the land was given him in its entirety, he shall render the *luzzi*-services. If the land was not given him in its entirety, but only a small portion was given to him, he shall not render the *luzzi*-services. They shall render them from his father's estate. If the land of the heir is vacated, and the men of the village give him other public land, he shall render the *luzzi*-services.

¶ 47a If anyone holds land by a royal grant, [he shall] not [have to render] *šaḫḫan*- and *luzzi*-services. Furthermore, the king shall provide him with food at royal expense.[33]

¶ 47b If anyone buys all the land of a man having a TUKUL-obligation, he shall render the *luzzi*-services. But if he buys only the largest portion of the land, he shall not render the *luzzi*-services. But if he carves out for himself idle land, or the men of the village give him land, he shall render the *luzzi*-services.

¶ XXXVI (= late version of ¶ 47a) If anyone holds land by a royal grant, he shall perform the *luzzi*-services. But if the king exempts him, he shall not perform the *luzzi*-services.

¶ XXXVII (= late version of ¶ 47b) If anyone buys all the land of a TUKUL-man, and the former owner of the land dies, the new owner shall perform whatever *šaḫḫan*-services the king imposes on him. But if the former owner is still living, or there is an estate of the former owner of the land, whether in that country or another country, he shall not perform the *šaḫḫan*-services.

¶ XXXIXa (= late version of ¶ 47) If anyone holds land by a royal grant, he shall perform the *luzzi*-services devolving on the land. If they exempt him from the palace, he shall not render the *luzzi*-services. XXXIXb If anyone buys all the land of a TUKUL-man, they shall ask the king, and he shall render whatever *luzzi*-services the king says. If he buys in addition someone else's land, he shall not render the *luzzi*-services of that. If the land is vacated, or the men of the village give him other land, he shall perform the *luzzi*-services.

¶ 48 A *ḫipparaš*-man renders the *luzzi*-services. Let no one transact business with a *ḫipparaš*-man. Let no one buy his child, his land, or his vineyard(s). Whoever transacts business with a *ḫipparaš*-man shall forfeit his purchase price, and the *ḫipparaš*-man shall take back whatever he sold.

¶ XL (= late version of ¶ 48) If a *ḫipparaš*-man renders the *luzzi*-services, let no one transact business with a *ḫipparaš*-man. Let no one buy his child, his land or his vineyard(s). Whoever transacts business with a *ḫipparaš*-man shall forfeit his purchase price, and the *ḫipparaš*-man [shall take] back whatever he sold.

¶ 49 [If] a *ḫipparaš*-man steals, there will be no compensation. But [if] ..., only his ... shall give compensation. If they (i.e., the *ḫipparaš*-men) [were] to have to give (compensation for) theft, they would all have been dishonest, or would have become thieves. This one would have seized that one, and that one this one. [They] would have overturned the king's authority(?).

¶ XLI (= late version of ¶ 49) [If] a *ḫipparaš*-man steals, they will impose upon him no [compensation, or else only his ...] will [make compensation.] If [the *ḫipparaš*-men had been required ...] [*Continuation broken away.*]

¶ 50 The ... [man] who ...-s in Nerik, Arinna or Ziplanta, and he who is a priest in any town ... their houses are exempt, and their associates render the *luzzi*-services. In Arinna when the eleventh month arrives, [the house of him] at whose gate an *eyan* (tree or pole) is erected is likewise exempt.

¶ 51 Formerly the house of a man who became a weaver in Arinna was exempt, also his associates and relatives were exempt. Now only his own house is exempt, but his associates and relatives shall render the *luzzi*-services. In Zippalantiya it is just the same.

¶ 52 A slave of a Stone House, a slave of a prince or a person entitled to wear a reed-shaped emblem(?)—any of such people who hold land among TUKUL-men, shall render the *luzzi*-services.

¶ 53 If a man having a TUKUL-obligation and his associate live together, if they have a falling out, they shall divide their household. If there are on their land 10 persons, the man having a TUKUL-obligation shall receive 7 and his associate 3. They shall divide the cattle and sheep on their land in the same ratio. If anyone holds a royal grant by tablet, if they divide old land, the man having a TUKUL-obligation shall take 2 parts, and his associate shall take one part.

¶ 54 Formerly, the ... troops, the troops of Sala, Tamalki, Hatra, Zalpa, Tashiniya and Hemuwa, the bowmen, the carpenters, the chariot warriors and their ...-men did not render the *luzzi*-services, nor did they perform *šaḫḫan*-services.

¶ 55 When (a delegation of) Hittites, men owing *šaḫḫan*-services, came, they did reverence to the father of the king, and said: "No one pays us a wage. They say to us: 'You are men required to perform your jobs as a *šaḫḫan*-service!'" The father of the king [stepped] into the assembly and declared under his seal: "You must continue to perform *šaḫḫan*-services just like your colleagues."[34]

¶ 56 None of the coppersmiths is exempt from participating in ice procurement,[35] construction of fortresses and royal roads, or from harvesting vineyards. The gardeners render the *luzzi*-services in all the same kinds of work.

¶ 57 If anyone steals a bull—if it is a weanling calf, it is not a "bull"; if it is a yearling calf, it is not a "bull"; if it is a 2-year-old bovine, that is a "bull." Formerly they gave 30 cattle. But now he shall give 15 cattle: 5 two-year-olds, 5 yearlings, and 5 weanlings. He shall look to his house for it.

¶ 58 If anyone steals a stallion—if it is a weanling, it is not a "stallion"; if it is a yearling, it is not a "stallion"; if it is a two-year-old, that is a "stallion." They used to give 30 horses. But now he shall give 15 horses: 5 two-year-olds, 5 yearlings, and 5 weanlings. He shall look to his house for it.

¶ 59 If anyone steals a ram, they used to give 30 sheep. Now he shall give [15] sheep: he shall give 5 ewes, 5 wethers, and 5 lambs. And he shall look to his house for it.

¶ 60 If anyone finds a bull and castrates it, when its owner claims it, the finder shall give 7 cattle: 2 two-year-olds, 3 yearlings, and 2 weanlings. He shall look to his house for it.

¶ 61 If anyone finds a stallion and castrates it, when its owner claims it, the finder shall give 7 horses: 2 two-year-olds, 3 yearlings, and 2 weanlings. He shall look to his house for it.

¶ 62 If anyone finds a ram and castrates it, when its owner claims it, the finder shall give 7 sheep: 2 ewes, 3 wethers, and 2 sexually immature sheep. He shall look to his house for it.

¶ 63 If anyone steals a plow ox, formerly they gave 15 cattle, but now he shall give 10 cattle: 3 two-year-olds, 3 yearlings, and 4 weanlings. He shall look to his house for it.

¶ 64 If anyone steals a draft horse, its disposition is the same.[36]

¶ 65 If anyone steals a trained he-goat or a trained deer or a trained mountain goat,[37] their disposition is the same as of the theft of a plow ox.[38]

¶ 66 If a plow ox, a draft horse, a cow, or a mare[39] strays into another corral, if a trained he-goat, a ewe, or a wether strays into another pen, and its owner finds it, he shall take it back in full. He shall not have the pen's owner arrested as a thief.

¶ 67 If anyone steals a cow, they used to give 12 oxen. Now he shall give 6 oxen:[40] he shall give 2 two-year-old oxen, 2 yearling oxen, and 2 weanlings. He shall look to his house for it.

¶ 68 If anyone steals a mare, its disposition is the same (i.e., 2 two-year-olds, 2 yearlings, and 2 weanlings).

¶ 69 If anyone steals either a ewe or a wether, they used to give 12 sheep, but now he shall give 6 sheep: he shall give 2 ewes, 2 wethers, and 2 (sexually) immature sheep. He shall look to his house for it.

¶ 70 If anyone steals an ox, a horse, a mule, or an ass, when its owner claims it, [he shall take] it in full. In addition the thief shall give to him double. He shall look to his house for it.

¶ 71 If anyone finds an ox, a horse, or a mule, he shall drive it to the king's gate. If he finds it in the country, they shall present it to the elders. The finder shall harness it (i.e., use it while it is in his custody). When its owner finds it, he shall take it in full, but he shall not have the finder arrested as a thief. But if the finder does not present it to the elders, he shall be considered a thief.

¶ 72 If an ox is found dead on someone's property, the property-owner shall give 2 oxen. He shall look to his house for it.

¶ 73 If anyone ... s a living ox, that is the same as a case of theft.

¶ 74 If anyone breaks the horn or leg of an ox, he shall take that ox for himself and give an ox in good condition to the owner of the injured ox. If the owner of the ox says: "I will take my own ox," he shall take his ox, and the offender shall pay 2 shekels of silver.

¶ 75 If anyone hitches up an ox, a horse, a mule or an ass, and it dies, [or] a wolf devours [it], or it gets lost, he shall give it in full. But if he says: "It died by the hand of a god," he shall take an oath to that effect.

¶ 76 If anyone impresses an ox, a horse, a mule or an ass, and it dies at his place, he shall bring it and shall pay its rent also.

¶ 77a If anyone strikes a pregnant cow, so that it miscarries, he shall pay 2 shekels of silver. If anyone strikes a pregnant horse, so that it miscarries, he shall pay 3[41] shekels of silver. ¶ 77b If anyone blinds the eye of an ox or an ass, he shall pay 6 shekels of silver. He shall look to his house for it.

¶ 78 If anyone rents an ox and then puts on it a leather ... or a leather ..., and its owner finds it, he shall give 50 liters[42] of barley.

¶ 79 If oxen enter another man's field, and the field's owner finds them, he may hitch them up for one day until the stars come out. Then he shall drive them back to their owner.

¶ 80 If any shepherd throws a sheep to a wolf, its owner shall take the meat, but the shepherd shall take the sheepskin.

¶ 81 If anyone steals a fattened pig, they used to pay 40 shekels of silver. But now he shall pay 12 shekels of silver. He shall look to his house for it.

¶ 82 If anyone steals a pig of the courtyard, he shall pay 6 shekels of silver. He shall look to his house for it.

¶ 83 If anyone steals a pregnant sow, he shall pay 6 shekels of silver, and they shall count the piglets: for each 2 piglets he shall give 50 liters of barley. He shall look to his house for it.

¶ 84 If anyone strikes a pregnant sow a lethal blow, its disposition is exactly the same.

¶ 85 If anyone cuts out a piglet and steals it, he shall give 100 liters of barley.

¶ 86 If a pig enters a grain-heap, a field, or a garden, and the owner of the grain-heap, field, or garden strikes it a lethal blow, he shall give it back to its owner. If he doesn't give it back, he shall be considered a thief.

¶ 87 If anyone strikes the dog of a herdsman a lethal blow, he shall pay 20 shekels of silver. He shall look to his house for it.

¶ 88 If anyone strikes the dog of a dog trainer (or: hunter?) a lethal blow, he shall pay 12 shekels of silver. He shall look to his house for it.

¶ 89 If anyone strikes a dog of the enclosure(?) a lethal blow, he shall pay one shekel of silver.

¶ 90 If a dog devours lard, and the owner of the lard finds the dog, he shall kill it and retrieve the lard from its stomach. There will be no compensation for the dog.

¶ 91 [If] anyone [steals bees] in a swarm, [formerly] they paid [... shekels of silver], but now he shall pay 5 shekels of silver. He shall look to his house for it.

¶ 92 [If] anyone steals [2] or 3 bee hives, formerly the offender would have been exposed to bee-sting. But now he shall pay 6 shekels of silver. If anyone steals a bee-hive, if there are no bees in the hive, he shall pay 3 shekels of silver.

¶ 93 If they seize a free man at the outset, before he enters the house, he shall pay 12 shekels of silver. If they seize a slave at the outset, before he enters the house, he shall pay 6 shekels of silver.

¶ 94 If a free man burglarizes a house, he shall pay in full. Formerly they paid 40 shekels of silver as fine for the theft, but now [he shall pay] 12 shekels of silver. If he steals much, they will impose much upon him. If he steals little, they shall impose little upon him. He shall look to his house for it.

¶ 95 If a slave burglarizes a house, he shall pay in full. He shall pay 6 shekels of silver for the theft. He[43] shall disfigure the nose and ears of the slave and they will give him back to his owner. If he steals much, they will impose much upon him; if he steals little, they will impose little upon him. [If] his owner says: "I will make compensation for him," then he shall make it. But [if] he refuses, he shall lose that slave.

¶ 96 If a free man breaks into a grain storage pit, and finds grain in the storage pit, he shall fill the storage pit with grain and pay 12 shekels of silver. He shall look to his house for it.

¶ 97 If a slave breaks into a grain storage pit, and finds grain in the storage pit, he shall fill the storage pit with grain and pay 6 shekels of silver. He shall look to his house for it.

¶ 98 If a free man sets fire to a house, he shall rebuild [the house]. And whatever perished in the house—whether it is persons, [cattle, or sheep], it is damage(?). He shall make compensation for it.

¶ 99 If a slave sets fire to a house, his owner shall make compensation for him, and they shall disfigure the slave's nose and ears and return him to his owner. But if the owner will not make compensation, he shall forfeit that slave.

¶ 100 If anyone sets fire to a shed, he shall feed his (sc. the owner's) cattle and bring them through to the following spring. He shall give back the shed. If there was no straw in it, he shall (simply) rebuild the shed.

¶ 101 If anyone steals a vine, a vine branch, a ..., or an onion/garlic, formerly [they paid] one shekel of silver for one vine and one shekel of silver for a vine branch, one shekel of silver [for one *karpina*, one] shekel of silver for one clove of garlic. And they shall strike a spear on his [...] [Formerly] they proceeded so. But now if he is a free man, he shall pay 6 shekels [of silver]. But if he is a slave, he shall pay 3 shekels of silver.

¶ 102 [If] anyone steals wood from a [...] pond, [if] he steals [one talent (= 30.78 kg) of wood], he shall pay 3 shekels of silver; if he steals 2 talents (= 61.56 kg) of wood, [he shall pay] 6 shekels of silver; if he steals [3] talents (= 92.34 kg) of wood, it becomes a case for the king's court.

¶ 103 [If] anyone steals plants, if it is 0.25 square meters [of planting], he shall replant it and [give] one shekel of silver. [If it is 0.5] square meters of planting, he shall replant it and pay 2 shekels of silver.

¶ 104 [If] anyone cuts down a pear(?) tree or plum(?) tree, he shall pay [... shekels] of silver. He shall look to his house for it.

¶ 105 [If] anyone sets [fire] to a field, and the fire catches a vineyard with fruit on its vines, if a vine, an apple tree, a pear(?) tree or a plum tree burns, he shall pay 6 shekels of silver for each tree. He shall replant [the planting]. And he shall look to his house for it. If it is a slave, he shall pay 3 shekels of silver for each tree.

¶ 106 If anyone carries embers into his field, catches(??) it while in fruit, and ignites the field, he who sets the fire shall himself take the burnt-over field. He shall give a good field to the owner of the burnt-over field, and he will reap it.

¶ 107 If a person lets his sheep into a productive vineyard, and ruins it, if it has fruit on the vines, he shall pay 10 shekels of silver for each 3,600 square meters.[44, 45] But if it is bare, he shall pay 3 shekels of silver.

¶ 108 If anyone steals vine branches from a fenced-in vineyard, if he steals 100 vines, he shall pay 6 shekels of silver. He shall look to his house for it. But if the vineyard is not fenced in, and he steals vine branches, he shall pay 3 shekels of silver.

¶ 109 If anyone cuts off fruit trees from their irrigation ditch, if there are 100 trees, he shall pay 6 shekels of silver.

¶ 110 If anyone steals clay from a pit, [however much] he steals, he shall give the same amount in addition.

¶ 111 [If] anyone forms clay for [an image] (for magical purposes), it is sorcery and a case for the king's court.

¶ 112 [If] they give [to an *arnuwalaš*-man] the land of a man having a TUKUL-obligation who has disappeared, [for 3 years] they shall perform no [*šaḫḫan*-services], but in the fourth year he shall begin to perform *šaḫḫan*-services and join the men having TUKUL-obligations.

¶ 113 [If] anyone cuts down a vine, he shall take the cut-down [vine] for himself and give to the owner of the vine the use of a good vine. The original owner of the cut-down vine shall gather fruit from the new vine [until] his own vine recovers. ...

[*¶¶ 114 and 118 too broken for translation. ¶¶ 115-117 lost in a lacuna.*]

¶ 119 If anyone [steals] a duck (lit., pond bird) trained (as a decoy) [or] a mountain goat trained (as a decoy), [formerly] they paid [40] shekels of silver, but now [he shall pay] 12 shekels [of silver]. He shall look [to his house for it].

¶ 120 If anyone steals ...-ed birds [...], if there are 10 birds, he shall pay one shekel [of silver].

¶ 121 If some free man steals a plow, and its owner finds it, he shall put [(the offender's) neck] upon the ..., and [he shall be put to death] by the oxen. So they proceeded formerly. But now he shall pay 6 shekels of silver. He shall look to his house for it. If it is a slave, [he shall pay] 3 shekels of silver.

¶ 122 If anyone steals a wagon with all its accessories, initially they paid one shekel of silver, [but now] he shall pay [... shekels of silver]. He shall look [to his] house [for it].

¶ 123 If [anyone steals a ..., ... Now he shall pay] 3 shekels of silver. He shall look to his house for it.

¶ 124 If anyone steals a ... tree, he shall pay 3 shekels of silver. He shall look to his house for it. If anyone loads a wagon, [leaves] it in his field, and someone steals it, he shall pay 3 shekels of silver. He shall look to his house for it.

¶ 125 If anyone steals a wooden water trough, he shall pay [...] + one shekel of silver. If anyone steals a leather ... or a leather ..., he shall pay one shekel of silver.

¶ 126 If anyone steals a wooden ... in the gate of the palace, he shall pay 6 shekels of silver. If anyone steals a bronze spear in the gate of the palace, he shall be put to death. If anyone steals a copper pin, he shall give 25 liters of barley. If anyone steals the threads (or strands of wool) of one bolt of cloth, he shall give one bolt of woolen cloth.

¶ 127 If anyone steals a door in a quarrel, he shall replace everything that may get lost in the house, and he shall pay 40 shekels of silver. He shall look to his house for it.

¶ 128 If anyone steals bricks, however many he steals, he shall give the same number a second time over. If [anyone] steals stones from a foundation, for 2 stones he shall give 10 stones. If anyone steals a stela or a ... stone, he shall pay 2 shekels of silver.

¶ 129 If anyone steals a leather ..., a leather ..., a [...], or a bronze bell(?) <of> a horse or a mule, formerly they paid 40 shekels of silver, but now [he shall pay] 12 shekels of silver. He shall look to his house for it.

¶ 130 If anyone steals [...s] of an ox or a horse, [he shall pay ... shekels of silver.] He shall look to his house for it.

¶ 131 If [anyone steals] a leather harness(?), he shall pay 6 shekels of silver. [He shall look to his house for it.]

¶ 132 If a free man [steals ..., he shall pay] 6 shekels of silver. [He shall look to his house for it.] If he is a slave, [he shall pay 3 shekels of silver.]

¶ 133 If a free man [steals ...,] he shall pay [...] shekels [of silver. He shall look to his house for it. If he is a slave, he shall pay ... shekels of silver.]

¶ 142 [If] anyone drives [..., ... anyone steals] its wheel(s), he shall give 25 liters of barley [for each] wheel. [If he is a slave, he shall give ... of barley] for each wheel.

¶ 143 If a free man [steals] copper shears(?) [or] a copper nail file(?), he shall pay 6 shekels of silver. [He shall look to] his house [for it]. If it is a slave, he shall pay 3 shekels of silver.

¶ 144 If a barber gives copper [...s] to his associate, and the latter ruins them, he shall replace [them] in full. If anyone cuts fine cloth with a ..., he shall pay 10 shekels of silver. If anyone cuts [...], he shall pay 5 shekels of silver.

¶ 145 If anyone builds an ox barn, his employer shall pay him 6 shekels of silver. [If] he leaves out [...], he shall forfeit his wage.

¶ 146a If anyone offers a house, a village, a garden or a pasture for sale, and another goes and obstructs(?) the sale, and makes a sale of his own instead, as a fine for his offense he shall pay 40 shekels of silver, and buy [the ...] at the original prices. ¶ 146b[46] [If] anyone offers a [...] person for sale, and another person obstructs(?) the sale, for his offense he shall pay 10 shekels of silver. He shall buy the person at the original prices.

¶ 147 [If] anyone offers an unskilled person for sale, and another person obstructs(?) the sale, as the fine for his offense he shall pay 5 shekels of silver.

¶ 148 [If] anyone [offers] an ox, a horse, a mule, or an ass [for sale], and another person preempts(?), as the fine for his offense he shall pay ... shekels of silver.

¶ 149 If anyone sells a trained person, and (afterwards, before delivery) says: "He has died," but his (new) owner tracks him down, he shall take him for himself, and in addition the seller shall give 2 persons to him. He shall look to his house for it.

¶ 150 If a man hires himself out for wages, his employer [shall pay ... shekels of silver] for [one month. If a woman] hires herself out for wages, her employer [shall pay ... shekels] for one month.

¶ 151 If anyone rents a plow ox, [he shall pay] one shekel [of silver] for one month. [If] anyone rents a [..., he shall pay] a half shekel of silver for one month.

¶ 152 If anyone rents a horse, a mule, or an ass, he shall pay one shekel of silver [for one month].

¶ 157[47] If a bronze axe weighs 1.54 kg,[48] its rent shall be one shekel of silver for one month. If a copper axe weighs 0.77 kg, its rent shall be ½ shekel of silver for one month. If a bronze ...-tool weighs 0.5 kg, its rent shall be ½ shekel of silver for one month.

¶ 158a If a free man hires himself out for wages, to bind sheaves, load them on wagons, deposit them in barns, and clear the threshing floors, his wages for 3 months shall be 1,500 liters of barley. ¶ 158b If a woman hires herself out for wages in the harvest season, her wages shall be 600 liters of barley for 3 months' work.[49]

¶ 159 If anyone hitches up a team of oxen for one day, its rent shall be 25 liters of barley.

¶ 160a If a smith makes a copper box weighing 1½ minas, his wages shall be 5,000 liters of barley. ¶ 160b If he makes a bronze axe weighing 2 minas, his wages shall be 50 liters of wheat.

¶ 161 If he makes a copper axe weighing one mina, his wages shall be 50 liters of barley.

¶ 162a If anyone diverts an irrigation ditch, he shall pay one shekel of silver. If anyone stealthily takes water from an irrigation ditch, he/it is ... ed. If he takes water at a point below the other's branch, it is his to use.

¶ 162b [If] anyone takes [...], whoseever [...] he prepares, [...]. [If] anyone [...s] sheep from a pasture, [... will be] the compensation, and he shall give its hide and meat.

¶ 163 If anyone's animals go crazy(?),[50] and he performs a purification ritual upon them, and drives them back home, and he puts the mud(?) (used in the ritual) on the mud pile(?), but doesn't tell his colleague, so that the colleague doesn't know, and drives his own animals there, and they die, there will be compensation.

¶ 164 If anyone goes to someone's house to impress something, starts a quarrel, and breaks either the sacrificial bread or the libation vessel,

¶ 165 he shall give one sheep, 10 loaves of bread, and one jug of ... beer, and reconsecrate his house. Until [a year's] time has passed he shall keep away from his house.

¶ 166 If anyone sows his own seed on top of another man's seed, his neck shall be placed upon a plow. They shall hitch up 2 teams of oxen: they shall turn the faces of one team one way and the other team the other. Both the offender and the oxen will be put to death, and the party who first sowed the field shall reap[51] it for himself. This is the way they used to proceed.

¶ 167 But now they shall substitute one sheep for the man and 2 sheep for the oxen. He shall give 30 loaves of bread and 3 jugs of ... beer, and reconsecrate (the land?). And he who sowed the field first shall reap it.

¶ 168 If anyone violates the boundary of a field and takes[52] one furrow off the neighbor's field, the owner of the violated field shall cut off a strip of his neighbor's land 0.25 meters deep along their common boundary and take it for himself. He who violated the boundary shall give one sheep, 10 loaves, and one jug of ... beer and reconsecrate the field.

¶ 169 If anyone buys a field and violates the boundary, he shall take a thick loaf and break it to the Sungod [and] say: "You ... ed my scales into the ground." And he shall speak thus: "O Sungod, O Stormgod. No quarrel (was intended)."[53]

¶ 170 If a free man kills a snake, and speaks another's name, he shall pay 40 shekels of silver. If it is a slave, he alone shall be put to death.

¶ 171 If a mother removes her son's garment, she is disinheriting her sons. If her son comes back into her house (i.e., is reinstated), he/she[54] takes her door and removes it, he/she takes her ... and her ... and removes them, in this way she takes them (i.e., the sons) back; she makes her son her son again.[55]

¶ 172 If anyone preserves a free man's life in a year of famine, the saved man shall give a substitute for himself. If it is a slave, he shall pay 10 shekels of silver.

¶ 173a If anyone rejects a judgment of the king, his house will become a heap of ruins. If anyone rejects a judgment of a magistrate, they shall cut off his head.

¶ 173b If a slave rebels against[56] his owner, he shall go into a clay jar.

¶ 174 If men are hitting each other, and one of them dies, the other shall give one slave.

¶ 175 If either a shepherd or a foreman takes a free woman in marriage, she will become a slave after either two or four years. They shall ... her children, but no one shall seize their belts.[57]

¶ 176a If anyone keeps a bull outside a corral,[58] it shall be a case for the king's court. They shall sell the bull. A bull is an animal that is capable of breeding in its third year. A plow ox, a ram, and a he-goat are animals that are capable of breeding in their third year. ¶ 176b If anyone buys a trained artisan: either a potter, a smith, a carpenter, a leather-worker, a fuller, a weaver, or a maker of leggings, he shall pay 10 shekels of silver.

¶ 177 If anyone buys a man trained as an augur(?), he shall pay 25 shekels of silver. If anyone buys an unskilled man or woman, he shall pay 20 shekels of silver.

¶ 178 The price of a plow ox is 12 shekels of silver. The price of a bull is 10 shekels of silver. The price of a full-grown cow is 7 shekels of silver. The price of a yearling plow ox or cow is 5 shekels of silver. The price of a weaned calf is 4 shekels of silver. If the cow is pregnant with a calf, the price is 8 shekels of silver. The price of one calf is 2 (variant: 3) shekels of silver. The price of one stallion, one mare, one male donkey, and one female donkey are the same.

¶ 179 If it is a sheep, its price is one shekel of silver. The price of 3 goats is 2 shekels of silver. The price of 2 lambs is one shekel of silver. The price of 2 goat kids is ½ shekel of silver.

¶ 180 If it is a draft horse, its price is 20 (variant: 10) shekels of silver. The price of a mule is 40 shekels of silver. The price of a pastured horse is 14 (variant: 15) shekels of silver.[59] The price of a yearling colt is 10 shekels of silver. The price of a yearling filly is 15 shekels of silver.

¶ 181 The price of a weaned colt or a weaned filly is 4 shekels of silver. The price of 4 minas of copper is one shekel of silver, of one bottle of fine oil is 2 shekels of silver, of one bottle of lard is one shekel of silver, of one bottle of butter/ghee is one shekel of silver, of one bottle of honey is one shekel of silver, of 2 cheeses is one shekel [of silver], of 3 rennets is one shekel of silver.

¶ 182 The price of a ... garment is 12 shekels of silver. The price of a fine garment is 30 shekels of silver. The price of a blue wool garment is 20 shekels of silver. The price of a ... garment is 10 shekels of silver. The price of a tattered(?) garment is 3 shekels of silver. The price of a ... garment is 4 shekels of silver. The price of a sackcloth garment is one shekel of silver. The price of a sheer/thin tunic is 3 shekels of silver. The price of an ordinary tunic is [... shekels of silver]. The price [of one] bolt of cloth weighing 7 minas is [... shekels of silver]. The price of one large bolt of linen is 5 shekels of silver.

¶ 183 The price of 150 liters of wheat is one shekel of silver. The price of 200 liters [of barley is ½ shekel of silver.] The price of 50 liters of wine is ½ shekel of silver, of 50 liters of [... is ... shekels of silver. The price] of 3,600 square meters of irrigated(?) field is 3 [shekels of silver. The price] of 3,600 square meters of ... field is 2 shekels of silver. [The price] of a field adjoining(?) it is one shekel of silver.

¶ 184 This is the tariff, as it was ... ed in the city.

¶ 185 The price of 3,600 square meters of vineyard is 40 shekels of silver. The price of the hide of a full-grown ox is one shekel of silver. The price of 5 hides of weanling calves is one shekel of silver, of 10 oxhides is 40 shekels of silver, of a shaggy sheepskin is one shekel of silver, of 10 skins of young sheep is one shekel of silver, of 4 goatskins one shekel of silver, of 15 sheared(?) goatskins is one shekel of silver, of 20 lambskins is one shekel of silver, of 20 kidskins is one shekel of silver. Whoever buys the meat of 2 fullgrown cattle shall give one sheep.

¶ 186 Whoever buys the meat of 2 yearling cattle shall give one sheep. Whoever buys the meat of 5 weanlings shall give one sheep. Whoever buys the meat of 10 calves shall give one sheep. Whoever buys the meat of 10 sheep shall give one sheep. Whoever buys the meat of 20 lambs shall give one sheep. [If] anyone buys the meat of [20] goats, he shall give one sheep.

¶ 187 If a man has sexual relations[60] with a cow, it is an unpermitted sexual pairing: he will be put to death. They shall conduct him to the king's court. Whether the king orders him killed or spares his life, he shall not appear before the king (lest he defile the royal person).

¶ 188 If a man has sexual relations with a sheep, it is an unpermitted sexual pairing: he will be put to death. They will conduct him [to the] king's [court]. The king may have him executed, or may spare his life. But he shall not appear before the king.

¶ 189 If a man has sexual relations with his own mother, it is an unpermitted sexual pairing. If a man has sexual relations with his daughter, it is an unpermitted sexual pairing. If a man has sexual relations with his son, it is an unpermitted sexual pairing.

¶ 190 If they ... with the dead—man, woman—it is not an offense. If a man has sexual relations with his stepmother, it is not an offense. But if his father is still living, it is an unpermitted sexual pairing.

¶ 191 If a free man sleeps with free sisters who have the same mother and with their mother—one in one country and the other in another, it is not an offense. But if it happens in the same location, and he knows the women are related, it is an unpermitted sexual pairing.[61]

¶ 192 If a man's wife dies, [he may take her] sister [as his wife.] It is not an offense.[62]

¶ 193 If a man has a wife, and the man dies, his brother shall take his widow as wife. (If the brother dies,) his father shall take her. When afterwards his father dies, his (i.e., the father's) brother shall take the woman whom he had.[63]

¶ 194 If a free man sleeps with slave women who have the same mother and with their mother, it is not an offense. If brothers sleep with a free woman, it is not an offense. If father and son sleep with the same female slave or prostitute, it is not an offense.

¶ 195a If a man sleeps with his brother's wife, while his brother is alive, it is an unpermitted sexual pairing. ¶ 195b If a free man has a free woman in marriage and approaches her daughter sexually, it is an unpermitted sexual pairing. ¶ 195c If he has the daughter in marriage and approaches her mother or her sister sexually, it is an unpermitted sexual pairing.

¶ 196 If anyone's male and female slaves enter into unpermitted sexual pairings, they shall move them elsewhere: they shall settle one in one city and one in another. A sheep shall be offered in place of one and a sheep in place of the other.

¶ 197 If a man seizes a woman in the mountains (and rapes her), it is the man's offense, but if he seizes her in her house, it is the woman's offense: the woman shall die.[64] If the woman's husband discovers them in the act, he may kill them without committing a crime.

¶ 198 If he brings them to the palace gate (i.e., the royal court) and says: "My wife shall not die," he can spare his wife's life, but he must also spare the lover and 'clothe his head,'[65] If he says, "Both of them shall die," they shall 'roll the wheel.'[66] The king may have them killed or he may spare them.

¶ 199 If anyone has sexual relations with a pig or a dog, he shall die. He shall bring him to the palace gate (i.e., the royal court). The king may have them (i.e., the human and the animal) killed or he may spare them, but the human shall not approach the king. If an ox leaps on a man (in sexual excitement), the ox shall die; the man shall not die. They shall substitute one sheep for the man and put it to death. If a pig leaps on a man (in sexual excitement), it is not an offense.

¶ 200a If a man has sexual relations with either a horse or a mule, it is not an offense, but he shall not approach the king, nor shall he become a priest.[67] If anyone sleeps with an *arnuwalaš*-woman,[68] and also sleeps with her mother, it is not an offense.

¶ 200b If anyone gives his son for training either as a carpenter or a smith, a weaver or a leatherworker or a fuller, he shall pay 6 shekels of silver as the fee for the training. If the teacher makes him an expert, the student shall give to his teacher one person.

Telipinu Edict ¶ 49: And a case of murder is as follows. Whoever commits murder, whatever the heir himself of the murdered man says (will be done). If he says: "Let him die," he shall die; but if he says: "Let him make compensation," he shall make compensation. The king shall have no role in the decision.

Telipinu Edict ¶ 50: Regarding cases of sorcery in Ḫattuša: keep cleaning up (i.e., investigating and punishing) instances. Whoever in the royal family practises sorcery, seize him and deliver him to the king's court. But it will go badly for that man (C adds: and for his household) who does not deliver him.

Notes

1. See Friedrich 1959: 48–61.

2. English translations of King Telipinu's edict may be found in Sturtevant and Bechtel 1935 and in Bryce 1982.

3. The latest edition of this text is Hoffmann 1984.

4. No manuscript of the laws ¶¶ 1–100 dates from the intervening Middle Hittite period (ca. 1500–1400). For laws ¶¶ 101–200, manuscript q, commonly regarded as OH, is definitely later than the other OH manuscripts of the laws and might possibly be MH.

5. The significance of this phrase has been much debated. I favor the view that the person entitled to make a claim in the case is entitled to recover damages from the estate of the perpetrator.

6. Given the price of a slave, this fine of 2 minas (= 80 shekels) seems inordinately high.

6a. OH manuscript. NH reads "a Hittite merchant."

7. Hittite: 100 *gipeššar* = 3.3 IKU = 3 acres = 1 hectar, worth about 8.25 shekels of silver according to ¶ 183. The fine in the late version (all his land plus 60 shekels) is much higher.

8. Or perhaps: "he shall take those very (people who inhabit the village)."

9. Cf. LU ¶ 22, LE ¶ 42, LH ¶¶ 196, 198, 200, 201.

9a. Later variant: 6 shekels.

10. "30 minas." Perhaps a scribal error for "30 shekels." See also in ¶ XIII.

11. Perhaps a scribal error for "15 shekels."

12. Remainder of the paragraph in manuscript C reads: "he shall pay 20 shekels of silver."

13. Remainder of the paragraph in manuscript C reads: "he shall pay 10 shekels of silver."

14. Since the victim is a free person, "owner" probably indicates only the head of his household.

14a. Or: "the claimant shall confiscate the entire house of the abductor."

15. So the OH manuscript. The NH manuscript substitutes: "shall pay one year's wages: 100 shekels of silver for a man, 50 shekels of silver for a woman."

16. Although the Hittite wording cannot support the translation "brings impurity into a vessel or vat," yet the act referred to must be urinating or in some other manner defiling the vessel and its contents.

17. Another manuscript reads "[the victim] ta[kes] 3 shekels of silver."

18. So the OH manuscript. The NH manuscript has: "for the palace."

19. Another manuscript reads: "The victim [takes three shekels of silver]."

20. Another manuscript reads: "divorces."

21. That is, she shall be paid for the number of children she has borne?

21a. Variant: and he/she has a son.

22. Another manuscript reads: "As soon as (*kuššan*) he runs off ... they (i.e., the parents) shall compensate ..."

23. Another manuscript reads: "But if it is not the wish of the father and mother."

24. Another manuscript adds: "who runs off with her."

25. Another manuscript has a singular verb.

26. So the OH manuscript. The NH manuscript substitutes: "If a foreman or a herdsman."

26a. So OH manuscript. NH reads: If an overseer or a herdsman elopes with a free woman and does not pay a brideprice for her, she will become a slave for (only) 3 years.

27. One NH manuscript has "releases," while another has "casts off," "rejects."

28. A later manuscript reads "they declare the land of the TUKUL-man vacant."

29. A later manuscript reads "men will work it for the village."

29a. Or: on a business trip.

30. A later manuscript adds: "And as hire he shall pay 12 shekels of silver. As the hire of a woman he shall pay 6 shekels of silver."

31. Another manuscript reads: "on someone's land or house."

32. That is, the principal heir shall inherit the *luzzi*-obligation.

33. Literally, "shall take bread from his table and give it to him."

34. Presumably only a delegation of the men subject to the *ILKU*-obligation appeared before the king.

35. Post-OH manuscripts omit "ice procurement."

36. Literally, "is this very (same)."

37. That is, decoys used by hunters.

38. A later copy incorrectly substitutes "its compensation is the same as that for a he-goat."

39. NH text: "jenny."

40. The OH manuscript omits: "Now he shall give 6 oxen."

41. A NH manuscript reads: 2.

42. Hittite: 1 *PARISU.*

43. Another manuscript reads: "They."

44. Hittite: 1 IKU, which equals 30 *gipeššar.*

45. Two late manuscripts add: "He shall look to his house for it."

46. ¶ 146b is omitted in the post-Old Hittite copies.

47. The OH manuscript q shows that there was no gap in which four additional laws (¶¶ 153–156 in Hrozný's numbering) might fit. We preserve the traditional numbering of ¶¶ 157–200 for convenience of reference.

48. So the OH manuscript. The NH manuscripts describe lighter axes, for the same rent, yielding a higher rental rate.

49. A NH manuscript has: "He (the employer) shall give 600 liters of barley for two months' (work)."

50. The translation "are smitten by a god" proposed by (Friedrich 195: 75) and others is unsatisfactory, since the word ought to mean literally "to make oneself divine" or "to be made divine." The translation "are branded" (Goetze 1969: 195) is impossible.

51. A later manuscript reads "take."

52. A later manuscript reads "drives."

53. The meaning of these two sayings is obscure. I offer here a literal translation. The second may be a disavowing of evil intention. The field-owner accidentally transgressed the border with his neighbor, not intending to steal land from him.

54. It is unclear if the actor in the following clauses is the mother or the son.

55. Hittitologists are divided in their interpretation of this law. I have resorted to a literal translation in order not to obscure the data, confusing though they may be. The alternation of "son" and "sons" is unexpected, but it is unmistakably in the text and is probably an original. The referent of "them" in the penultimate clause cannot be the untranslatable items in the preceding sentence, because they are nouns, while the pronoun "them" is animate.

56. Literally, "exempts/frees himself from."

57. The significance of this gesture is unknown.

58. Literally "dispenses with a bull's corral."

59. For what follows, another manuscript substitutes: "The price of a yearling filly is 15 shekels of silver. The price of a gelding(?) or a mare is [...] shekels of silver. The price of 4 minas of copper is one shekel [of silver]."

60. Literally, "sins." So also in ¶¶ 188–190, 199–200.

61. One NH manuscript mistakenly adds: "It is not an offense."

62. Another version reads: "If a woman's husband dies, his partner shall take his wife." See Hoffner 1997:151, n. 539.

63. A NH manuscript adds: "There is no offense."

64. Cf. Deut. 22:25f.

65. The significance of this gesture are unknown.

66. The nature and significance of this action is unknown.

67. That is, he has committed no punishable crime, but he has become so defiled by the incident that he may not enter the king's presence or ever become a priest.

68. Perhaps a woman who has been taken captive in war.

Sources for Hittite Laws

Editions are Hrozný 1922, Neufeld 1951, Imparati 1964, and Hoffner 1997. **Translations** without accompanying critical transliteration and variants are Sturtevant and Bechtel 1935, Hoffner 1963, Goetze 1969, Haase 1979, von Schuler 1982, Haase 1984. Systematic commentary on the laws may be found in Hoffner 1963, and detailed and valuable commentary on individual laws in Güterbock 1961.

Bibliography for Hittite Laws

Beal, Richard Henry

1988 "The ^{GIŠ}TUKUL-institution in Second Millennium Hatti." *AoF* 15: 269–305.

Bryce, Trevor, R.

1982 *The Major Historical Texts of Early Hittite History.* Queensland, Australia: University of Queensland.

Cornil, Pièrre

1987 "Textes de Boghazköy. Liste des lieux de trouvaille." In *Hethitica VII,* Bibliothèque des cahiers de l'institut de linguistique de Louvain, No. 36, pp. 5–72. Louvain–Paris: Peeters.

Friedrich, Johannes

1959 *Die hethitischen Gesetze.* Documenta et Monumenta Orientis Antiqui 7. Leiden: E. J. Brill.

Goetze, Albrecht

1969 "The Hittite Laws." In *Ancient Near Eastern Texts Relating to the Old Testament,* 188–197. Princeton, NJ: Princeton University Press.

Güterbock, Hans Gustav

1954 "Authority and Law in the Hittite Kingdom." *JAOS* Suppl. 17 (July–September): 16–24.

1961 Review of Johannes Friedrich, *Die hethitischen Gesetze* (Leiden: Brill, 1959) in *JCS* 15: 62–78.

1962 "Further Notes on the Hittite Laws." *JCS* 16: 17–23.

Güterbock, Hans Gustav, and Harry A. Hoffner, Jr.

1989 *The Hittite Dictionary of the Oriental Institute of the University of Chicago.* Vol. L–N. Chicago: The Oriental Institute.

Haase, Richard

1979 *Die keilschriftlichen Rechtssammlungen in deutscher Fassung.* 2d ed. Wiesbaden: Otto Harrassowitz.

1984 *Texte zum hethitischen Recht. Eine Auswahl.* Wiesbaden: Reichert.
Hoffmann, Inge
1984 *Der Erlaß Telipinus.* Texte der Hethiter 11. Heidelberg: Winter.
Hoffner, Harry A., Jr.
1963 "The Laws of the Hittites." Ph.D. dissertation, Brandeis University.
1981 "The Old Hittite Version of Laws 164–166." *JCS* 33: 206–9.
1995 "Legal and Social Institutions of Hittite Anatolia." In *Civilizations of the Ancient Near East.* Ed. J. M. Sasson et al., pp. 555–70. New York: Scribners.
1997 *The Laws of the Hittites. A Critical Edition.* Documenta et Monumenta Orientis Antiqui, vol. 23. Leiden: E. J. Brill.
Hrozný, Frédéric
1922 *Code Hittite provenant de l'Asie Mineure (vers 1350 av. J.-C.). 1er partie. Transcription, traduction française.* Hethitica. Tome 1er. Première partie. Paris: Librairie orientaliste Paul Geuthner.
Imparati, Fiorella
1964 *Le leggi ittite.* Incunabula Graeca 7. Roma: Edizioni dell'Ateneo.
Laroche, Emmanuel
1971 *Catalogue des textes hittites.* Vol. 75, Études et Commentaires. Paris: Klincksieck.
Marazzi, Massimiliano
1982 "Nota sul testo KBo XXII 61 (=CTH 291)." SMEA 22: 67–68.
Neufeld, E.
1951 The Hittite Laws. London: Luzac.
Otten, Heinrich.
1965 *Das Gelübde der Königin Puduhepa an die Göttin Lelwani.* Studien zu den Boğazköy-Texten 1. Wiesbaden: Otto Harrassowitz.
Otten, Heinrich, and Vladimir Souček
1966 "Neue hethitische Gesetzfragmente aus dem Grossen Tempel." *AfO* 21: 1–12.
Pritchard, James B., ed.
1969 *Ancient Near Eastern Texts Relating to the Old Testament. Third Edition.* 3d ed. Princeton, NJ: Princeton University Press.
Sturtevant, Edgar H., and George Bechtel
1935 *A Hittite Chrestomathy.* William Dwight Whitney Linguistic Series. Philadelphia: Linguistic Society of America.
von Schuler, Einar
1982 "Die hethitischen Gesetze." In *Rechtsbücher.* Ed. Otto Kaiser. Texte aus der Umwelt des Alten Testaments I/1, pp. 96–123. Gütersloh: Mohn.
Watkins, Calvert
1973 "Hittite and Indo-European Studies: The Denominative Statives in *-e-*." *TPS* 1971: 51–93.

Glossary for Hittite Laws

ḫipparaš

In laws ¶¶ 48–49 and their late parallels we learn of a class of people called *ḫipparaš*. The word is without cognate in Hittite and without a clear etymology. In the Main Version of the laws, which stems from the OH period, the *ḫipparaš*-man renders the *luzzi*-services. In the late parallel to ¶¶ 48 (XL) the opening words have been modified to "If a *ḫipparaš*-man renders *luzzi*." If the text is in order here, we must assume that it was no longer the case that all persons in this category were subject to *luzzi*. In the late parallel, *ḫipparaš* is rendered by the Akkadogram *asīru*, "prisoner." The *ḫipparaš* may not sell anything he owns, which suggests that perhaps as a prisoner of the crown all that he was or possessed belonged to the king. For the same reason, if he steals, he must return the stolen items, but he cannot be fined, since anything he might give to pay the fine would be the king's.

luzzi and *šaḫḫan*

In laws dealing with land tenure or ownership two terms occur denoting obligations required of holders or owners of certain types of land. The terms, *šaḫḫan* and *luzzi*, have been claimed to denote "feudal" obligations. But one cannot indiscriminately apply a model of medieval European society to Hittite society. The conditions were quite different. The issue is further complicated by the fact that our documentation doesn't always make it clear to whom the *luzzi* or *šaḫḫan* was rendered. *luzzi* is clearly at times, and possibly always, a service rather than a transfer of goods (i.e., a tax). It is often translatable by the French word corvée. *šaḫḫan*, which seems to be rendered at times by the Akkadogram *ILKU*, is more difficult to pin down, but it too may well have been always in the form of services. In ¶ 55 men owing *šaḫḫan* = *ILKU* are refused wages (*kuššan*) for their services on that basis. It is also unclear if in the later stages of Hittite law (in the Late Parallel

Version) there was any distinction between the two. We have adopted the translation of "*šaḫḫan*-services" and "*luzzi*-services," merely as a means to distinguish the two while indicating that they were probably services rather than transfers. To the extent that (during the early period?) the two types differed, the scribes indicated this by the choice of verbs. One "performs" (Hittite *išša*-) *šaḫḫan*, whereas one "renders" (literally, "carries" or "lifts," Hittite *karp*-) *luzzi*.

TUKUL-obligation.

In addition to *šaḫḫan* and *luzzi*, a third category of obligation toward the state devolving on holders of land is the TUKUL-obligation, from Sumerian GIŠTUKUL. The man owing it is the LÚ GIŠTUKUL "man of the TUKUL." Although GIŠTUKUL usually means "weapon," at times it seems to denote non-military services, as in Queen Puduḫepa's vow.[1] Goetze's translation (in Pritchard 1969) of LÚ GIŠTUKUL in the laws as "craftsman" reflects this concept. The obligation of such a person according to ¶ 40 is to "hold" (Hittite *ḫar*-) the GIŠTUKUL. Because of the uncertainty in determining the nature of this obligation, we have rendered it "the TUKUL-obligation."[2]

Notes

1. Otten 1965: 44f. with n. 4 ("Handwerk"), including dairyman, baker, bee-keeper.
2. For a thorough discussion of the TUKUL-obligation, see Beal 1988.

Index for Hittite Laws

(Numbers refer to ¶s, not pages.)

Sources

The sources listed provide the reader with two categories of references for the Sumerian and Akkadian collections. First, for each law collection, there are references to *selected treatments.* The treatments include one or more of the following: full editions, transliterations, translations, and commentaries on the entire composition or major portions of it. Some of the law collections have received wide scholarly and popular attention and have been translated into several modern languages, and a complete bibliography of treatments is neither possible nor desirable here. Rather, the selection provided is intended to refer the reader to the *editio princeps,* to the most reliable or the most current editions available in modern European languages, and to treatments with critical philological or legal commentaries. Second, publication data for the *copies and photographs* of the cuneiform tablets used in the reconstructions of the law collections are listed, along with the cuneiform tablet sigla. This information is primarily for the cuneiformist, but may prove useful to the reader who compares the editions here with earlier ones. The few notes referring to textual variants identify sources by these sigla.

1. Laws of Ur-Namma (LU)

Selected treatments: Kramer and Falkenstein 1954; Szlechter 1955; Gurney and Kramer 1965; Finkelstein 1969a, 1969b; Yıldız 1981; Römer 1982; Kramer 1983; van Dijk 1983; Saporetti 1984: 21–25; Yaron 1985; Sauren 1990.

Copies and photographs:

A (Ni 3191): Kramer and Falkenstein 1954: pls. 4–7; Kramer 1976: pls. 128–29.

B (U.7739(+)U.7740 [IM 85688(+)IM 85689]): Gurney and Kramer 1965: 18; Finkelstein 1969a: 69, 71.

C (Si. 277): Yıldız 1981: 88, 90, pls. 2–4.

2. Laws of Lipit-Ishtar (LL)

Selected treatments: Steele 1948, 1950; Kramer 1950; Civil 1965; Szlechter 1957–58; Lutzmann 1982; Saporetti 1984: 27–34.

Copies and photographs:

A (AO 5473): de Genouillac 1930: pls. 72–73 No. 34.
B (UM 29–16–55 + 29–16–249): Steele 1948: 433, 440 + I (N 1791): Civil 1965: 9 pl. 1.
C (UM 29–16–230): Steele 1948: 436 + H (N 3058): Steele 1950: 490 + N 7085.
D (CBS 8284): Lutz 1919: pl. 108 No. 101.
E (CBS 13632 + 13647): Lutz 1919: pl. 107 No. 100.
F (CBS 8326): Lutz 1919: pl. 109 No. 102.
G (UM 29–16–218): Steele 1950: 444.
J (CBS 2158): Civil 1965: 9–10 pls. 1–2.
K (N 3320): Civil 1965: 10 pl. 2.
L (CBS 6802, unpublished).
M (UM 29–15–448, unpublished).
N (BM 54326 [82–5–22,478], unpublished).
O (CBS 11352, unpublished).
P (2N–T 440 [UM 55–21–71]): Civil 1965: 11 pl. 3.
R (AO 10624): de Genouillac 1925: pl. 4 No. C4.
S (Ni 9770): Kramer, Çığ, and Kızılyay 1969: 182.
T (A 32768 = N9–215): Biggs 1969: 40 No. 49 (+) (CBS 9556): Legrain 1926: No. 47.

3. Laws of X (LX)

Selected treatments: Michalowski and Walker 1989.

Copies and photographs:

Michalowski and Walker 1989: 396.

4. Laws About Rented Oxen (LOx)

Selected treatments: Civil 1965: 6–8; Roth 1980; Saporetti 1984: 37–38.

Copies and photographs:

A (N 5119): Civil 1965: 11.
B (3N–T 903,139): Civil 1965: 12.
C (N 963): Civil 1965: 12.
D (N 4938): Roth 1979: 362; Roth 1980: 145.
E (N 6079+6918): Roth 1979: 361; Roth 1980: 146.
F (N 5265): Roth 1979: 361; Roth 1980: 146.

5. Sumerian Laws Exercise Tablet (SLEx)

Selected treatments: Clay 1914, 1915: 18–27; Finkelstein 1966, 1969c; Petschow 1967; Roth 1980; Saporetti 1984: 36–37.

Copies and photographs:
(YBC 2177): Clay 1915: pl. 16 No. 28.

6. Sumerian Laws Handbook of Forms (SLHF)

Selected treatments: Roth 1979.
Copies and photographs:
(FLP 1287): Roth 1979: 358–60.

7. Laws of Eshnunna (LE)

Selected treatments: Goetze 1948a, 1950, 1956; Landsberger 1968; Yaron 1969/1988; Finkelstein 1970; Borger 1982a; al-Rawi 1982; Saporetti 1984: 41–48; Eichler 1987.
Copies and photographs:
A (IM 51059): Goetze 1948a: pls. 1–2; Goetze 1948b: pls. 1–2; Goetze 1956: 187–93.
B (IM 52614): Goetze 1948a: pls. 3–4; Goetze 1948b: pls. 3–4; Goetze 1956: 194–97.
C (Haddad 116): al-Rawi 1982: 119, 1984: Arabic Section 97–98.

8. Laws of Hammurabi (LH)

Selected treatments: Scheil 1902: 11–162; Harper 1904; Meek 1950a; Laessøe 1950; Driver and Miles 1952, 1955; Petschow 1965; Finet 1973; Borger 1979, 1982b; Saporetti 1984: 49–92.
Selected copies and photographs: Publication details of copies and photographs of manuscripts published through 1952 are found in Driver and Miles 1955: 1–2; for publication details of copies and photographs of manuscripts published through 1979, see Borger 1979: vol. 2, pp. 2–4. Copies of several of the duplicates are reproduced, in their original autograph copies, in Ungnad 1909 and in Bergmann 1953. Borger's manuscript sigla (A–Z, a–t) are used in this edition, to which I add those sources published since 1979.
Louvre stela: Scheil 1902: pls. 3–15; Harper 1904; Ungnad 1909; Deimel 1930; Bergmann 1953: 1–37.
A (AO 10237): Nougayrol 1951: pl. 1.
B (BM 34914): Wiseman 1962: 164–65.
C (BE 35271): Bergmann 1953: 52.
D (K 10778): Laessøe 1950: 182.
E (VAT 10079): Schroeder 1920: No. 190.
F (VAT 10132 (+) 10875): Weidner 1952/53a: 323–24 and pl. 16.
G (VAT 10691): Schroeder 1920: No. 192.
H (VAT 13050): Schroeder 1920: No. 191.
I (no museum number): Boissier 1926: pl. 1.

J (K 4223 (+ K 9054 + K 13979) + Sm 1008A): Meissner 1898: 505 and 511 = Bergmann 1953: 46–47.

K (no museum number): Nougayrol 1958: 155 stone fragment 9.

L (K 10483): Meissner 1898: 507 = Bergmann 1953: 46.

M (no museum number): Nougayrol 1958: 154 stone fragment 8.

N (K 8905): Meissner 1898: 507 = Bergmann 1953: 46.

O (YBC 6517): Stephens 1937: No. 34.

P (AO 7757 + DT 81 + Rm 2,388 (+) Rm 277): Laessøe 1950: pl. 1 + Meissner 1898: 513 and 515 + Laessøe 1950: 175 (+) Meissner 1898: 517 and 519 = Bergmann 1953: 48–49.

Q (no museum number): Scheil 1908: pl. 9 No. 1 = Ungnad 1909: 36, Bergmann 1953: 44.

R (no museum number): Scheil 1908: pl. 9 No. 2 = Ungnad 1909: 37 left, Bergmann 1953: 45.

S (CBS 15284): Poebel 1914: No. 93 and pls. 108–109 = Bergmann 1953: 41.

T (K 10485): Meissner 1898: 507.

U (no museum number): Scheil 1908: pl. 9 No. 3 = Ungnad 1909: 37 right, Bergmann 1953: 45.

V (Ni 2358): Langdon 1914: No. 22 and pls. 2–3 = Bergmann 1953: 42–43; Finkelstein 1969d: 12–13.

W (VAT 991): Ungnad 1909: 42 = Bergmann 1953: 51.

X (no museum number): Scheil 1921: 148; Dossin 1927: No. 200.

Y (YBC 6516): Clay 1915: No. 34.

Z (VAT 1036): Ungnad 1909: 42 = Bergmann 1953: 51.

a (VAT 10104): Schroeder 1920: No. 7.

b (Sm 1642): Meissner 1898: 511 = Bergmann 1953: 47.

c (Sm 26): Meissner 1898: 509 = Bergmann 1953: 47.

d (no museum number): Nougayrol 1958: 153 stone fragment 6.

e (K 11571+ 91-5-9,221): Meissner 1898: 509; King 1901: 46–47 = Bergmann 1953: 47, 49.

f (K 6516): Weidner 1952/53: pl. 16.

g (no museum number): Nougayrol 1958: 154 stone fragment 7.

h (no museum number): Nougayrol 1958: 152 stone fragment 4.

i (K 1100 + K 10884): Nougayrol 1966: 90.

j (K 15046): King 1914: 152.

k (K 17335).

l (K 19559).

m (K 19879).

n (Sm 1640).

o (Rm 369).

p (BM 16567).

q (BM 59776): Sollberger 1964: 130.

r (BM 78944 + BM 78979): Finkelstein 1967: 40–41.
s (U 13622): Gadd and Kramer 1966: No. 401.
t (Ni 2553+2565): [used by Driver and Miles 1955: 1 from unpublished copy; quoted in part by Finkelstein 1967: 39 n. 2 and 48] Donbaz and Sauren 1991: 16–19, pls. 1–2.
u (L.78.79): Arnaud 1983: 253.
v (BM 59739): Lambert 1989: 98.
w (CBS 1511): Sjöberg 1991: 224–25.
x (K 11795).
y (no museum number): al-Qit 1985: 143 No. 4.

9. Neo-Babylonian Laws (LNB)

Selected treatments: Peiser 1889; Meek 1950c; Driver and Miles 1955: 324–47; Petschow 1959; Szlechter 1971, 1972, 1973; Borger 1982d; Saporetti 1984: 117–20; Roth 1989a: 29–34.

Copies and photographs:
(BM 56606 [82-7-14,988]): Peiser 1889: pl. 7.

10. Middle Assyrian Laws (MAL)

Selected treatments: Driver and Miles 1935; Weidner 1937/39; Meek 1950b; Cardascia 1969; Saporetti 1979; Borger 1982c; Saporetti 1984: 93–116.

Copies and photographs:
MAL A—a (VAT 10000): Schroeder 1920: No. 1; Weidner 1937/39: pl. 4.
b (K 10135): Postgate 1973: pl. 12 No. 4.
MAL B—(VAT 10001): Schroeder 1920: No. 2.
MAL C+G—(VAT 10093+10266): Schroeder 1920: No. 6 + No. 143; Weidner 1937/39: pl. 3.
MAL D—(VAT 9575): Schroeder 1920: No. 3.
MAL E—(VAT 9839): Schroeder 1920: No. 4.
MAL F—(VAT 10109): Schroeder 1920: No. 5.
MAL J—(VAT 11153): Schroeder 1920: No. 193.
MAL K—(VAT 14388): Weidner 1937/39: pl. 5 No. 1.
MAL L—(VAT 14426): Weidner 1937/39: pl. 3 No. 2.
MAL M—(Assur 13221): Weidner 1937/39: pl. 6 No. 1.
MAL N—(Assur 23078): Weidner 1937/39: pl. 6 No. 2.
MAL O—(Assur 5732): Weidner 1937/39: pl. 5 No. 2.

11. Middle Assyrian Palace Decrees (MAPD)

Selected Treatments: Weidner 1954/56; Grayson 1972: 46–47, 52–53, 78, 100, 130–32, 139–40, 142, 152; Grayson 1976: 42–44.

Copies and photographs:
A (VAT 9629): Weidner 1954/56: pl. 7.
B (VAT 9614): Weidner 1954/56: pl. 8.
C (VAT 9571): Weidner 1954/56: pl. 9.

D (VAT 9491): Weidner 1954/56: pl. 8.
E (VAT 14407): Weidner 1954/56: pl. 12.
F (VAT 9652+9655+10402): Weidner 1954/56: pl. 10–11.
G (VAT 9140+12959): Weidner 1954/56: pl. 9
H (VAT 9567): Weidner 1954/56: pl. 12.
I (YBC 7148): Beckman and Foster 1988: 5 No. 2.

Bibliography

Arnaud, D.

1983 "Catalogue des Documents Inscrits Trouvés au cours de la huitième campagne (1978)." Pp. 229–90 in *Larsa et ʾOueili, Rapport Préliminaire.* Ed. by J.-L. Huot. Paris: Éditions Recherche sur les Civilisations.

Aynard, M.-J., and J.-M. Durand

1980 "Documents d'Époque Médio-Assyrienne." *Assur* 3: 1–54.

Beckman, G. M., and B. Foster

1988 "Assyrian Scholarly Texts in the Yale Babylonian Collection." Pp. 1–26 in *A Scientific Humanist: Studies in Memory of Abraham Sachs.* Occasional Publications of the Samuel Noah Kramer Fund 9. Ed. by E. Leichty et al. Philadelphia: The University Museum.

Bergmann, E.

1953 *Codex Ḫammurabi,* textus primigenius, editio tertia. Rome: Pontificium Institutum Biblicum.

Biggs, R.

1969 In *Cuneiform Texts from Nippur, Eighth and Ninth Seasons.* Assyriological Studies 17. Ed. by G. Buccellati. Chicago: University of Chicago Press.

Boissier, A.

1926 "Lipit-Ištar, législateur." *Babyloniaca* 9: 19–22.

Borger, R.

1971 "Gott Marduk und Gott-König Šulgi als Propheten. Zwei prophetische Texte." *Bibliotheca Orientalis* 28: 3–24.

1979 *Babylonisch-Assyrische Lesestücke.* 2 vols. 2nd ed. [1st ed. 1963]. Analecta Orientalia 54. Rome: Pontificium Institutum Biblicum.

1981 *Assyrisch-babylonische Zeichenliste,* 2 Auflage. Alter Orient und Altes Testament 33/33A. Kevelaer: Butzon & Bercker; and Neukirchen-Vluyn: Neukirchener Verlag.

1982a "Der Codex Eschnunna." Pp. 32–38 in *Rechtsbücher, Rechts- und Wirtschaftsurkunden Historisch-chronologische Texte.* Texte aus der Umwelt des Alten Testaments 1/1. Ed. by O. Kaiser. Gütersloh: Gerd Mohn.

1982b "Der Codex Hammurapi." Pp. 39–79 in *Rechtsbücher, Rechts- und Wirtschaftsurkunden Historisch-chronologische Texte.* Texte aus der Umwelt des Alten Testaments 1/1. Ed. by O. Kaiser. Gütersloh: Gerd Mohn.

1982c "Die mittelassyrischen Gesetze." Pp. 80–92 in *Rechtsbücher, Rechts- und Wirtschaftsurkunden Historisch-chronologische Texte.* Texte aus der Umwelt des Alten Testaments 1/1. Ed. by O. Kaiser. Gütersloh: Gerd Mohn.

1982d "Die neubabylonischen Gesetze." Pp. 92–95 in *Rechtsbücher, Rechts- und Wirtschaftsurkunden Historisch-chronologische Texte.* Texte aus der Umwelt des Alten Testaments 1/1. Ed. by O. Kaiser. Gütersloh: Gerd Mohn.

Bottéro, J.

1992 "The 'Code' of Ḫammurabi." Pp. 156–84 in *Mesopotamia: Writing, Reasoning, and the Gods.* Translated by Z. Bahrani and M. van de Mieroop. Chicago: University of Chicago Press. [English translation of "Le 'Code' de Hammurabi." *Annali della Scuola Normale Superiore di Pisa* 12 (1982): 409–44.]

Brinkman, J. A.

1966 Review of *Grammatik des Akkadischen*, by A. Ungnad. *Bibliotheca Orientalis* 23: 293–96.

1977 "Appendix: Mesopotamian Chronology of the Historical Period." Pp. 335–48 in *Ancient Mesopotamia: Portrait of a Dead Civilization*, by A. L. Oppenheim. Revised edition completed by E. Reiner. Chicago: University of Chicago Press.

Cardascia, G.

1969 *Les lois assyriennes.* Paris: Les Éditions du Cerf.

1980 "Égalité et inégalité des sexes en matière d'atteinte aux moeurs dans le Proche-Orient ancien." *Welt des Orients* 11: 7–16.

Civil, M.

1965 "New Sumerian Law Fragments." Pp. 1–12 in *Studies in Honor of Benno Landsberger.* Assyriological Studies 16. Ed. by H. G. Güterbock and T. Jacobsen. Chicago: University of Chicago Press.

1974–77 "Enlil and Namzitarra." *Archiv für Orientforschung* 25: 65–71.

Clay, A. T.

1914 "A Sumerian Prototype of the Hammurabi Code." *Orientalistische Literaturzeitung* 17: 1–3.

1915 *Miscellaneous Inscriptions in the Yale Babylonian Collection.* Yale Oriental Series Babylonian Texts 1. New Haven: Yale University Press.

David, M.
1939 "Zur Verfügung eines nichtberechtigten nach den mittelassyrischen 'Gesetzesfragmenten.'" Pp. 123–40 in *Symbolae ad iura orientis antiqui pertinentes Paulo Koschaker dedicatae.* Studia et Documenta ad iura orientis antiqui pertinentia 2. Leiden: E. J. Brill.

Deimel, A.
1930 *Codex Hammurabi, textus primigenius.* Rome: Pontificium Institutum Biblicum.

van Dijk, J.
1983 "Note on Si 277, a Tablet of the 'Urnammu Codex.'" *Orientalia* n.s. 52: 457.

Donbaz, V., and H. Sauren
1991 "Ni 2553 + 2565, A Missing Link of the Hammurabi Law-Code." *Orientalia Lovaniensia Periodica* 22: 5–28.

Dossin, G.
1927 *Autres textes sumériens et accadiens.* Mémoires de la Délégation en Perse 18. Paris: Librairie Ernest LeRoux.

Driver, G. R., and J. Miles
1935 *The Assyrian Laws.* Oxford: Clarendon. Reprint, Darmstadt: Scientia Verlag Aalen, 1975.
1952 *The Babylonian Laws: 1. Legal Commentary.* Oxford: Clarendon Press.
1955 *The Babylonian Laws: 2. Transliterated Text, Translation, Philological Notes, Glossary.* Oxford: Clarendon Press.

Durand, J.-M.
1993 "Le combat entre le Dieu de l'orage et la Mer." *Mari Annales de Recherches Interdisciplinaires* 7: 41–61.

Eichler, B.
1987 "Literary Structure in the Laws of Eshnunna." Pp. 71–84 in *Language, Literature, and History: Philological and Historical Studies Presented to Erica Reiner.* American Oriental Series 67. Ed. by F. Rochberg-Halton. New Haven: American Oriental Society.

Finet, A.
1973 *Le Code de Hammurapi.* Paris: Les Éditions du Cerf.

Finkelstein, J. J.
1961 "Ammiṣaduqa's Edict and the Babylonian 'Law Codes.'" *Journal of Cuneiform Studies* 15: 91–104.
1966 "Sex Offenses in Sumerian Laws." *Journal of the American Oriental Society* 86: 355–72.
1967 "A Late Old Babylonian Copy of the Laws of Hammurapi." *Journal of Cuneiform Studies* 21: 39–48.
1969a "The Laws of Ur-Nammu." *Journal of Cuneiform Studies* 22: 66–82.
1969b "The Laws of Ur-Nammu." Pp. 523–25 in *Ancient Near Eastern Texts Relating to the Old Testament.* 3d ed. with supplement. Ed. by J. B. Pritchard. Princeton: Princeton University Press.

1969c "Sumerian Laws." Pp. 525–26 in *Ancient Near Eastern Texts Relating to the Old Testament.* 3d ed. with supplement. Ed. by J. B. Pritchard. Princeton: Princeton University Press.

1969d "The Hammurapi Law Tablet BE XXXI 22." *Revue d'Assyriologie* 63: 11–27.

1970 "On Some Recent Studies in Cuneiform Law." *Journal of the American Oriental Society* 90: 131–43.

1981 *The Ox That Gored.* Transactions of the American Philosophical Society 71/2. Philadelphia: The American Philosophical Society.

Freydank, H.

1982 "Fernhandel und Warenpreise nach einer mittelassyrischen Urkunde des 12. Jahrhunderts v.u.Z." Pp. 64–75 in *Societies and Languages of the Ancient Near East: Studies in Honour of I. M. Diakonoff.* Ed. by M. A. Dandamayev et al. Warminster, England: Aris & Phillips.

1991 *Beiträge zur Mittelassyrischen Chronologie und Geschichte.* Berlin: Akademie Verlag.

1994 "Nachlese zur den mittelassyrischen Gesetzen." *Altorient Forschung* 21: 203–11.

Frymer-Kensky, T.

1977 "The Judicial Ordeal in the Ancient Near East." Diss., Yale University. Ann Arbor: University Microfilms.

Gadd, C. J., and S. N. Kramer

1966 *Literary and Religious Texts* 2. Ur Excavation Texts 6/2. London: The British Museum.

Gelb, I. J.

1955 "Notes on von Soden's Grammar of Akkadian." *Bibliotheca Orientalis* 12: 93–111.

de Genouillac, H.

1925 *Premières recherches archéologiques à Kich* 2. Paris: Librairie orientaliste Paul Geuthner.

1930 *Textes religieux sumériens du Louvre* 1. Textes cunéiformes, Musée du Louvre, Département des Antiquités Orientale 15. Paris: Librairie orientaliste Paul Geuthner.

Goetze, A.

1948a "The Laws of Eshnunna Discovered at Tell Harmal." *Sumer* 4: 63–91.

1948b "The Akkadian Law Code from Tell Harmal." *Journal of Cuneiform Studies* 2: plates I–IV.

1950 "The Laws of Eshnunna." Pp. 161–63 in *Ancient Near Eastern Texts Relating to the Old Testament,* 2d ed. 1955, 3d ed. with supplement 1969. Ed. by J. B. Pritchard. Princeton: Princeton University Press.

1956 *The Laws of Eshnunna.* Annual of the American Schools of Oriental Research 31.

Grayson, A. K.

1972 *Assyrian Royal Inscriptions 1: From the Beginning to Ashur-resha-ishi I.* Wiesbaden: Otto Harrassowitz.

1976 *Assyrian Royal Inscriptions 2: From Tiglath-pileser I to Ashur-nasir-apli II.* Wiesbaden: Otto Harrassowitz.

Gruber, M. I.

1989 "Breast-Feeding Practices in Biblical Israel and in Old Babylonian Mesopotamia." *Journal of the Ancient Near Eastern Society* 19: 61–83.

Gurney, O. R., and S. N. Kramer

1965 "Two Fragments of Sumerian Law." Pp. 13–20 in *Studies in Honor of Benno Landsberger.* Assyriological Studies 16. Ed. by H. G. Güterbock and T. Jacobsen. Chicago: University of Chicago Press.

Haase, R.

1965 *Einführung in das Studium keilschriftlicher Rechtsquellen.* Wiesbaden: Otto Harrassowitz.

Hallo, W. W.

1976 "Toward a History of Sumerian Literature." Pp. 181–203 in *Sumerological Studies in Honor of Thorkild Jacobsen.* Assyriological Studies 20. Ed. by S. J. Lieberman. Chicago: University of Chicago Press.

Harper, R. F.

1904 *The Code of Hammurabi, King of Babylon.* Chicago: University of Chicago Press.

van den Hout, T. P. J.

1987 "Masse und Gewichte, bei den Hethitern." Pp. 517–27 and 527–30 in *Reallexikon der Assyriologie* 7. Ed. by E. Ebeling et al. Berlin: de Gruyter.

Hunger, H.

1968 *Babylonische und assyrische Kolophone.* Alter Orient und Altes Testament 2. Kevelaer: Butzon & Bercker; Neukirchen-Vluyn: Neukirchener Verlag.

King, L.

1901 *Cuneiform Texts from Babylonian Tablets in the British Museum* 13. London: The British Museum.

1914 *Catalogue of the Cuneiform Tablets in the Kouyunjik Collection, Supplement.* London: The British Museum.

Kramer, S. N.

1950 "Lipit-Ishtar Lawcode." Pp. 159–61 in *Ancient Near Eastern Texts Relating to the Old Testament,* 2d ed. 1955, 3d ed. with supplement 1969. Ed. by J. B. Pritchard. Princeton: Princeton University Press.

1976 *Sumerian Literary Tablets and Fragments in the Archaeological Museum of Istanbul* 2. Ankara.

1983 "The Ur-Nammu Law Code: Who Was Its Author?" *Orientalia* n.s. 52: 453–56.

Kramer, S. N., M. Çığ, and H. Kızılyay

1969 *Sumerian Literary Tablets and Fragments in the Archaeological Museum of Istanbul* 1. Ankara: Turk Tarih Kurumu Basımevi.

Kramer, S. N., and A. Falkenstein
1954 "Ur-Nammu Law Code." *Orientalia* n.s. 23: 40–51.

Kraus, F. R.
1950 "Codex Hammu-rabi IV 32–44." *Wiener Zeitschrift für die Kunde des Morgenlandes* 51: 173–77.
1960 "Ein zentrales Problem des altmesopotamischen Rechts: Was ist der Codex Hammu-rabi?" *Genava* 8: 283–96.
1984 *Königliche Verfügungen in altbabylonischer Zeit.* Studia et documenta ad iura orientis antiqui pertinentia 11. Leiden: E. J. Brill.

Laessøe, J.
1950 "On the Fragments of the Hammurabi Code." *Journal of Cuneiform Studies* 4: 173–87.

Lafont, B.
1984 "Les prophètes du dieu Adad." *Revue d'Assyriologie* 78: 7–18.

Lambert, W. G.
1976 "Tukulti-Ninurta I and the Assyrian King List." *Iraq* 38: 85–94.
1989 "The Laws of Hammurabi in the First Millennium." Pp. 95–98 in *Reflets des deux fleuves, Volume de Mélanges offerts à André Finet.* Akkadica Supplementum 6. Ed. by M. LeBeau and P. Talon. Leuven: Peeters.

Landsberger, B.
1937 *Die Serie* ana ittišu. Materialien zum sumerischen Lexikon 1. Rome: Sumptibus Pontificii Instituti Biblici.
1949 "Jahreszeiten im Sumerisch-Akkadischen." *Journal of Near Eastern Studies* 8: 248–97.
1968 "Jungfräulichkeit." Pp. 65–103 in *Symbolae iuridicae et historicae Martino David dedicatae* 2. Ed. by J. A. Ankum et al. Leiden: E. J. Brill.

Langdon, S.
1914 *Historical and Religious Texts from the Temple Library of Nippur.* Babylonian Expedition of the University of Pennsylvania 31. Munich.

Legrain, L.
1926 *Royal Inscriptions and Fragments from Nippur and Babylon.* Publications of the Babylonian Section, University of Pennsylvania Museum 15. Philadelphia: The University Museum.

Leichty, E.
1989 "Feet of Clay." Pp. 349–56 in *dumu-e$_2$-dub-ba-a: Studies in Honor of Åke W. Sjöberg.* Occasional Publications of the Samuel Noah Kramer Fund 11. Ed. by H. Behrens et al. Philadelphia: The University Museum.

Lieberman, S. J.
1989 "Royal 'Reforms' of the Amurrite Dynasty." *Bibliotheca Orientalis* 46: 241–59.

1992 "Nippur: City of Decisions." Pp. 127–36 in *Nippur at the Centennial: Papers Read at the 35e Rencontre Assyriologique Internationale, Philadelphia, 1988.* Occasional Publications of the Samuel Noah Kramer Fund 14. Ed. by M. deJ. Ellis. Philadelphia: The University Museum.

Lutz, H. F.

1919 *Selected Sumerian and Babylonian Texts.* Publications of the Babylonian Section, University of Pennsylvania Museum 1/2. Philadelphia: The University Museum.

Lutzmann, H.

1982 "Aus den Gesetzen des Königs Lipit Eschtar von Isin." Pp. 23–31 in *Rechtsbücher, Rechts- und Wirtschaftsurkunden Historisch-chronologische Texte.* Texte aus der Umwelt des Alten Testaments 1/1. Ed. by O. Kaiser. Gütersloh: Gerd Mohn.

Meek, T.

1950a "The Code of Hammurabi." Pp. 163–80 in *Ancient Near Eastern Texts Relating to the Old Testament,* 2d ed. 1955, 3d ed. with supplement 1969. Ed. by J. B. Pritchard. Princeton: Princeton University Press.

1950b "The Middle Assyrian Laws." Pp. 180–88 in *Ancient Near Eastern Texts Relating to the Old Testament,* 2d ed. 1955, 3d ed. with supplement 1969. Ed. by J. B. Pritchard. Princeton: Princeton University Press.

1950c "The Neo-Babylonian Laws." Pp. 197–98 in *Ancient Near Eastern Texts Relating to the Old Testament,* 2d ed. 1955, 3d ed. with supplement 1969. Ed. by J. B. Pritchard. Princeton: Princeton University Press.

Meissner, B.

1898 "Altbabylonische Gesetze." *Beiträge zur Assyriologie* 3: 493–519.

Michalowski, P., and C. B. F. Walker

1989 "A New Sumerian 'Law Code.'" Pp. 383–96 in *dumu-e$_2$-dub-ba-a: Studies in Honor of Åke W. Sjöberg.* Occasional Publications of the Samuel Noah Kramer Fund 11. Ed. by H. Behrens et al. Philadelphia: The University Museum.

Moran, W.

1957 Review of *The Laws of Eshnunna,* by A. Goetze. *Biblica* 38: 216–21.

Müller, M.

1982 "Gold, Silber und Blei als Wertmesser in Mesopotamien während der zweiten Hälfte des 2. Jahrtausends v.u.Z." Pp. 270–78 in *Societies and Languages of the Ancient Near East: Studies in Honour of I. M. Diakonoff.* Ed. by M. A. Dandamayev et al. Warminster, England: Aris & Phillips.

Nougayrol, J.

1951 "Le prologue du Code Hammourabien, d'après une tablette inédite du Louvre." *Revue d'Assyriologie* 45: 67–79.

1957 "Les fragments en pierre du Code Hammourabien (I)." *Journal Asiatique* 245: 339–66.

1958 "Les fragments en pierre du Code Hammourabien (II)." *Journal Asiatique* 246: 143–55.

1966 "K. 10884." *Revue d'Assyriologie* 60: 90.

Oppenheim, A. L.

1977 *Ancient Mesopotamia: Portrait of a Dead Civilization.* Revised edition completed by E. Reiner. Chicago: University of Chicago Press.

Oppenheim, A. L., E. Reiner, et al.

1956– *The Assyrian Dictionary of the Oriental Institute of the University of Chicago.* Glückstadt: J. J. Augustin; Chicago: The Oriental Institute.

Otto, E.

1993 "Die Einschränkung des Privatstrafrechts durch öffentliches Strafrecht in der Redaktion der Paragraphen 1–24, 50–59 des Mittelassyrischen Kodex der Tafel A (KAV 1)." Pp. 131–66 in *Biblische Welten, Festschrift für Martin Metzger.* Orbis Biblicus et Orientalis 123. Ed. by W. Zwickel. Freiburg, Schweiz: Universitätsverlag; Göttingen: Vandenhoeck & Ruprecht.

Paul, S.

1990 "Biblical Analogues to Middle Assyrian Law." Pp. 333–50 in *Religion and Law.* Ed. by E. B. Firmage et al. Winona Lake, IN: Eisenbrauns.

Peiser, F. E.

1889 "Anhang." Pp. 823–28 in *Sitzungsberichte der Königlich Preussischen Akademie der Wissenschaften zu Berlin.*

1890 *Jurisprudentiae Babylonicae quae supersunt.* Diss., University of Berlin.

Petschow, H.

1959 "Das neubabylonische Gesetzesfragment." *Zeitschrift der Savigny-Stiftung für Rechtsgeschichte* 76: 36–96.

1965 "Zur Systematik und Gesetzestechnik im Codex Hammurabi." *Zeitschrift für Assyriologie* 57: 146–72.

1967 "Zu §3 des Fragments der Rechtssammlung YBT I 28." *Zeitschrift für Assyriologie* 58: 1–4.

1968 "Zur 'Systematik' in den Gesetzen von Eschnunna." Pp. 131–43 in *Symbolae iuridicae et historicae Martino David dedicatae* 2. Ed. by J. A. Ankum et al. Leiden: E. J. Brill.

Pfeiffer, R. H., and E. A. Speiser

1936 *One Hundred New Selected Nuzi Texts.* Annual of the American Schools of Oriental Research 16. New Haven: American Schools of Oriental Research.

Poebel, A.

1914 *Historical and Grammatical Texts.* Publications of the Babylonian Section, University of Pennsylvania Museum 5. Philadelphia: The University Museum.

Postgate, J. N.
1971 "Land Tenure in the Middle Assyrian Period: A Reconstruction." *Bulletin of the School of Oriental and African Studies* 34: 496–520.
1973 "Assyrian Texts and Fragments." *Iraq* 35: 13–36.
1982 "*Ilku* and Land Tenure in the Middle Assyrian Kingdom—A Second Attempt." Pp. 304–13 in *Societies and Languages of the Ancient Near East: Studies in Honour of I. M. Diakonoff.* Ed. by M. A. Dandamayev et al. Warminster, England: Aris & Phillips.

Powell, M.
1987 "Masse und Gewichte." Pp. 457–517 and 527–30 in *Reallexikon der Assyriologie* 7. Ed. by E. Ebeling et al. Berlin: de Gruyter.

al-Qit, R. A. M.
1985 "Specimens of Clay Tablets Discovered in Babylon." *Sumer* 41: Arabic Section 141–43.

al-Rawi, F.
1982 "Assault and Battery." *Sumer* 38: 117–20 (= *Sumer* 40 [1984]: Arabic Section 95–98).

Reiner, E.
1970 "Hammurabi god of kings? (*CH* iii 16)." *Revue d'Assyriologie* 64: 73.

Ries, G.
1983 *Prolog und Epilog in Gesetzen des Altertums.* Münchener Beiträge zur Papyrusforschung und antiken Rechtsgeschichte 76. Munich: Beck.

Römer, W. H. P.
1982 "Aus den Gesetzen des Königs Urnammu von Ur." Pp. 17–23 in *Rechtsbücher, Rechts- und Wirtschaftsurkunden Historisch-chronologische Texte.* Texte aus der Umwelt des Alten Testaments 1/1. Ed. by O. Kaiser. Gütersloh: Gerd Mohn.

Roth, M. T.
1979 "Scholastic Tradition and Mesopotamian Law: A Study of FLP 1287, a Prism in the Collection of the Free Library of Philadelphia." Diss., University of Pennsylvania. Ann Arbor: University Microfilms.
1980 "The Scholastic Exercise 'Laws About Rented Oxen.'" *Journal of Cuneiform Studies* 32: 127–46.
1988 "'She will die by the iron dagger': Adultery and Marriage in the Neo-Babylonian Period." *Journal of the Economic and Social History of the Orient* 31: 186–206.
1989a *Babylonian Marriage Agreements, 7th-3rd Centuries B.C.* Alter Orient und Altes Testament 222. Kevelaer: Butzon & Bercker; Neukirchen-Vluyn: Neukirchener Verlag.
1989b "Marriage and Matrimonial Prestations in First Millennium B.C. Babylonia." Pp. 245–55 in *Women's Earliest Records from Ancient*

Egypt and Western Asia. Brown Judaic Studies 166. Ed. by B. S. Lesko. Atlanta: Scholars Press.
1990 "On LE ¶¶ 46–47A." *Nouvelles Assyriologiques Brèves et Utilitaires*, No. 92.

Saporetti, C.
1979 *Le leggi medioassire*. Cybernetica Mesopotamica, Data Sets: Cuneiform Texts 2. Malibu: Undena Publications.
1984 *Le leggi della Mesopotamia*. Studi e manuali di archeologia 2. Firenze: Casa Editrice le Lettere.

Sauren, H.
1989 "Aufbau und Anordnung der babylonischen Kodizes." *Zeitschrift der Savigny-Stiftung für Rechtsgeschichte*. Romanistische Abteilung 106: 1–55.
1990 "á-áš, áš, aš." *Revue d'Assyriologie* 84: 41–43.

Scheil, V.
1902 *Textes élamites-sémitiques, deuxième série*. Mémoires de la Délégation en Perse 4. Paris: Librairie Ernest LeRoux.
1908 *Textes élamites-sémitiques, quatrième série*. Mémoires de la Délégation en Perse 10. Paris: Librairie Ernest LeRoux.
1921 "Sur une tablette de Suse portant un fragment du code de Hammurabi." *Revue d'Assyriologie* 18: 147–49.
1939 *Mission en Susiane, Mélanges Épigraphiques*. Mémoires de la Mission Archéologique de Perse 28. Paris: Librairie Ernest LeRoux.

Schroeder, O.
1920 *Keilschrifttexte aus Assur verschiedenen Inhalts*. Wissenschaftliche Veröffentlichung der Deutschen Orient-Gesellschaft 35. Leipzig: J. C. Hinrichs.

Sjöberg, Å. W.
1991 "Was There a Sumerian Version of the Laws of Hammurabi?" Pp. 219–25 in *Velles Paraules, Ancient Near Eastern Studies in Honor of Miguel Civil*. Aula Orientalis 9. Ed. by P. Michalowski et al. Barcelona.

von Soden, W.
1959–81 *Akkadisches Handwörterbuch*. Wiesbaden: Otto Harrassowitz.
1969 *Grundriss der Akkadischen Grammatik samt Ergänzungsheft zum Grundriss der Akkadischen Grammatik*. Analecta Orientalia 33/47. Rome: Pontificium Institutum Biblicum.
1974 "Duplikate aus Ninive." *Journal of Near Eastern Studies* 33: 339–44.

van Soldt, W.
1990 "Matrilinearität: A. In Elam." Pp. 586–88 in *Reallexikon der Assyriologie* 5. Ed. by E. Ebeling et al. Berlin: de Gruyter.

Sollberger, E.
1964 "A New Fragment of the Code of Ḫammurapi." *Zeitschrift für Assyriologie* 56: 130–32.

Steele, F. R.
1947 "The Lipit-Ishtar Law Code." *American Journal of Archaeology* 51: 158–54.
1948 *The Code of Lipit-Ishtar.* Philadelphia: The University Museum. (Also published as "The Code of Lipit-Ishtar." *American Journal of Archaeology* 52: 425–50.)
1950 "An Additional Fragment of the Lipit-Ishtar Code Tablet from Nippur." *Archiv Orientální* 18: 489–94.
Steinkeller, P.
1987 "The Administrative and Economic Organization of the Ur III State: The Core and the Periphery." Pp. 19–41 in *The Organization of Power, Aspects of Bureaucracy in the Ancient Near East.* Studies in Ancient Oriental Civilizations 46. Ed. by McG. Gibson and R. D. Biggs. Chicago: The Oriental Institute.
Stephens, F.
1937 *Votive and Historical Texts from Babylonia and Assyria.* Yale Oriental Series. Babylonian Texts 9. New Haven: Yale University Press.
Stol, M.
1979 "Kallatum als Klosterfrau." *Revue d'Assyriologie* 73: 91.
1988 Review of *Old Babylonian Letters from Tell Asmar,* by R. M. Whiting, Jr. *Archiv für Orientforschung* 35: 177–79.
1989 "Old Babylonian Ophthalmology." Pp. 163–66 in *Reflets des deux fleuves, Volume de Mélanges offerts à André Finet.* Akkadica Supplementum 6. Ed. by M. LeBeau and P. Talon. Leuven: Peeters.
1993a "Biblical Idiom in Akkadian." Pp. 246–49 in *The Tablet and the Scroll: Near Eastern Studies in Honor of William W. Hallo.* Ed. by M. E. Cohen et al. Bethesda: CDL Press.
1993b *Epilepsy in Babylonia.* Cuneiform Monographs 2. Groningen: Styx Publications.
Stuneck, M. A.
1927 "Hammurabi Letters from the Haskell Museum Collection." Diss., University of Chicago.
Sweet, R. F. G.
1958 "On Prices, Moneys, and Money Uses in the Old Babylonian Period." Diss., University of Chicago.
Szlechter, E.
1955 "Le Code d'Ur-Nammu." *Revue d'Assyriologie* 49: 169–76.
1957–58 "Le Code de Lipit-Ištar (I–III)." *Revue d'Assyriologie* 51: 57–82, 51: 177–96, and 52: 74–90.
1971 "Les Lois Néo-Babyloniennes." *Revue Internationale des Droits de l'Antiquité* 18: 43–107.
1972 "Les Lois Néo-Babyloniennes." *Revue Internationale des Droits de l'Antiquité* 19: 43–127.
1973 "Les Lois Néo-Babyloniennes." *Revue Internationale des Droits de l'Antiquité* 20: 43–50.

Ungnad, A.
1909 *Keilschrifttexte der Gesetze Hammurapis.* Leipzig.

Walker, C. B. F.
1987 *Cuneiform.* Reading the Past 3. Berkeley and Los Angeles: University of California Press and The British Museum.

Weidner, E.
1937/39 "Das Alter der mittelassyrischen Gesetzestexte." *Archiv für Orientforschung* 12: 46–54.
1952/53a "Drei neue Fragmente des Kodex Ḫammurapi aus neuassyrischer Zeit." *Archiv für Orientforschung* 16: 323–24.
1952/53b "Die Bibliothek Tiglatpilesers I." *Archiv für Orientforschung* 16: 197–215.
1954/56 "Hof- und Harems-Erlasse assyrischer Könige aus dem 2. Jahrtausend v. Chr." *Archiv für Orientforschung* 17: 257–93.
1957/58 "Die Feldzüge und Bauten Tiglatpilesers I." *Archiv für Orientforschung* 18: 342–60.

Westbrook, R.
1985 "Biblical and Cuneiform Law Codes." *Revue biblique* 92: 247–64.
1988 *Old Babylonian Marriage Law.* Archiv für Orientforschung Beiheft 23. Horn, Austria: Berger & Söhne.
1994 "The Old Babylonian Term *napṭārum.*" *Journal of Cuneiform Studies* 46: 41–46.

Wiseman, D.
1962 "The Laws of Hammurabi Again." *Journal of Semitic Studies* 7: 161–72.

Yaron, R.
1969 *The Laws of Eshnunna.* Jerusalem: Magnes Press; Leiden: E. J. Brill.
1985 "Quelques remarques sur les nouveaux fragments des lois d'Ur-Nammu." *Revue historique de droit* 63: 131–42.
1988 *The Laws of Eshnunna.* 2d rev. ed. Jerusalem: Magnes Press; Leiden: E. J. Brill.

Yıldız, F.
1981 "A Tablet of Codex Ur-Nammu from Sippar." *Orientalia* n.s. 50: 87–97.

Glossary

Adab. Central Mesopotamian city, seat of the worship of the mother-goddess Ninmaḫ; modern Bismāya.

Adad. God of the rains and violent weather, whose temple Eudgalgal was in Karkara.

Adad-nārārī I. Assyrian king, son of Arik-dēn-ili, reigned 1305–1274 B.C.E.

Aja. Goddess associated with light, consort of the sun-god Shamash, her temple Ebabbar was in Sippar.

Akkad. The north Mesopotamian city founded by Sargon I as capital of the "Sargonic Dynasty"; also, more broadly, used to refer to all of Babylonia; site of the temple Eulmash, dedicated to Ishtar. The "Akkadian Period," also known as the "Sargonic Period" (ca. 2300–2100 B.C.E.), saw the unification of much of settled Mesopotamia under one rule.

An. Father of the gods of the Sumerian pantheon, the sky god; Akkadian Anu.

Anshan. City in Iran, north of Persepolis; modern Tall-i Malyān.

Anu. See An.

Anunnaku. A term including all the gods of heaven, earth, and the nether world.

Ashnan. Sumerian god of agriculture and grain.

Ashur (Aššur). The patron deity of the city Assur and of the Assyrian nation.

Ashur-dan I. Assyrian king, son of Ninurta-apil-Ekur, reigned 1178–1133 B.C.E.

Ashur-nādin-aḫḫē II. Assyrian king, reigned 1400–1391 B.C.E.

Ashur-rēsha-ishi I. Assyrian king, son of Mutakkil-Nusku, reigned 1132–1115 B.C.E.

Ashur-uballiṭ I. Assyrian king, son of Erība-Adad, reigned 1363–1328 B.C.E.

Assur (Aššur). The capital city of the Assyrian empire in the second and early first millennia, situated on the Tigris River in northern Mesopotamia; *Libbi-āle,* "Inner City," is either another name for the city or a district within it; modern Qalʿat ash-Sherqāṭ.

awīlu (or later Babylonian *amēlu,* Assyrian *a'īlu,* and Sumerian lú). The term used for (1) the general, nonspecific, "person" as subject of a law provision, and for (2) a member of the highest privileged class, in contrast to a member of the *muškēnu-class* or to a slave.

Babylon. City in central Mesopotamia, seat of the second-millennium empire of the First Dynasty of Babylon (or Hammurabi Dynasty); modern Bābil.

bā'iru. Translated "fisherman"; see soldier.

bariga. A capacity measure equal to sixty silas; see the Table of Weights and Measures.

barleycorn. A weight measure, approximately 0.046 grams, equal to 1/180 of a shekel; a length measure, approximately 0.28 centimeters, equal to six fingers; see the Table of Weights and Measures.

Borsippa. Central Mesopotamian city, cult center of the god Nabû and, earlier, of Tutu, in the temple Ezida; modern Birs Nimrūd.

bur. A surface measure, approximately 6.5 hectares; see the Table of Weights and Measures.

commoner. The translation used here for Akkadian *muškēnu,* designating a class of protected persons with lesser rights and privileges.

cubit. A length measure, approximately 50 centimeters; see the Table of Weights and Measures.

Dadusha. An early ruler of the kingdom of Eshnunna.

Dagan. A West Semitic deity associated with grain, also worshiped in Mesopotamia and at Mari and Tuttul.

Damkina. Spouse of the god Enki, with a cult center in Malgium.

Dilbat. Central Mesopotamian city, seat of the worship of the god Urash; possibly modern Tall Dulaihim.

Ea. See Enki.

Eabzu. "House of the Subterranean Waters (Abyss)," temple of the god Ea/Enki in Eridu.

Eanna. "House of Heaven (of the god An)," temple of the goddess Ishtar (Inanna) in Uruk.

Ebabbar. "White House," or "House of Bright Light," the name of temples in Sippar and in Larsa dedicated to the gods Shamash and Aja.

Egalmaḫ. "Vast Splendid House," temple of the goddess Gula in Isin.

Egishnugal. "House Filled with (Moon) Light," temple of the moon god Sîn (Sumerian Nanna) in Ur.

Ekur. "Mountain House," temple of the god Enlil in Nippur.

Emaḫ. "Splendid House," temple of the goddess Ninmaḫ in Adab.

Emeslam. "House of the Warrior of the Nether World," name of the temple of the god Erra in Kutû, and of the temple in Mashkan-shapir.

Emesmes. Temple of the goddess Ishtar in Nineveh.

Emeteursag. "House Befitting the Hero," temple of the god Zababa in Kish.

Eninnu. "House of the Fifty (White *anzû*-birds)," temple of the god Ningirsu in Girsu.

Enki. Sumerian god of subterranean waters, associated with magic and wisdom, whose main city was Eridu and whose temple there was Eabzu; Akkadian Ea.

Enlil. Patron god of the city Nippur, whose temple was the Ekur; consort of the goddess Ninlil; one of the most important deities of the Sumerian pantheon.

Enlil-nārārī. Assyrian king, son of Ashur-uballiṭ, reigned 1327–1318 B.C.E.

ensi-ruler. A term for ruler (Sumerian).

***ēnu*-lord.** A term for ruler, also a term for high priest (Akkadian; Sumerian en).

Eridu. A city in southern Mesopotamia, seat of the god Enki (Akkadian Ea) and his temple Eabzu; the city to which kingship was said to first descend from heaven; modern Abu-Shahrēn.

Erra. A war-god, patron deity of Kutû.

Esagil. "House with a Lofty Top," temple of the god Marduk in Babylon, inspiration for the biblical "Tower of Babel."

Eshnunna. Capital of an early-second-millennium kingdom between the Tigris River and the Zagros Mountains; modern Tell Asmar.

Eudgalgal. "House of the Fierce Storms," temple of the god Adad in Karkara.

Eulmash. Temple of the goddess Ishtar in Akkad.

Ezida. "Righteous House," temple of the god Nabû (earlier of Tutu) in Borsippa.

finger. A length measure, approximately 1.66 centimeters; see the Table of Weights and Measures.

Girsu. Site of the temple Eninnu for the god Ningirsu; modern Tello.

Ḫaja. Divine consort of the goddess Nisaba.

Hammurabi (or Hammurapi). Sixth king of the First Dynasty of Babylon, reigned 1792–1750 B.C.E., among whose many military, economic, and political accomplishments is the largest and most famous cuneiform law collection.

Ḫursagkalamma. "(House of) the Mountain of the World," temple of the goddess Ishtar in Kish.

Id. The deity of the river; see River Ordeal.

Igigu. The chief gods of the pantheon.

iku. A surface measure, approximately 0.36 hectares; see the Table of Weights and Measures.

Inanna. Sumerian goddess associated particularly with the arts of love and war; Inanna was important in many Sumerian and Akkadian cities, especially Uruk with its temple Eanna; Akkadian Ishtar.

Inner City. Akkadian *Libbi-āle*, a name for the Assyrian capital city Assur.

innkeeper. The woman innkeeper, Akkadian *sābītu*, appears in the laws in her capacity as a money-lender and creditor.

Ishkur. Sumerian god associated with rainstorms, identified with the Akkadian god Adad.

Ishtar. See Inanna.

Isin. A city in southern Mesopotamia, prominent in the late third and early second millennia with the rise of the Isin Dynasty and the Isin-Larsa Period (also known as the Early Old Babylonian Period, ca. 2000–1800 B.C.E.); site of the temple Egalmaḫ dedicated to Ishtar; modern Ishān Baḫriyāt.

Karkara. A center of worship of the storm-god Adad.

Kesh. A city in central Mesopotamia, as yet unidentified, probably in the vicinity of Adab.

Kish. A city in central Mesopotamia, center of worship of the god Zababa; modern Tall al-Uḥēmir.

kulmašītu. A member of a group or class of minor temple dedicatees, with special privileges; Sumerian nu-bar.

kur. A capacity measure, approximately 300 liters; see the Table of Weights and Measures.

Kutû. Central Mesopotamian city, cult center of the god Erra and his temple Emeslam; modern Tall Ibrahīm.

Lagash. Center of the important state of Lagash; modern al-Hibā.

Larsa. City in southern Mesopotamia; modern Sinkara.

Libbi-āle. See Assur.

Lipit-Ishtar. Ruler (1934–1924 B.C.E.) in the First Dynasty of Isin, a Sumerian dynasty based in southern Mesopotamia.

Lushmu House. A palace of the Middle Assyrian rulers.

Malgium. City on the east bank of the Tigris River, exact location unknown, that resisted but was defeated by Hammurabi's forces; a cult-center of the gods Enki and his spouse Damkina.

Mama. A name of the mother-goddess.

Marduk. Chief god of Babylon, whose temple there was Esagil.

Mari. Large and important early second-millennium site on the middle Euphrates, a center of the worship of the god Dagan; modern Tall al-Ḥarīrī.

marriage prestations. The customary and obligatory exchanges of gifts at marriage, and the terms for the gifts, vary through time and dialects: *biblu* (in the LE, LH, and MAL) and níg-dé-a (in the LU), "ceremonial marriage prestation," is given on behalf of the groom to the bride's father; *nudunnû* (in the LE, LH, and MAL), "marriage settlement," is given by the husband to the wife, but the same term later (in the LNB) refers to the "dowry" given by the bride's family to the groom; *šeriktu* (in the LE and LH) and *širku* (in the MAL), and sag-rig$_7$ (in the LL), "dowry," is given by the bride's father to the groom; *terḫatu* (in the LE, LH, MAL), "bridewealth," is given by the groom to the bride's father; *zubullû* (in the MAL), "bridal gift," is given by the bride's father to the groom. (Note that in contemporary Old Babylonian transactional documents, the prestations identified by the labels *nudunnû* and *šeriktu* are reversed; and see Roth 1989b: 246–48.)

Mashkan-shapir. City on the Tigris River; modern Tall Abu-Duwari.

merchant. Translates Akkadian *tamkāru*, and refers to a person engaged in trade and mercantile activities, often in the laws functioning as a creditor.

mina. A weight measure, approximately 500 grams, equal to 60 shekels; see the Table of Weights and Measures.

miqtu. A member of a social or economic class of persons, possibly under royal patronage.

muškēnu. See commoner.

nadītu. A member of a group or class of Old Babylonian temple dedicatees, with special inheritance privileges and economic freedoms; some groups lived in cloisters or compounds, others married but were not permitted to bear children; Sumerian lukur.

Nanna. Sumerian moon-god, patron deity of the city Ur whose temple there was Egishnugal; Akkadian Sîn (or Suen).

Nergal. God of the nether world, closely identified with Erra, worshiped at the Emeslam at Kutû.

Ninazu. A Sumerian god, son of Enlil, worshiped at Eshnunna.

ninda. A length measure, approximately 6 meters; see the Table of Weights and Measures.

Nineveh. Assyrian city, capital of the Assyrian empire in the eighth century B.C.E.; site of the Emesmes temple for Ishtar; modern Mosul.

Ninisina. Sumerian patron goddess of the city Isin, associated with healing arts.

Ninkarrak. A Sumerian goddess associated with the healing arts.

Ninlil. Consort of the god Enlil.

Ninsun. A Sumerian bovine goddess, important in the cities of Ur and Uruk where the rulers claimed descent from her.

Nintu. A name of the mother-goddess.

Ninurta. Sumerian god, associated with vegetation and also with warfare.

Ninurta-apil-Ekur. Assyrian king, descendant of Erība-Adad, reigned 1191–1179 B.C.E.

Nippur. An important city in the third and second millennia, located in central Babylonia, cult center of the god Enlil and his temple Ekur; modern Nuffar.

Nisaba. Sumerian goddess, patron of the scribal arts and learning, and of grain.

nisku. A class of persons, probably of menial or lower-class status.

Nunamnir. A name of the god Enlil.

Nuzi. A mound in the area of ancient Arrapḫa (modern Kirkūk); the mid-second millennium tablets reveal a mixture of native, Hurrian, and Babylonian social and linguistic patterns; modern Yorghan Tepe.

overseer. Translation of Assyrian *uklu* (Babylonian *aklu* or *waklu*), in common contexts the term is used of persons in charge of military groups, artisans, and workers, and of high political and military leaders; it is also a royal title or honorific of Assyrian kings from the fifteenth through the seventh centuries.

Processional Residence (Akkadian *ḫūlu*). A part of the women's quarters in the Middle Assyrian palace; see MAPD note 6.

qadištu (Assyrian *qadiltu*). A member of a group or class of minor temple dedicatees, with special privileges; Sumerian nu-gig.

rēdû. See soldier.

reed. A length measure, approximately 3 meters; see the Table of Weights and Measures.

River House. A palace of the Middle Assyrian rulers.

River Ordeal. A judicial process in which, for a case without clear evidence or witnesses, the deity of the river is asked to judge the claims of disputing parties; both parties apparently can survive the process, although usually only one party will "turn from" (i.e., refuse to undergo) the ordeal and is declared the loser or guilty party.

sar. A surface measure, approximately 0.0036 hectares; see the Table of Weights and Measures.

seah. A capacity measure, approximately 10 liters; see the Table of Weights and Measures.

sekretu. A member of a group or class of temple dedicatees, with special privileges, sometimes living in cloistered groups.

Shalmaneser I. Assyrian king, son of Adad-nārārī I, reigned 1273–1244 B.C.E.

Shamash. Sun-god; see Utu.

shekel. A weight measure, one-sixtieth of a mina, approximately 8.33 grams; see the Table of Weights and Measures.

Shulgi. A king of the Third Dynasty of Ur, son of Ur-Namma, ruled 2094–2047 B.C.E.

sila. A capacity measure, approximately 1 liter; see the Table of Weights and Measures.

Sîn. See Nanna.

Sîn-muballiṭ. Fifth king of the First Dynasty of Babylon, reigned 1812–1793 B.C.E., father of Hammurabi.

Sippar. A city in northern Lower Mesopotamia, cult center of the sun-god Shamash and his consort Aja; modern Tall Abu-Ḥabba.

soldier. Translation of Akkadian *rēdû*, usually in the phrase *rēdûm u bāʾirum*, "soldier and fisherman," a designation of a person granted land rights in exchange for service for the state; both the soldier and the fisherman are *nāši biltim*, "state tenant."

Sumer. Southern Mesopotamia; the phrase "Sumer and Akkad," refers to all of southern Mesopotamia.

Sumukan. Sumerian god of wild game animals.

Sumu-la-el. Second king of the First Dynasty of Babylon, reigned 1880–1845 B.C.E.

Susa. Capital city of Elam, in southwestern Iran; modern Shūsh.

šiluḫlu. A dependent agricultural worker; the duties and privileges of persons so identified are unclear.

šugītu. A member of a group or class of temple dedicatees, with special privileges, but always inferior to a *nadītu*.

Tiglath-pileser I. Assyrian king, son of Ashur-rēsha-ishi I, reigned 1114–1076 B.C.E.

Tishpak. Chief god of the city of Eshnunna.

Tukultī-Ninurta I. Assyrian king, son of Shalmaneser I, reigned 1243–1207 B.C.E.

Tuttul. A city at the mouth of the Baliḫ on the upper Euphrates. Also, a city on the middle Euphrates, cult center of the god Dagan; probably modern Hīt.

Tutu. God of the city of Borsippa, with a temple, Ezida, there.

ugbabtu. A member of a group or class of priestesses, with special privileges, sometimes of royal lineage; Sumerian nin-dingir.

Ur. An important city in Mesopotamia, probably the Biblical "Ur of the Chaldees," city of the moon-god Nanna (Akkadian Sîn); center of the Ur III Dynasty (also known as the Third Dynasty of Ur or as the Neo-Sumerian Period, ca. 2100–2000 B.C.E.); modern Tell al-Muqayyar.

Urash. Patron deity of the city Dilbat.

Ur-Namma. A king and founder of the Third Dynasty of Ur, ruled 2112–2095 B.C.E.

Uruk. City in southern Babylonia, cult center of Anu and Ishtar; biblical Erech, modern Warka.

Utu. Sumerian sun-god, patron deity of justice, with important cult centers in Sippar and in Larsa; Akkadian Shamash.

wife. The translation of Akkadian *aššatu* and Sumerian dam; the designation of a full legal spouse, owing her husband exclusive sexual rights, entitled to economic support, whose children will be his heirs. "First-ranking wife" translates Akkadian *ḫīrtu* and Sumerian (dam) nitadam, terms designating the wife with primary rights (including preferential inheritance rights for her children).

Zababa. God associated with warfare; patron deity of the city Kish, where he had a temple, Emeteursag.

Zabala. Modern Tall Ibzeḥ.

Zarpanitu. Spouse of the god Marduk of Babylon.

Indexes

Locators are given to the Introduction (Intro) and to the law collections, in the order in which they are presented in this volume (LU, LL, LX, LOx, SLEx, SLHF, LE, LH, LNB, MAL, MAPD) and to the parts of the editions of the law collections, viz., introductory paragraphs (intro), prologue (prol), law provision (¶ and number [or column and line numbers for the SLHF]), epilogue (epil), and colophon (including subscript or date); the addition of "n" to a citation refers to the pertinent endnote.

No index references are given to the general front matter or to the Glossary. The Index of Selected Legal Topics and Key Words applies almost exclusively to the law provisions within the collections, occasionally to their prologues or epilogues. This last index (which combines headings for key words with headings for social and legal categories) should serve as a preliminary tool for further research but is not intended to be comprehensive or exhaustive.

1. Deities

Adad: LH prol, ¶¶ 45, 48, epil; MAL B ¶ 18
Addu: Intro
Aja: LH prol
An: LU prol; LL prol
Anu: LH prol, epil
Anunnaku: LH prol, epil
Ashnan: LL epil, LX epil
Ashur: MAPD ¶¶ 8n, 10
Dagan: LH prol
Damkina: LH prol
Ea: LH prol, epil
Enki: LX epil; LH prol
Enlil: LU prol; LL prol, epil; LX epil; LE prol; LH prol, epil
Erra: LH prol
^{d}GUD.DUMU.^{d}UTU ("Bull-the-Son-of-the-Sun-God"): MAL A ¶ 47
Ḫaja: SLEx colophon
Id: LH ¶¶ 2, 132; MAL A ¶¶ 17, 22, 24–25
Igigu: LH prol
Inanna: LL prol
Ishkur: LX epil
Ishtar: LH prol, epil
Mama: LH prol
Marduk: Intro; LH prol, ¶ 182, epil
Nanna: LU prol
Nergal: LH epil
Ninazu: LE prol; LH prol
Ninisina: LL prol
Ninkarrak: LH epil

2. Persons

3. Places
Countries, cities, rivers, mountains

Libbi-āle (Inner City [i.e., Assur]): MAL A ¶ 24n; MAPD ¶¶ 2–3, 6, 20
Malgium: LH prol
Marad: LU prol
Mari: Intro; LH prol
Mashkan-shapir: LH prol
Nineveh: LH prol
Nippur: LU intro n; LL prol; LH prol
Sippar: LU intro n; LH prol
Sumer: LU prol; LL prol, epil; LH prol, epil
Susa: Intro
Ṣupur-Shamash: LE prol
Tigris River: LU prol; LE prol
Tuttul: LH prol
Ur: LU prol; LL prol; LH prol
Uruk: LL prol; LH prol
Uṣarum: LU prol
Zabala: LH prol

4. Temples and Palaces

Eabzu: LH prol
Eanna: LH prol
Ebabbar: LH prol, LH epil
Egalmaḫ: LH prol
Egishnugal: LH prol
Ekur: LL epil; LH prol, epil
Emaḫ: LH prol
Emeslam: LH prol
Emesmes: LH prol
Emeteursag: LH prol
Eninnu: LH prol
Esagil: LH prol, epil
Eudgalgal: LH prol
Eulmash: LH prol
Ezida: LH prol, prol n
Ḫursagkalamma: LH prol
Inner Quarters: MAPD ¶¶ 8, 20
Lushmu House: MAPD ¶ 6
Processional Residence: MAPD ¶¶ 8–9, 20–21
River House: MAPD ¶ 6

5. Selected Legal Topics and Key Words

abortion and miscarriage: LL ¶¶ d–f; SLEx ¶¶ 1'–2'; LH ¶¶ 209, 211–14; MAL A ¶¶ 21, 50–53. *See also* assault
absence. *See* desertion
abuse and mistreatment: LH ¶¶ gap s, 116, 245; MAPD ¶ 18. *See also* assault
accusation, slander, and testimony: LU ¶¶ 13–14, 28; LL ¶¶ 17, 33; LH ¶¶ 1–4, 9–13, 26, 126–27, 131–32, 161; LNB ¶ 2; MAL A ¶¶ 17–19. *See also* denial, oath and ordeal, speech offenses
adoption, fosterage, and apprenticeship: LL ¶¶ 20a–20c; SLHF iv 25–30; LE ¶¶ 32–35; LH ¶¶ 185–93; MAL A ¶ 28. *See also* children and minors
adultery. *See* sexual offenses
agriculture and agricultural offenses. *See* animals, fields, hire of persons, irrigation, natural catastrophe, orchards, rates
alteration of terms: LNB ¶¶ 8–9
animals: MAL C ¶ 8. *See also* hire
dog: LE ¶¶ 56–57
donkey (ass): LOx ¶ 8; LE ¶ 50; LH ¶¶ 7–8, 224–25, 244; MAL C ¶¶ 4–5
goat: MAL C ¶ 6b
horse: MAL C ¶¶ 4–5; MAL F ¶ 2
lion: LOx ¶¶ 7–8; SLEx ¶ 9'; SLHF vi 16–22, vi 32–36; LH ¶¶ 244, 266
onager: LNB ¶ 4
ox: SLHF v 45; LE ¶¶ 40, 50; LH ¶¶ 7–8, 224–25, 241–43, 245, 262–63; MAL C ¶¶ 4–5
ox, death of: LOx ¶¶ 6–9; SLEx ¶ 9';

CPSIA information can be obtained
at www.ICGtesting.com
Printed in the USA
BVHW082338170919
558725BV00003B/3/P

9 780788 503788